KU-354-795

THE QUIET SHOWMAN

Novels by Montague Haltrecht

JONAH AND HIS MOTHER
A SECONDARY CHARACTER
THE DEVIL IS A SINGLE MAN
THE EDGWARE ROAD

THE QUIET SHOWMAN

Sir David Webster and the Royal Opera House

MONTAGUE HALTRECHT

COLLINS
St James's Place, London
1975

William Collins Sons & Co Ltd
London · Glasgow · Sydney · Auckland
Toronto · Johannesburg

First published 1975
© 1975 Montague Haltrecht

ISBN 0 00 211163 2

Set in Monotype Garamond
Made and Printed in Great Britain by
William Collins Sons & Co Ltd Glasgow

CONTENTS

ILLUSTRATIONS

ACKNOWLEDGEMENTS

I am grateful to the following for permission to quote from the works mentioned:

Boosey & Hawkes for quotations from the letters of Ralph Hawkes and H. W. Heinsheimer; Calder & Boyars Ltd for extracts from Stendhal's *Life of Rossini*, transl. Richard Coe; the Victoria and Albert Museum for extracts from 'Royal Galas' by Michael Wood and from 'The Trojans and Rafael Kubelik' by Lord Harewood, from *Covent Garden: 25 Years of Opera and Ballet*, the Catalogue of the exhibition held at the Museum in 1971; Hamish Hamilton Ltd for extracts from *At the Piano* (c) 1966 by Ivor Newton; 5000 *Nights at the Opera* (c) 1972 by Rudolph Bing; *A Life in the Theatre* (c) 1959 by Sir Tyrone Guthrie; Frank Hauser for two lines from his unpublished translation of Molière's *Le Misanthrope*; Hutchinson & Co. Ltd for extracts from Sir Thomas Beecham's *A Mingled Chime* and from his foreword to Stephen Williams's *Come to the Opera*; MacGibbon & Kee for extracts from Peter Brook's *The Empty Space*; the Society of Authors on behalf of the Bernard Shaw Estate for an extract from Shaw's *Music in London*, 1890–4; the Author's Literary Estate and Chatto & Windus for an extract from Lytton Strachey's *Elizabeth and Essex*.

I should also like to thank all those who have allowed me to quote from their letters, or from letters in which they hold the copyright.

M.H.

INTRODUCTORY NOTE

I'm grateful to the Royal Opera House and to General Administrator John Tooley for facilities extended to me, and particularly for access to the Archives. The archivist is Terry Benton and the office is in the daily charge of Boris Skidelsky, who made constant visits most agreeable. I owe a great deal to the late Muriel Kerr, Sir David's secretary and personal assistant throughout his term, and to everyone else who gave up their often valuable time to talk to me, and not even primarily about themselves. Everybody I saw appears in the book with the exception of Professor Kenneth White, who helped me with reminiscences of Sir David's Liverpool years, and to whom I'm not less grateful in spite of the omission. My extra thanks to Lord Harewood who was not only among those who gave up time to talk to me, but also read the typescript before publication and gave me his detailed and invaluable comments. I must also mention Harold Rosenthal's *Two Centuries of Opera at Covent Garden* (Putnam, 1968), which it was most comforting to have at hand. Mr Rosenthal was Covent Garden's first archivist, so I owe him thanks too for the facilities I enjoyed there. Helen Nickson typed the book, and Elizabeth Walter spent many hours at Collins editing it.

Wherever it's seemed natural I've given the names of operas in English. I haven't a scheme, and they're given in the original language where that seems more natural. Hence *Marriage of Figaro*: but the hero of *Bohème* remains in Italian as Rodolpho. One or two of the less well-known operas are borderline cases, and I've decided on *Coq d'Or* rather than *The Golden Cockerel*, though it's *Woman without a Shadow* and not *Die Frau ohne Schatten*. Verdi's opera is given in Italian as *Otello*, but the character is referred to as Othello. And the Debussy opera appears first as *Pelléas et Mélisande* because it is then on a list of French operas, all of them given their original titles: but when it's mentioned again later it's always *Pelléas and Mélisande*. Only pedantry could insist on logic in the matter.

M. H.

PROLOGUE

David Webster · the man · his task · his achievement

No hero of an opera house can ever be said to have gone entirely unsung. But if we are about to sing a song of David Webster, it can at least be claimed that the song has not hitherto been sung loudly enough.

Already an echo comes back, David Webster, why David Webster? Who was he? What was special about him? What was he and what did he achieve that such a claim should be made on his behalf? He ran an opera house. No small thing. Even so, he wasn't an artist. He was only an administrator.

His home town, Liverpool, has not as yet decided to honour him. Liverpool doesn't count him among its most distinguished sons, while his contemporary, the composer Alan Rawsthorne, has been honoured with a university doctorate. And this would have seemed the right order of things to David Webster. He was always happy to see the artist honoured before the administrator. Not that he wasn't one for the honours – he loved them, and by the end of his career had amassed more than a few. He made an entrance once at a private view in a fashionable London art gallery, Robert Fraser's, wearing the gorgeous blue riband of the Chevalier de la Légion d'Honneur, newly acquired, and with that air of smugness and excellent digestion more familiar among beauty queens. But much as he loved honours for himself, it was the artist rather than administrator he wanted to see acknowledged.

For his achievements, as he often said, were based on the sweat and talent of his artists, and his pleasure was the consciousness that he had created conditions in which they could function. He was to be seen, often almost invisible, *behind* his artists. He was weightily unassertive, and it would almost be possible to write his life story in terms of his artists' achievements alone, excluding him altogether. It's not *quite* possible, but his shade would no doubt nod appreciation of the effort and accept it as recognition of a kind. His success in his role is almost best acknowledged by *not* applauding him in it: and he had selected his role with as much deliberation as the artists whose trust and admiration he gained. Being not clearly in view, and not fully understood, made a direct appeal to that elusive irony which was, defensively, a large part of his make-up. He was a man apart. If others made demands on him, it was not for himself to make demands on his own behalf. His closest relationship, refuge and succour for the essentially lonely, was with the role he had created for himself.

When he retired in 1970, artists and the Covent Garden staff commissioned a painting of him, and he himself chose David Hockney to execute the commission. The original plan was to show Webster with his hat on the back of his head – it was characteristic of him, that hat on the back of his head, at a cautiously jaunty angle, turning him almost into a blurred parody of a rake. He was to have been seen against a background of the Covent Garden market, the setting of his opera house. But the painting we have is less significantly Sir David Webster and more patently another in the Hockney canon, and this itself is curiously appropriate. Sir David is seen in profile, sitting on a cheap iron-framed chair, the kind that can be stacked. The chair is not at all of the kind that anyone could associate with him. He is facing a table with flowers on it which takes up quite half the canvas – the flowers float, David Webster floats, both the flowers and the administrator are objects caught in space. Except for the physical details, it's the same painting as the one by Hockney of Christopher Isherwood, with Sir David in place of Isherwood, balanced by flowers instead of Don Bachardy, and with that chair and table in place of the sofa in the earlier painting. It's not our Sir David quite, but it's a good painting, though whether a portrait is also a good painting is not always the sitter's first consideration. When Rembrandt painted his *Night Watch*, some of the burghers complained that their faces were in shadow. But Rembrandt was more concerned with composition and the balance of light and shade than with simply recording his sitters, who were reduced to merely elements of the whole. Sir David would have considered this order of precedence correct. He too is subordinated to the demands of the composition, like Rembrandt's burghers, but in his case the subordination itself is eloquent of the man. And in any case, to have had him full flush to the audience, confronting them directly, would not have been appropriate at all.

He was Sir David Webster, opera knight; and he was also a knight on a chessboard, one step back, one step to the side. He was happy, if that is the right word, not to be known. It was as a tyro aged forty-one that he first came to the Opera House, and it was only at this point that he permitted his story to begin. His colleagues at the Opera House weren't made privy to what had gone before. To people he'd known earlier who were not involved in his new life he became henceforth a necessarily occasional visitor from another and strange world to them. There's nothing in the early years to justify a book being written about him. He was outstanding at university, but there are many who are bright there, equally bright, and who continue brightly in after-life, with successful and useful careers, who none the less don't make such a mark on their times that their contribution has to be recorded.

Webster's fellow-students at Liverpool had recognized very soon that he was someone who was going to have a career. The question was what. Even if music was his great love, it didn't have to be opera. At first it looked very much as if it wouldn't be. At university he'd studied economics and after university he was a success in business. During the war, again with great success, he worked for the Ministry of Supply, and before the Covent Garden offer came he'd already signed to work for Sir Robert Barlow as his assistant and putative heir at Metal Box – with a starting salary of £10,000 a year, more than he was to get at the Opera House after twenty-five years' service. But even if he'd risen to become Sir Metal Box in his turn people would hardly have wanted a book about him.

It's possible to imagine that he might have gone another way altogether, and become a diplomat. He could certainly have been of use in the Trades Union movement, for he had a 'socialist' conscience – socialist in inverted commas because he didn't have any definite political affiliations and is the harder to define as one because even in the 'thirties, when cloth-caps were in, there was nothing at all 'cloth-cap' about him. Opera-hat if you like.

For all his 'socialist' leanings he chose the Royal Opera House. Like any traditional opera house it is an emblem of privilege and class-separation. It is precisely because of such associations that not so long ago a befurred and bejewelled first-night audience was pelted with mud on their way in to La Scala, Milan. There's not a better picture of the tiara-set on show than in the celebrated theatre-scenes in Proust's *The Guermantes Way* – the aristocracy is set in an aspic of privilege, and given full credit for the glamour, the more so because Proust remains an outsider, at a distance from them. Webster too was an outsider in this world, or in such of it as survived after the Second World War, and had he been a reading man he might well have identified himself with the author-hero, who remains respectfully bemused if at the same time covertly satirical.

But he also recognized that, on the very simplest level, we have to have an opera house. It is right, and necessary, that *The Mastersingers* and *The Marriage of Figaro* and *Otello* be performed. These works are as central to European culture as the Acropolis or Botticelli's *Primavera*. They *must* be made available. The question of *to whom available* was one that exercised David Webster. If he responded to royalty he also loved his audience up in the gallery, and soon after his appointment he declared that his aim was 'to make the house popular, not just aristocratic'. Pre-war opera had been international, dressy and exclusive. Such opera as wasn't exclusive had not been glamorous. He wanted to create an opera which was both glamorous and popular.

The house had been a dance-hall for servicemen during the war, and Desmond Shawe-Taylor, writing in *Vogue*, noted that 'the beautiful old building can doubtless be held to have "done its bit" – like a prima donna gallantly tackling "Roll Out the Barrel" in the NAAFI'. When Webster took it over it was still shabby, a mere shell of a building. But to him it was beautiful even before it was refurbished: one of the most beautiful of buildings, one which inspires devotion, in its artists, its staff, its audiences. It opens a perspective on to a world of vanished elegance, and this elegance Webster was determined should be preserved and enjoyed.

One could almost say Webster's *People* rather than his audience, for in a sense he was a self-appointed pupil of the pioneering Lilian Baylis of the Old Vic, who was wont to talk unceasingly of 'My People', for whom only the best, she never tired of asserting, was good enough. Sir David's People were most particularly the people up there in the amphitheatre and gallery, even more than royalty and the aristocracy and the rich whose patronage was of especial importance in his early, building days at the Opera House.

The feeling of exclusiveness, of the house and the whole world of opera, was very strong in 1946 when Webster reopened Covent Garden, and something which much concerned the new boss with his 'socialist' conscience. This exclusiveness is nicely parodied in a little incident of the early post-war years. Royalty was expected at a performance of *Tiresias*, the bisexual ballet choreographed somewhat ahead of its time back in 1951 by Frederick Ashton. Fonteyn was disturbingly passionate as Tiresias exploring sex as a woman, and threatened to turn Opera House into hot-house. On Constant Lambert, responsible for the scenario as well as the music, devolved the task of writing a synopsis for the programme. 'Enclosing the *Tiresias* libretto,' he wrote to the press officer, Michael Wood: 'I have done my best to make the point of the story clear to the gallery while keeping it concealed from Royalty. A very difficult task I assure you.'

If the house itself was 'exclusive', the very act of opera itself could be construed as similarly tainted. There is a huge range of works in the opera repertory, which incorporates the musical equivalent of all species of drama, classical as well as boulevard; one roof gives shelter to the classical and the commercial, the frivolous and the highbrow. With Wagner in the repertory opera can't be accused, in an obvious sense, of being altogether frivolous, but there is an apparent separation from the real world which can make it seem irrelevant. Totalitarian states, assuming that it is irrelevant, tend to be benevolent towards opera, as well as ballet, because they feel them to be so removed from ordinary life as not to be disturbing or provocative. Opera is often preferred remote. The heroine of Verdi's *La Traviata* is a courtesan, and the first audiences, in 1853, would have found her more acceptable as a figure of their own day if she had been vilified. Verdi, however, presents her most tenderly, and before it could achieve success the opera had to be played in the costume of an earlier period. In its still comparatively early days, back in the eighteenth century, Doctor Johnson had notably dubbed opera 'an exotic and irrational entertainment', and in our own day we have J. W. Lambert, literary editor of the *Sunday Times*, commenting with great love in a radio programme on 'this dotty and elevating art form'.

Very occasionally opera does have an immediate relevance. Bellini was an Italian patriot and in his *Norma* the chorus of Druid warriors shouting for the expulsion of the Romans was easily applied to the anti-Austrian ferment of the time. The Risorgimento owes much to the inspiring strains of Verdi, and Auber's *Masaniello* had the distinction, if not perhaps markedly any other, of actually inciting a revolution, for after its first performance at La Monnaie in Brussels on 5 August 1830 the audience stormed out of the theatre and instantly took to the barricades. But one can scarcely imagine Webster mounting an opera at Covent Garden hoping to send its audience out burning to cast votes in a local election. (*Masaniello*, incidentally, is the opera with a non-singing ballerina heroine who finally leaps from a balcony in Naples to her death in the crater of Vesuvius – which happens to be some eight miles away. Dotty indeed!)

So the Opera House, and opera itself, on this deeper level presented a fascinating challenge, and it was taken up by a man who relished difficult situations because coping with them allowed him the fullest exercise of his talents. A huge task, undertaken by a man whose experience of administration had been mainly in business. Yet barely ten years later he could write in *Music and Musicians*: 'To the Londoner of 1939 the idea of opera and ballet for eleven months a year would have been unthinkable. Today the Opera House is accepted as part of the normal life of the town. That surely is an achievement.'

It is indeed an achievement, and in a sense too thoroughly, too quietly achieved for the good of his own reputation. The Opera House, organized in a completely different way from any it had previously known throughout its long history, enjoys huge international prestige: its acclaim resounds and his name is lost in the din. He didn't mind, as the noise pleased him. But he wasn't falsely modest, not modest at all, and his quiet smile was no disclaimer. He knew the measure of his achievement.

He wasn't an elusive personality, still less an enigmatic one. But he was complex. In each decade of his life, at least until his last, he seemed to be very thoroughly of his time. In the 'thirties he was 'socialist', and also the socialite. He had his collapsible opera-hat, a flat disc which, when you gave a bang to the edge, concertinaed out shinily. In the 'forties he was your full Shaftesbury Avenue toff. Shaftesbury Avenue then meant Tennant's and Binkie Beaumont, and Rattigan's *While the Sun Shines*, and there was Hermione Gingold and her bitchy intimate revues, and the Ivy restaurant was *the* theatre-rendezvous. And then through into the 'fifties. Barbara Goalen's era, when the fashion model stalked with blank black elegance against plush; and if the plush seemed rather often to be that of the Opera House it could have been because Barbara Goalen was a close friend of David's, and was often photographed there. He could move with the times because he had such a refined sense of time.

As to the bringing in of an audience more and more representative of the nation as a whole – bringing them in to savour opera on the grandest level – this is perhaps still not fully achieved, but the movement is in the right direction. The complete renewal of the gallery seating, under Webster's watchful eye, was a part of that movement. The top balcony, the amphitheatre, used to give way, after only six rows, to an entirely separate gallery cut off from the main part of the house. This was made up, apparently, of shabbily upholstered benches, but the gallery-goer knew that they weren't benches at all, but merely strips of upholstered board on huge, barely concealed stone steps: and narrower strips, carrying small numbered enamelled discs to indicate each person's allotted space, also saved him pressing back against naked stone. From downstairs in the house, or from the stage, this entire gallery, holding five hundred or so people, a quarter of the entire audience, appears to be a tiny pocket almost outside the house proper, somewhat like a lopsided teat on a massive bottle. In 1964 all this was changed. The barrier between amphitheatre and gallery was ripped out, comfortable tip-up seats were installed, and the whole area became known henceforth as amphitheatre, upper and lower. Glamour had finally infiltrated the remote areas of the house, and with the removal of the barrier former galleryites were made to feel that they were not merely distant spectators but, now, participants in the activities of the house. This alteration had been devoutly wished by Webster – it helped him 'embrace' his audience. And a cruel fact of the matter is that the alterations were only finally willed on the governors in the interests of safety. Money had to be spent would they or no, and

Webster had his opportunity to make the alterations in the way he'd long wanted to.

He has to be recreated, this complex man. Lunches, thousands of them, at the Savoy Grill, where he had his own table. He wasn't one for the canteen, though later, when his regime at the Opera House was fully established, and he himself greatly esteemed, he would occasionally make an entrance there. A hush would fall, and he would be enhaloed in the respect accorded him. The flower end of the Crush Bar in the Opera House was familiarly known as David's corner, where he and his friends would drink, through all the intervals, nothing but Dom Perignan champagne. He was a man for champagne, and lived rather too well for his own good. But he always had. When he ran the Bon Marché store in Liverpool before the war, he was to be spotted in the confectionery department digging into the chocolates . . . sampling the wares. He was greedy and he didn't take enough exercise. He was at the Opera House among the most exercised people in the world, the ballet company, and he didn't even walk anywhere. Towards the end of his life he'd maybe take a stroll along the front at Brighton, where after his father's death his mother came down to live, but that was all.

There was also David Webster in the privacy of his own well-appointed home, supper balanced on his knee, perhaps, and ready to be dropped in on as casually as might be by a variety of friends: and there'd often be a choice of three home-baked pies, memories of Ma's simple fare.

And he was a shy man. It was partly from his very shyness that he derived his sympathetic understanding of his artists, which was totally unenvious and uncompetitive. He could write, again in *Music and Musicians*, that 'Criticism is good for institutions, but criticism of artists must be tempered with pats on the back and recognition.' This is especially admirable in a man who had himself suffered so deeply from criticism.

The accompanist Ivor Newton has suggested, in his autobiography *At the Piano*, 'that the wealthy lover of art gave something to the world which has never been replaced. The practical enthusiasm and personal interest of the great patron went beyond anything an official cultural programme can give.' Webster's career stands as a challenge to this dictum. Newton may be right in the main – but Webster at least, using public money, *did* give his artists precisely 'that practical enthusiasm and personal interest', and they were part of the basis of his success in dealing with them.

He was gallant in his shyness. When he walked through the market, which in some ways it's a pity to have lost from the Hockney painting, he drew himself up to his full and not so very considerable height, making the most of himself. As the years passed, and he continued at the Opera House, he of course became known to the people in the market. He appeared to them friendly, and not unnecessarily grand, but still very slightly remote, as though he knew that his authority would be diminished here too by familiarity. His shyness made it easier for him to be a trifle aloof-seeming. All this was appreciated by many he worked with. 'Do you know,' he once said to Geraint Evans, 'you've never invited me to your home?' 'When you retire and you're not my boss any more,' Geraint Evans answered, acknowledging his appreciation of the Webster persona, and abetting him in the maintaining of it, 'I'll invite you then, that's the first thing I'll do.'

He was complex, many-tiered like his Opera House – jaunty, bravely the showman, with a thumb in his waistcoat pocket, and perhaps in the later years a trace of dandruff on the shoulders of the well-cut, now slightly crumpled suit. And across his waistcoat was the delicate chain of his wafer-thin gold fob-watch. He was a man who had undertaken a gigantic task and succeeded in it. And he translated himself into a tiny Colossus bestriding the market, as was his right.

PART ONE

Foundations

CHAPTER I

Birth in Scotland · education in Liverpool · amateur theatricals · political opinions · Sunday school superintendent

David Webster was born on 3 July 1903, a summer baby. More particularly a festival baby. In July of that year Bayreuth was once more tuning up, shortly to welcome visitors again to its annual jamboree, and Bayreuth's Wagner, along with Mozart, whose spirit and works dominate nearby Salzburg, can be made to stand in jointly as his godfathers. During that same year Melba was again giving her Mimi and Juliet at Covent Garden, and it is possible to imagine her voice as the most beautiful and significant raised at baby Webster's christening.

Webster can be claimed as a son of Liverpool, but he was actually born north of the border, in Dundee. His father was a commercial traveller in grocery, and it was when he was appointed area manager for Reckitt's that he brought his family down with him to Liverpool. Ernest Newman, later famous as music critic of the *Sunday Times*, and an authority on Wagner, was a native of Liverpool, and he too can be registered as one pronouncing an unconscious benediction on that Dundee christening, for 1903 was the year when, giving up commerce for the world of music, as David Webster himself was one day to do, he joined the staff of the Midlands Institute of Music in Birmingham.

Wee David was only ten years old when he was removed from Dundee, but he took a something Scots down south with him, something much more than a Dundee accent which he was still able to hit off perfectly, when he chose, even in his later Empire-building days. And not that meanness either, which conventionally, and offensively, is still often attributed to the Scots – though Webster was well aware of this legend. The Scots bass David Ward shared not only initials with him but also his birthday, and each year over a long period the two DW's would exchange the same initialled birthday cards, a nice send-up of their imputed national characteristic.

The something Scots is altogether subtler. It might have been derived in part at least from a disciplined childhood – which, however, he could have had were he born somewhere else. But young David had this special characteristic, that he would tell you, precisely and once only, whatever he had to say to you. By not being prepared to repeat himself, or to elaborate, he impressed on his audience the importance of what he had to say and his own importance too. Goethe once wrote a long letter to a friend, and ended by apologizing – he hadn't had time, he explained, to write short. Webster conveyed the impression of having condensed his speech before uttering, one of the reasons why, later, he was a non-pareil among after-dinner speakers.

More specifically one might say that there was something Scots Presbyterian about him which made him not only a man of words – few and well-chosen – but also, finally, very much a man of his word. A decision once made, he stood by it. He was hardly a *young* young man, even in his Liverpool schooldays, or at university there. He often appeared pompous, particularly to those who didn't have the wit to divine his future importance, of which his youthful self-importance was merely the shell. Guilelessly, but not by any means unconsciously, he had from his early years almost put himself into inverted commas, 'David Webster, Man of his Word': and it was this which was to enable him later on to play the English gentleman to foreigners. Maria Callas was interviewed once at London Airport arriving after a not particularly spectacular but much-headlined difference with Rudolph Bing of the Metropolitan Opera, New York. Her contrasting good relations with David Webster were commented on. 'Ah, yes,' she explained, her words travelling usefully round the world. 'But David Webster is a gentleman.' Though here in England the word gentleman is still too bound up with the question of birth, and not everyone would allow him to be one. At least one colleague in his Royal Opera House days was sometimes, in moments of exasperation, to be heard complaining, 'The fellow's *not* a gentleman!' But he was the very idea of the English gentleman to foreigners, which gave him a useful persona for dealing with them.

He was also devout. Soberly devout. His parents never drew the blinds on Sundays, they remained closed, and the family lived through the Sabbath in a dim light, pious goldfish. In Liverpool David joined the Sefton Park Presbyterian Church, a liberal church with nothing narrowly Calvinist about it, and later he served as Sunday school superintendent. This soberest side of himself he kept private when he reached London, not because of provincialism but because of his fear of being thought provincial. But he never, throughout his London days, lost the habit of praying to God in difficult times. At the Opera House, when things were going badly on stage he would pace up and down behind the grand tier, flushing pinkly, and muttering – and it was usually God he was muttering to.

His own favourite memory of his Scottish childhood was being taken to see Pavlova dance. He hadn't, like so many others, been inspired with the desire to become a dancer himself, but he did owe to the ballerina an anecdote that he loved to repeat in after years. As number succeeded number through the evening, the applause for her had become ever more tumultuous, but after *The Dying Swan* a hushed, awed silence gripped the theatre. It was too much for a lady in a nearby stall, who couldn't restrain herself. 'Well,' she whispered excitedly, 'don't you think she's exactly like Mrs Wishart!'

Liverpool proved a very satisfactory stopover for David Webster. The city was small enough, local enough, for a young man to make himself accepted in it as kingpin, while still large enough to be a cultural centre – and this long before the Beatles and the Merseyside poets brought to it a special and fairly brief celebrity in the 'sixties. 'God intended me to shine,' Dame Edith Evans once reputedly informed another actress who had complained to her that she was being mercilessly overshadowed in a scene they shared, 'and shine I must!' David Webster had to shine too, and he did. Liverpool saw his protracted education, which certainly didn't end with his university days. Here in Liverpool he flexed muscles and prepared himself, learned his strengths and increased them. He made himself into *somebody* in Liverpool: he was prepared to move to London when the right opportunity presented itself, when he was certain of being somebody there too. The story of his early life can be read as the story of the provincial arming himself for the assault on the Big City. He might have been ready earlier, but the important thing is that he was ready when at last that opportunity did present itself.

He seemed never to have been young, even when he *was* young. At school, certainly by the time he came to university, he was already a kind of father-figure, judiciously good-humoured, pompous but also kind, with a detachment anything but youthful. It seemed natural for him to assume that what he was doing was more interesting than what anyone else was doing and, while he was a courteous listener, it was his own activities that were usually the subject of conversation.

His parents recognized very soon that they had between them produced something out of the ordinary. His father didn't know what, exactly. His mother was prepared to sit back, proud and imperturbable, to wait and see. This mother, not a warm and outgoing woman, nor given to being responsive, was not an easy woman to impress, nor easily disturbed. There was a likelihood that he was not for their sphere, that in his future life he would be driven beyond them into worlds not theirs. But she didn't seem frightened of losing him. She wasn't possessive, which in itself could be disturbing for David. She seemed happy, as far as anyone could judge, to watch him at a distance, and certainly didn't expect, or even want, to be a part of his social life. She was imperturbable and David would have liked to draw a response from her, with the result that finally it was he who was possessive of her. If he was tied at all, it wasn't she who tied him – he tied himself.

Webster was educated at Holt School, and in 1921 won a scholarship which took him to Liverpool University. The 'twenties were beginning, an exciting period, subsequently dubbed the Jazz Age and embodied in the dazzling figure of F. Scott Fitzgerald; a generation had been erased in the war just ended, and the future was with Webster's generation. A responsibility to replace the dead heroes devolved on Webster and Co., and he was gaily eager to accept it. He was a natural for an arts course at university, but he elected, as a better preparation for his future, to study economics instead. His choice of subject was a happy one, for his confirmed brilliance in economics released him from any inhibiting fear of money. He was freed to imbibe, in due course, the lesson that business is no impersonal art, that it is not the history of man in relation to the ledger, but is finally another branch of the art of personal relations, people more than figures.

Even so, his studies were by no means the most important part of his university life. Within the year Webster had become Secretary of the University Guild, and also Chairman of the Dramatic Society: and dividing himself for his two functions he wrote to himself and back again and had the correspondence published in the university magazine. The Secretary of the Dramatic Society was a girl who later married the novelist John Brophy, and she played opposite her Chairman in a play called *Fogerty's Fairy* by W. S. Gilbert. In the course of the action David had to kiss her. 'In those days he was a great one for flirting with the girls,' she volunteered. 'He and I were quite sweet on one another.'

In his second year David held auditions for Shaw's *Arms and the Man*, and gave the part of Sergius to a new boy, Joe Hodgkinson, who, as it turned out, in the future was to be helpful to him in his Opera House career; while he cast himself, already, with a kind of foresight, dipping into the chocolates, as Bluntschli, the Chocolate Soldier. A lightsome flamboyance was as much a part of the young David as the Florida Water he always wore, or that watch on its chain of which he appreciated the full picturesque value, and which he later sported bravely in Covent Garden market. When he played Bluntschli he didn't have confidence in his memory. The play's climax is Bluntschli's big speech, and he prepared for it, very much in the style of Mrs Patrick Campbell, by jotting down parts of it on bits of paper and leaving them here and there about the stage, behind chairs, under vases, on shelves. It wasn't only that he didn't trust his memory: typically, he also didn't intend to overtax himself unnecessarily. At one performance a mischievous cast shifted the papers about. They were not rewarded by any outward show of distress. Young Hodgkinson, on stage with him, admiringly noted his resourcefulness and the unflappability which was to become famous. Webster might appear to have been taking his revenge when it was the turn of J. M. Barrie's one-acter *The Twelve Pound Look*. Again he spread his bits of paper about. This time the papers were left where they were – but he found that he himself had muddled them, so he walked off stage, whispering coolly to the unfortunate actress left behind to cope alone, 'Winnie, I'm just going off to look at the book.' (Joe Hodgkinson must have taken pity on poor Winnie, for later he swept her up in consoling holy matrimony.)

David Webster both acted and directed while at university, and the list of plays gives off a whiff of the period. *Portrait of a Man with Red Hair*, Benn Levy's adaptation of the Hugh Walpole novel, in which David played the lead. There was *Musical Chairs* by Rodney Ackland, and Ashley Dukes's *The Man With a Load of Mischief*, a favourite of Webster's. He directed A. A. Milne's *The Dover Road* as well as appearing in it: he was proud of being, as it were, actor-manager on this occasion, and was puffed up with pride throughout the period of rehearsal and performance. Unfortunately he didn't have time to learn his lines properly. The *Liverpool Daily Post*, perhaps of the opinion that pride ought to have a fall, judged that 'on the whole, Mr Webster was not as good as Mr Milne'.

He wasn't highbrow, but didn't admit it to himself – he liked to be thought of as having a wide range of interests not dully *confined* to the highbrow. And with some reason. The future Mrs Brophy had the impression that he came from a home 'without much culture' but adds that he was 'very quick to pick up cultural things – especially about music, for example'. He was interested in what was current, the best of its kind in its own age, which is the only time when much that is merely good can be enjoyed at all. The expressionist drama of Ernst Toller caught his fancy, but he also enjoyed popular theatre. He was up-to-date, swingingly as we might say in the 'seventies, and his contemporaries, who regarded him as a vital force, relied on him to lead them to all that was latest in the drama, in the same way as they looked to Alan Rawsthorne in the musical field – though there was little comparable musical excitement at the university. The breadth of Webster's sympathies, together with his sense of what goes in the theatre, marked him out already as a real theatre-man; and when a universities drama festival was held at Oxford, at the J. B. Fagan Theatre, his friends were not surprised in the least to see David Webster's production win it.

He had the easy but not necessarily deep culture of the café society. It is only in the light of his future career that his theatrical activities at university earn themselves special prominence, for he himself didn't know where his future was to lie. He certainly wasn't deliberately preparing himself for the role of musical administrator, much less for the running of an opera house.

To his friends, none the less, he did seem set for a career in the theatre. When after university he went into business they all felt he had let them down, all the more because there had been a distinct possibility of their group founding a theatre company to storm the capital: the dream had been endorsed by many a smoke-wreathed late-night discussion, stimulated by black coffee and that release of adrenalin occasioned by contemplation of future glory. People in Webster's later life tended to be amazed that a businessman, coming late into the theatre, could successfully build an opera company from nothing and bring new and continuous life to the empty shell of an intermittently great house. But his career can also be interpreted as having always been the theatre, interrupted by a long spell in business; and throughout his business career his interest in theatre and music, and his participation in these arts, continued.

At university, as Secretary of the Guild, and after his first year as President, he constantly showed that he knew how to get people to do things for him, and the stewards of the Guild too regarded him as a grown man, not a boy. This was partly because he was somewhat portly from the very beginning, but mainly because he had learnt how to create that father-figure manner to go with the portliness – a rhythm of movement, an unassertive weightiness and gravity – which used a possible disadvantage to good effect. He was soft, and inclined to be flabby, but he had also a certain delicacy; and if anyone later on was tempted to recall him as a gangling youth he knew how to destroy that memory.

He had no interest in learning for its own sake, he confined himself to absorbing what was useful to him. He was interested in Toller, and later also in Capek, because he was deeply interested in political ideas. Prominent on his bookshelf, but also read – in his university days at least, he did read a certain amount – was Fülöp-Miller's *Mind and Face of Bolshevism*. And he went farther afield than Oxford for the drama festival. He was one of the delegates from Liverpool University at the first international student gathering after the war, which was organized by the International Student Service, later absorbed into the World University Service, and which took place in Budapest. Budapest then represented *Mittel*-Europa at a very particular point in its history, the Bela Kun revolution in Hungary having been a spin-off from the Russian Revolution, and Horthy having been put in power after a communist dictatorship lasting nine months. Webster was brought into contact with top students from all over the world and he benefited richly from the contact. Such a mind-broadening experience was all the more valued by a mere provincial.

This was another side of him than the bright young theatre-man. The 'socialist' side was also shown by the earnest young man who ran a Sunday school in Liverpool's dockland, where the boys in the interest of hygiene had to have their hair cropped, leaving only a quiff on top; and he was also associated with the Nile Street University Settlement, which had been modelled on Toynbee Hall in London. Here he saw poverty and the urgent housing problems, and he experienced the extra tensions created by the large numbers of coloured immigrants. A. A. Milne and J. M. Barrie alone aren't enough to invoke the David Webster of his student days.

He left university in 1924. He didn't go into the theatre and he didn't become a diplomat. Twenty years were to pass before he began to be thoroughly himself, and only hindsight sees him to have been preparing himself through these two decades, so that in 1944, the war ending and he ready for his assault on London, he seemed, with his accustomed quietness, to be no more than gathering together the threads.

CHAPTER II

A Liverpool businessman · Bon Marché's manager · more amateur theatricals · ballet and opera · famous names · London visits · travels abroad

David Webster graduated in economics and went on to read education, part of the time in Oxford as well as Liverpool. He began, but didn't complete, a thesis on the place of drama in education, and he looked about for a job instead. An administrative job in education was a possibility, but he also thought about going into insurance, because the father of one of his friends was General Manager of the biggest insurance company in England and would have held doors open for him. But it also happened that another friend was Advertising Controller for Liverpool's Lewis group of stores, and David went in with him instead.

He didn't have strong vocational urges and he certainly didn't feel he was committing himself for life. Webster wasn't, in fact, from the very beginning a man given to long-term planning. He went into Lewis's thinking only that Lewis's was *now*. And he didn't stay on the advertising side long. He soon went over to merchandising, not in Lewis's itself but in Bon Marché, the sister-store, to begin with merely walking the floor. He then became a Departmental Manager, and from there was promoted to become General Manager – and this when he was still a year or two short of thirty, and at a salary of something like £7000 a year.

Lewis's, a kind of Liverpool equivalent of Selfridge's, was large and comprehensive and necessarily impersonal, while Bon Marché was smaller, a little-sister fashion-store with some aspirations to class. Before Webster it was also somewhat provincial, even tatty, but during his tenure he justified its aspirations. *Bon marché* is French for cheap, and a store so-called in France is the equivalent of Woolworth's or a dime-store: but by the time Webster had done with it, Liverpool's Bon Marché could be regarded as an equivalent of Marshall and Snelgrove in London. The name Bon Marché certainly didn't translate itself into cheap to the crowds who passed in the 'thirties, or stopped to gawk. It had a something French about it, it had style and chic, it was of course rather expensive, not within the reach of everybody's pocket. But it did have something extra . . .

While Webster reigned here supreme, Fred Marquis – later Lord Woolton – ruled at Lewis's. Later admirers and colleagues of the two men would have had difficulty envisaging them meeting in another guise altogether in darkest dockland, but in fact Marquis had been Resident Social Worker at the Nile Street Settlement, which is where Webster first encountered him. The Social Worker had seen the potential in the Sunday School Teacher, who in his turn had responded to something in the Social Worker. Marquis was another formidable provincial who rose through trade, and he too was eventually to storm the capital as a proven businessman. If like Webster he hadn't appeared provincial in the provinces, in the big city he too was wary, needing the reassurance that he was better prepared, better armed, than any competitor. Marquis, the first non-Jew at his level in what had been a Jewish family business, encouraged Webster and finally appointed him his successor as General Manager of Lewis's. When he left Webster took over from him, and the move to the larger store was an advance for the younger man both in status and salary: but Webster regretted Bon Marché none the less, for there he had been able to impose himself more. It was also more fun, which was one of the reasons he had stayed on so long. It paid well and he had enjoyed it as well.

At Bon Marché Webster embarked on a life of selling which was by no means interrupted when he was seconded to the Opera House. The location had changed, and the merchandise, and 'the store' was somewhat different, but there was a continuity. As it happens, Webster wasn't the only opera house manager with store experience. Rudolph Bing, when he had already put in time with Glyndebourne Opera, did his stint at Peter Jones in Sloane Square in 1941, and afterwards was assistant to the Director of Selling for all the twenty or so stores in the group. You have to know how to sell whatever it is you're selling, and neither was the poorer for his store experience.

Reinforcing his training in economics, it made Webster more than ever a man not afraid of money. It had no mystery for him, no glamour, especially after he had proved himself capable of commanding a large salary. 'Making money,' he would say, 'is only a knack.' A necessary and large part of his success as an opera administrator was in the handling of money – of money, and of the people, at the Arts Council and in the Treasury, who themselves handled money and had to be persuaded to part with it. What from the point of view of many money-people is merely an artistic flair wouldn't have been enough on its own to keep the house open.

Bon Marché was just right for Webster, big enough to impress but still small enough, and he imposed himself very thoroughly. God had to intercede if you wanted to see Marquis at Lewis's, but Webster at Bon Marché was very approachable. He was known for his fairness and for his love of people: from the beginning he showed himself a wonderful boss. Even so, he learned a lesson from Marquis, for in his prime at the Opera House he deliberately created the impression of a certain remoteness which added to his distinction.

But in Liverpool, for all that he'd seemed so mature even as a student, he was actually young, and young in a particular period. He was a Bright Young Thing, store or no store; as accustomed to striped blazers as to dinner-jackets, as much at home under a straw boater as under an opera-hat. He wasn't one of those ambitious young men who abandon gaiety when they enter into one of the respectable professions. He didn't dedicate himself grimly and humourlessly, but remained a Bright Young Thing whatever.

There was gaiety in the store itself. He imported it. One of his innovations was the bargain basement, which was definitely fun. And it was important for, giving the public the treat of shopping at Bon Marché in the 'thirties, the time of the Depression and the Jarrow March, it spread glamour a little beyond the circle of the affluent.

He also arranged exhibitions of paintings in a gallery beside the restaurant, and in the restaurant he held lectures and readings. An up-to-the-minute attraction was Edith Sitwell, in gold tissue and leopard-skin, reading *Façade* (ever after he thought her 'a much maligned woman'!). Webster also arranged fashion-shows, a daring novelty, and he conducted them himself, of course stylishly. 'Ladies,' he rallied his paying public, 'if you will insist on stuffing yourselves with cream cakes in our restaurants don't imagine you can walk on to the fashion floor and find something suitable off the peg.' The ladies were somehow flattered. They regarded with ironic sidelong glances the bulging figures of their neighbours without seeming to be conscious of their own – and meanwhile not one, but two, departments of the store had been advertised. Webster had a positively wilful confidence in what he was selling, which he learned and, once learnt, possessed for his entire life. Whether it was dresses and cream cakes or operas and opera-singers.

He conveyed confidence too to those involved with him. It was his personnel management which showed him perhaps most satisfyingly as the diplomat that might have been. At the store once he noticed that some of the girls were badly made-up. He didn't prowl the departments making personal comments, nor did he issue directives from a safe distance. What he did was gleefully to inform the girls that free tuition in make-up was going to be made available to any of them who wanted it.

He was a familiar figure about the store, but he didn't have to act grand to maintain his dignity, because the respect he inspired already made other people keep their distance from him. He had, as has been noted, more than a touch of pomposity: but this seemed natural to him, and he was appreciated for being able to be very much himself with everyone, without loss of dignity. In a lift he began to sing a popular song of the day, 'I took one look at you . . .' and a salesgirl who happened to be in the lift with him nearly fainted with surprise. This was, after all, the Guv'nor!

He conveyed that, once he'd engaged someone to do a job for him, that man or woman had his complete trust. A new employee was at once left alone to get on with his job unimpeded – but he or she was also expected to justify that trust. Webster was famous for getting the best out of his staff. 'I do very little,' he boasted later, 'besides engaging the best available staffs in each department and then I leave it to them.' It was no small boast, really. Napoleon could have said the same thing. Webster happened by this time to have arrived at the Opera House, but his boast could be applied to his management of either 'store'.

He also contrived to give people a sense that, if he left them alone to get on with their jobs, how they did them was none the less noted. They were thoroughly overseen by an often invisible overseer. And an overseer, what's more, who could on occasion be dangerous, and even brutal in abruptly dismissing anyone who revealed himself as incompetent or talentless. He particularly disliked dismissing people, and as he also hated to have an easy atmosphere disrupted, to have the sweetness of his troupe soured, he never wanted to keep people on to work out their notice. 'If they're going, let them go at once.'

Webster wasn't slow to realize that at Bon Marché he was coping with some of the same sort of problems that face an administrator in the theatre. Becoming successful in a new field had brought its excitements, but he'd become successful almost too early, and after a couple of years as manager, while he was still hardly into his thirties, he couldn't help wondering sometimes if he shouldn't be moving on, perhaps coming nearer to fulfilling his friends' expectations by finding himself a job in the theatre.

But he now had a great deal to lose. On the local scene David Webster of Bon Marché was a great figure, and he loved being a great figure. And if he had a capacity for enjoying life, he also had money enough and freedom enough to go ahead and enjoy it.

His life was not by any means confined to the store. He was also right at the centre of the Sandon Studios Society, which gave him opportunities both to act and to direct. The Sandon had originally been founded by artists, both professional and amateur, to provide life classes, and a sympathetic group of patrons had been created by inviting those interested in the arts to join as well. Class-divisions at this time were rigid, and the Society was middle-, preponderantly upper-middle class: it was self-consciously exclusive, with a humour inclined to be waggish, and in the 'thirties, the period of the Depression, also a kind of refuge. A history of the Sandon has been published which contains a note from George Melly, the writer and jazz-singer: 'The Sandon is so much a part of my early memories that it is hard for me to think of it as a real place. It has the mythical precision of the stories of Beatrix Potter. It carried an aura of immense sophistication.'

And so too, for George Melly, did David Webster. It was 'Uncle David' who, having played the mighty role of Macbeth at the Sandon, and not at all badly, coached young George when *he* played Lady Macbeth at Stowe.

In 1924, alongside Alan Rawsthorne, Webster appeared in the Sandon production of Molière's *Georges Dandin.* ('Mr David Webster as Monsieur de Sotenville,' said the *Liverpool Post*, 'was able to preserve an aristocratic hauteur even in a nightgown with his wig awry.') He directed the Sandon's *Cherry Orchard* in 1929, which was early days for Chekhov in England, and the Coventry Nativity Play at the Philharmonic Hall. He also did *The Beggar's Opera.* At the Sandon again in 1932 there was Bridie's *Tobias and the Angel*; Webster had the pleasure of mounting Toller's *Masses and Man*, which he had so long admired; and Drinkwater's *The Storm* mustn't be forgotten, if only because of the notice which appeared in the *Post and Mercury*, praising George Melly's mother Maud for her 'sincere and virile display as the grief-stricken wife'.

By no means confining his activities to the Sandon, Webster got his own ventures going too at the David Lewis Theatre, drawing for casts on the various dramatic societies on Merseyside: and all in all the list represents a goodly and parallel range, Shakespeare and Chekhov on the one hand, Bridie and Drinkwater on the other. In 1936 there was Eliot's *Murder in the Cathedral* which, reported the *Church Times*,

> was played for three nights last week to crowded audiences at the Central Hall, Liverpool . . . The atmosphere was wonderful, the stillness of the audience being a tribute to the way the skilful performers merged themselves into their parts, and made the play live. Mr David Webster was the Producer, and took the part of the Saint with dignity and restraint. One only wished that all clergy could preach sermons in the perfect manner of his Christmas address.

The rest of the article discusses the singing of the Plainchant from the Salisbury Antiphoner – it shows Webster already adept as producer of poetic drama with musical accompaniment, which after all is a possible definition of quite a number of operas. Elizabeth Latham, while she was the Opera House's stage manager, came across this notice and showed it to David Webster. Flushed out into the open just this once, just for a moment, Webster blushed shyly but happily, recalled to the past he never himself voluntarily recalled for anyone's instruction.

David Webster could act, often very well. It is not every actor who can cope with Beckett in *Murder in the Cathedral*, let alone with Macbeth. He never contemplated a career as an actor, however, and the reason is not far to seek. Simply, he was not of heroic stature. He wasn't likely either to become a matinée idol or to have a chance with the great roles such as Hamlet or Antony. He wasn't going to measure up to Gerald du Maurier or to John Gielgud, a close friend from this period. He'd have to make do as a character actor, and this would have meant waiting until middle age to 'come into his own' – and his own, as character actor, wasn't going to be enough.

Besides, Webster's talents and interests were possibly too wide-ranging, too various for him to have been happy applying himself with that single-minded concentration the actor's career demands. His interests overflowed into revue and cabaret as well, and into Victorian music-hall, which was not yet dead. (Seeing Marie Lloyd was a treasured memory.) Revue and cabaret were very much of that day, which, if it was the Jarrow March and Capek, and Chekhov at the Vic, was also Noel Coward and Gertie Lawrence, and Jack Buchanan and Delysia and Maurice Chevalier – who between them created an escapist world as potent as that of Hollywood to minister to the unassuageable hungers of the Depression. Webster loved it all. He would settle himself at the piano and pound out Beethoven's 'Appassionata' with enormous vigour and enjoyment, but he was also liable to pick out a tune from one of the Cochran revues which had caught his fancy. 'Love is like a fountain, Flowing cool and clear,' he'd sing tunelessly.

Revue was naughty. It was David's delight to sit in the canteen at Bon Marché writing revues with his friend Alfred Francis, whose family were the largest confectioners in Liverpool and who later was on the Board at the Old Vic. Maud Budden too, whose husband was assistant to the Head of the School of Architecture, wrote and performed in many of the revues – 'Readers of the Liverpolitan are not strangers to Maud Budden's brilliance,' Webster commented in 1932, combining the role of critic with his various other roles. And in 1934 the Sandon put on *Masquerade*, a programme of 'song, ballet and absurdity in the manner of the Chauve-Souris', of which the opening number was 'Cascara Sagrada'. This was followed by a ballet with music by the distinguished conductor Eugene Goossens, who some years before had been for a short time a member of the Society, and later there was another ballet with music by Alfred Francis. A one-act play by Strindberg was also a part of the entertainment on offer.

The same atmosphere – without the Strindberg – pervaded a fashion parade organized by Maud Melly at the Rialto, the local dance-hall. She called it the Liverpool Lovelies, Bon Marché did the clothes, and one of the buyers wowed them by dressing up as Princess Marina: and finally Billy Moss, an actor from the Playhouse, emerged from the loo done up as the Duke of Kent.

Every Christmas the Sandon put on a cabaret, and one of their most successful sketches was a send-up of the Epstein sculpture 'Genesis', which had recently been on exhibition in the Society's gallery – and had not been to everyone's taste. The sculptor Tyson-Smith, another member, made a cast of 'Genesis', and the sketch began with Billy Moss as a clergyman, deliciously scandalized by the outrageous avant-gardery as well as by the too-too-shocking blasphemy. 'Well,' he justified himself plaintively, 'how can I criticize if I don't see it first?' Then on came Two Flighty Girls (portrayed by middle-class ladies) to register their shock at the impact of modern sculpture depicting the horrors of childbirth. They blanched under their make-up. 'I dunno,' said one of them, 'as I'm going in for a family. I think I'll tell my boy-friend I'd rather 'ave a career.' A hole had been left in the plaster-cast for David Webster's head, which was now spot-lit in a lurid green light as with relish he imitated birth-pains. He was well into labour when a voice agonizedly besought the audience, 'For Godsake! Is there a doctor in the house?' Blackout!

On the other hand, Alfred Francis got him involved with the Ballet Club, and the Blackpool Stage Drama Festivals showed him, if he needed to be shown, the growing appeal of ballet. In the mid-'thirties Ninette de Valois sent some of the principals of her young ballet company up to Liverpool to dance with the Ballet Club, and the whole of *Giselle* was given, as well as the second act of *Swan Lake* and the third of *Nutcracker*. David Webster by this time was Chairman of the Club, and it was his pleasure to watch one of de Valois's assistants rehearse the amateur corps de ballet and then himself to welcome the dancers, who were no less than the young Margot Fonteyn and Robert Helpmann. John Hart did the Russian Dance in *Nutcracker*, and William Chappell was the Strange Player in the fourth ballet, *The Haunted Ballroom*. De Valois herself came up to see the final performance and she attended the reception afterwards, though she didn't carry away any impression of Webster, whom she had encountered only briefly, and she didn't, when they later met again on a very different basis, remember having previously met him at all. Frederick Ashton, whom Webster had first met on one of his visits to London, and who had already been in Liverpool before to produce a revue at the local dancing school, also produced for the Ballet Club; and on another occasion de Valois herself produced *Coppélia* for them.

Webster's visits to London were likewise a part of his continuing education, and he was by no means a stranger to London when he eventually arrived there to stay. Far from it. Most of his London trips were in search of pleasure, and he was hell-bent for the opera or a concert. But sometimes he combined pleasure with business. In 1931, shortly after he'd become manager of Bon Marché, he was in London recruiting staff, and at a party in Berkeley Square he met a young man who was working for Shellmex BP. James Cleveland Belle was only twenty-one and had recently been transferred to London from Cardiff. He made an impression, and David suggested he make another move – why didn't he apply for a job with Bon Marché? Jimmy asked how much money. 'Two pounds a week, not more than three.' But Jimmy was already earning four, and he wasn't interested. Later, a first-class ticket to Liverpool arrived for him through the post – from David Webster. The idea of first-class rail travel gained the day, Jimmy never having travelled first before. (David, as usual, knew his man. If it had been a second-class ticket he wouldn't have gone.) Soon Jimmy was working at Bon Marché: and thus began a friendship which was to last forty years.

All through the 'thirties they were often to be seen together racing for the 4.10 train from Liverpool. They'd change into evening clothes on the train and present themselves immaculate at the opera or concert or at a first night, there'd be supper afterwards at the Savoy Grill or the Café Royal, and then indefatigably back they'd go on the sleeper, to be once more, refreshed, at the store next morning. There was one time they were on the train five nights in a row for the week of Toscanini concerts at the Queen's Hall, and a few weeks after that it was five nights in a row again, but this time for Duke Ellington. These trips were another important feature of this life-style Webster had found for himself, and it was one he was naturally reluctant to abandon for an uncertain future. Through these trips he continued to keep up with what was new and what was best, and his friends continued to rely on him to keep them informed, as they had in the university days.

As for opera – the Liverpool Repertory Opera Company was founded in 1924, owing much to the energy and idealism of Edith Rose, and it was the most ambitious effort in the history of music in Liverpool so far. Its aim was: 'to place opera within reach of all by means of low prices of admission (3d. to 2s. 4d.) and to create an opera-going public with the hope of the establishment of a permanent opera.'

The company had £500 a year from the Carnegie Trust and support from local business organizations, which gave young Webster an early and useful lesson in the matter of outside support for the arts. But a permanent opera, unfortunately, was not established. The General Strike in 1926 – the year also in which Ninette de Valois joined Lilian Baylis at the Old Vic Theatre – saw the company almost halfway through its brief career, which lasted five years, and it was no longer in operation to give solace during the Depression.

Besides offering Webster invaluable experience of opera, it showed him that the highest reaches of the theatrical arts had not necessarily to be the prerogative of those already privileged in other ways, and when he went to the Opera House at last he was already confirmed in his sense of mission. Edith Rose, as well as that tawny insistent parakeet of a great lady, Lilian Baylis, were important figures in his imaginative life and provided him with guide-lines.

It is appropriate that the most popular opera presented in Liverpool – and produced by David Webster – was Rutland Boughton's *The Immortal Hour*, which was repeated over three or four seasons. For Rutland Boughton, who died as recently as 1960, made a brave and systematic attempt to establish an English school of opera (after the manner of the Wagnerian music-drama; his single-mindedness and energy even saw the establishment for a while of his own Bayreuth at Glastonbury). And Boughton's attempt was only one of a number over the years – but English opera, and opera in English, had been mostly left to touring companies, and it was not always presented on the highest level.

John Tobin, later of the London Choral Society, was another leading spirit, and usually the conductor. Webster had the lion's share of production; though William Armstrong, Director of the Playhouse, was invited to take charge of a second work by Rutland Boughton, *The Queen of Cornwall*. Webster produced Gustav Holst's *The Golden Goose* (it happened that both Boughton and Holst were represented, very briefly, in the Covent Garden season of 1924). The work of most of the other composers, including Gervase Hughes, Joseph Holbrooke and Sir Charles Stanford, was harder to come by elsewhere.

The most startling of all the productions in Liverpool, however, wasn't an English work at all. It was Stravinsky's *The Soldier's Tale*, a novelty, as it turned out, more durable than most. Webster produced, and also, seated before a large beer barrel to one side of the stage, pointedly spoke the Narrator's part. In the Sandon history John Tobin writes:

> This music was novel in spirit and in the demands it made on the small orchestra. At one rehearsal the percussion player, endeavouring to fulfil Stravinsky's requirements that he should play four different instruments within the space of one bar, got so involved and contorted that, with a sudden cry of 'To hell with these bloody drumsticks!' he threw them to the floor and wept.

While the *Daily Telegraph*'s doubting comment was that:

> Of course it arrests attention; oddities inevitably do arrest attention. But it may be questioned whether in this long essay in wilfulness there is anything that will interest the public in ten or twenty years' time.

The successful businessman found the world more and more opening up to him. There were further treats. For their fortnight's holiday David and Jimmy would put the car on the train and then motor through the Rhineland, which they loved, to Salzburg. Salzburg became a yearly pilgrimage, and David took pleasure in introducing Jimmy to the famous Mozart performances there, which were all the more exhilarating because in the 'thirties Mozart performances, certainly on this level, were not matters of everyday. Another Salzburg highlight was Toscanini's *Otello*, which in Webster's canon stood equal with the famous Bruno Walter performances of Strauss's *Rosenkavalier* at Covent Garden. Toscanini was one of Webster's great heroes, and he would judiciously make appraisal of his discipline, his steadfast devotion to the work in hand, his generous disregard of himself in favour of the composer. These were sterling example and inspiration to the future impresario.

And there was Broadway – the Great White Way. The name alone set the juices flowing. Liverpool was linked to New York by luxury liner, and that too had its significance, for the liner then was the equivalent of today's jet aeroplane. The international set in those days took to the water – it was the heyday in films of the shipboard romance, with Alice Faye as the heroine, or Carole Lombard, and if not them then probably Constance Bennett. *The* line was the Cunard, and when David Webster went up the gang-plank at Liverpool on to the *Laconia*, perhaps, or the *Franconia*, he was even then contributing his mite to the Opera House, for it was none other than Lady Cunard herself who was behind many a Beecham Covent Garden season. On the crossings there was champagne, and gaiety, and stars to jostle elbows with. But in the midst of it all, a happy Webster was none the less, with his 'socialist' conscience, at moments uncomfortably aware that the stewards serving them were being paid around thirty shillings a week and relied on the flow of tips to bring up their families.

For one of his first trips to New York, before he had risen to be boss of Bon Marché, Webster had to travel economy-class; he had just enough money to last him a couple of weeks. He made the most of his height as he walked the streets, determined not to be overawed by skyscrapers.

As luck would have it, Mrs Patrick Campbell was playing in New York, and her young admirer presented himself in her dressing-room with an introduction from his friend William Armstrong, Director of the Playhouse. Mrs Pat remembered Billy Armstrong well. It was while he was touring with her in *Hedda Gabler* that the Board had appealed to Armstrong to become their Director. 'I could have made him a great actor,' Mrs Pat reminisced. 'But he threw away the chance, he became a little man who sits in an office and makes lists.' Webster asked if she would condescend to dine with him. 'Well, no,' she said, barely giving the matter her attention. 'I won't eat. But I'll sit with you while *you* eat.' David Webster was puffed with pride as he stood outside the stage-door beside her. The great lady trod lightly, as though on an invisible carpet of ermine, across the pavement and into the taxi which came gliding all but unbidden to the kerb. She murmured, as she settled herself inside, the name of New York's most expensive restaurant. The buildings inclined their lofty heads as the taxi sped between them. In the restaurant she once more avowed her intention not to eat. Young David exhorted her. 'A very little, then,' she conceded. 'Perhaps the breast of *something which once flew*.' The most expensive dish in the most expensive restaurant in New York was forthwith placed before her. More hesitantly, David asked her if she wanted anything to drink. His sigh of relief, when she refused, was not audible. But it was premature. 'Perhaps a little champagne?' was her next utterance. She was trying out the word merely, but David stiffened. The word, alas, had sounded well on the restaurant air. 'Yes, a little champagne,' she said, yielding to his entreaty. The drawn cork was thunder in poor David's ear, and it was indeed a poor David who eked out the remainder of his stay in New York.

If he liked meeting stars, it was already no new experience for him. Like any large provincial centre, Liverpool had its particular venues where there was entertaining, parties and suppers, and the *crème de la crème* were present; people of distinction, the artists, the intellectuals, the grace and the beauty and the wit, assembled under the roofs, mainly, of those with enough money to splash about and entertain in some style. David, naturally, was at all such gatherings. Everybody who was anybody in Liverpool met Everybody passing through. At Maud Melly's, David first met Desmond Shawe-Taylor, then with the National Trust, his own musical life also in the future. In 1930 an introduction from Nigel Playfair's widow brought Anthony Gishford, one of the Hawkes' family – Hawkes of the music publishers Boosey and Hawkes – into his circle, and this contact was later to prove unexpectedly important in his life.

David's position, not hard-won but worked for with relish, enabled him to meet Everyone. Since their arrival in Liverpool he'd lived with his parents in a small terraced house sporting an aspidistra and old Victorian furniture, which weren't fashionable then. This was not a background against which he cared to be seen, and he hadn't taken people home – had even allowed some of them to imagine that he was for the time being not with his parents but in anonymous lodgings. It was different after he'd moved with them into a fine early Victorian house overlooking Princes Park. The new house was given a sophisticated decor, bang-slap up-to-date, with Matthew Smith white walls, and he was now himself in a position to entertain in fine style. If he was the suavest of guests, as a host he was quite superb. He knew how to arrange parties, how to make them go. His interiors might have been created entirely with an eye to their aptness as a background for parties. In London later, his parties were as celebrated as his after-dinner speeches, and in both capacities, as host and speaker, he made an admirable figurehead for his Opera House. It's impossible to estimate how much Opera House business was conducted the more easily and concluded the more happily because of the sense of well-being and the impression of pleasant personal relations established at the parties in his own home over which he presided so charmingly.

All this had very serious aspects. The best way to get to know an art is to practise it – as an amateur of exalted status, Webster most assiduously *did* practise – and another useful means is contact with artists. It was partly through William Armstrong that David was brought into such frequent and easy contact with the visiting actors, and indeed the two of them, Webster and Armstrong, were the twin centres of Liverpool's intellectual life throughout this period. It perhaps needs to be explained why David wasn't on the Board of the Liverpool Playhouse, for he was everywhere else rapidly earning for himself the title of Liverpool's Number One Busybody. It was because yet another of his activities was writing reviews in the local newspapers, so he couldn't qualify. But this didn't prejudice his friendship with Armstrong, and nor did his vociferousness at the meetings of the Playhouse Circle, held in the Playhouse on Sunday nights. Webster and others would demand more modern and advanced plays, while Armstrong, with the same kind of responsibilities as Webster was going to shoulder one day at the Opera House, patiently explained that he was also concerned with not emptying his theatre.

Webster learned from the artists he met, and he had a respect for them based on a knowledge of what they really are. It was to stand him in good stead.

One of his early artists was Frederick Ashton who, in 1926, when he was in a revue, *Riverside Nights*, received his first-ever fan-letter from David Webster. The fan-letter was followed by an invitation to lunch, and lunch was at one of the big hotels in Northumberland Avenue, the Metropole it might have been. Young Freddie, a busy professional, with his way still to make, and more used to milk-bars, was very much impressed by the way this assured younger man who was his host coped with waiters and wine-lists, almost ostentatiously at his ease.

He and Webster didn't lose touch after that first meeting. But it was more than his poise in a restaurant that Ashton responded to. Ashton was, after all, and always had been, a pro of pros. While he worked for the Ballet Rambert he had to get a new ballet on for £15 (!), making his living meanwhile outside the ballet, in revues mainly. It was tough. He worked for George Black at the Palladium, in Charlot revues for C. B. Cochran, he arranged shows for the Crazy Gang. At the Trocadero restaurant he appeared in their annual revue every night over the whole year. In brief, he had the kind of seasoning which produced a pro not likely to be over-patient with amateurs. But his very background provided a meeting-point, for it had the very flavour of the world in which Webster, store manager though he might be, was most vividly alive. And, cleverer than most, the future Sir Frederick was quick to divine in his young host that potential which produced the future Sir David. He continued to be impressed by David's authoritativeness, so impressed that when, towards the end of the war, he had the idea of starting a regional ballet company, it was David he thought of for the company's Director.

David, in fact, had made a point very early of learning to cope with living high. The restaurant is almost as much a scene of Webster's life as the Opera House itself. In his university days his friends had admired his poise and assurance, and had even then seen him coping with restaurants, even with Liverpool's Adelphi, a restaurant all of four stars. And from the first he had automatically taken cabs. It hadn't been long before he was informing Jimmy Cleveland Belle, almost echoing his admired Mrs Pat, that for them in the future it was to be nothing but first-class hotels and the best champagne. It was part of his armoury, a kind of shell for a man who seemed to have been born without one.

Mrs Pat had made a great impression. So too did another superbly talented monster enormously admired by Webster – Sir Thomas Beecham. Along with Toscanini and Bruno Walter, it was Beecham more than any other who revealed to Webster, through the 'twenties and 'thirties, the great works of the musical repertory.

The first encounter with Beecham was at one of the Sandon suppers. The year was 1937, Beecham was in Liverpool with his opera company, so who more natural for guest of honour? This was one of the Sandon's most memorable evenings. It happened that some of the reviews for the company's performances had been not entirely favourable. It wasn't so much the musical standards, but rather that in matters of ensemble and acting, of scenery and costumes, there were undoubtedly deficiencies. Beecham, who loved controversy, had started a correspondence in the *Liverpool Daily Post* with a characteristically witty letter, and the paper's music critic, A. K. Holland, had mentioned David Webster in a subsequent article. In another paper Webster – almost inevitably, he was in on everything – had written a notice of Delius's *Koanga*, complaining that the orchestra had been given only one rehearsal, and that Oda Slobodskaya, the heroine, 'looked like a corner cupboard with a vase on top'.

In his speech at the Sandon dinner Beecham demanded that copies of the *Liverpool Daily Post* in which the letters and articles had appeared should be burnt by the hangman on St George's Hill plateau. He wouldn't let the subject rest. 'And who,' he growled, 'is this David Webster?' Alfred Francis, present at the supper, would have been pleased to give him a clue, for he had dubbed the subject of Beecham's enquiry, affectionately, 'The Caterer'; and he might, indeed, inadvertently have prompted Beecham, who in later years in London was wont to use a somewhat modified, and certainly coarser, version of the nickname. Had he foreseen the future that night at the Sandon, and had the least idea how he and Webster were going to clash, Beecham might well have asked that Webster be burnt along with the copies of the newspaper. On second thoughts, he probably wouldn't have. There were further uses for David Webster, for Tommy always enjoyed having someone to break his lance against.

CHAPTER III

The war · Lewis's · the Liverpool Philharmonic · Covent Garden leased by Boosey and Hawkes · post-war plans · Webster asked to take charge

When war was declared on 3 September 1939, David and Jimmy were on the *Aquitania* in the middle of the Atlantic, on their way back from a holiday in New York. Originally they'd planned to fly to Budapest, where their friend Benjie Bruce, whose career as diplomat had ended when he married the glorious Tamara Karsavina (ballerinas in those days being out of bounds), was now the Bank of England's representative. He'd been going to book a car for them to motor down to the Black Sea, but the political situation had made them change their minds, and they'd decided on America instead, as otherwise it might be a long time before they saw their friends there again.

The trip back was somewhat eerie. They had to sail through the night in darkness, with no one even allowed to smoke on deck. And soon after war was declared they had news of the sinking of the *Athenia*, which unnerved everybody, and especially the crew, many of whom had sailed with the *Aquitania* in the First World War, when she'd been narrowly missed no less than three times. Could they expect to be as lucky again in a second war? With one accord everybody – passengers, officers and crew alike – took to drink, and before long the impeccable Cunard liner declared itself out of champagne. But at least they arrived safely in Southampton in beautiful weather. At Waterloo they heard their first air-raid siren, though they didn't have their first experience of blackout till they were back in Liverpool. It was very strange after New York. 'If a black man were to cross the road now,' said David ruminatively as they were driving home after dinner, 'he wouldn't have a chance.' At these words there was a bump and they stopped the car. Close examination in the darkness established that, sure enough, they'd knocked over a black man – or so, at least, they were later to claim. He wasn't hurt and he didn't upbraid them. Instead he apologized, which added to the strangeness of it all.

Shortly afterwards Webster was moved from Bon Marché to Lewis's, and when news reached him that his new store had been bombed he was soon on the spot to see the huge building being reduced to one-eighth of its proper size: it thus fell to him in his early days there to reorganize the store on a much-reduced basis. He'd been officially urged not to join up on the grounds that he'd be called for if he were needed, and it was a year or two later that Fred Marquis, now, as Lord Woolton, Minister of Food, had him seconded to the Ministry of Supply. He was sent scurrying about the country with a brief to increase productivity in ammunition factories employing somewhere between fifteen and twenty-five thousand people each, and he did in fact devise a method which proved so successful that the professionals were reluctant to trust it. They claimed that not only were the figures false but also that the goods being produced were inferior. Eventually they had to concede that the figures were accurate and the goods actually of a higher standard. Webster also gave lectures on morale and absenteeism, the latter being markedly reduced when he arranged days off for women whose husbands were on leave.

Another important wartime contribution, though, had to do with music. This was his championing of the Liverpool Philharmonic Orchestra, and it was his contribution to the arts of peace which certainly had the more lasting effect. The old Philharmonic Hall had been burnt down in 1936, but the merchants, lawyers and other people who formed the committee had had the foresight to keep the hall well insured, and aided by civic financial support, much more generous than was then usual, the Hall had been rebuilt, and reopened in July 1939 with a magnificent concert conducted by Beecham. Webster was by now a member of the committee. He had returned from America, however, to find it all but decided that the fine new hall must be closed, this being considered no time for music-making.

Webster protested. He felt that, on the contrary, music was now more than ever important. He was right. In England at this time an extraordinary spirit was being created, the Second World War inspiring a positive rage to preserve. Throughout the Blitz in London, for example, Myra Hess's famous lunchtime recitals at the National Gallery drew crowds, and intrepid soloists made impossible journeys through the blackout to entertain people in the most uncomfortable and unlikely venues. Troops on leave, displaced persons almost, would flock to concerts, and ENSA (Entertainments National Service Association) took ballet and opera to people who'd never had the chance to see them before. Ninette de Valois ascribes the wartime and early post-war boom in ballet partly to the fact that the public had little else to spend its money on, but it was also one aspect of this frantic drive to preserve and perpetuate a tradition which in the case of ballet was not even, as yet, firmly planted. And religion, its power already weakened, suffered a further blow during the war, so that the comfort and inspiration people might once have found in going to church they now looked to find in music.

Webster fought to keep the Philharmonic Hall open. There was much wrangling, but only a single resignation, and the committee went ahead to frame their winter concert programme. But with a vital difference.

The Liverpool Philharmonic had not hitherto been a permanent orchestra, but a nucleus only of local players augmented by large numbers of players from the Hallé in Manchester. It had given no more than one concert a fortnight through the autumn and winter seasons. With the threat of imminent invasion it wasn't thought right to take people away from their homes and families, so David Webster proposed, and enthusiastically promoted, a most outrageous solution – nothing less than the formation of a permanent and full-time orchestra. That was to be the Philharmonic Society's ultimate aim, though it was not fully achieved for some years. It's not surprising that Webster met with opposition. But he had a much more acute sense of the times than anyone about him, and he saw that in some respects conditions were favourable to the enterprise. He considered that Liverpool ought to have its orchestra, but he also felt strongly that he had a duty to provide musicians with work.

He prevailed. Concerts were given throughout the war, thirty-two of them in the first wartime season, though the second half of the season could only be confirmed when they found themselves, which they had by no means taken for granted, still surviving at Christmas. Artists accepted special fees, and concerts were retimed to begin at 6.30 p.m., to end, hopefully, before the bombers arrived. There was an important, and significant, announcement at the head of the slim prospectus for the 1939/40 season: 'The rule regarding evening dress has been waived for the time being.' No one had been allowed in to hear the Liverpool Philharmonic before without white tie and tails, but this was changed now and forever.

Webster became Chairman of the Orchestra in 1940 and served till 1945. The concerts were attended by factory workers, and by members of the forces who were admitted at very low prices, and who subsequently sent grateful messages from all over the world. Malcolm Sargent became chief conductor. Soon concerts were being given not only in the Philharmonic Hall but also round the district, in schools, in churches, in factories and hangars – anywhere a space could be cleared and a reasonable acoustic obtained. The orchestra played outside Liverpool for the first time in its history, often on Sundays when the pubs were shut, the streets pitch-dark and no proper food to be found. 'The orchestra plays better when it's hungry,' was one of Sargent's most quoted as well as most unfortunate remarks. Webster didn't himself work better when he was hungry, and Sargent made

The Royal Opera House, Covent Garden, when used as a wartime dance hall

Left: Ljuba Welitsch, Constance Shacklock and Peter Brook during rehearsal for *Rosenkavalier*, 1949
Below: Beryl Grey rehearsing the Spanish dance for the new production of *Carmen*, 1949

amends fully, to him at least, when from a tour of Portugal he sent him a crate of huge golden oranges.

The orchestra in the long run didn't suffer from the continuous battles with A. K. Holland of the *Liverpool Daily Post*, with whom not so long before Webster had been ranged in the attack on Beecham's opera company. Conditions, indeed, were so good for the making of music that they were able to supplement the basic repertory with modern works. Michael Tippett's first Symphony was given its world première, and Bartok's Concerto, shortly after its first performance in America, was given for the first time in Britain by the Liverpool orchestra. And there was no shortage of works by Britten and Mahler, all of them new to Liverpool audiences, as well as novelties by Malipiero, Bax, Atterberg and Roy Harris.

Movement of artists was necessarily restricted, and this caused problems with guest conductors and soloists. Henry Wood was among the guest conductors in 1941, and Charles Munch and Roger Desormière were among those who came once Europe was opened up again. But conditions, as Webster had foreseen, worked in favour of stabilizing the main body of the orchestra. After the worst of the provincial air-raids at the end of 1941 the bombing was more and more concentrated on London, so that a secure post in a large provincial city had its attractions for members of a scattered profession. Henry Holst, one of the outstanding orchestral violinists of the day, leader of the Berlin Philharmonic under Furtwängler in the 'twenties and latterly with Toscanini in Lucerne, was a great acquisition; and his authoritative presence in Liverpool made Webster's task easier in 1943 when he tried to strengthen the growing orchestra further by incorporating into it the dozen or so players of the BBC Salon Orchestra, which the Corporation was on the point of disbanding. He had to act quickly. The Salon Orchestra was a wartime unit based for convenience and safety in Evesham in Worcestershire, and it included some of the most distinguished British instrumentalists of the day. Among those who now joined Holst in Liverpool were Anthony Pini the 'cellist, Reginald Kell the clarinetist, and the violinist David Wise.

These principals made an enormous difference to the orchestra, which under Sargent's direction grew slowly into a full-time body. Planning problems became more complex as a result, and Webster gained further valuable experience coping with them. The Philharmonic finally became a full-time orchestra in the last year of the war, and some of the enjoyable complexity of the organization involved is suggested by the foreword he wrote in the programme for the 1945/6 season, the first year of peace:

Programme making is anybody's game until it comes to arranging fifty or sixty of them for practical use, for at that point many factors raise their ugly heads: how long is the work? Does that make too long a programme or too long a half? Can any soloist play that work or is interested enough to learn it? Can they do it on that date which is the only one the conductor can accept? Is that the right work for that conductor? Won't that make too brilliant a programme? Is the contrast too violent or not strong enough? Are there too many bits in this programme? Are there too many different styles in that one? Everything in the first half is in the same key. That piece only lasts five minutes and takes eight extra players including two who have come from London and they will cost too much. That piece can't be played before a clarinet concerto because the First Clarinet must be fresh for his solo work. Are the parts in England?

These are the daily problems of musical administration, and from 1943 onwards Webster was more and more involved in them.

And in 1943 he was forty. The war wasn't going to last forever, and when it did end finally his work at the Ministry would end with it. Victory began to seem certain. Was he going to remain involved in musical administration? He pondered his future. If he went back to merchandising now it would probably be for the rest of his life.

Jimmy Cleveland Belle had been released from the Signal Corps to go to the Cotton Board, blue-print for the Council of Industrial Design. Jimmy had become highly respected in the world of business, and his future was certainly going to be in London. In fact it wasn't long before he was business consultant for three or four firms, and shortly a Director of Horrocks and Aquascutum, eventually also becoming Vice-President of the Incorporated Society of London Fashion Designers. David didn't want to remain behind in Liverpool. If there was one thing certain, it was that the time had come at last for both of them to make the assault on the Big City.

And then Sir Robert Barlow of Metal Box, who'd met Webster in the course of his work with the Philharmonic, made his excellent offer. This would bring Webster down to London, and with a bang. A contract was drawn up. There'd be other problems to absorb him than those of musical administration, but in a private capacity he'd continue to enjoy the concert and the theatre, and such opera as there was. Musical administration was becoming something like a drug, it was in his veins – would he suffer withdrawal symptoms? No, he was decided. He signed.

But meanwhile there were events shaping in London which were to prove of moment, more than might have been guessed at the time, in the whole future artistic life of the country. They were certainly to prove important in Webster's own life. Mecca was making a good thing out of the Covent Garden Opera House as a dance-hall, but their lease was due to expire in December 1944. They weren't going to relish giving it up, and the agreement was that they should be allowed to renew the lease unless the house was required again for its original purposes. This didn't seem likely with the war still on. But Philip Hill, chairman of the proprietors, Covent Garden Properties Ltd, felt strongly that it ought to be given back, and he was prepared to take a smaller rent than the one Mecca paid. His first approach was to Harold Holt, the concert agent. Before the war Holt had been the English agent of the Russian-American impresario Sol Hurok, and at the outbreak of war the two men had been about to organize together an opera season at Covent Garden. Would Harold Holt like to take charge now? But he would have to convert the dance-hall first, and it would be harder to assemble an opera company than in 1939. He already had enough responsibilities, and he declined. He mentioned it to Leslie Boosey with whom he was lunching at the Cafe Royal – was it of any interest to him? Indeed it was. Boosey forthwith enlisted the support of Ralph Hawkes, his partner in the music firm (both men, incidentally, were directors of Holt's agency): and very soon, fired by the idea of a rescue operation, he was drawing up terms of agreement.

The firm most generously decided that they were prepared to spend a considerable amount of money in the interests of music and opera. They took the lease of the Opera House, since Mecca were pressing for a decision; but as they weren't able to undertake the promotion of actual ballet and opera seasons at once, there was more than a little awkwardness to contend with. The Duke of Bedford was enlisted, for his family had the Bedford Box in perpetuity, and by the terms of Mecca's lease it was reserved for Covent Garden Properties Ltd, who had given an undertaking to retain it for his use. It was argued against Mecca that the box entailed rights to the actual ground beneath it. It worked out finally that Boosey and Hawkes were granted the lease from 1 April 1944, for five years, and they granted Mecca Cafés a licence to continue using the theatre as a dance-hall until September 1945.

By then Boosey and Hawkes had issued their manifesto.

> We hope to re-establish Covent Garden as a centre of opera and ballet worthy of the highest musical traditions. The main purpose will be to ensure for Covent Garden an independent position as an international opera house with sufficient funds at its disposal to enable it to devote itself to a long-term programme, giving to London throughout the year the best in English opera and ballet, together with the best from all over

the world. If this ambition can be realized it is felt that it will prove to be a great incentive to artists and composers, since it will offer to them an opportunity for experience in the performing and writing of operas on a scale equal to that which has prevailed so long on the Continent but has been lacking so long in our musical life here in London.

Brave words, carefully assembled and in tune with the times. Most generously, Boosey and Hawkes were prepared to meet the rental, and at an agreed price to sub-let the theatre to the non-profit-making company who would take charge of the house; and also to pay the rates, as well as the insurance both of the building and of its stores, scenery and costumes, together with management expenses and the salaries of the front-of-house staff.

David Webster could not have been considered for the key post were it not for his work with the Philharmonic, which had made him nationally known. It was Anthony Gishford who first suggested him for it. As soon as he heard from his cousin, Ralph Hawkes, about the Covent Garden lease being acquired, Gishford wrote to Webster, whom after their first meeting in Liverpool he'd seen from time to time on the London trips: 'Would you like your name put forward?'

Webster had already been told about the scheme by Lady Cunard, who was certain Beecham was going to get the job. In fact all that had happened was that Beecham had taken out options on a number of singers for a season of international opera, and had applied to Harold Holt for the use of Covent Garden for either May through to July 1945 or else from May to mid-October. But – if it happened at all – he was merely going to be in charge of the one, privately sponsored season, not permanently in charge: for all his long, earlier associations with the house he wasn't being thought of for the job. And that season never did take place.

When Gishford's letter came, in February 1944, Jimmy was as excited about it as David. He was proud that his friend's abilities were being acknowledged in high places, and he didn't doubt that if David were given the job he would make something tremendous of it.

But he also foresaw something of the strains involved, and he did worry about these on his friend's behalf.

Gishford arranged a lunch at the Ritz Grill for Ralph Hawkes to meet David Webster. This was 6 April 1944. Webster was overflowing with ideas, and he and Ralph hit it off together instantly. After lunch Gishford went back to the War Office, where he was still working, and left David and Ralph, still talking excitedly, to wander off together, up Bond Street, along Oxford Street and into Upper Regent Street, where Boosey and Hawkes had their offices. That's the time it took for Ralph to be convinced that he had the man for the job. But it was for *him* to convince David that he must give up Metal Box even if he'd already signed.

Jimmy was delighted that Ralph Hawkes had shown himself a man of perception, immediately recognizing in David the right man, the *only* man. Inevitably it would mean a drop in salary – but this didn't worry him. If it fell to him to support their life-style, or in any way to support David and – *if* he took the job, that is – relieve the new strains as far as was within his power, this was pleasure for him. But in some ways he saw the future more clearly than David. 'You realize, don't you,' he put it to him, 'you won't be a private person any longer? We'll never be able to walk out of a theatre again in the middle of the performance if we want to.'

It was true. David wouldn't be free to criticize even implicitly. And when they were in a foreign city, and went to the opera, they weren't free just to slope off afterwards and do the town. They were expected to go backstage politely, and often have supper with the singers – splendid artists maybe, but not always ideal supper companions. This might be enjoyable every now and then, but it was going to be *always*.

Even opera and music weren't going to be the same any more. When they'd been to Salzburg before the war they'd paid the hotel doorman well over the odds for tickets, there was no other way. 'Now there'll be tickets for the asking, but will you want them?' Over-involved professionally, David would be having enough and more than enough already – he'd have to restrict himself so there'd be some relish left for all the music he *had* to hear.

At first, and for years to come, there were many who were doubtful about David's appointment. A mere amateur they called him, a business-man; his very presumption was a source of wonder and scorn and drew the harshest of criticism. The criticism, in the face of which he maintained silence, hurt, for Webster wasn't one to shrug it off pain-lessly. This was part of the inevitable strains which to some extent undermined his health eventually and shortened his life. It drove him further into an obsessive secretiveness, though this was up to a point natural to him, if only as a provincial 'covering up'. But he also 'covered up' because he didn't want to give anyone ammunition to use against him. If he was evasive about himself, he was also almost pathologically reluctant to commit himself to specific aims and attitudes, which made him tend to exaggerate his tendency to delay. He was to become the great pragmatist, sensitive to prevailing winds and ready to bend with them or to resist them, as seemed best at that moment: he never lost the outsider's apprehensiveness, and he also believed that the results he achieved were all that could speak for him adequately and finally justify him.

Jimmy didn't dissuade David and he didn't try to. Didn't want to. He had felt it his duty to make one or two points, not more. David was released by Barlow and he accepted the offer of Covent Garden. A contract was drawn up, and his appointment was to run from 5 August 1944 through to 31 December 1945, with an option of renewal for a further twelve months. Even now his whole life wasn't signed away to music. For a while, David and Jimmy were in London three or four nights at a time, always at the Savoy (which then charged them a guinea a night). Then Jimmy rented a house in Weymouth Street, which he later bought, from the Chairman of Yardley's, and he began to furnish it. David had no time to contribute, but he approved everything Jimmy did. Jimmy created a stable background for him while David, who had an office at his disposal in Boosey and Hawkes in Upper Regent Street, prepared. In July 1945 Douglas Lund, who was later to be the Opera House Accountant, came in as his assistant. It was on 22 October 1945 that Mecca finally handed over the building. And at last David Webster's real life and career began in earnest.

CHAPTER IV

Webster at Covent Garden · rejects Sadlers Wells Opera but retains Ballet · secures subsidy from Arts Council · unsatisfactory negotiations with BBC · hopes for private monies dashed by taxation

David Webster entered the Opera House with the words of Melba's farewell speech ringing in his ears – 'My darling public, at all costs keep Covent Garden as your opera house – for my sake': though Webster was dedicating himself to work not so much for Melba's sake as for that of the darling public. He was greeted by Frank Ballard, who had been there before the war and had stayed on in charge through its metamorphosis, in spite of having frequently to retreat in despair to the upper reaches of the house to escape the sound of the dance-music he detested. But he had never ceased to hope for restoration, and he welcomed Webster as his deliverer.

From the outset Webster didn't try to make things easier for himself. If he succeeded in his task it would be against the odds – but even at the beginning he seemed to be stacking the odds against himself still further. His very first big decision, flouting reasonable expectation, was to reject the Sadlers Wells Opera, a going concern, as the basis for his new opera; and with this rejection he seemed almost to be inviting failure.

The Sadlers Wells Opera Company, with almost endless provincial tours, had gallantly survived the war, clinging, like the other arts, with desperate tenacity. Tyrone Guthrie managed both Sadlers Wells and the Old Vic through this testing period, and when the opera company gave a short season at the New Theatre in February 1941 he wrote that:

> Lancashire has encouraged us to believe that the effort to keep Sadlers Wells alive is not unjustified; that upon this company of singers and players, familiar and loved at the Old Wells, may be founded the National Opera of hereafter; that this Company is the isthmus, small but strong, linking the continents of the past and the future.

This seems a most reasonable expectation. A division of slender operatic resources was surely an absurdity, and there were many who agreed with Guthrie when he later wrote in his autobiography, *A Life in the Theatre*:

> I think it was a mistake, at the end of the war, that public money was used to found at Covent Garden another opera company, thus dividing in two the available funds, talent and support, which was barely sufficient for one.

Anticipating opposition, Guthrie, together with Professor Dent, a member of the Sadlers Wells Board, in November 1944 drew up and signed a Memorandum of Opera Policy. Their point was that in its present stage of development English opera should lay particular stress on literary aspects, on acting and presentation. They ended, interestingly, with the suggestion that what was practical for England, as well as 'characteristic', was a kind of 'opéra comique': which is to say, opera on a small scale.

Now Webster had had experience of small-scale opera in Liverpool, and he by no means despised it. But what he envisaged, what he felt with a virtually crusading fervour to be the right thing for Covent Garden, was opera on a much grander scale, with an altogether different level of aspiration. His dream was to compete in the international stakes, and eventually to match his company with the biggest and best. Such a dream seemed at this time virtually an impossible one, and to achieve it would certainly be in defiance of probability. But he was convinced, and all the more after the Memorandum, that this higher level of ambition would not be possible if Sadlers Wells were involved.

Guthrie thought the company 'had many excellent singers, many distinguished productions had been given . . . There were, in my opinion, the elements of a splendid ensemble.' If the chorus were reinforced, it seemed to him, then there was little enough to justify rejection. But he also admitted that 'even the excellencies of the company were worthy rather than exciting; a little dowdy, a little stodgy; they were something which no theatrical performance can afford to be – snob-repellent.'

This too is near the heart of the matter. Webster wasn't repelled simply because he was a snob, and indeed he wasn't repelled at all. But he did emphatically reject the dowdy and spurn the stodgy. For his own opera he absolutely required excitement and glamour.

There was also the point, though not the main one, that he wanted to be king-pin in his own organization, all the more if he was going to impose his unlikely ambitions for opera, ambitions which he could hardly risk explaining in detail even to his colleagues. If he'd taken on the Sadlers Wells Opera then there would be people within the organization whom he'd have had to acknowledge as his seniors: and in fact it was going to be a long time before he lost his nervousness of anyone who had been connected with opera in England before or during the war.

If he began from nothing, anything that was ultimately achieved would be seen to be *his* achievement and no one else's; though at the same time as rejecting it he was jealous of Sadlers Wells simply for being a going concern already.

In the original draft of the Memorandum, Guthrie and Dent also suggested that Sadlers Wells be given a clear field for five years as far as subsidy was concerned, and that Covent Garden should be used only for visiting companies and, possibly, for an occasional production drawing on the joint resources of Sadlers Wells and the Old Vic.

Webster watched developments anxiously, and sometimes wondered whether he'd been wise to give up Metal Box. A committee had been formed at Covent Garden, preceding the Covent Garden Trust which was created later, in February 1946, and they were considering the Boosey and Hawkes plan. Webster had asked that Lord Keynes be approached for Chairman, and Leslie Boosey and Ralph Hawkes went to Washington to see him: happily, he was prepared to move over from CEMA (Council for the Encouragement of Music and the Arts, and forerunner of the Arts Council), where he was also serving as Chairman. Keynes was an economist, but he was also a member of the Bloomsbury Set, with whom he had passed many an evening watching the Diaghileff Ballet. He had been particularly taken with the ballerina Lydia Lopokova ('wittiest, most graceful and most vivacious of all soubrettes' in the words of Arnold Haskell), and she had eventually become his wife. He had served as Treasurer to the Camargo Society which through the early 'thirties had helped keep classical ballet alive after the death of Diaghileff in 1929. Keynes was the man above all others whom Leslie Boosey hero-worshipped, and in Keynes Webster found his main ally and support.

Keynes was quite definite that what was needed for Covent Garden was not a musician in charge but a businessman with a deep feeling for the arts, a Webster rather than a Beecham. In all his years of involvement with opera, Beecham, spending huge sums of money, had never managed to build up a permanent organization. But Keynes had faith in David Webster.

Like Keynes, Webster was not only good with money but had shown a marked propensity for involving himself in the arts. Their tastes and temperament coincided most satisfactorily, and their harmonious relationship was no small factor in the organizing, as well as the financing, of the operation. Webster could not have chosen a Chairman more pat to his purpose; and indeed Guthrie could have been aiming equally at Keynes with his phrase 'snob-repellent'.

The Covent Garden Committee's first move was to invite the Sadlers Wells Governors to join them in discussion of the Boosey and Hawkes plan for Covent Garden. A possibility when negotiations were opened was that the Sadlers Wells Ballet might go into Covent Garden intact, while the opera company be used as the nucleus only of a larger company. The Sadlers Wells Governors were at least induced to withdraw their 'exclusivity' clause from the Memorandum, which was something, but Webster most decidedly didn't want the Sadlers Wells Opera. He recognized, however, that this was only a first move.

To his relief, the Governors themselves found reason to hesitate. Under the terms of their charter, the Sadlers Wells Theatre – which had been commandeered by the Borough of Finsbury and used during the war as a rest centre – was intended 'for the recreation and instruction of the poorer classes', and had to be priced low to make it available for 'artisans and labourers'. The people of Finsbury had subscribed money, and they had a right to performances in their own theatre. It wouldn't answer, transferring the two companies to Covent Garden and perhaps using the Sadlers Wells Theatre only for a school. It was suggested that if Sadlers Wells combined with Covent Garden to provide performances at Covent Garden 'at suitable prices' the terms of the trust would be fulfilled, and the school established at Sadlers Wells Theatre could meantime give performances there as well as in the provinces. Discussions continued and a further compromise was suggested, Covent Garden to take over the opera company and Sadlers Wells eventually to house a company which would mount chamber works.

A solution seemed near, hardly one that David Webster was going to be happy with. The Sadlers Wells Trust wanted to take on the running of Covent Garden themselves, and they were prepared to admit some of the Covent Garden Committee to their ranks, but only such of the Committee as they themselves approved – which hardly represented to David Webster a satisfactory balance of power! He persuasively put the objections to Lord Keynes, insisting that Sadlers Wells's function was to serve its own Borough, while what he envisaged for himself and Covent Garden was an institution serving the nation at large. If the Covent Garden Committee registered itself as a charitable trust it was only because CEMA, in a major move, had allowed theatrical performances of a high-aspiring 'cultural' nature to be exempt from entertainments tax. But Sadlers Wells, as he wrote to Lord Keynes in January 1945, was 'a far more parochial affair', and 'by the terms of their trust they are charitable within the more specific meaning of the term'.

The attitudes of the two parties, fortunately for Webster, and also for the future of opera in England, were not to be reconciled. The Covent Garden Committee, keen to have the ballet from Sadlers Wells, were looking for changes in scope, direction, policy and personnel before they were prepared to take on the opera company, while on their side the Sadlers Wells Governors were concerned for their name and tradition and, quite apart from their responsibility as a charitable trust, didn't want to see either lost in the new Covent Garden.

Further complications were caused by the intervention on the scene of John Christie, who before the war had established the celebrated annual summer seasons of festival opera at Glyndebourne, his estate in Sussex. After the summer of 1939 Glyndebourne had become the home of evacuees, but he was now planning an International Glyndebourne, its first performances to be in Canada, and his larger plan was a single management comprising his own opera together with both Sadlers Wells and Covent Garden. He also had a vision of a National Council of Music to oversee the production of all musical performances in England. It happened that Christie had been at Eton with Keynes, and the two men had detested one another and still did. Christie wanted to come on the Covent Garden Board, and intimated that Leslie Boosey had invited him. Boosey, however much Covent Garden might be indebted to him and his firm, and although he himself was a member of the Board, was not of course empowered to issue such an invitation, and Keynes refused even to entertain the idea of Christie.

The threat from Christie was not a very serious one, and Webster's main fear, once he had seen negotiations break down and Sadlers Wells Opera going its own way, was that he would lose the Sadlers Wells Ballet. He saw that the ballet was already of a standard to bring lustre to his house, and at the same time he was convinced that the larger house was essential to the company if it was to be elevated to the same international status he had already envisaged for his opera.

Fortunately, for all practical purposes the Sadlers Wells Ballet was already separate from the organization Lilian Baylis had built up. (This included not only the opera and ballet, but also the Old Vic Theatre Company, which likewise had operated during the war on a very low budget in the provinces.) Ninette de Valois had joined Lilian Baylis, in 1926, in the first place only to teach movement to drama students and to arrange choreography for the Shakespearian productions, but her ballet had developed from these small beginnings. She had had to fight for audiences, which is one of the reasons she had considered it important to send some of her dancers to Liverpool to work with the Ballet Club there. After Diaghileff – even against De Basil, whose company had incorporated some of the remnants of Diaghileff's, and was thus international and could command an audience – British ballet in swaddling clothes, which was what de Valois had to sell, seemed humble and unexotic.

But her company had survived, and it continued to develop. The boom conditions of wartime especially favoured her, and she seized the opportunities they offered the more determinedly because she was fully aware that they couldn't last forever.

She was therefore dismayed when she found that Guthrie wanted her ballet to finance its sister company, the Sadlers Wells Opera. He tended to see the ballet as suited by its very nature to being only the younger sister, and he considered that the organization as a whole ought to benefit from what he took to be the comparatively easy success of the ballet during the war. But de Valois, to ballet what Florence Nightingale had been to the nursing profession, had not survived her Crimea to see herself traduced in this manner. She fought – and as a result the ballet and opera had virtually parted. Bronson Albery, along with Guthrie, had become joint Administrator of the Old Vic and Sadlers Wells, and his theatre, the New (renamed the Albery in 1973), became their London home. And it was he, together with de Valois, who in effect ran the ballet company.

The pioneering de Valois was fiercely protective of her ballet, having already seen it threatened once. She too recognized that Covent Garden provided the setting she now required for it, and she saw that the moment of greatest test had come. Her ballet would have to prove itself a major company. But once again there was a danger that her company might be forced to subordinate itself to the needs of the organization as a whole, its success exploited not for its own benefit but to finance the opera. So she hesitated.

Webster at the time was anxiously following the negotiations with the Sadlers Wells Governors, and here at least he could make himself felt. Where the ballet was concerned he could have less effect. Discussions centred on what had effectively become a ballet triumvirate – de Valois herself, Constant Lambert, the company's Musical Director and artistic conscience, and, as the third and still junior partner, Webster's old friend Frederick Ashton. There was a possibility that the ballet might instead go under Albery's management to His Majesty's Theatre. Frederick Ashton threw in his weight in favour of Covent Garden. Webster waited – and prayed. In the end he got his ballet.

Negotiations, with the Sadlers Wells Governors as well as with de Valois and the Sadlers Wells Ballet, had a happy outcome. What Webster wanted Webster got. But both the young ballet and the new opera needed money to support them, and in the end none of this would have served any purpose at all if money hadn't been forthcoming.

CEMA, forerunner of the Arts Council, has so far been mentioned only in passing. But CEMA was the vital element: and it has to be stated firmly that the establishment, at last, of the principle of state subsidy for the arts was by far the most important result of the changes the war had brought about in the country's attitude to art and artists. There had been a small preliminary gesture in 1931, when Ramsay MacDonald's socialist government had arranged that, through the BBC, Covent Garden should be paid the sum of £25,500, a fraction of their licence money. And even this sum was reduced finally to £15,500: and two years later the National Government had withdrawn the grant as part of its economy measures.

The real start was made in 1939, when William Williams, General Secretary of the Institute of Adult Education, called together the heads of the various institutes of education in London. He reminded them that in the last war anyone not in uniform had been branded a coward. It mustn't happen in the new war. 'We must persuade the government,' he urged, 'that the artist has a part to play in the war effort.' He drafted a memorandum insisting on the artist's value in boosting morale and providing entertainment. This time artists must be properly used. And so began a revolution – for it was no less than that – which followed its course in a very quiet, very English way. Lord De La Warr, the President of Education, read the memorandum. He was disturbed by it, and he and his parliamentary secretary, Kenneth Lindsay, decided to send it to Tom Jones, Secretary of the Pilgrim Trust. This curious institution had been founded with American money to sustain the British way of life, and the British way of life was, admittedly, now under fire. Tom Jones persuaded his trustees to find £25,000 for an experiment, to send out artists to sing and dance and variously perform in areas where evacuees were thickest. And three months later Tom Jones phoned Lord Keynes at the Treasury: and the Treasury now contributed its mite so that the experiment could continue for another three months.

And on the basis of these funds from the Pilgrim Trust and the Treasury, the Government – and particularly the Labour Leader in the Coalition, Attlee – approved the setting up of CEMA. The King granted a Royal Charter, Mary Glasgow was seconded from the Board of Education to become Secretary, and Lord Keynes was the inspiring and indefatigable Chairman. After the second three months had passed, Tom Jones informed Keynes that the Pilgrim Trust was making a strategic withdrawal; CEMA had come into existence, and it was the sole responsibility of the Treasury to keep it alive and nourished.

One is tempted even to define the birth of the Arts Council as the most important event in the arts since the birth of Shakespeare. And yet it was scarcely seen to be born at all. It was as though its non-existence was an insignificant fact, not noted – and then one day there it suddenly was, where before there had been nothing. To begin with the grant was small, and its continuance by no means guaranteed. It is difficult to imagine today that there can have been a time when the arts in England received no government subsidy at all, for now it is a right. The Arts Council is an independent body under the wing of the government, and yet outside the government, so that there is a measure of freedom here not enjoyed abroad, where state theatres, directly answerable to a Ministry of Culture which makes the appointments, often groan under the weight of an 'unwritten' censorship – toe the line or else no money! The Arts Council is more flexible in its workings, it is made up of individuals, and it was especially personal, and more informal, in its early days when it was smaller and more uncertain.

With CEMA from the beginning were Joe Hodgkinson and his wife Winnie, making a welcome reappearance in the Webster story. Joe was chosen by Mary Glasgow to be Honorary Treasurer, supervising the financial side of the operation – Winnie later went off to look after the Ballet Rambert, but Joe stayed on to become North West Region Manager. Sergius had still a vivid memory of the Chocolate Soldier's cool assurance and unflappability, but he didn't have to work at convincing the new people, who were instantly convinced by the Soldier himself. Bill Williams eventually succeeded Mary Glasgow, and Sir Alan Barlow took over as Chairman when Keynes became Chairman of the Covent Garden Committee.

If money was to go on being given, it had to be justified by the use to which it was put. And it was David Webster, more than anyone else, who justified it. He was the Art Council's first main beneficiary and he did put their money to good use. His success at the Opera House is important therefore not only in the history of opera in England but as finally confirming the precious principle of government arts subsidy. It was no longer possible, after his success, for subsidy to be withheld – and when the National Theatre was at last founded, after prolonged discussion, in 1963, it was partly on the basis of Webster's success, which ensured that money had to be found now for institutions of this stature. Had Webster failed, the consequence of his failure might have been felt for a long time, and a long way beyond the Opera House. There were even those who saw possible advantages to the new project, if only in prestige, of putting in the Opera House Administrator as first boss of the National.

But the National Theatre was twenty years away, and for the present, while he had still barely more than amateur status, Webster was having to deal on equal terms with people of long experience and huge authority in the arts and in government. He'd prepared himself well. Not one of those meals in first-class restaurants had been wasted, nor the socializing and the liner crossings, and he was already accustomed to moving freely among top people – though not to closing with them in such a deadly arena as the one he'd now entered. Formidable men abounded who had to be won over. There were formidable men on the Covent Garden Committee, and it says much that Professor Dent was prepared to come on to the Board at Covent Garden and to serve the new opera enthusiastically. After negotiations were concluded there was no rancour left behind to sour relations with Guthrie either, and diplomatic Webster was able to benefit without prejudice from his services as a director.

The involvement with Sadlers Wells, and the still uncertain outcome of negotiations, didn't make for easy dealing with CEMA. At the beginning of the war the Sadlers Wells Opera had been subsidized by the Carnegie Trust (who had given the Liverpool Repertory Opera Company £500 a year during its five years' existence); but at the beginning of 1943 CEMA took both the opera and ballet companies into 'association' as part of an agreement by which in the future CEMA was to handle the professional arts and the Carnegie Trust the amateur. The opera and ballet were modestly supported, as was the Old Vic – though Guthrie was very conscious that the humble operations of the touring Old Vic didn't have enough glamour for Keynes, whom he thought, 'great man though he was . . . a "sucker" for glamour'.

At the beginning of 1945 Keynes wrote to Sir Alan Barlow at CEMA on the question of subsidy for Covent Garden:

> Sadlers Wells Opera and Ballet have, in fact, more than paid their way. But that is because, at any rate in the case of opera, their ambitions have been moderate.

If not actually immoderate, his ambitions for Covent Garden, like Webster's, were certainly not modest. And CEMA *must* help.

> It is rather astonishing, I think, that it should be possible to plan something so big on such *a very reasonable* financial basis . . . This is a long way the best concerted effort ever adumbrated in this country. It would be a major disaster, really not to be contemplated, that this opportunity should not be taken.

CEMA, with opera so large on their horizon, decided to treat it as a category on its own, separate from music and drama, and to ask the Treasury for £40,000 – £25,000 for Covent Garden and £15,000 for Sadlers Wells. Unfortunately, at this time, the possibility of Sadlers Wells Opera being incorporated into Covent Garden still appeared strong, especially to the Treasury who didn't yet know Webster well; and so, regarding the two as involved in one venture, the Treasury offered only £25,000 in all. CEMA had therefore to decide after all not to segregate the grant for opera, but to allot money to the opera as it thought fit from their total grant.

Webster worked out with Mary Glascow how much money he'd need. It came to £10,000 to open the house, and £60,000 for new productions: he envisaged, high-vaulting, an initial season of six to eight months, with running costs at roughly £5000 a week. £7000 was not a huge sum for restoring the building, but he cut it to £4750 to take in essentials only. It was as well that Webster had learnt not to be frightened of money.

In September 1945 CEMA gave the Covent Garden Committee a non-recurrent grant of £25,000, and the annual subsidy was fixed at the same figure; while the Treasury offered an extra £30,000 if CEMA would make up their £25,000 to £30,000, to which they agreed, though the extra £5000 was not immediately available. Boosey and Hawkes agreed to underwrite expenses, and also to give £10,000 on permanent loan. Webster had prayed, as usual, and he'd been answered. All other negotiations, whatever their outcome, would have been pointless if these had failed.

Sadlers Wells Opera meanwhile had secured a grant to enable them to open their own theatre in June, but they still weren't ruled out for Covent Garden. Separate subsidy, however, seemed to confirm the division, and by the end of the year that division was final. There was in fact also a further upheaval in which happily Webster had no part. Peter Pears and Joan Cross, after a row with Sadlers Wells, seceded from the company, though they were engaged as guests for further performances of Britten's new opera *Peter Grimes*, which had reopened the theatre. Pears and Cross, together with Eric Crozier, formed the English Opera Group, which in June 1946 made its first appearance with another new Britten opera, *The Rape of Lucretia*: and Webster was pleased to note that the dream of a chamber opera company had not had to be abandoned either. The English Opera Group, in fact, was one of the earliest visitors to his Opera House, in the summer of 1948.

Webster had money – and the Sadlers Wells Ballet too – for an initial period of four years; while the ballet school remained under the guidance of the Governors of Sadlers Wells, who also sponsored a new, smaller ballet company for the Sadlers Wells Theatre which it was planned to present the following spring.

Not that Webster could rest, particularly when it was a question of money. Sadlers Wells was helped by the local borough because it was a local theatre, but Covent Garden had no luck with the London County Council or the Greater London Council, partly because his was not a local theatre, but also because at this time the 1951 Exhibition was being planned, and this, including the building of the Festival Hall

Karl Rankl

Left: Marion, Lady Harewood with David Webster and Jimmy Cleveland Belle
Below: Benjamin Britten, Peter Pears and David Webster during the early 1940's

in 1949, was the Council's major effort, taking most of their available funds.

Keynes also brought up the matter of the BBC, which in the past had been a patron of the arts of a sort. They'd helped to subsidize the pre-war international seasons at Covent Garden by buying broadcasting rights – in 1938, for example, they'd paid £7600, transmitting about fifteen of the thirty-five performances. The orchestra had been given £706. 5s., and the singers nothing at all, which left the sponsoring company almost £7000 in credit. The BBC's attitude was now different. An official body having taken on the responsibility of subsidy, they felt that their obligation was at an end, though in principle they were prepared to allow a margin between opera expenses and what they paid. Currently Sadlers Wells was being paid £100 for each opera broadcast, of which 12s. 6d. went to every member of the company, the singers as well as the orchestra now being entitled to benefit. Keynes was hardly thinking along the same lines. He suggested that Covent Garden go for a lump sum of £10,000 a year, and not less than £7500, in return for which the BBC would be allowed to broadcast whichever and as many performances as they wanted. But this arrangement seemed to the BBC too much like subsidy again. They flatly refused. Difficult to say how much difference their agreement might have made to the Opera House fortunes: but it's not overstating the case to say that the history of the performing arts is written in terms of negotiations of this kind, that £10,000 more or less can make all the difference to institutions on this level, and that history is finally written in terms of the few personalities involved in such negotiations.

The BBC was never closed with satisfactorily. For *The Fairy Queen*, the production incorporating both opera and ballet which preceded the debut of the opera company proper, Webster was offered £250, which gave the Opera House £100 after the artists had been paid their pennies. This trifling sum seemed to him all the more disproportionate when he learned that the BBC had paid about £5000 for two studio performances of *The Valkyrie*. To make matters worse, the BBC was shortly to approach Kirsten Flagstad to do the opera for them in English – at the very time when he was about to approach her himself and invite her to give the opera in English at Covent Garden. A broadcast from Covent Garden instead of a studio performance, even if the BBC paid for it handsomely, would still be a large saving for them.

The worst blow – if the new undertaking had failed, then this would have appeared in retrospect the *coup de grâce* – came with Dalton's Finance Bill at the beginning of 1946. Lord Keynes had been approaching rich people, exhorting them to give the Opera House deeds of covenant, which was not to make exorbitant demands on them at a time when deeds could be made from money liable to surtax. In America private support of the arts comes from gifts made by the rich from surtax, which is still allowed there – so that the arts in America are supported indirectly from government money, since the surtax would otherwise be paid to the state. But they are supported haphazardly. Keynes happily saw himself with the best of both worlds, with subsidy from CEMA, not lavish but still subsidy, reinforced by private monies which would not be spent according to the whim of the rich patron but would be distributed by the official body receiving government support. He had had some subscriptions promised, and one of them was going to yield as much as £25,000 a year. Dalton's Bill decreed simply that people couldn't make a deed of covenant with *surtax*. £25,000 – and more – was lost at a stroke. It was a bitter blow. But Webster wasn't one to brood. It was money lost that he'd never had. His prayers were now redirected entirely to the success of the ballet company's *Sleeping Beauty*, whose first night was rapidly approaching.

Would the still fledgling ballet, without as yet a proven, fully authoritative ballerina, make an impact in the house – or would it be daunted by the sheer size and grandeur of its new setting? Webster had recognized the size of the house as a challenge, and it was going to be a challenge too for de Valois and her ballet. The fortunes of his house depended on de Valois's success or failure. Had he been wise to put such faith in the ballet? And was de Valois right to bring her ballet to the house, or was her particular ambition for it misguided? Guthrie certainly was one who thought so, and even after she had achieved the success she'd aimed at he succinctly wrote down the case against: the move to Covent Garden

> certainly gave de Valois what she had a perfect right to demand: scope, financial and artistic, to exploit the current vogue for ballet, to build up the efficiency of her company, to make it world-famous and to establish a British National, or as it has become, a Royal Ballet at Covent Garden.
>
> These were aims with which I could not, and cannot entirely sympathize. Covent Garden I have always regarded as an artistic graveyard; its cubic capacity is enormous but it holds a comparatively small audience; it is 'grand' – and the grandeur certainly pays a dividend on the three or four occasions when royalty is present in full regalia – but on most nights of the week when the audience is just the usual middle-class crowd, of which all ordinary modern audiences are composed, the building's grandeur is just an inappropriate and wildly costly memorial to bygone glories. Covent Garden has the quality of swallowing up all but the most powerful and penetrating performers and performances. It is essentially a 'star' house. Great personalities can dominate it and be seen to advantage; but the minor talent, the subtle effect, the delicate work go for nothing at all.

> De Valois has been aware of this and has deliberately broadened the style of her ballet to suit the house. In the process, much of the old repertoire which suggested at one time that some significant content might be developed became, in the new and vast surroundings, quite ineffective. Without content, ballet has no right to the pretension that it is an art on an equality with opera or drama. In my opinion ballet has got above its station and should have been content to remain no more than an adjunct to the opera.

These words of Guthrie's, even acknowledging that he perhaps never 'tuned-in' to ballet, are not lightly to be dismissed.

Webster none the less saw the house as right, even essential, for *his* purposes, and his hopes for English opera were not so very different from what de Valois's had been for the ballet. His success finally was as unlikely as hers. Indeed, he learned an enormous amount from her: if imitation is famously a form of flattery, then he must be marked down as one of her greatest admirers. Meanwhile, anxiously and enviously, he watched her assembling her forces, identifying her success with his own.

CHAPTER V

Reopening of the House · *The Sleeping Beauty* · Ashton's *Symphonic Variations* · staffing problems · the search for a musical director · Goossens and Walter proposed · Rankl appointed

---

The Opera House reopened on 20 February 1946. David Webster had answered certain criticisms in advance in an article in the *Arts Council Bulletin*:

> Those who may regret that Covent Garden is not opening with opera should perhaps reflect on two points. First, that it augurs well for the new regime at Covent Garden that its first company should be one whose dancers and choreographers are British, whose productions are largely designed by British artists, and many of whose scores are contributed by British composers. Secondly, that to prepare an opera company largely British in personnel, of a quality in any way worthy of the singing traditions of Covent Garden takes time. It is therefore too early to talk at length on the prospects of opera given by a resident company. Other things may be said: while foreigners will not be excluded from the company, British artists will be given first chance; that the operas will be given in English; that every encouragement will be given to our own composers; and that the Covent Garden Opera Trust will on its own behalf and on behalf of opera in England combine with other authorities to set up a first-class school of training for opera.

Webster would have preferred not to make a statement, but he was bound to, if only in order to justify continued subsidy. Hence his insistence that English money was going to be used for the benefit of English art, and not merely to import foreigners for the delight of a tiny section of public. It was not going to be opera as before. In the first year of peace even the most restrained use of foreigners could easily give offence: but if the patriotism running high demanded tact, Webster also knew how to use it for his advantage.

The establishment of two separate operatic organizations, as expected, drew fire. A month before the reopening Desmond Shawe-Taylor was writing in the *New Statesman*:

> In Sadlers Wells we have a rough and unofficial, but promising, Volksoper; in Covent Garden the empty shell of a Staatsoper. The resources of both, singers included, ought to be combined under a single artistic direction . . . How are we to escape from this course of perpetual mediocrity and provincialism? Only, I think, by pooling our slender resources,

> pocketing our pride, and submitting to the direction of musicians and producers who know the whole complex business of opera inside out, and retain in their blood the pre-war standards of a good continental opera house.

He noted that Glyndebourne had used foreigners – Carl Ebert, actor turned director, Fritz Busch, conductor, Rudolph Bing, administrator – to reach and maintain its standards. Webster had emphasized the opportunities that would go to the English but had been careful not to rule out the possibility of employing foreigners in order to help the English artists make the best use of them.

Meanwhile the dance-floor had been taken up and the carpets from before the war beaten and relaid. Seats were brought out of store, they were reconditioned and put back in place. The house was done over in purple and gold, though there was no money for elaborate redecoration. In any case there was a shortage of materials in England and severe rationing restrictions. The staff, including the stage-hands and cleaners, contributed from their own small stock of clothing coupons to provide pink silk to shade the electric candles set along the balconies, which toned with the new Regency wallpaper. The house was understaffed, and most were inexperienced in their different fields – but there was a joyous sense of adventure. Whatever happens to warclouds after war was happening, and the reopening of the Opera House helped it happen. The seasons of the Old Vic at the New Theatre, led by Ralph Richardson and Laurence Olivier, had just the right bravura swing to them, and the reopening of the Opera House too held something of the excitement of a new dawning, confirming, along with peacetime, a new era, hopefully, for the lyric arts in England.

David Webster, calm paterfamilias to children many of them scarcely younger than himself, and some older, watched work in progress. He stood at the back of his theatre, in nobody's way, and his eye travelled over the rows of seats. In the gloom common to any unlit theatre, and particularly cavernous in the huge Opera House, he wondered how it would look 'on the night'. Would the scene dazzle and delight? How would it match people's memories of the old days? Across the rows of seats his eye went to the vast stage with its mighty proscenium arch. Would the little company fill the stage *brilliantly*? If he had doubts, it was only Jimmy who was made privy to them.

The Sleeping Beauty was going to need four huge sets and umpteen costumes, and everybody's efforts right up to the first night would be entirely absorbed by it; since work couldn't start on the other ballets till after the first night, it would therefore have to run for an inordinate number of consecutive performances, a month of them at least.

Webster wouldn't start small – he started as he intended to go on. Stacking the odds against himself had already become something of a trademark. Fonteyn was not yet established as a ballerina, and in any case wouldn't be able to dance Aurora every night, and the shortage of male dancers alone could prove embarrassing if not downright disastrous; the scenery would be on show every night and might have to impress its splendour on the audience without much support from the dancers. He had many discussions with Frederick Ashton, and they agreed that Oliver Messel, a darling of Shaftesbury Avenue, should be entrusted with the supremely important task of designing the work. Webster was excited about having Messel at the Opera House, as he still had vivid memories of the first-ever all-white set C. B. Cochran had commissioned from Messel for a production of Offenbach's *La Belle Hélène*. Messel and the success of *The Sleeping Beauty* fixed the lesson firmly in Webster's mind that if the artists were of doubtful quality, spend your money, put the emphasis, on presentation.

The production costs for *The Sleeping Beauty* were £12,814, in 1946 a gargantuan sum. But Messel proved a marvellous choice. His delicate colour sense combined with an engaging fancifulness: the baroque elaboration of his sets and costumes invited the audience to revel in a non-functional splendour, and there was a feeling of expense lavished for its own sake, a luxury indeed in those years of austerity. The decors were also much abused, being considered by many to be vulgar and fussy as well as ostentatious. But they worked triumphantly well none the less, and Messel was noted by Webster as a future designer for his opera.

The opening was itself a miniature campaign. It was planned mainly by Anthony Gishford, who had suggested himself as Public Relations Officer for the Opera House (and remained for a year or so before going to work for Boosey and Hawkes), and by Michael Wood who was brought in in the first place as his assistant. Everybody was involved. If the House Manager wanted to find his secretary, Audrey Longley, she was as likely as not to be located up in wardrobe, sewing on sequins, together with Ruth Lynam, perhaps, who didn't actually have a specific job but was supposed to be helping de Valois. Wardrobe had an allocation of clothing coupons, but there was a panic because there weren't enough gloves to go round in one scene. And on the first night costumes for the last act were still coming in at the stage-door as the curtain rose on the Prologue.

There was a mainly invited first-night audience, and the guest list had been left to Webster and Lord Keynes. If formal dress wasn't insisted on it was as much because of clothes rationing as to make a social point. But the point was made just the same, as it had been with the Liverpool Philharmonic wartime concerts. There were not many tiaras on view besides those of the Queen and Queen Mary, though Webster had reinvented the scene somewhat by the time he came, much later, to recall the evening in a broadcast:

> *Everybody* wore tiaras and a great deal of jewellery, and one felt, if called upon to come down to the orchestral pit and divest themselves of their jewellery, there might have been enough to dispose of quite a bit of the national debt.

That is how, in those starved days, one might have felt. Even one tiara was startling. There were some few tails, and a goodly sprinkling of lounge suits among the dinner-jackets. Cyril Connolly, though not converted to balletomania by the experience, was there in a dark blue smoking-jacket. Arnold Haskell, a moving spirit, with Keynes, of the Camargo Society fifteen years earlier (and responsible for introducing the word 'balletomania' into England), had been laid up with a poisoned arm, but the nurses at the Royal Free Hospital had put his arm in splints and insisted that he go. Webster's mother was there with Edith Rose, and so was Maud Melly with George. The Royal Family, George VI and the two princesses along with the Queen and Queen Mary, were to be received by Lord Keynes and Lydia Lopokova. There was no one more apt for the duty. Lopokova had danced in Diaghileff's stupendous but ill-fated production of *The Sleeping Beauty* at the Alhambra in 1921, shortly before de Valois herself became a member of the company. Lopokova had first danced the role of the Lilac Fairy and had later also taken her turn in the ballerina role. The ballet at one time, she confesses with great humour, was performed under the title of *The Sleeping Princess*, Diaghileff having told her that it couldn't possibly be called 'The Sleeping Beauty' if *she* was the heroine. The ballet was now performed under its almost proper name (accurate translation from the French would make it *The Beauty in the Sleeping Wood*): Fonteyn was the Beauty, and the world awoke after the nightmare of the war years. If the ballet had been untimely in 1921, it was wonderfully appropriate to this time and this occasion.

Webster mingled quietly with the audience. The Royal Family had a side box, and Queen Mary entered first. 'What, no food?' were her first words as she scanned the annexe. Pre-war the Royal Family had had their food brought in by servants, but rationing post-war did not spare the highest in the land.

And then, suddenly, there was a terrible moment of sad, grotesque comedy. About to receive the king and queen and the princesses, Lord Keynes suffered a minor heart-attack. Lydia Lopokova bundled him behind a door and sent at once for David Webster, whose nerves, for all his calmness, were already overstretched. He summoned his reserves of diplomatic skill and, though meeting his royal guests for the first time, conducted them with consummate ease and graciousness to their box. He then went anxiously back to satisfy himself that Keynes was being looked after. He was somewhat reassured, and certainly did not for the moment anticipate serious consequences.

The curtain rose. If *The Sleeping Beauty* failed, the failure would resound. But it succeeded. It succeeded hugely. The audience roared and all but wept its gratitude. It was as though the ballet had wrested them from that long nightmare of war, rescued them from the encircling gloom of the austerity present. *The Sleeping Beauty* confirmed to them the survival of civilization and its arts. The stage was flower-bedecked, and the curtain-calls continued. The curtains parted yet again and de Valois stepped out into view of the audience. It was twenty years since she had first gone to Lilian Baylis at the Old Vic. This was a fulfilment.

Webster was quietly in the audience, and the very theatre itself was for him the Beauty that was awakened. It was a huge personal success for him too. Sir Kenneth Clark, a member of the Board, wrote him:

> One more word of congratulation on your marvellous achievement. It was a miracle. We all basked in the reflected glory and took what credit we could, but in the end it was all back to you.

But success for a night was one thing, maintaining it quite another. Michael Wood the very next morning was asking Webster, 'What do we do now? We've only worked for the first night.'

What they did was set to work on a triple bill to be mounted in a month's time, while a succession of different dancers took their chances in *Sleeping Beauty*. On the second night a young Russian dancer, married to an Englishman, had a triumph as the Blue Bird, and a year or two later, under her married name of Violetta Elvin, she was Aurora, following Moira Shearer, Pamela May and Beryl Grey in the role and making up, with them, the company's first generation of ballerinas.

The company and its emerging stars settled into their new home. Ashton watched rehearsals and performances from the stalls, from the side of an upper balcony, from the back of the gallery – from everywhere. 'You're not registering in this big house,' he one day told Fonteyn. 'You must hold the positions longer.' There was no danger, with this supremely musical dancer, that her phrasing would be distorted.' Hold positions longer, you've got to show them clearly.' It was a discovery that was as important for this expanding career as her first-night success as Aurora – it was a turning-point in her relationship with her choreographer and opened the door to her future greatness.

The success of Fonteyn in the house, and Ashton's, are barely separable. More than any other artist her success is associated with Covent Garden, and the fame and glamour of the house seemed often to be *her* fame and *her* glamour: David Webster, glorying in her glory, could also register with satisfaction that she had found her ultimate fulfilment in *his* house, and might not have become what she did become in a humbler setting.

At the beginning of April there was a crisis. Ashton was preparing a new ballet, but Michael Somes, partnering Fonteyn, hurt his knee, and it had to be postponed. Robert Helpmann's *Adam Zero* had therefore to be brought forward. Like his earlier *Miracle in the Gorbals* it had a scenario by Michael Benthall, and Helpmann agreed to have the ballet ready in time if Benthall, then Major Benthall in charge of Welfare in Hamburg, could be flown over to direct it. Webster secured his release for the occasion. *Adam Zero*, like *Miracle*, was set to a score commissioned from Arthur Bliss, and again the company was offered a change from classical dancing. It was also notable for anticipating some of the features of theatre in the future: like the musical *Hair*, for example, in the 'sixties, it used technical resources, lights and scaffolding and so on, in full view of the audience, a daring innovation in 1946. The ballet had a further importance because Webster, watching Benthall working, fixed him in his mind as someone to use in the future to direct operas for him.

And then came the Ashton ballet, *Symphonic Variations* – the masterpiece of the first season by the Sadlers Wells Ballet at Covent Garden. It is a masterpiece created for the Opera House and for the company's dancers, and almost of itself defines a style of English dancing. In a sense the ballet was created as a contrast to the work Helpmann was doing: Helpmann's work was the resistance against which he worked, inspired by another ideal altogether. *Symphonic Variations* is a serenely lyrical ballet in which Ashton sublimely used the huge space newly at his disposal, placing the dancers so perfectly, in such purposeful relationship to that space about them; his lean, spare but emotionally charged choreography is at one with that of his designer Sophie Fedorovich, who in *her* work was known as the great eliminator. The ballet confirmed Ashton's position in the company. And where *The Sleeping Beauty* saw the stage filled with scores of dancers, *Symphonic Variations* saw it filled as effectively with six, so that the two ballets together seemed to confirm the wisdom of the move to Covent Garden.

The house had opened with success. That success had been maintained after the first night, and the season, amazingly, continued to be extended.

But it was an Opera House without opera: without even, as yet, a

Musical Director. The opera's first night was still to come, and that was the night towards which Webster was working, to which he'd been working from the moment he'd gone to Boosey and Hawkes in their Regent Street offices, to which he continued to work, with its applause dinning gratefully in his ears, right through the ballet season.

He now had at least the basis of an orchestra in the one accompanying the ballet, the nucleus of which had been drawn from the band used during the ballet's wartime seasons at the New Theatre. But there was much, very much, to be done. Above all, there was still the key man, the Musical Director, to be appointed. This had been a matter of constant discussion and negotiation over the entire year preceding the opening of the house, for until a Musical Director had been found the real work of building an opera company could hardly begin.

Even the house itself was still understaffed, and often appointments depended on securing people's release from the forces. There'd been hardly anyone he could call on from before the war. Frank Ballard was now Chief Machinist, and his assistant was Ted Lilley, who'd been a props boy in 1937. There was a returning electrician who at once became *Chief* Electrician, and a carpenter, and a man who'd operated the curtains on the stage. And a stage doorman. These few at once acquired a kind of senior status. There was also a fireman from before the war. Not much to build on. The box office had to be started from scratch. Frequently Webster was taking on people who hadn't done the job before, and his experience of hiring staff for Bon Marché was proving invaluable, for he had to match people he was meeting for the first time with jobs whose requirements he as yet hardly understood himself, whose very names were sometimes mysterious. Chief Machinist was the new name for Master Carpenter, the man who was both head of the stage crew and also in charge of the workshops and the carpenters who build the sets. As he delved into unexplored corners of the Opera House, it was hard for anyone to assess what exactly Webster did and didn't know about. In a way he was pleased to have a team about him who couldn't measure his regime against the pre-war seasons. There was a sense of embarking on an adventure together, the new Administrator with his staff.

Pre-war Frank Ballard had had a hundred and twenty people working under him on the stage, and for the opening Webster had only been able to supply him with thirty-five. Which is why Webster had to grab at staff as they presented themselves. He made some strikingly apt choices. Peter Waller had been working at the Grosvenor Hotel when he was recruited by the American Red Cross in London who needed someone who knew about catering. Webster invited him to be his House Manager. Muriel Kerr, also from the American Red Cross, went to see Webster just before Christmas in 1945. He at once recognized her as a most promising receptacle for confidences – as it were, a briefcase with a secure zip only waiting to fasten itself over secrets. She was unobtrusively steadfast, that was apparent to him at once, and she had a great potential for loyalty. It wasn't long before the boss was asking his future secretary, 'When can you start?' She gave in her notice at the Red Cross, and on 23 January was sitting beside her new boss in the small office with one desk and the one telephone on it.

By this time Peter Waller too had an assistant, Bill Fleming-Williams. Michael Wood had come in with Anthony Gishford, swelling the small group in the large house, and Leonard Grant was taken on as Douglas Lund's assistant. David Webster, and the Opera House, commanded loyalty. People came to work for him, and continued to work for him, who could have earned larger salaries elsewhere. Muriel Kerr was still with him when he retired, and remained at Covent Garden until her death early in 1975. Leonard Grant and Michael Wood from among these first people also remained with the organization, Grant eventually succeeding Lund as Opera House Accountant, and Michael Wood, having succeeded Gishford as Press Officer, eventually taking charge of the Royal Ballet School.

This was already the basis of an organization, and Webster was at the centre of it, happy to feel a family round him in a house pulsating with activity.

And what of the musical staff? Joseph Shadwick came in as Orchestral Leader, making replacements and additions from among those who like himself were returning members of His Majesty's Forces. There was still no Chorus Master. And still no Musical Director. That was the most important, the crucial, appointment, and it was yet to be made. They couldn't get along much longer without a Musical Director.

At the beginning of 1945 Ralph Hawkes, running Boosey and Hawkes's New York offices, had written:

> There are, of course, numerous conductors here who are falling over themselves to get to London but I have seen all the top-notchers and, when the time is ripe, I think we shall be able to get what we want, but I must stress the fact that unless something is done by the end of March, we shall have a job to get Szell for he is already a very rising star at the Metropolitan and elsewhere and is very sensible of his success. Bruno Walter can be had in 1946 if we want him.

Bruno Walter! David Webster, when still merely a visitor in the house, had often been entranced by Bruno Walter's famous performances of *Rosenkavalier*. Lotte Lehmann had been the Marschallin, with

Elizabeth Schumann as Sophie and Richard Mayr as Ochs. This was the most famous of all between-the-wars productions, the very hallmark of Vienna. It would be 'rather wizard' if he could have that same Bruno Walter as his Musical Director. It was a possibility to savour.

Ralph Hawkes added that: 'Goossens can be had earlier and he might be of very great assistance in our commencing efforts.'

It was precisely because David Webster was already known to be dilatory that Hawkes felt it necessary to stress that they move fast. Webster's was a guarded personality, and it sometimes seemed that he would have liked nothing better than to seal himself within an envelope and launch himself into the world 'under plain covers'. His dilatoriness was an essential part of this personality, for to commit himself to a decision was a form of 'declaring' himself.

But his dilatoriness also became one of his strengths. His stock phrase was, 'See me in ten days' time.' It seemed that his door was never shut, that you could see him whenever you wanted to – but you couldn't. When there was a complication to be sorted out, a complaint or a grievance, he'd ask Muriel Kerr for the details first and assess the situation in unassailed privacy. The altogether invaluable Miss Kerr, ideally protective of her boss's weakness, was the one who sensed the right time for confrontation, and no one was better tuned-in to Webster's way of making weakness appear only under the guise of strength.

If he could, in a particular crisis, make rapid decisions and implement them with speed, she knew that he usually, when there was no immediate crisis, preferred to wait and see, hoping that the problem would disappear in the interim or solve itself. It often did. He was certainly in no hurry to answer most letters – 'If you wait long enough,' he claimed, 'they answer themselves.' Sometimes, of course, they didn't, and he was the loser by the delay.

But never was his dilatoriness more constructive than here, in this all-important question of the appointment of a Musical Director. He couldn't, *wouldn't* move fast. The wrong choice and the whole enterprise might be in ruins. If he had sometimes to grab at staff, Webster wasn't going to grab when it was a question of Musical Director, however gratifying it might be to him to have the great Bruno Walter in the house. Approaches were made, and a twelve months' contract was actually proposed to Walter, with a fee of £10,000. Like an animal alert to danger, Webster sensed the atmosphere, he sniffed out motive and meaning. He registered Walter's reluctance – such a contract would have committed him exclusively to England for a prolonged period, and he didn't want such a complete turnabout. He'd become too closely associated with America and, besides, he was close on seventy. He was perhaps prepared to come to England in the spring or summer of 1946, for three or four months only.

Bruno Walter had just given *Fidelio* with a cast of young American singers, but it was only after hearing the singers, he explained in a letter to H. W. Heinsheimer, Ralph Hawkes's New York representative, that he'd fixed on the opera for them. 'I cannot say,' he further explained, 'I will conduct *Tristan*, *Don Giovanni*, *La Forza del Destino*. I will have to know which cast will be available and then will determine which operas to present.'

Webster had to acknowledge, sadly, that Walter simply hadn't grasped the basic facts of the situation – he was being approached to work in a house where managing to get enough silk to make the lampshades had itself seemed a major achievement.

And Walter also wanted Carl Ebert, Glyndebourne's Artistic Director, to come to Covent Garden. Ebert in his turn was keen that Glyndebourne and Covent Garden should amalgamate and that Glyndebourne's Administrator, Rudolph Bing, should also come to Covent Garden. Which would leave David Webster where?

Webster may have had but one desk to strum his fingers on, but his one telephone, and Miss Kerr's letters, from the first days connected him with the great. He was not intimidated. The desk-man, which he essentially was, is a being of another world, and in this world Webster was virtually an artist. Of another kind than the one who depends on his brush or his pen or his voice, but still, arguably, an artist. The desk-man's skill is deployed in negotiations, and it is here that he exercises power. The artist proper creates his own material, and shapes it for his purposes. The desk-man shapes actual events so that their outcome – their final form – is as near as possible to the ideal.

In the matter of Musical Director, Webster, as so often in the future, delayed constructively. There was no Bruno Walter for Covent Garden, not even for a three or four months' period as guest. There was no Ebert and no Bing, and George Szell's success with *The Mastersingers* at the Metropolitan at the end of 1945 put him too effectively out of the running. Hawkes had put forward Eugene Ormandy's name, 'the best young conductor in this country after Toscanini, Walter, Koussevitsky and Stokowski'. But Bruno Walter had suggested that, himself refusing, Eugene Goossens should come into the reckoning, perhaps with William Steinberg also involved.

The thinking was still on a grand scale. There was nothing provincial about the thinking. Sir Eugene Goossens, who had composed the music for a ballet in the Sandon Society's *Masquerade* in 1934, was seriously pursued. He was offered £5000 for a twelve months' engagement. This had been too long a period for Bruno Walter, but it was too short for Goossens. He was subsequently offered two years. Ralph Hawkes urged Webster to get Goossens to sign. But negotiations continued, with Webster still reluctant to conclude. The house was open, the ballet's first season was under way, and still no contract had been signed. And in March 1946 Goossens himself broke off negotiations. 'Webster's own statement,' he wrote to Ralph Hawkes,

> embodies my biggest misgiving when he says 'not that England is entirely devoid of good singers, but there are naturally few of them, and those few, for obvious reasons, are not well-schooled in opera'. In other words, unless 'those few' not 'well-schooled' in opera prove susceptible within a reasonable amount of time, either their places must be taken by the foreign artists (with imperfect diction) – thus defeating the main idea of the project – or else the whole idea of opera in English must be abandoned. It is the prospect of shouldering the responsibility of making bricks without straw that alarms me a great deal . . .
>
> I cannot safely undertake the responsibility for a project the artistic outcome of which I cannot foresee and consequently take full musical responsibility for. The real paucity of experienced operatic material (how could it be otherwise after what England has endured in the war?) plus my natural fear that after so much preliminary work the calibre of the artists themselves might prove an insuperable handicap to the success of the company, are the strongest reasons for my decision.

What he couldn't 'help adding (certainly in no spirit of recrimination)' is highly relevant:

> all this could virtually have been written many months ago had the true statement of fact I requested at that time have been forthcoming from London. It might indeed have materially changed the whole situation.

It was as well that the situation was not changed, though just how it might have been changed by Webster's moving faster is hard to see. Webster, knowing that the job he had to offer was neither a sinecure nor glamorous, had had to take soundings: and moving faster could not have turned it into a sinecure or increased its glamour. At most an exciting building job was on offer. What had come through to him in the course of negotiations spread over more than a year was that, while neither of them would say so, both Walter and Goossens were thinking in terms of the Grand Season as before. Goossens was saying you can't have a company without foreigners, and you can't have foreigners unless you let them sing in a foreign language.

Webster had also come to see that it was going to be no good going to men who had established careers and much to lose. These weren't the men to relish 'the responsibility of making bricks without straw'. At this early stage celebrities from abroad were out, and the best thing was probably to use what there was at home – Constant Lambert, Malcolm Sargent, Walter Susskind, and occasionally maybe even that disruptive Titan Beecham. But it became increasingly clear to him that above all IT WAS NO USE HAVING A MUSICAL DIRECTOR WHO WOULDN'T DO THE SPADEWORK.

During this year of negotiations Webster had showed his hand would he or no – already inviting comparison with Queen Elizabeth I, whom Lytton Strachey, in *Elizabeth and Essex*, most memorably describes:

> In reality, she succeeded by virtue of all the qualities which every hero should be without – dissimulation, pliability, indecision, procrastination, parsimony. It might almost be said that the heroic element chiefly appeared in the unparalleled lengths to which she allowed these qualities to carry her.

Webster, true, had not had the opportunity to show himself parsimonious in the course of these negotiations. But the comparison stands. If always cautious, like Queen Elizabeth, about spending public money, there was also, in his parsimony, an often striking contrast with the lavishness of his personal living style.

Webster's final selection of Musical Director fell on one who, after Walter and Goossens, represented an apparently alarming decrescendo. It was not even one of the English conductors. After the great names spoken with such pleasure he made the descent to . . . to whom? To one Karl Rankl. And who under the sun, people were soon asking, might this Karl Rankl be?

CHAPTER VI

Spadework · Beecham's criticisms · chorus assembled · English singers and English opera · Webster's ambitions

Rankl was born in Austria in 1898, and he studied in Vienna, where he was a favourite pupil of Schoenberg; Webern was another of his teachers. He joined Weingartner's staff at the Vienna Volksoper in 1922 as coach and choirmaster, in 1925 went to Reichenberg as Opera Director, moved on to Königsberg in 1927 and, most importantly, from 1928 to 1931 was Klemperer's assistant at the Kroll Opera in Berlin. Subsequently he was Musical Director of the State Opera in Wiesbaden, but had soon to leave Germany because of the Nazis, directing the opera first in Graz and then in Prague, before being forced to flee again in 1939.

The world face of music had changed since the rise of the Nazis – a tentative analogy can be made between the sack of Constantinople in 1453, and the dispersal of its scholars, and the Anschluss of 1933 and the dispersal of musicians. Europe, and in particular Germany, had been the acknowledged musical centre of the world, but after 1933 musicians fled in greater and greater numbers, taking with them their talents and musical tradition. America was the greatest beneficiary, with Bruno Walter, Toscanini and Klemperer settling in the United States, while Kleiber and Busch worked mainly in South America during the war; and hence Bruno Walter, in the course of his negotiations with Covent Garden, felt confident to forecast that, where Central Europe had been the cradle of opera before the war, after the war it was going to be England and America. This hardly seemed likely in England, at any rate, in 1945. Had one or two of the 'greats', had only Bruno Walter himself, decided to settle in England rather than America, things might have looked different.

Rankl was one of the few refugee musicians who had chosen to come to England, and Webster had an exact idea of what he could contribute. Somewhat in the manner of his first boss Weingartner, Rankl was the very type of the old German Kapellmeister – he was an all-round musician who could equally well compose or conduct a symphony, even if his symphonies weren't masterpieces and he was not a virtuoso conductor. But he had conducted the Liverpool Philharmonic during Webster's chairmanship and shown himself good enough. What was crucially important was that he measured up to

Desmond Shawe-Taylor's not unexacting definition of the kind of men the Opera House needed – men 'who know the whole complex business of opera inside out, and retain in their blood the pre-war standards of a good continental opera house'. It was impossible, long negotiations had already proved it out of the question, to get men as well equipped as Rankl who were also 'great' conductors and would bring prestige to Covent Garden. For England, at that time, Rankl was the man. He has our gratitude.

There is more history in Rankl's five years at the Opera House than in any other period of Webster's quarter of a century tenancy. Amazing progress was made. Not much more than a scratch orchestra had become by 1951 an orchestra which, adequately rehearsed, and under a good conductor, could play magnificently. There was no chorus, it can't be repeated often enough, and Rankl created one. There was almost nothing. There were bits and pieces of old scenery, much of which couldn't be used, and some of it which, for the sake of economy, had to be. Beecham was among those who didn't welcome Rankl, and now he claimed that this old scenery belonged to him. He had been Artistic Director of the Covent Garden opera seasons from 1932 until the war, and when Covent Garden Estates Ltd leased the house to Covent Garden Trust he was prepared to make an issue – Betty Humby Beecham wrote that her Tommy was about to sue. Webster forwarded her letter, and was relieved to hear from Covent Garden Properties Ltd that:

> As far as we are concerned the whole of the scenery and costumes owned by this company and included in the lease to you were acquired by us from the liquidator of the previous company, and we do not admit that Sir Thomas Beecham has any interest therein.

This was but a foretaste of the Beecham tactic. Beecham was not pleased with what was happening at the Opera House – he had been used to being in charge there, the house had been financed by private monies, and he had lost large sums in it, his own and other people's. His plans for his international season in 1945 had foundered, and the options on the singers had lapsed on 1 January; but, asserting his status, for a while he had continued, as H. W. Heinsheimer described to Ralph Hawkes, confidently 'big-mouth' about the scheme. Not altogether without relish, Webster – an adversary, but also a friend, with inscribed books from the man to prove it – waited for further broadsides.

Rankl had not much of an orchestra to begin with. And no chorus at all. No costumes, no productions. Every opera had to be mounted fresh, if that not always appropriate word may be allowed. More than that – almost everyone involved in a new production had to be taught the opera. Imagine mounting a production of *Siegfried* with an orchestra of whom some ninety per cent didn't know the score, had never played a single note of it. Rankl had to teach the orchestra, teach the chorus, teach a team of singers most of them not only new to the work but even new to the stage. Many of the producers engaged, whatever their credits in the theatre, were new to opera. Even the repetiteurs, most of them, weren't experienced – it became a question of the Musical Director having to teach the teachers. An average of six new productions a year were mounted during Rankl's five years, thirty or so in all; and in his final year there were six new productions along with twenty-one revivals, making twenty-seven operas altogether in repertory. Rankl was in the toils of the repertory system, with single performances of many works in alternation popping up here and there throughout the season. He took on a task which Walter wouldn't, which Goossens wouldn't; it's wrong, altogether wrong, to judge Rankl only as a conductor; quite simply, he did the spadework; and no one willing to do it could have done better.

Rankl was appointed at last in April 1946. The ballet company was entering on its third month of consecutive performances and Webster was going into his sixth month at the Opera House. Norman Feasey, another of the small band with experience of the House pre-war, came in as Chief Repetiteur. Four repetiteurs in all were needed, and by November two more had been found, one of them George Malcolm.

And the singers? In the summer Webster and Rankl were in America looking out for singers, and extensive auditions were held in London and in the major provincial cities. Some two thousand were seen and heard, and by early August the auditions were nearly complete. A chorus of seventy was engaged – in Webster's own words, 'the first instalment of a dream come true'. Rankl met Douglas Robinson when he was in Leeds holding auditions, and he invited him to audition for the post of Chorus Master: Robinson took charge of a rehearsal in Morley College in London in September, with the chorus augmented for the evening by professionals from Westminster Abbey and St Paul's, and he did so well that he was offered the job, in which he continued until 1974.

The chorus assembled for the first time in the Crush Bar at Covent Garden on 20 October, a year after Mecca had handed over the empty building in its wretched state. There were singers from all walks of life, Welsh miners and northern factory workers and schoolmasters among them: some of them had only recently been demobbed, three came from the Carl Rosa Opera Company and one from Sadlers Wells, but in all only five or six of them had ever been on a stage before.

There were good musicians among them, and some who didn't know what a sharp or flat was. On the 28th they were introduced to their new Chorus Master. Rankl proudly demonstrated the quality of the voices he had found by making each of them in turn, that afternoon, stand and sing scales – all the first sopranos and tenors had top Cs, and even Ds, some of them. Rankl was rightly proud. 'You have,' he said, 'the finest collection of voices in the world. It is up to you to make them into a chorus.' It was this chorus that was the basis of the first-ever permanent company to work at Covent Garden.

If there were fine voices to be had for the chorus, why then was the engagement of principals to present such problems? The answer is to be found in the miserable history of the English singer, on whom had been fostered 'second-place mentality'. Inferiority in the field of opera had always been taken for granted, with few protestants. Opera singers constituted a minority group driven to believing the propaganda directed against themselves: and consequent lack of opportunities ensured that their level of achievement appeared to justify the propaganda. But Webster had undertaken to champion them, and if he aroused bitter opposition it was partly because people resented his attack on received ideas. Who was he, a business-fellow from out-of-London, a provincial, to fly in all their faces and, almost worse, eventually to confound them with his success? Criticism of him was bitter, and continued bitter – and it was partly suppressed hysteria based on a natural resentment that expectations had been confounded. Bad enough for Webster had he failed. But even the very success of this haberdasher from Liverpool put them all to shame.

Webster's achievement can only be appreciated against a background of the history of the English singer, indeed of the English musician. Pre-war even an all-English orchestra would have been unthinkable: but the atmosphere defiantly prevailing during the war had helped, and now (1975) we have five major English orchestras in London alone. The rise of the English singer and of English opera are part of a general rise in the status of the English musician. But there was more opposition to the unacknowledged English singer, and it was far harder to win opportunities for him. That was the problem. In 1955 Webster, in *Music and Musicians*, wrote: 'I have seen nothing in the last ten years to make me doubt the possibility of a great crop of English opera singers, given opportunity, experience and encouragement.'

He's proved right in his expectations, which were the same in 1944. But it was an act of the greatest courage, foresight, will – what have you – an act of great faith, to base the fortunes of his company on singers without experience, with only an inferiority complex to define them.

Every now and then someone had found something good to say about the English singer's potential, and as often as not it was a foreigner.

In 1826 Weber came to England to take up his post as Musical Director at Covent Garden, and he saw a performance of his opera *Der Freischütz*. He had the highest praise for Mary Ann Paton and John Braham, who sang the leads, and he wrote to his wife: 'There are several good tenors here and I really cannot see why English singing should be so much abused. The singers have a good Italian education, fine voices and expression.'

But about the same time, in his *Life of Rossini*, Stendhal was writing: 'No truly honest observer, venturing into Italy from abroad, could dare for one instant to deny the hopeless absurdity of presuming to train singers or compose elsewhere than under the shadow of Vesuvius.'

Indeed, the whole story is told in the invitation issued in 1862 to Charles Santley – the first English Figaro and a renowned Don Giovanni – to appear twice at Covent Garden in the role of Di Luna in *Il Trovatore*. He was offered no engagement, not even a fee. It was considered that the compliment of permitting an Englishman to sing at the Opera House beside highly paid foreign artists was itself sufficient. The non-engagement became a kind of general audition for Santley; and a successful one, for within a week or two the impresario Maplesson was offering him a contract for a season at His Majesty's.

There'd been occasional attempts – gallant attempts – to improve this situation. Such English opera as there was had been, much of it, traditionally supplied by touring companies, in the early years of this century, for example, by the Carl Rosa or the Moody-Manners. (In a Ronald Firbank novel the Miss Chalfonts of Ashringford are discovered 'standing before the announcements of the Lilliputian Opera House, where', they note deprecatingly, 'never came anything more exhilarating than Moody-Manners or Mrs D'Oyley Carte'.) Richter's English *Ring* cycles at Covent Garden in the first decade of this century did nothing, finally, to break the succession of one international season after another, in which English singers for the most part were only allowed to appear insignificantly. It was 1911 before even an all-English chorus was assembled.

Beecham, early in his career, was for a time a champion, and the prospectus of his first important opera season, in 1910, while boasting the supremacy of the foreign singers he'd engaged, also added: 'It is believed that many of the native artists engaged are likely to attain similar successes if the same chances are afforded them.'

And in his last night speech after his short 1919 season at Drury Lane he proclaimed it his ambition to 'establish not only opera in

English but English opera!' (And he spoke too of his hopes of having opera at Covent Garden all the year round – something never before achieved in the theatre's entire history.)

Through the 'twenties he was liable to come out in support of English opera and English artists, hot in their defence, for example, when in 1928 the novelist Hugh Walpole launched an attack on them. 'Our singers,' he stoutly maintained, 'are equal to any in the world.'

But eventually he gave up on them, and through the 'thirties he was committed to international opera. In his autobiography, *A Mingled Chime*, published in 1944, he wrote that:

> English voices are unlike those of other nations; really robust tenors and true dramatic sopranos hardly exist among us, and high baritones are as rare as a perfect summer. The best among them are of comparatively moderate volume, pure and excellent in tone but lacking in power and brilliance in comparison with those of Italy, Germany and France.

He went on to suggest, much in the vein of Professor Dent and Tyrone Guthrie in their manifesto of that same year, that a smaller theatre, something along the line of the Opéra Comique in Paris, would suit English voices better.

Beecham didn't persevere, and it wasn't through him, but through David Webster, that English singers were given their chances. It was he who had the stamina to persist: though it must be emphasized that what Beecham was writing in 1944 was nothing extraordinary, it was quite in accord with received ideas. In size and style and scope, in vigour and temperament, the English singer seemed anything but an *opera*-singer. Oratorio, perhaps. In fact, here the English singers had already excelled, having had the chance here, as never in opera, to explore their potential fully.

All the more credit then, against this background, to Webster and to Rankl as well, who in 1947, interviewed in *Bandwagon* by Charles Reid, was making statements which *were*, for the time, extraordinary. 'The English,' he stated firmly, 'are temperamentally as well equipped for opera as any other nation . . . Once the music grips them they let themselves go . . . as effectively as any Neapolitan who ever clung to a top note.'

If this was madness in 1947, his points were still not proven by the end of his five years at Covent Garden, though there was by then a hopeful sign or two. But by the 'seventies they have at last become commonplace.

A problem for Webster and Rankl was that English singers, like other persecuted minority groups, were reluctant to give up their identity as second-class citizens. Percy Heming, who was attached to the production staff, summoned the principals in their first week of rehearsals at the house and told them, 'this company has been formed for you young artists'. This was itself a revolutionary statement – that English singers were no longer there merely to provide a backing to show off distinguished foreigners. Heming paused for the words to register. 'The company has been formed for *you* young artists, put all you've got into it. Make a go of it!'

Webster had to persuade them that a decent future could be secured in opera as well as in oratorio. There had been occasional English singers who had won international status for themselves. Eva Turner and Alfred Piccaver between the wars, and of course Dame Nellie Melba herself, since Commonwealth artists are normally also considered 'English' singers: but these were exceptions, and considered virtually honorary foreigners. Isobel Baillie, heroine of more than a thousand *Messiahs*, was the very type of an English singer. To make Webster's task the harder, the English are not so much unmusical as too musical by half, and the many choral societies in England and Wales – most numerous where life was toughest – were the obvious source of income for singers whose opportunities for employment in opera were then extremely uncertain. No one could be certain that the house would remain open, or even that if it did it would not revert to international seasons. In March 1947 a memorandum, prepared by Professor Dent, was presented to the Board:

> If we are to make opera more important than oratorio in this country, it will inevitably take a good many years and we must be prepared to face a long and gradual transition period.

Webster was distressed to find his English singers taking to the night trains between rehearsals or performances for engagements in the provinces, but he couldn't stop them. He didn't have enough to offer them, not at first, neither a certainty of continuous employment nor enough money.

It was, then, more than mere snobbery which had made David Webster want an alternative to the kind of work Sadlers Wells provided. The idea of opera on a small scale at Sadlers Wells appealed to him, but this could only be a second wing of the English opera. It could only promote local singers locally, and he knew that his singers must be trained up to compete on the international stages if they were to acquire confidence. And if eventually they were to aspire to Vienna and La Scala and the Metropolitan, then only a house of the same size and stature in England, which meant Covent Garden and nowhere else, could give them their testing ground. This was a totally opposed view to that expressed by Eric Crozier when he was forming the English Opera Group:

> the best way to achieve the beginnings of a repertory of English opera is through the creation of chamber opera, requiring small resources of singers and players, but suitable for performances in large and small opera houses or theatres.

Webster's ambitions were encapsulated in Beecham's long-ago words 'to establish not only opera in England but English opera'. He felt that there was no national repertory of English operas because there was no national opera house. Only a national opera house could attract and inspire composers, and it had to be based on singers of international stature.

He was committed to open with a company made up of English singers only – the term, normally taken to include Commonwealth artists, he stretched slightly to include also an American or two. It hadn't taken him long to discover that almost all of them were either almost totally inexperienced or else 'over-the-top', and he was well aware of the nature of the material he had to deal with. At the end of the company's first season Desmond Shawe-Taylor wrote in the *Statesman* that:

> the impression persists that the authorities at Covent Garden are curiously indifferent to the actual sound made by the human voice; and curiously unaware of where to look for the best English singers.

But Webster was anything but indifferent, and he'd looked long and thoroughly. He was constantly upset by people imagining that there was treasure he'd overlooked: in 1950 it was suggested to Lord Baldwin that deserving English singers were being overlooked in favour of foreigners, and Baldwin passed on the suggestion, for what it was worth, to the Chairman of the Board, whom in this instance Webster had little difficulty in reassuring.

> Trefor Jones is naturally well known to us. He is no more a young man and in figure smaller than Svanholm and as far as he is concerned I don't think that even platform shoes would give him the dignity of a Parsifal. Frankly, I doubt if he could ever have sung a Parsifal here, but he certainly could not now.

Webster could not altogether avoid a touch of impatient comic irony when he refuted a second charge of neglect:

> Baldwin mentioned Widdop. It is a great grief to me that Walter Widdop was passed [*sic*] when he could be used at Covent Garden – he died about a year ago!

Webster had also found that the occasional singer neither inexperienced nor 'over-the-top' – nor dead – was not necessarily to be had easily. At the beginning of 1945, many months before he had even moved into the Opera House, he cabled from his office in Upper Regent Street to Ralph Hawkes in New York: 'Are there any singers of British nationality doing star work in America besides Brownlee?' There was only one, Arthur Carron of the Metropolitan, who had been known here before the war as Arthur Cox of Sadlers Wells. Carron was worried about the news that had reached him that Sadlers Wells might be amalgamating with Covent Garden, and in answer to a preliminary enquiry he wrote to Heinsheimer:

> I did not work hard in America for six years to become again a member of Sadlers Wells. Will you have an English or an international company? I do not want to go down after my Metropolitan years.

He preferred to wait till the new regime at Covent Garden had established itself.

If the new opera company was to be made up entirely of English singers for its debut, it was not going to be long before guests were introduced into it – foreign guests of the highest international standard. This was Webster's intention from the beginning. He knew all along that he could not bring on his own singers unless they had the experience of working alongside foreign singers – the experience and the inspiration. They needed to learn various styles, and they needed to be inspired to aim high.

Webster knew in advance that his company, unleavened by guests, could not rise above a level of mediocrity. But he had none the less to make good his intentions towards English singers and English opera by presenting, prematurely, an all-English opera company, partly to convince the singers themselves. The public, as well as the Treasury, would have to be shown that the company could not yet achieve a decent level unaided, and after a first season would no doubt welcome guests in its ranks; but in spite of the presence of foreign singers, he would have imposed the idea of a future *English* company. This is not to say that Webster looked forward to failure. On the contrary he feared it. But he was planning, long in advance, to capitalize if necessary on the company's failure, or at the very least comparative failure, which must be allowed to make its point. He was quite conscious of beginning in one way in order to continue in another.

And he could have had no better example than that of Ninette de Valois, who was working near him in the house. De Valois had shown superb confidence in promoting her own artists. Markova had been the star of the Vic-Wells Ballet, but when she left the company in 1935 de

Valois, with invisible braggadocio, had proceeded *not* to invite another guest star to lead the company. She was asked why she hadn't, for example, invited Spessivtseva to take Markova's place. 'If I do that,' she had answered, 'I will rob all my young dancers of their self-confidence and we shall never have a national ballet.' She had decided, coolly, that the time was right for creating the company's star from its own ranks, and she had selected the young Fonteyn for promotion. Fonteyn had been given opportunities, and had developed into the star that de Valois had judged the company needed.

Webster didn't expect to found a national opera in a single season. He was going to present a company of English singers and to introduce, as soon as was both feasible and tactful, star guests into their ranks. He was going to have to judge when his own singers were ready for promotion, but he was determined to bring them up eventually to the level of the guest singers. And then at last English composers would have a company to compose for. They would compose operas for the singers he had brought on, or for their heirs – in Webster's own time, or in time to come – but the day would come when English composers would begin at last to create a repertory of native English operas.

CHAPTER VII

Ballet to the fore · Ballet Theatre and the San Carlo Opera · *The Fairy Queen* · Massine

After Rankl's appointment, no energies were spared in putting the opera company together. It was priority. But if Webster was looking forward, apprehensively, to presenting the company, he was also happy to delay as long as was reasonable, and a bit longer. He wanted the house well and truly warmed first.

So he wasn't only shopping about for singers for his own company, he was in the market for entire guest companies. It would be no bad thing for the opera public to taste the pleasure of an *Opera* House again, and acquire the habit of coming back: and it would be best if they had already acquired the habit before the new opera presented itself. The public was enjoying ballet, and they ought also to have some opera on a higher level than he could hope to offer at first. If their appetite for opera were whetted, they might even be more, rather than less, tolerant of his new company, and eager for the house to be kept open even if the home company's first ventures weren't exemplary.

David Webster at his desk was in touch with the world. Even in the autumn of 1944, with the war still on, a visit by the Russian opera and ballet was being contemplated. Lord Keynes wrote to Webster: '*The Fountain of Bakhchisarai* I have seen done in Russia. It is not quite first class but well worth seeing.'

It was a film of this ballet that was the first sight most of the Western world was vouchsafed of Ulanova, and the ballet was included in its repertory when the Bolshoi Ballet at last came to Covent Garden twelve years later.

And Sir Anthony Eden – as though further to demonstrate, if proof were still needed, the importance of contact at government level – himself suggested a visit by the Bolshoi. In January 1945 the British Ambassador to Moscow, Sir Archibald Kerr, reported to Keynes:

> Eden's suggestion was made and Molotov's consent given in that glow of brotherhood that comes with food and wine . . . No answer means 'no' – a polite form of saying no. And I think that the reason is probably a physical one – the business of moving the corps de ballet from Moscow to London would be very formidable, and, so long as everything in the Soviet Union is set aside in the interests of the Red Army, I don't think that there is any chance of getting your attractive plan on foot. If Hitler

is finished this year it would not be impossible to get it moving next year.

There was a possibility of a visit by the Royal Opera from Stockholm. The Swedes, with guilt feelings about the war, offered to come for nothing, profits to go to some deserving English charity (and Webster was quick to suggest Covent Garden as the deserving charity). In March 1945 Kenneth Clark was in Stockholm, and Webster asked him to reconnoitre. 'We shall need a real coloratura soprano,' he wrote, 'and a bass who can act. We are all right for the "statuesque" bass, but we have not actually got an actor bass.'

It was early days, with Mecca still in the house, but Webster already knew the local situation thoroughly and was not naïve about the problems he'd be facing.

The Swedish Company, however, like the Bolshoi, didn't come until 1956, and at the beginning of 1946 the Paris Opéra and the Opéra Comique seemed the most likely visitors. They were to bring an interesting programme of novelties – novelties, that is, to English audiences – Lalo's *Le Roi d'Ys* and Dukas' *Ariane et Barbe Bleu*, Debussy's *Pelléas et Mélisande*, Gounod's *Mireille*, and a triple bill composed of Ravel's *L'Heure Espagnole*, Fauré's *Masques et Bergamasques*, and Ibert's *Angélique*. A big financial loss would be sustained, inevitably, but as Webster wrote to Lord Keynes:

> From our angle I think the main reason for facing the possibility of a loss is that we are bringing opera of a good standard to London, which is something we set out to do.

Negotiations, absurdly, broke down. Webster had proposed that the two companies bring a Chief Machinist and four others with them to London, but they insisted on no less than twelve. Webster persuaded the administration to a compromise, and they agreed to cut the number to eight. The visit might still have taken place if they'd been prepared to bring only one company, or even to do without the Opéra Comique's chorus – the financial loss had to be kept within limits. But it was probably as well that the visit was cancelled, since the fare on offer was somewhat insubstantial for an audience many of whom had still to make acquaintance with the basic repertory. In the quarter of a century since only *Pelléas* and the Ravel have made any headway here.

After the Russian, the Swedish, the French, Webster was more or less reduced to German or Italian companies, the more obvious choices since the German and Italian works are the basis of the repertory. But as they had been so recently our enemies, there was the worry of possible political embarrassment. To the public of those days the opera-singer was still the Italian singer. A whole generation was growing up, well before long-playing records, with a tiny stock of 78s, and many people forty years old or more salivate nostalgically at the mere memory of those red labels (HMV) and mauve labels (Columbia). Spinning on them were Caruso and Gigli, Tito Schipa and the honorary Italian Björling, and Richard Tauber and Elisabeth Schumann. The world's top companies were then, of course, La Scala Milan and the Vienna State Opera; and it is difficult to realize in the 'seventies just how great was their pre-eminence.

Webster divined that the forces, who had flocked to the opera in Naples and Rome in the last couple of years of the war, would take more kindly to the idea than the stay-at-homes. If it had to be a German or Italian company, therefore, he favoured the San Carlo, which had, after all, been opened by the British Army Authorities in 1943 and was officially named the General Mediterranean Forces San Carlo Opera Company, Naples. From early 1945 British soldiers had been used as extras, and the *Tosca* firing squad was usually commanded by a British officer.

Even so, Webster wondered – was it tactful to bring over the company before 1947 at the earliest? He was emboldened by the continuing success of the Sadlers Wells Ballet and, though still nervous, he decided to risk it and bring forward the visit to the autumn of 1946. He of course recognized the dangers that attached to having his own singers inevitably overshadowed in advance, but other considerations too weighed with him. He needed time, he wanted to keep the house open, and he was concerned that people at least realize, or have recalled to them, the potential of the art of opera, which his own company at first could hardly be expected to realize fully. The best of the visitors must establish a standard which his own singers, however much discouraged, would have to aim at. (Webster felt differently four years later. When La Scala itself came to Covent Garden in 1950, he insisted that the guest company appear only after his own had finished its season: his singers were just beginning to gain in confidence after their four consecutive seasons and he wasn't going to have their chances with the audience prejudiced.)

The San Carlo included the baritone Tagliabue, a particular forces favourite, and the prima donna was Margherita Carosio, the finest Italian soprano of the day. Luigi Infantino was also in the company, not to mention, because Webster's eye going down the list could hardly be expected to note it in the spring of 1946, the young Mario del Monaco in *Tosca* and *I Pagliacci*. And, most important, Gigli was to reappear for a performance or two. Eager as he was to present Gigli, Webster wondered if there'd be trouble on account of his wartime record. The Board, men of standing in the world, and well placed to know, reassured him. Besides, the Italians tactfully expressed their desire to give the opening performance in aid of a British Forces charity, and their request was granted.

Negotiations were going ahead too with the Vienna State Opera, and even before it was clear which conductors would be in charge, the political records of both the young Herbert von Karajan and of the veteran Knappertsbusch had to be looked into. The Vienna State did come, in the summer of 1947, without, as it happened, either of them.

While the San Carlo was booked to follow on immediately after the visit of the American company Ballet Theatre, due to open at the house on 4 July, the home ballet company's season had been frequently extended till it was actually into its fifth month, and could have gone on running had the American company not been coming. The house, meanwhile, was being kept open without a break.

Ballet Theatre's visit was important if only because it was brought over under the aegis of impresario Sol Hurok, with whom a most fruitful collaboration now began. It was Hurok who was to present the Sadlers Wells Ballet on its American tours, expertly managing and promoting the still-young company when its success was by no means automatic, and exploiting its success ably when, on the strength of that first tour, it had become a highly exploitable commodity. The prestige of that success helped Webster get the Opera House grant increased, and the cash that flowed into the house from the tour contributed to both the prestigious ballet company itself and to the at-first fumbling and stumbling opera company. Webster was steadfast, in spite of constant protest, in refusing to publish separate accounts for the two companies. The grant was given to him for the Opera House, and not for the benefit of one or other company in it. No comparable grant would have gone to the ballet had it found a home of its own elsewhere. And besides, it was opera that was Webster's love, and that weighed with him. He didn't love the ballet as he loved his opera, though he was careful not to give anyone reason to suspect that he didn't. He was certainly proud of the ballet, and he couldn't *not* warm to its success. He wanted, he absolutely required, the *best* ballet company, his opera too ultimately had to be the best: and with both together he would have the best of all possible houses.

Ballet Theatre was led by Alicia Alonso, Nora Kaye and André Eglevsky. The modern American works, particularly those of Agnes de Mille (*Rodeo*, *Fall River Legend*) and Jerome Robbins (*Interplay* and, especially, *Fancy Free* on which the film *On the Town* was based), made a great impression, and the company gave London its first post-Diaghileff glimpse of a Balanchine work, *Apollo*. But they didn't shine in the classics. (Nor, a year later, did the Ballet Russe when they came to Covent Garden – so that the Sadlers Wells success in reviving the classics, their much greater sensitivity to style and atmosphere, was notably reaffirmed.)

And then came the San Carlo Opera. These were exciting days. If the Italian company had a success, it was not for its overall standard of production. But the audience was delighted to hear authentic Italian voices: they had a glamour, they evoked a nostalgia for the pre-war international seasons which made David Webster still more anxious about his own test yet to come. Carosio had her triumphs, and Tagliabue predictably had a warm welcome from the almost-sold-out houses. Del Monaco made his mark, and a new baritone, Paolo Silveri, was noted. The seven-week season ended on 19 October, there was a short tour, taking in, owing to the shortage of suitable theatres in the provinces, a couple of Butlin's Holiday Camps and the Davis Theatre, Croydon, and then the company returned to Covent Garden for four extra performances, which brought Gigli back to London. There were two *Bohèmes*, and he appeared twice in both *Cavalleria Rusticana* and *I Pagliacci* on the one evening. His daughter Rina sang opposite him in the *Bohèmes* and the *Pagliaccis*. As soon as Gigli was announced to appear there was chaos both inside and outside the box office. The all-night opera- and ballet-queues – the new season by the Sadlers Wells Ballet, due to open again a couple of weeks after Gigli's appearances with the San Carlo, was booking at the same time – became entangled with each other, thousands of people were unable to obtain tickets, and the house could have been sold out at least twenty times. The evening of the performances ticket touts were offering three guinea seats for twelve guineas and six guinea boxes for twenty-five. Webster reported to Ralph Hawkes that Gigli:

> is of course no actor and his own performances are little, if anything, removed from concert performances, and they have perhaps little to do with the art of Opera, but his singing is terrific. I think tenors of this sort have more in common with the largest tomato in the show or a prize marrow rather than anything else, but they are very enjoyable none the less.

The debut of Webster's own opera company was inevitably coming nearer. His instinct for delay here had some justification. There had been long discussions about the possible ways of introducing it to the public for the first time. Eighteen months before Ralph Hawkes had suggested they play safe and perhaps present Flecker's *Hassan*, a poetic drama with music, or an operetta, possibly *Die Fledermaus*: something that wouldn't strain slender resources. (He'd also wondered about importing an entire American company to do Gershwin's *Porgy and Bess*, but Webster, an early enthusiast of jazz, was rather more sympathetic to the idea than the Board, who when he put it to them threatened to resign almost *en bloc.*)

Webster wanted to play safe, and decided that it would be unwise to present the company unsupported. If it could be presented in conjunction with the ballet it wouldn't be inviting judgement on its first appearance, and the ballet would guarantee it a measure of success. He wanted Purcell's *King Arthur*, but the Board again protested – how many consecutive performances could audiences be expected to take?

The choice fell finally on another Purcell work, *The Fairy Queen*, to give the house its fourth first night within a year. *The Fairy Queen* was not only, like *King Arthur*, by the father of English opera, but also had the advantage of a text based on a Shakespeare play – the opera company would be leaning not only on the ballet but on Shakespeare as well. Furthermore, the character of Oberon gave a leading acting/miming role to a hero of the ballet company, Robert Helpmann, which would increase its chances with the audience.

Webster was keen to bring out the masque-aspects of the work. The masque was an entertainment which put emphasis on spectacle and staging more than on the music and singing, and was defined by its moving spirit Inigo Jones as 'Pictures with light and motion': Inigo Jones rather than Purcell had been senior partner when the work was created. *The Fairy Queen* was also particularly appropriate for half-introducing the company since it hinted at what was to come, an opera in which for several seasons the emphasis was going to be on lavish presentation.

Indeed, as in the course of rehearsals it became clear to what extent it was to be an evening of more masque, less music, Webster suggested that Constant Lambert rather than Karl Rankl should conduct the opening performance: and that the opera company's Musical Director was not in charge of the company's first appearance further confirmed that the opera was a junior partner in the venture, its real debut still to come. Rankl would hardly be expected to conduct subsequent performances when he'd agreed to relinquish the first night, and it was Geoffrey Corbett who alternated with Lambert.

The Fairy Queen was moderately successful through its twenty-three performances, but was only once revived afterwards, for the Festival of Britain in 1951, mainly because opera and ballet in the house had their separate destinies. The chorus, heard for the first time, made a favourable impression. Titania, opposite Helpmann's Oberon, was Margaret Rawlings, who was also Lady Metal Box, her husband being that same Sir Robert Barlow who had contracted Webster to become his assistant and heir-apparent. When her contract was being made out for her *Fairy Queen* appearances, Barlow suggested that his wife's payment shouldn't be made in money but in tickets, his way of helping the new company.

It had been generally assumed that Joan Cross would be singing in the production. She ought to have been, if only as an acknowledgement of her contribution to English opera throughout the 'thirties, when she'd stayed with the Sadlers Wells as their star and inspiration. Her purity of voice could hardly be emulated, but her constant, careful musicianship, her taste and style and idealism, could be; and she had helped to establish the company on firm foundations. For a while, before her secession along with Peter Pears, she'd been director of the company. Not till cast-lists were pinned on the notice-board was it learnt that she'd been overlooked, and this perhaps gives a measure of the chaos out of which was to emerge order of a kind; also, perhaps, (she was a very outspoken lady), it gives a measure of Webster's nervousness at this time of people with pre-war experience of opera.

The Fairy Queen opened on 12 December 1946, and the opera company's first production, *Carmen*, was being prepared to open on 14 January 1947. The opera's real first night was perilously near, and before it arrived Webster had made a further move to secure the house in the event of a flop.

He's already been alerted to the possibility of having Danilova as a guest artist with the ballet. Like Lydia Lopokova, Danilova was a former Diaghileff ballerina, though much her junior when they had both danced in the 1926 season, and Lydia was with Lord Keynes when they had tea with her and Balanchine in March 1946. 'We had a long chat,' Keynes reported to Ninette de Valois,

> finding them at least as adorable and very little changed. George seemed scarcely changed at all. Danilova, of course a good deal older and very much more now in appearance la femme fatale.

Danilova had suggested that she come to Covent Garden as a guest in *Coppélia*; and if it could be arranged, it would be a pleasure to look forward to. But the great shortage, particularly in England where war service had interrupted training, was of male dancers. The importance in this period of an Eglevsky cannot be exaggerated, and in the autumn Hurok, already considering taking the company to the United States, was doubtful unless at least two male dancers of the level of Eglevsky could be secured for it. Eglevsky was pursued, but he couldn't be secured.

But another name had come up – that of Leonid Massine. Massine had still an enormous glamour, he was a legendary figure, his career stretching back to Diaghileff in his prime: and de Valois saw in him the most valuable of all the possible acquisitions. It wasn't a question of the American tour – when that was finally arranged, it had to be on very particular terms, dictated by de Valois, and Massine was no part of them. But he was a character dancer of quite extraordinary vividness, with a kind of definition and linear precision not often looked for, or met, outside painting. And he was more than a dancer. He was also a creator of character ballets, which de Valois badly needed to enlarge the company's still slender repertory. She needed him as a dancer, but as a choreographer too and also as a teacher. She was often in years to come to resist the introduction into the company of guests who would rob her dancers of their opportunities and confidence – but Massine at this stage she *wanted*.

The task of approaching him fell to Webster, a task made easier because Massine was already in the country, appearing in *A Bullet in the Ballet*, a stage version of the novel by the chess expert S. J. Simon and the ballet critic Caryl Brahms. The play failed before reaching London, a not unimportant accident in the history of the Opera House. He was therefore open to offers, and Webster, leavening parsimony, which was essential, with love and admiration which were involuntary, made his offer charmingly, and was not resisted. However much a weapon in his hands, Webster's love and admiration for artists were genuine, and recognized as genuine by the artists who inspired them. He gave the impression, not a false one, that he had a warm nest prepared for them. The implicit plea, 'Come Home, Leonid Massine, we need you,' was not an easy one to resist, and many another fine artist was to yield to such a plea in years to come, usually not at all to his cost.

Massine's very presence in the house would be an inspiration, not only to the dancers but even to the singers who, as they passed to and fro from their dressing-rooms, would catch glimpses of him practising on stage or rehearsing the company. Massine brought something to the Opera House which a few years later Maria Callas was also to bring – if he was a dancer he was also a Presence, a reminder and an embodiment of the possibilities and the highest aspirations of his art.

One living legend, Gigli, had already been presented. A second, Massine, was promised. He would be there to win back the house, and help secure its future, whatever happened on the evening of 14 January 1947 when the curtain rose at last on *Carmen*.

CHAPTER VIII

Waverley becomes Chairman of Covent Garden Trust · first opera production · *Carmen* in English · a less than splendid reopening · *Manon* · erosion of confidence · Beecham's broadsides etc.

The death of Lord Keynes in April 1946, only two months after the reopening of the house, had been a grievous blow to Webster. Keynes had accorded him respect, had treated him as an equal even, and he had brought, as well as his experience and acumen and enormous prestige, a huge relish to their tasks. Webster felt his death as a private sorrow, and he found himself without his best support at a time when he was only beginning to assemble his opera company.

But Webster had been fortunate enough to find his successor in Sir John Anderson, later Lord Waverley, whose prestige actually matched Keynes's – this massy proconsular administrator, perhaps best remembered as the Home Secretary who introduced Anderson shelters during the war, had been Chancellor of the Exchequer in his time, and Lord Privy Seal, as well as Governor of Bengal. He stood tall in the establishment. The choice was Webster's, but his triumph lay not so much in chosing him as in persuading him to undertake the job. Waverley wasn't an arts man, but he knew about money, and he had had to be convinced that the undertaking was important in terms of national prestige, since only the grandest scheme could have attracted him and been permitted to make further demands on his energies. Webster had generally to underplay the extent of his ambitions, but Waverley might not have capitulated to less.

It was obvious that Covent Garden was going to be permanently short of money, and Waverley had first to have some sort of guarantee of government support, all the more because remission of Super Tax reduced the likelihood of money coming from private sources. It was arranged that Kenneth Clark would see the Chairman of the Arts Council while Waverley would pursue his enquiries through the Exchequer. Waverley knew there would be a fight, since the government, while wanting Covent Garden re-established, was also going to be reluctant to finance it. But he demanded assurance. Webster waited anxiously, for on government response depended the whole future. On 1 August the Chancellor, Dalton, wrote to Waverley:

> The assistance which the Covent Garden Trust receives from the Exchequer will, of course, come to it through the Arts Council. You will

> understand that in general I should wish the Council to feel themselves responsible for the allocation of the funds which Parliament puts at their disposal, and to plan their work ahead in the expectation of an assured but limited grant. I recognize, however, that the magnitude of the Covent Garden undertaking and the difficulty in present circumstances of estimating its future needs, places it in a special position, and that the State will be assuming a definite obligation to see to it that, subject to others playing their part, Opera is not let down.

On the strength of this letter Waverley decided that he would be one of those playing their part. On 16 August he accepted the Chairmanship: and, apart from a year when he was absent and Kenneth Clark stood in for him, he remained Chairman until his death in 1958.

It was a stroke of good fortune that a Labour Government was in power through these early years, the Left being better disposed at that time to giving money for the arts. Such a grant is regarded as partly educational, since it helps to make available to a wider range of the population the best products of the imagination and intellect of mankind throughout its history – a Labour Government is more prepared to regard the arts as a legacy from the past which must be shared, and fostered in the present as a benefit and pleasure to all (or at least to all those for whom they *are* a benefit and pleasure). When in his turn Sir Stafford Cripps became Chancellor of the Exchequer he too, once persuaded that the undertaking was a worthwhile one, and not merely foolhardy, proved a friend, happy to concur with the spirit of Dalton's letter. Waverley, of course, his allegiance once given, was unshakeable. He was accustomed to carrying the Dalton letter about with him in his pocket, ready to brandish at appropriate moments. Not only David Webster but the rest of us as well have to be grateful that, with the decline in private wealth and the end of private patronage, Lord Keynes and now Waverley intervened, and that the Chancellors were sympathetic.

The chain of command in the organization was fairly clear. According to the terms of agreement, the Administrator's job was most importantly 'the general supervision, preparation and co-ordination of all productions sponsored by the body now known as the Covent Garden Council'. Board meetings were conducted by the Chairman, and it was the Administrator's duty to advise the Board and carry out their recommendations. (The Board members at the beginning were, besides Sir Kenneth Clark and Professor Dent, and of course Leslie Boosey and Ralph Hawkes, Samuel Courtauld, Sir William Walton, Sir Stanley Marchant and Sir Steuart Wilson.) After the meetings it was the Board's recommendations that Webster passed on to the members of his staff.

Webster was entirely clear in his own mind that in fact the decisions were his. He was happy that the Board should discuss, but he was jealous of his powers, which he construed as virtually encompassing those of Artistic Director as well. 'I'm the Administrator,' he would say, 'and I'm here to administrate! After all, I'm the one who has to take the criticism.' Waverley was certainly not less welcome as Chairman because he was no arts man. Webster had ideas about his own function, and was grateful to a Chairman who limited his. Many years later Webster was to write to the third Chairman about his two predecessors: 'The first was an inspiration, the second a huge tower of strength in the privacy of our affairs and in public representation, but *he left all details to me*.'

Which allowed the Quiet Showman to envisage himself also as a hidden dictator. Covent Garden was *his* house, as he saw it, and really no one else's.

Waverley was mighty in the establishment – close to the government, close to where the money was. He was idiosyncratic in one unexpected particular, having a bee in his capacious bonnet about tube trains. If he was phoned with a problem he would instruct whoever it was to 'Come in fifteen minutes,' and then add, 'No taxis! Come by tube.' Webster learned to lie beautifully. Once, with Douglas Lund, he came to tell Waverley that the Opera House needed a £15,000 overdraft from their bank, Coutts, if they were to get through the season, but they couldn't offer any security. 'No problem,' said Waverley, adjusting his voice-level to the office confines. 'It's Jasper Ridley, isn't it? Chairman of Coutts?' Lund nodded. 'Tell him you come from Waverley.' Lund did, and as Waverley had foretold, though Lund had been less sanguine, the bank's Chairman on that say-so, without security, made the money instantly available.

Waverley 'left all details to me', said Webster. But for all that, there had to be results. Waverley expected results all the more as a reward for the trust he'd given, which was much the same as Webster's attitude when he himself gave anyone his confidence. If there were failures he had all the more right to be incensed because he wasn't himself responsible.

Webster was fortunate in having the support of such a man when the curtain, at last, rose on the new opera company's first opera, *Carmen*. It was 14 January 1947, and Edith Coates was Carmen. Kenneth Neate was Don José and Audrey Bowman Micaela, while Escamillo was Denis Noble, well known from before the war. *Carmen* happened to be the Chairman's favourite opera, and Beryl Grey was his favourite dancer, and beyond *that* his tastes were rather vague.

Alas, as the evening unfolded, it wasn't long before Webster saw that he was going to need support. From the very start the opera didn't go well, and with the entry of Carmen herself doubts were confirmed. Webster had had doubts all along: if he hadn't communicated them he had not been able to suppress them entirely, and now they were being justified. The evening proceeded somewhat dankly, and increasingly a pall hung over the intervals. The unqualified success of the evening was Waverley's favourite Beryl Grey in the last act Spanish dance, hardly enough to salvage the wreck.

Webster was never able to accept criticism of anything that happened in his Opera House. Even if Jimmy at home in Weymouth Street were to suggest that a particular performance had not been good enough, Webster was liable to go dumb and, raining or not, take an unhappy turn or two round the block. Even to criticize this opening *Carmen* was to criticize *him*. He loved his company already. It was his. He loved them for getting on an opera at all. Wasn't that in itself an achievement?

Waverley wanted results, but he didn't expect miracles. Both men reluctantly absorbed the atmosphere at the party afterwards, which was given at the Savoy, and in honour of Sir Stafford Cripps. It was full of people whispering together, dutifully cracking their faces into smiles, and when voices were raised heartily they had unmistakable notes of defiance in them. This was the normal atmosphere of an after-a-flop party. But Waverley still had confidence in the future. And while Webster had *hoped* – though not perhaps for another *Sleeping Beauty* – he had none the less gone some way towards insuring himself, almost unconsciously, against . . . against what? An evening, at any rate, of something *less* than splendour. He wouldn't articulate for himself such words as failure, flop. But he'd not trumpeted this occasion as he had the *Sleeping Beauty* opening, and it hadn't been an evening of personal invitation and royalty. He was ready to argue that the house had been kept continuously open for a year, and there had been a varied and often exciting spread of wares, so that *one* bad performance – if it really had been so bad – wasn't necessarily an event of magnitude. The new ballet season was currently in progress, and Massine was already in the house, due to make his first appearance with the company the following month. In the summer Webster had the Ballet Russe to offer his public, and after that, hopefully, the Vienna State Opera. One poorish performance, surely, could be absorbed into the continuum of the house? The public had no reason to complain.

He moved quietly about among the guests at the party. A word here, a word there. Waverley was reassuring, benign even, and Sir Stafford Cripps was friendly enough, though people in the main were being anxiously benevolent or over-heartily congratulatory.

And next morning the critics were less than congratulatory, while reviews collected over the following days offered little consolation. Goossens, refusing to take on the job of Musical Director, had explained that he was alarmed by 'the prospect of shouldering the responsibility of making bricks without straw', and, precisely echoing him, 'Bricks without Straw' was the heading of Desmond Shawe-Taylor's *Statesman* review: it contained severe strictures on the quality of the bricks so obtained. Shawe-Taylor was distressed by a Carmen 'so determined to prove herself the toughest moll in Seville that she constantly allows her tone to become raucous and unsteady, and as soon as that happens, *entre nous tout est fini*'. Philip Hope-Wallace, in the *Guardian*, judged the performance 'hard-working, handsome, heavy-handed'. He is an appreciative critic who is usually constructively ready to look for what is to be enjoyed in any performance, even if it fails to measure up to the best, but he felt constrained, in *Time and Tide*, to make a further contrary point or two:

> We all wish the Covent Garden Trust success, but that must not stop me from describing their first effort, a *Carmen* in English, as a dire penance for anyone who really loves this epitome of the Gallic spirit . . . Edith Coates, a good Verdian and a hard worker with plenty of power and temperament, did not spare herself. There were moments when one rather wished she had.

The Observer complained that 'one listens in vain for anything that may justly be called a full and true Bizet voice'. Webster could hardly persuade himself that he'd had a good press – though here and there was some praise for Rankl, who had gallantly entered where Goossens more wisely, perhaps, judging by results, had feared to tread, and praise too for the chorus. That might be something to build on for the future. But for the present? The headline for Stephen Williams's notice in the *Evening News* read, 'This British Carmen is all wrong.'

In spite of himself, Webster hoped for a reversal with his second production, Massenet's *Manon*. Another French opera – had this been a wise choice? *Carmen* had shown that the French style didn't come easily to English singers. But he had Heddle Nash to offer in it, a bit 'over-the-top' maybe, but surely a beloved singer who'd be welcomed. Heddle Nash was the main reason for the production. His recording of the Dream Song from *Manon* was well known and widely admired. But of *Manon*, alas, the *Statesman*'s Desmond Shawe-Taylor had 'not much to say, the production being no more than a handsome frame for a non-existent picture. The principals are frankly inadequate . . .'

Webster had hoped that the comparative failure of *Carmen*, which he now acknowledged, at least to himself, would be absorbed into the success of this second production. He scanned the notices, and he couldn't help, at moments, being bitter, for standards were being set that a new, young company couldn't reasonably be expected to attain. The critics, he felt, were merely protecting themselves, demonstrating their credentials. They would be doing much better to involve themselves sympathetically with the adventure. Criticism could be turned back on the critics with Molière's ironic words (from *The Misanthrope*):

> The greater one's love the less the flattery;
> To pardon nothing is the sign of love's integrity.

But it wasn't just flattery he craved. There was, surely, good to be found in his *Carmen*, and in *Manon* too?

New productions were mounted at the rate of one a month. Webster was already coming to dread reactions to them. More difficult now for a single production to reverse what was coming to be almost a trend. The public was aware of the critical attitudes. How could they involve themselves sympathetically when they weren't being given a lead?

Thank God for *Swan Lake* and *Sleeping Beauty*, and for Massine's *The Three Cornered Hat* and *Boutique Fantasque*, in which Massine was appearing himself. The Vienna State had been definitely booked to follow Ballet Russe into the house. It was barely three months after that *Carmen* first night and already Webster was waiting for reviews of his fourth opera, *Rosenkavalier*. It was much the same story again. 'I cannot help asking myself,' said Ernest Newman in the *Sunday Times*,

> whether the people in charge at Covent Garden are not making the mistake of flying too high on their trial trip. What seems to me principally wrong there just now is the low overriding standard of taste in the productions.

He at least admitted that the singing, note by note anyway, was mostly satisfactory. On the other hand, though: 'The singing of the Marschallin never offended the ear, where it mostly failed was in psychological insight.' He said of the company generally: 'The shortcomings were not primarily due to technical inexperience but to lack of dramatic and psychological insight.'

To sum up these first few months – disaster. 'The critics don't appreciate the problems,' Webster mourned. Singers, and particularly in thin times, such as 1947, when the shortage of singers was notorious everywhere, couldn't be type-cast, as in the straight theatre, with the juvenile playing only juvenile parts and the character-lady the character-parts. They had to take on parts according to their vocal range. Edith Coates was the equivalent of a 'character-lady'. In this very first season she had a great success as Azucena in *Trovatore*, which was much more her style of gipsy than Carmen. But she was leading mezzo in the company and Carmen is a leading mezzo role, so she'd had to do it. And Webster was grateful to her. Virginia McWatters, Manon, and Doris Doree, the Marschallin, were both from New York, where McWatters, indeed, had made something of a sensation with Zerbinetta's fiendishly difficult coloratura in Strauss's *Ariadne on Naxos*. He and Rankl had held extensive auditions in New York the previous summer and these two singers had seemed prizes when they were engaged. Webster had thought of mounting *Ariadne* at Covent Garden for McWatters the following season – out of the question now. But where were singers to be had for their roles in English? McWatters also sang Sophie in *Rosenkavalier*, and when she had to be replaced Webster even flew out to Vienna in the hopes of finding a singer there prepared to do the role for him in English. No luck. He was none too pleased on his return to find that it had already been arranged for him to audition one Leni Lynn, 'the Hollywood Coloratura' – hardly suitable, surely? But eventually he was grateful just to have someone who could get through the part. And it wasn't because, in the words of Desmond Shawe-Taylor, the authorities were 'curiously indifferent to the actual sound made by the human voice'.

Webster by now had come to realize and accept that critics and audiences were not prepared to lend support to a venture for its own sake, or for the sake of fostering its future. They wouldn't support the house simply for the pride and pleasure of being in on something new. Maybe, he forced himself to admit, there were faults in his productions – yet standards *would* improve. Patience. But it obviously wasn't going to be like the Continent, where with one town or region in competition with another, civic pride ensured the local company warm support and partisanship.

Webster was silent in the face of that huge volume of criticism which was to be aimed at the Opera House, and at himself personally, over the years to come. But it affected him deeply. If silent, he was not the less painfully storm-racked.

Audiences only came to be entertained. So be it. The press as a whole, or so he saw it, had no sense of responsibility either. They weren't going to help, they preferred to remain absolute in their standards. So he had no alternative but to pretend that the opera was achieved from the very beginning. It was policy as well as instinct not to acknowledge criticism by answering it. There was also no shortage of criticism in the house itself – the very corridors rustled with whispers.

Webster knew that his only answer could be achievement. It could hardly be a matter of months. He was all the more pleased, therefore, to be able to present Eva Turner, this first season, in her famous role of Turandot. She had been an undisputed international star, an exception among English singers. The company by now was, naturally enough, dispirited, and beginning to wonder whether they would ever be able to make good Webster's hopes for them: they were all too ready to accept that English singers were not the stuff stars are made from, and to regard Eva Turner, a star torn from their ranks, as an isolated case, the exception to prove the rule.

But to Webster she represented the level of achievement he was aiming at. He watched the faces of his young artists as they listened to her huge voice, which was still capable of rolling thrillingly round his theatre. They turned awe-struck to look at the rather short figure in their midst from whom it came. She was warm, friendly, encouraging. Yes, she represented their level of aspiration. Just as Webster had wanted.

Even if people had known the nature of Webster's ambitions for his company they wouldn't have had confidence in him. They thought they were going to have to settle for opera on the level of those first performances, whereas what Webster had in mind was more or less unprecedented in Opera – but was usual in ballet. In Diaghileff's day there had been only one organization in the West and dancers had been raised within the ranks. Fonteyn had risen within the ranks. That's how ballet works. When in the 'sixties John Cranko went to Stuttgart to take charge of the ballet there he had to persuade the Germans, who had no ballet traditions of their own, that ballet always has made its own stars, and that you can and should promote artists within the organization.

Opera has another story to tell. On the Continent, even today, a singer tends to rise by being invited to another opera house as guest, and coming back as a star to his own house only after successes outside it.

What Webster was determined to do was to develop his singers in much the same way that up to that time only ballet companies had developed their artists. Sometimes singers were miscast, or overparted, simply because he had no one else to fill a role: but whatever, they were being given experience and stretched and that was what mattered, and if singers had to be brought on too fast sometimes, Webster could persuade himself that ultimately even that was for the best. He never wavered in his belief that, so long as he could continue to provide his singers with opportunities, eventually they would prove themselves equal to them. English singers were going to rise from the ranks – they had virtually nowhere else to come from.

The most forceful criticism, perhaps because his vocal timbre was so singularly penetrating, always seemed to come from Beecham. He was something of a leader for the opposition, no doubt spurred by his feelings that he was being wrongly, even maliciously, excluded. He wasn't the only one to feel this. V. N. Lucas wrote in the *New English Weekly*:

> It may be that there is somewhere lurking a new genius of an impresario, but until one such arrives it is as futile to discuss opera in England without Sir Thomas Beecham as it would be to consider the British War Cabinet without Mr Winston Churchill.

Futile it most definitely wasn't, whether Webster does or does not qualify for election as a 'genius of an impresario'. But such statements weren't going to discourage Beecham from uttering. He uttered.

> Probably at no time during the last seventy years has this branch of the musical art declined to so low a level in England . . . We are in a pitiable plight . . . We have touched rock-bottom, and if we are to have opera again of any consequence we shall have to rebuild from a crude beginning.

This in February 1948 (in his foreword to Stephen Williams's *Come to the Opera*), when the opera company was just entering into its second year. Building, and not rebuilding, from nothing. Beecham's pre-war years at the house, Webster reflected, had left him with nothing – or, if he didn't count that scenery, simply a few more years added to all those that had gone before of neglect of the English singer, and that present sense of inferiority with which he was having to grapple. Beecham, spending large sums of private money, his own and other peoples, had never managed to establish a permanent organization. How would he have fared, in charge of post-war Covent Garden, with the small sums of public money available? If a permanent organization was to be established, and the subsidy continue, it was not so much futile as essential, surely, to leave Sir Thomas Beecham out of the reckoning! Furthermore, Beecham was given to referring privately about town to Webster as 'that homosexual haberdasher'. Not pleasing. Though in spite of everything Webster felt able to handle Beecham, and it was the public pronouncements which upset him more. Personal hurt he considered his own affair, no one else's. And what was more important was that Beecham might still, some time or another, be of enormous value to the house as a conductor.

The public utterances were dangerous in themselves and because they encouraged others. Criticism continued, from all sides, as though ratified by Beecham's, and its tone seemed to have been set early and definitely; as the huge backlog piled up it could be seen to have changed remarkably little over many years. Ten years later the *Daily*

Telegraph was opening its columns to receive a letter which ran:

> What were the qualifications of the administrators of Covent Garden at the time of their appointment? The public were told one had been managing director of a departmental store and enthusiastic supporter of an amateur opera company in Liverpool. Is this sufficient qualifications for any person occupying an important seat on the selection committee?

This letter – written in 1957, not 1947! – is signed by one Thomas Bartram, which seems curiously, and appropriately, like an elided Thomas Beecham, Bart! The point, though, is that by this time, by 1957, what had Webster's qualifications at the time of his appointment to do with anything at all? His 1957 qualifications were what counted, and by now he had kept the house open for ten years, and he was already seen to be succeeding in his plans for it.

At the beginning, when Webster had had no prestige of his own, he'd relied greatly on the prestige of Keynes and Waverley. But he'd not, unfortunately, had prestige to bring to the support of his Musical Director. In the autumn of 1946 the Incorporated Society of Musicians had strongly registered their protest at the appointment of a foreigner, and had demanded that in future all appointments of foreign Musical Directors be barred. The area of discontent had spread the following summer, when the Vienna State arrived, and members of the Society surrounded the Opera House with banners proclaiming the legend, 'British Orchestras Second to None!' Again, local musicians were not only being threatened, but threatened by yesterday's foes!

And then there was Beecham, of course. At a Foyle's Literary Luncheon in June 1948 he uttered his most celebrated phrase of the era when he complained of English singers' 'pleasant but woolly voices that cannot carry beyond the fourth row of the stalls'; and he went on to express amazement that anyone had had the temerity to appoint a foreigner in high musical places.

> I say the Italians, the French, the Germans, and other countries, would not dare to put a foreigner in charge of a national institution. We put them in everywhere and not a voice is raised. I know half a dozen people who could do a damn sight better than some who are making a mess of things ... We proclaimed to the world that we could not govern our own musical institutions. Covent Garden is the laughing-stock of the world!

Toting himself even more deliberately into the picture, he also said:

> I don't get a farthing from anyone and have not the slightest intention of receiving it. I have done many things in my life, but I have never made myself a public crook, as nine-tenths of the public organizations of this country are doing by taking money which they should not receive from people who cannot afford it.

Actually, he had in the past taken many farthings from people, but they were private farthings. A lot of people, Lady Cunard prominent among them, had kept him well supplied so that he could continue with his operatic ventures. And in the Christmas of 1939, a few months after war was declared, when he went to America, he had kept himself going by contacting Lady Cunard's friends there and telling them she'd suggested that, if he needed money, they'd be happy to supply him – the authority for which story was Emerald Cunard herself. Beecham, a splendid buccaneer in his way, had flourished in another era, the era of private enterprise and private wealth. He couldn't accommodate himself to the idea of public subsidy, particularly when such money as there was didn't seem to be finding its way into *his* purse.

Nor did he seem able to refrain from thundering. He was in Cape Town later that summer of 1948, and even there, some seven thousand miles from London, he felt obliged to give it as his opinion that the proposal to keep Covent Garden as a National Opera House was

> just another momentous piece of asininity on the part of the British government . . . There can be no national opera in England when there are no composers and no singers. To talk of national British opera is pure humbug.

Rankl toiled, without much encouragement: he soon became more used to hostility than to appreciation, though Webster, a fellow-sufferer, supplied such appreciation as he could. Webster was no less upset than Rankl himself when Beecham, in January 1949, a few months after that Foyle's Luncheon, renewed his attack. The annual conference of the Incorporated Society of Musicians was being held in the Clarence Room of the Hotel Metropole in Brighton, and on 5 January Beecham set off a hugely publicized row when, in a notable set-piece, he inveighed against

> the strange and un-English way of doing things . . . The national opera is to be established and controlled by a body from which the leaders of the musical profession in England have been carefully excluded. I don't think the word 'racket' is out of place.

He demanded an enquiry. And he very particularly inveighed against Rankl, whose appointment he thought 'the mystery of mysteries, a fantastic dream'. (Those who had appointed him he designated 'nitwits'.) This was really the Beecham show-stopping aria of the 'forties, and seemed to bring down the house. Waverley, the same evening, made a statement: 'Sir Thomas's great gifts as a musician are well known. Unfortunately, he has another gift too – that of an unbridled tongue.'

While addressing the conference the following day, Sir Steuart Wilson was more specific in rebutting charges:

> What is sad in this controversy is to recall the fact that the British National Opera Company broke up largely because we were unable to persuade Sir Thomas Beecham to believe in English opera singers. He threw his hand in, paused a little, and then went in for international opera.

With heavy irony he continued:

> Now it is obvious to you that your job is to chuck out the lot of these doddering old trustees, including me, get in a fine new lot who won't employ any English singers, or else pull down Covent Garden and let us do opera in pocket size, suited to our national corporeal failings.

Beecham continued his attack with an article in the *Daily Telegraph* a fortnight later, in which he summed up what he took to be

> the precise situation of the new project. In the short space of two years an immense amount of public money has been lightly expended on a National Opera scheme in a structure where neither the best English works nor our English singers, not to forget the English language itself, can be heard to advantage.

Rankl refused to comment.

This was something of the atmosphere in which Webster and his foreign Musical Director worked to build. But a measure of sacrifice was needed if English opera was to be encouraged, and both men knew it. Submitting to Beecham, and to other criticism, was one aspect of that sacrifice. Beecham, in one testing situation, actually showed himself less willing to expend himself. Incensed at his exclusion – in a directorial role – from Covent Garden, he had offered his services to Christie at Glyndebourne. At a time when Covent Garden was manifesting its faith in native talent, Christie, also wanting to show willing, had suggested that they too make extensive use of young English singers. Small voices would certainly be able to fill the tiny theatre in Sussex more easily than the huge spaces of Covent Garden, but Beecham didn't altogether approve the scheme, and Lady Beecham framed his objection forcefully. 'He is now being asked to be a kind of nurse in a species of musical kindergarten.' Which was it, precisely. Her husband himself couldn't have put it better. They are the very words to be applied, but admiringly, to the gallant and smarting Rankl at a larger house.

Webster was left in no doubt as to the atmosphere in which he and his Musical Director were going to have to work. The means, not of averting but of surviving disaster, had now to be considered.

CHAPTER IX

Webster rallies · foreign guest artists · Flagstad, Hotter, Schwarzkopf · a director of productions needed · Tyrone Guthrie's *Peter Grimes* · guest conductors suggested · Rankl's opposition · Sadlers Wells Ballet goes to America · Peter Brook appointed

---

'While foreigners will not be excluded from the company,' Webster had written in the *Arts Council Bulletin* in January 1946, 'British artists will be given first chance.' He'd carefully left the door open to foreigners.

After *Carmen* it was clear that one or two at least were going to be necessary. In March Webster opened discussions with the Board, and the names Flagstad and Hotter and Schwarzkopf were touted. In May he first approached the Ministry of Labour to discuss permits, but with Equity in support, the Ministry for a time promised to be immovable. Webster persisted. The future hopes of British artists, which Ministry and Equity were apparently protecting, in fact depended on their giving way. They did give way, and a principle seemed shakily to have been established.

Waverley's wife Ava was meanwhile proving invaluable. She was of that generation of hostesses who were themselves liable to be called 'great', and she wasn't slow to see what her contribution had to be. Webster at first seemed a very odd sort of administrator to her. A haberdasher, no less – or, rather, no more. Webster showed yet again that he knew how to get on with the people it was important to get on with, and where necessary to ingratiate himself. Ava Waverley could not doubt his love of the Opera House, nor that he too had an apparently quite old-fashioned love of glamour. Both of them, the Lady and the haberdasher, recognized that the English are a nation for pageantry, and that a parade of celebrities at Covent Garden would bring a glamour to the house that the performances themselves didn't as yet. Lady Waverley was indefatigable, and it was a fine stroke for her to have been able to entice the Duchess of Kent to the house so early, and Henry Moore was also an acquisition. Another campaigner was Kenneth Clark's wife Jane. In July 1947, in spite of the current poor standard of performance, she could write from Somerset Maugham's Villa Mauresque, where the Clarks were staying, 'On the seventeenth I have the Duke of San Lucar, Massigli, the Sitwells coming . . .' – the lists continued down the years. They needed to. Patronage of this order did attract customers.

And meanwhile catering, and the bills for entertaining, presented their own problems, which fell within the province of House Manager Peter Waller (who was the first, at Covent Garden, to organize catering in a West End theatre: and he had Webster's permission, while still at Covent Garden, to organize the huge complex in the Royal Albert Hall). After the *Carmen* first-night party, given by Boosey and Hawkes, he was ordered to conduct an enquiry. How had 115 people managed to do away with 805 drinks? A rather obvious pun on the name of one of the hosts was difficult to avoid. On the matter of the Royal Box suppers Waller wrote to Webster:

> Our weekly allocation of points from the Ministry of Food for the whole Opera House is 750. When a tin of tongue is opened for use in the Royal Box this requires 268 points. From time to time we are able to get a fresh tongue, but criticism then arises of the colour when served, and the amount of pickling that has taken place.

These were small matters which had bearing on the large. Entertaining was important, and it helped: but it wasn't long before it became apparent that box-office receipts plus the grant weren't going to cover running expenses, and that overdraft facilities would have to be extended.

For the kind of presentation Webster was aiming at cost money. *The Sleeping Beauty* had shown him how audiences at this time responded to lavishness – and he knew that, all other considerations apart, for some years to come lavishness of presentation was going to have to make up for deficiencies in performance. Scenery might have to console audiences for what went on in front of the scenery.

Besides, audiences brought up on cinema could not be expected to endure what they had in the past. Bernard Shaw has painted a grim picture in *Music in London*:

> There is only one period – 'The Past'; only two sets – 'Exterior' and 'Interior'. In *Martha* I have seen Queen Anne alive, with her ladies in Victorian dress, her retinue Plantagenet, the buffo bass in eighteenth-century full-bottomed wig, and the chorus in tights from *Trovatore*.

Covent Garden in its pre-war international seasons might not have been offering anything quite as crude as that – but Charles Moore, the stage director and an accomplished linguist fluent in four languages, had been in charge of all productions, which were stock productions, standard throughout the opera houses of the world. Singers usually knew their roles and their moves before they arrived at the house. This wasn't going to do today.

So Webster wondered whether he oughtn't to engage a Director of Productions. Bruno Walter had suggested Ebert, who at Glyndebourne had been an equal partner with the Musical Director. Ought that to be the pattern for Covent Garden? Webster wanted a Shaftesbury Avenue man. *Turandot* in the first season, directed by Michael Benthall and with designs by Leslie Hurry, was a tinsel-and-glitter affair, and had a sort of 'razzmatazz' success. It wasn't tasteful, but its vulgarity didn't offend Webster as much as it did some others. Webster knew what went in the theatre, and this went, after its fashion. Ashton's *Manon*, Joan Cross's *Rosenkavalier*: both were tasteful, but given the standard of performance, neither had registered strongly. *Turandot* registered, and so did *The Magic Flute* with its deliberately showy and theatrical Messel designs, though it had been disastrously produced by Malcolm Baker-Smith: when the production was replaced by subsequent ones Webster always harked back regretfully to the Messel designs. Definitely, the way was Shaftesbury Avenue.

He'd already had problems getting a Musical Director who'd accept the conditions, and he expected to have the same problems with a Director of Productions. Keeping the costs down in the face of directors with ambitious budgets was going to become more and more an obsession, though he did sometimes achieve lavish effects relatively cheaply. Jay Pomeroy's last seven operas at the Cambridge Theatre cost on average £17,500, while Webster managed even the tinsel-and-glitter *Turandot* for £11,680. Pomeroy was using private money, he'd spent £100,000, and by the middle of 1948, two years and 687 performances later, he was poorer to the tune of £231,250, and the company had to be wound up. There was nothing left.

This wasn't going to be allowed to happen at Covent Garden. Keeping costs down *had* to be an obsession. Seeing that the orchestra didn't go into overtime was also an obsession. The orchestra contract stipulated three-hour sessions, eleven of them in all, with only seven performances. The remaining four were for rehearsals, and a great deal of juggling was needed. Like his old friend William Armstrong at the Liverpool Playhouse, Webster had become, in the words of Mrs Pat, 'a little man who sits in an office and makes lists'. On these lists depended so much. It didn't help that when an opera was mounted for the first time it was new to most of the orchestra – but rehearsal time could not be extended. Webster had to bear the burden of constantly playing host to Rankl; he had to console him for the entirely inadequate conditions under which he had to work, and congratulate him for getting on shows week after week, in spite of everything, in spite of criticism and overt hostility, through the greater part of the year. It would be the same story again, playing host to a Director of Productions.

Rankl undertook his duties nobly, smarting at the restrictions but understanding the need for economy. He was working with Webster for a common aim. Would a Shaftesbury Avenue man similarly commit himself? Be prepared to work within limitations? And what limitations! Constance Shacklock, highly praised by an otherwise censorious Ernest Newman for her Annina in the first *Rosenkavalier* performances ('she sings well, moves with an ease and grace that are a joy to the spirit no less than the eye'), was very soon promoted to major roles. But when she took on for the first time the huge role of Octavian in *Rosenkavalier*, an important date both for her career and for a house dedicated to bringing on local talent, she was allotted only one stage rehearsal and no orchestral rehearsal at all. Joan Hammond went on stage to sing Leonora in *Fidelio* for the first time at the Opera House having been merely led round the stage with the stage director pointing out to her the main positions. She went through one great scene wondering if she was going to be able to find her way off at the end of it. She did sing again at the Opera House – but there were offers which she refused because of these conditions (and in 1955 a petition signed by three hundred of her deprived fans was handed in at the stage door. Webster defensively claimed that, taking in offers to appear with the company on its provincial tours, he had made her in all no less than sixty-seven offers since 1947.) Indeed, it sometimes seems surprising that the company got through at all. One week in 1950, for example: *Traviata* was revived on 20 October with a 'general rehearsal' for the first three acts and the fourth not rehearsed or lit at all: *Boris Godunov* went on the next evening with the snow effects not rehearsed: and next evening it was the turn of *Bohème*, with no complete run-through, no rehearsals at all with sets, and no lighting rehearsal.

Webster knew the conditions in 1947, and he knew about costs, which could only rise. He had to be chronically mean. Frederick Ashton stayed on the same salary from 1945 until he became Assistant Director of the Ballet Company in 1952, and Webster never suggested a rise. And Ashton had to fight with him to get royalties per performance for choreographers: to begin with, ballets had belonged to the house for their first five years. Webster in his office made lists, knowing that conditions could not improve quickly. On the contrary. The repertory had to be enlarged, and for a while conditions were more likely to get worse. Coping with the stacks of scenery alone would be a problem. And how would the guest singers fit into the company? Opera is the unwieldiest of the arts.

Webster made approaches to Benthall and Tyrone Guthrie. Would they commit themselves to Covent Garden? Would either of them become his Director of Productions? Guthrie at least agreed to take on a production or two for him. But he wouldn't make any commitment beyond.

Webster talked . . . and he prepared to greet his guests. The Italian Silveri was the first to appear with the company, in *Rigoletto*, which opened the second season on the last day of October 1947. He was already known from the San Carlo season, and he was predictably robust and warm and authentic. And Flagstad was expected. A Guthrie, a Flagstad, these were what he needed. And a Flagstad might help him attract a Guthrie. After Gigli, after Massine, with Flagstad he now had a legendary figure of his very own, working with his own company and collaborating with his own artists. He could hear in advance the gasps of amazement that must greet her first appearance – just wait till his audiences experienced the sheer splendour of her tone!

How did his baby company secure such a prize? It was simply that, as with the founding of the Liverpool Philharmonic Orchestra on a permanent basis, Webster appreciated the particular conditions which could be made to work for him. Singers at this time often needed to live down a 'Nazi' past. A taint could attach to singers who had merely, early in their careers, stayed on in Europe to work, when their more celebrated senior colleagues left Europe confident that they could continue their careers abroad. There were many different degrees of fellow-travelling. Flagstad herself had gone back to Norway for the last two years of the war to be with her husband, who was accused of being a collaborator (and who died after the war while still waiting to be brought to trial). The King of Norway himself insisted that he was innocent, but Flagstad had been helped by the Germans to get back to Norway, and Norwegian Americans had demonstrated outside the Carnegie Hall when she first appeared there after the war. Webster was more concerned about his guest artists' present achievements than about their past, and their reputations in this aspect concerned him only in so far as they affected the house. Were there going to be demonstrations here too? Would his audiences, and his company too, accept them? Hostility might be directed against any German or Austrian whatever his supposed record during the war. Hans Hotter and Elisabeth Schwarzkopf were expected, and Schwarzkopf in particular was the subject of rumours, albeit rumours never confirmed. Walter Legge, founder and Artistic Director of the Philharmonic Orchestra and Artistic Director of Columbia Records, was helpful in securing visas, so Webster was confident at least that they'd be arriving.

Another reason singers were prepared to come was that conditions in Europe, and particularly in Germany and Austria, were dreadful. There was rationing in austere Britain, and when the American company, Ballet Theatre, had come to Covent Garden a couple of years earlier they had all brought extra suitcases crammed with tins of food: but to German guests it appeared a land of plenty. Italians were more difficult to come by at this time, partly because conditions in Italy were not so fearful as in Germany, and also because in the main they were less disciplined, unwilling to learn their roles in English and to co-operate with an English company. The German repertory was from the beginning less of a problem than the Italian, and Webster was the more appreciative of a Silveri or, shortly, Margherita Grandi, who (born in Tasmania, as it happens) had the large sweep and compelling forward beat and energy of the true Italian dramatic soprano.

Webster was relieved to find, when Flagstad duly arrived at the beginning of 1948, that his company were prepared to accept her unreservedly. But she was awesomely imperturbable, and he divined that her great reputation alone was more than enough to intimidate them. The atmosphere at the first rehearsal of *Tristan and Isolde* was therefore somewhat uncertain – but came the moment, early in the opera, when Brangane has to approach Isolde and take her hand. Young Shacklock moved forward hesitantly. When not in full cry the diva was not, as it happened, at all the implacable princess or warrior-maid, and she saw her young colleague's nervousness. 'It's all right, my dear,' she said kindly, 'you can touch me. I am quite human.' They both laughed, and all was well. The international star and the beginner moved towards each other in harmonious accord, and that touching of hands can be the symbol for the company of those days. Hans Hotter was apprehensive about how the company would receive him, but he was warmly welcomed: he responded gratefully to friendliness, and barriers were broken down. Webster was proud of his company, for their welcome was *his*.

Flagstad and Hotter were paying the house an enormous compliment by agreeing to learn their roles in *Valkyrie* in English. (In fact, each had agreed when told that the other had already consented.) Webster returned the compliment by mounting *Tristan* in German, the first foreign opera to be performed in the original language. Hotter, who was still some way from his God-like prime, was handicapped by singing in English, and in later seasons all performances of *The Valkyrie* and the other *Ring* operas, as well as *Tristan*, were done in German. This was not only a compliment to these particular artists, but also Webster's announcement that he was prepared to be flexible in the matter of language, though the *principle* of opera in English, remained for many years to come.

Flagstad and Hotter were won for the house. For three or four years, until her retirement, Flagstad was a regular visitor, and it was Covent Garden that she chose for her one hundred and fiftieth Isolde – the huge wreath which Webster proudly presented to her on stage at the end of the evening was also something of a symbol, a suitably magnified wedding-ring to seal the marriage of singer and house. Hotter, the great Wotan of his day, soon seemed to be almost a company member, certainly to his audiences who were as welcoming as the company had been of these artists bringing to them their talent and style and tradition.

Webster did not exactly love singers. It was more *their talent* he loved. From the very first, even with the restrictions of a limited budget and a raw young company, singers coming to the house felt that their talent was gratefully accommodated – that Webster had created a sympathetic atmosphere in which they were encouraged to work. Certainly they found less of that damaging and distracting intrigue they came to expect in some other houses.

Webster kept an eye on things from afar, capitalizing on a useful remoteness. He was more intimately casual when he met singers in the street, away from the Opera House, than when he saw them in the corridors or in his office. In the street they weren't so likely to talk business – above all, they weren't likely to ask him for more money. He didn't have it to give, and he was very fearful of unguarded moments in which he might commit himself. He didn't often visit singers in their dressing-rooms, nervous that in the emotion of the moment, and on their territory, he'd commit himself to something he'd afterwards regret. He had all the more to be remote because he was emotional and easily moved. But singers felt noticed. Everybody felt noticed. He only visited Edgar Evans in his dressing-room twice in twenty-five years, but once he wrote to him from Rome, where he was holding auditions, after seeing bad notices in the English papers – 'As long as I'm pleased it doesn't matter what *they* say.' Webster made a point of being on stage for a few minutes sometimes during rehearsals, allowing himself to be known to his guests. He looked more like a banker than the Intendant his guests would naturally expect, and he had to make his charm work all the harder for him. He knew what impression he wanted to make, and was determined to make it even if he no longer had the benefit of distance to put him in favourable perspective.

Flagstad he watched over. One of his worries was that there was no heroic tenor really a match for her. The best in the world at this time was Set Svanholm who, in the words of Philip Hope-Wallace in *Time and Tide,* 'bounds about, is by no means bad-looking, and a joy to eyes reared on Melchior'. Webster got Svanholm for her, but, whatever his advantages, height wasn't one of them. There was a supper party in Weymouth Street when Flagstad and Fonteyn got chatting together. 'Svanholm!' the singer exclaimed. 'He is so little! He comes up to *here*!' She roughly indicated the level of David Webster's waist. Webster, making embarrassed noises of sympathy, wondered if the tenor's platform shoes could safely be made any higher. Came the moment when the ballerina decided she was not to be outdone. 'You're lucky,' she said at last. 'You should try being *carried* by Alexis Rassine. He only comes up to *here*!' And she pointed even lower.

Flagstad was of the pre-war generation, and so was Frederick Schramm, who directed her in *Tristan* and *The Ring*. Schramm gave Constance Shacklock Brangane's moves – '*Wagner* wants you here,' he would say – and Shacklock, allotted two rehearsals for moves for the entire opera, marked them in her score and went home and learned them. 'Now,' said Schramm proudly, 'you can do Brangane anywhere in the world.' Pre-war, given a team of Leider and Lehmann, Thorborg, Schorr and Melchior, and given different attitudes and expectations, it worked well in a way. Post-war, it worked when Flagstad in her glory was on stage. This was Wagner and this was Flagstad. But it was no way for the rest of the repertory.

By late spring 1948 Flagstad had come and gone, the operation a success. Hopes for the future revived. Especially, too, since the beautiful young Elisabeth Schwarzkopf had declared a wish to stay in England; for a while she became a member of the company. Eventually, too, she married Walter Legge, which confirmed her residence here. Her very presence was an inspiration. Like Hotter, she had first been seen as a member of the Vienna State Opera, and had first appeared with the Covent Garden company as Pamina in *The Magic Flute*. The performance had magic at any rate in one of its components! It was Schwarzkopf who showed the company how to sing Mozart – and seldom can instruction have been provided in lovelier form. Simply, her way was the right way. And, moreover, she sang in consistently excellent English, and in this set the example to all other foreign singers. She was prodigiously industrious, soon a byword (once, to replace Erna Berger in *Rigoletto*, she learned the role of Gilda in English at just over twenty-four hours' notice!). She sang a variety of roles, several of which are not associated with her in her later career. And not all of them suited her equally well. But she not only extended herself, she also enormously helped the company with its rapidly expanding repertory.

Webster watched her rehearsing Violetta in *Traviata*, with Guthrie her director. The Italian style didn't suit her ideally, but she was game, and good, as he had known she would be. He had certain reservations about Guthrie. He knew, quite as well as the critics, the danger of taking opera directors from the theatre. The problem is that with our sensibilities heightened by the music we resent lapses into the mundane, the *merely* realistic. And a producer can't work on the libretto as he would on the text of a spoken play because the 'feel' of the production must correspond with the music. Though he took trouble to learn musical terms, Guthrie was not a musician, and indeed Webster had had doubts about him for Britten's *Peter Grimes*, Guthrie's first opera at the house.

But Guthrie above all knew what would work in the theatre, and he could make his effects with great sureness even if they were sometimes obtrusive. One piece of business, the entrance of one of the demi-mondaines in the first act party scene, carried on shoulder-high by her admirers, was vulgar. This was nothing to do with the world of the French Second Empire, and was to transform a demi-mondaine, an elegant creature at home in the drawing-room, into a trollop. But at least it wasn't dull. Webster *saw* that it wasn't dull. He knew there'd be many, certainly among the critics, who wouldn't like the effect. But Guthrie evidently considered it more important, at all costs, to create some kind of life than to risk dullness – he needed to achieve a party atmosphere, and Schwarzkopf certainly responded. Not everyone did. During rehearsals Guthrie carried a whistle round his neck which he blew shrilly when things went wrong. He blasted off at the tenor Kenneth Neate. 'Kenneth,' he asked, 'haven't you ever been to a party?' The tenor claimed he had. 'All I can say, then,' Guthrie quietly berated him, 'is that you don't go to the same sort of parties *I* do.'

To the critics much in the production was going to appear merely fidgety and unmusical. But Webster *knew*, none the less, that he was right to want a Guthrie or a Benthall for his Director of Productions. He hadn't been able to get either, and his choice had fallen instead on the new 'enfant terrible' of the straight theatre – Peter Brook. The idea, he was sure, was right. But was it going to work out?

Would it, to begin with, work out with Rankl? Would Brook insist on an equal partnership with the Musical Director, and if so would Rankl accept such an arrangement? Rankl was making headway. In spite of everything, the orchestra was improving. The unfortunate tradition of orchestral substitutes had to be fought – before the war players would regularly send in substitutes not only to rehearse but even to play for them; it was accepted practice when a more lucrative engagement offered itself, and the conductor didn't always know on the night who would be there following his beat. Such attitudes still prevailed, and orchestral players of quality were not easy to come by. Webster knew that they had to be given a sense of being prestigiously employed, that they too were being asked to participate, and somewhat ingloriously, in a building operation. There was so much less glamour in the orchestra pit than with one of the concert orchestras who shared the limelight with their conductors. And there were players who considered it a demeaning chore to have to accompany the ballet as well night after night, endlessly repeating often mediocre scores. But they would only learn respect for the house, Webster felt, if they could be forced to take their duties in it seriously. They must not be let off rehearsals. In 1947 half the orchestra left, and in 1948 forty out of the ninety contracts were not renewed.

The pity of it was that Rankl, who trained the orchestra, had never made himself loved. He had no favourites – something that couldn't be said of Webster – and he worked everyone so that everyone felt fully stretched. But he was very nervous and his nervousness communicated itself. He felt insecure and frightened, and if he feared things would go wrong he tended to be overwhelmed, rather than to marshal his energies for the attempt to get things right. The orchestra often felt itself to be merely harried: Webster hovered the while with entirely concealed anxiety, trying to ease relations where possible and, within the limits of the budget and a still not entirely adequately manned house, to make conditions the best possible for co-operation. He was hovering one morning in the auditorium as Rankl began a rehearsal. There was something wrong. 'What does it take,' Rankl barked at the leader, Joseph Shadwick, 'to wake you up in the morning?' 'Beecham's pills,' Shadwick unkindly replied.

Things improved, the orchestral organization was strengthened. Morris Smith became Orchestral Manager and was then upped to a newly created post, Orchestral Director, while his assistant Honor Thackrah was promoted to become Orchestral Manager. Shadwick resigned and was replaced as leader by Thomas Matthews, who was thus joining an apparently stable organization with a sense of continuity and growth.

In spite of criticism, Rankl could feel with some justification that progress was being made: and the criticism came in such huge volume partly because the house was so ludicrously over-exposed, at this time as at all times. There are so many events in an opera house. New productions, first appearances of old productions in new seasons, revivals with cast changes – all come under review. And Covent Garden also had the ballet. It was as though a statement of accounts had to be delivered two or three times a week, while any art ideally needs long periods of entirely decent obscurity. Even repertory companies in the spoken theatre have only a handful of press-nights in an entire year.

Before the end of 1947, the opera company's first year, star conductors for guests were already being considered. William Walton spoke for all, though not precisely, when he commented at a Board meeting that Rankl 'lacked personality'. Of course Webster would have liked to approach Tullio Serafin there and then, a maestro who had first appeared at Covent Garden in 1908: or, on the other hand, a young Karajan who was still to become Lord of the Ring in Vienna. But Professor Dent put the case cogently:

> I know nothing of Karajan – but I am very much against inviting any German conductor, even if Rankl wanted him. It is obvious that German opera is what Rankl does best, and is most at home in. After all the work he has done it would be most insulting to ask an outside German 'star' to conduct Wagner operas . . . Another reason for not inviting a German is that they are all extremely arrogant and tiresome to deal with, expecting the whole regular routine upset to give them chances of extra rehearsals . . . In any case I think our Opera Company is at present not really established enough to profit by a star conductor from outside – they all need much more continuous training in ordinary routine work, singing, speaking, enunciating, acting, deportment, ensemble and general acquisition of the standard repertory.

If Rankl was short on glamour, then glamour was a commodity the orchestra pit would have to do without for another year or two. It was for David Webster, one to dip a toe hesitantly in the surf before plunging headlong, to gauge when the company really was 'established enough to profit by a star conductor from outside'. And he'd have to reckon with Rankl. It was Webster, of course, as tactful as he was tardy, who was given the task of discussing the matter with Rankl and a most delicate matter it turned out to be. Rankl, as a result, was present at the Board meeting on the last day of the year, 1947, and he nodded impatiently while the distinguished gentlemen, going through the motions of asking his advice and help, formally expressed their gratitude to him. And then he had *his* say. Foreign guest singers *ought* to be engaged, though only until the resident company was better. But beware of employing another foreigner as conductor. He was set against star conductors of any kind. His supporting staff was excellent, and if the Board wanted to help him then let them add to the supporting staff. It was left that Webster discuss the matter further with him. Clarence Raybould was considered a possible successor to Reginald Goodall as assistant to Rankl – Goodall, first conductor of *Peter Grimes* at Sadlers Wells, and therefore coming to the house with an aura, had not proved a great success as a house-conductor, though his value as teacher was always appreciated. But Raybould refused to come except on equal terms with Rankl, so in the end it was Peter Gellhorn who became assistant musical director, while Warwick Braithewaite became an additional staff conductor.

Webster, while accommodating to Rankl's wishes, also significantly reinforced the Board's vote of confidence by offering him, immediately after that painful Board meeting, a further three years in office. His services were secured until 1951, up to which point Webster was fairly sure they would still be invaluable. The intrusion of guest conductors was but postponed, it had to come; but he hoped to be able to continue using Rankl even then, though only on terms which coincided with the best for the house as a whole.

But a Director of Productions had to be now. And it was going to be Peter Brook whatever.

And overall was money, on which everything depended and continued to depend. The Arts Council Grant continued to rise after the first year, even if the Opera House money was always, and remains to this day, extremely meagre – not in terms of the total grant received by the Arts Council from the Treasury, but against the needs of grand opera and against the money enjoyed by foreign houses. For the 1948/9 financial year the grant had become £120,000, no small rise – but in January 1949 Webster reckoned the running costs of the house to be £400,000! Paris that year gave its opera £600,000 – five times as much as the Royal Opera House received – Buenos Aires received £30,000 for a short season, and Vienna gave its treasured house a guarantee against loss. These figures are eloquent. Every year provides figures just as eloquent, but there will be no need to give them again. £120,000 in 1948 at least showed a hopeful trend, and Webster knew that the more money paid by the Treasury the less the likelihood of their withdrawing funds. Waverley would from time to time reassure him by drawing Dalton's letter from his pocket.

In the Garden, finance was always the thorniest of bushes. One problem is that there aren't more middle-priced seats, which could have been sold more easily at a time when the top-price seats weren't selling too well. The cheap seats sold best (there were 500 gallery seats at 2s. 6d.), but at this point prices were having to relate too closely to concert and West End theatre prices, so that in effect opera was being sold too cheap. (By the 'sixties prices were not only much higher but also much higher relatively.)

And the orchestra ought always to have been larger. Even by the mid-'fifties it was considered necessary to hire extra players as often as three and four times a week: once survival became less a matter of doubt, then of wonderment, it became all the more important to improve standards, for survival alone was no longer a sort of justification in itself. But in the early days, when closure seemed always imminent, Frank Ballard would every week whisper to David Webster wryly, 'Well, how much longer will we be open?' Webster, sagely non-committal, tried to allay doubt with humour.

The ballet boom lasted just long enough, just into the 'fifties (it coincided more or less with Rankl's term at the house). The ballet company made its first trip abroad in October 1946, to Vienna, and was henceforth a welcome visitor anywhere in Europe. Hurok in America had almost at once begun to make wooing noises. But after first demanding an Eglevsky or two to strengthen the company, he went on to ask for Markova to lead the company in America, partnered by Dolin: and later stipulated Danilova with Frederick Franklin. But de Valois insisted 'no Fonteyn, no Sadlers Wells in America'. She emphasized her point by inviting first Markova and Dolin, then Danilova and Franklin, to be guests with the company, but only at Covent Garden. Webster negotiated with Hurok, and a possible four months' tour in the autumn of 1948, to take in the New York Golden Jubilee celebrations, was cancelled because the proposed New York venue was the City Centre, whose stage was too small to allow *Sleeping Beauty* and *Giselle* to be presented properly, and they were both essential for the company's debut. Webster insisted on the right conditions, so the first tour didn't take place until 1949: the ballet then had Fonteyn as its star and the Metropolitan as its New York setting. Webster had gone across to handle negotiations, and this was one of his personal successes, the only complaint coming from Lord Waverley, that the name Covent Garden did not figure largely enough in the publicity. More tours followed, which made a vital contribution to the support of the opera company, especially in the early years before rising costs cut the profits. Webster felt this to be a fair return for what he had contributed to the ballet company.

Ashton's development was a great joy of these years, but one of Webster's regrets was that he did not succeed in bringing Benjamin Britten into closer association. 'Fortunate century that saw this spirit rise in its midst!' Ludwig of Bavaria once exclaimed, meaning Wagner. If Webster didn't perhaps feel quite so intensely about Britten, he did, years later, say to Anthony Gishford, 'I would like to live long enough to see the next wave of really original talent in the arts. I would like to know who is going to be the next Frederick Ashton, who the next Benjamin Britten.' He had instantly seen in *Peter Grimes* the latest addition to the standard repertory, one of the few works of the first half of the twentieth century likely to survive. He'd acquired it almost at once for Covent Garden, but Britten, alas, was already committed to a policy of chamber opera. Had he looked to Covent Garden rather than to the English Opera Group as the company for which to compose, the prestige of the house would have been enormously advanced, and his work would have been an inspiration which Webster had to look elsewhere to provide. Webster saw *Peter Grimes* as the cornerstone of a national repertory, and was convinced that had Britten turned to

Covent Garden there would have been the possibility at last of beginning to build such a repertory, even before he'd created a company of the necessary stature to inspire composers to compose for it. Uncertain of Britten, Webster decided to commission an opera from Arthur Bliss, and for the libretto he called in, not a hack, but no less than J. B. Priestley, one of the notable English playwrights of the day.

Meanwhile further troubles were threatening. His own contract would shortly come up for renewal – it had barely a year to run – and Boosey and Hawkes's lease on the Opera House came to an end in December 1949. Jay Pomeroy, his regime at the Cambridge Theatre also coming to an end, was entering the lists in the early summer of 1948, already making an offer for the lease. His plan was to have dancing for six months of the year, and six months of international opera as pre-war. Were his offer to be accepted, Webster could have no prominent place in the house in the future, while his efforts would be assigned to the casualty list along with all previous attempts to establish English opera on a regular basis.

He didn't feel very strong in opposition. But he remained unflappable and he calmly welcomed Brook. If there were conflict he was going to do his best to support Rankl. But, such as it was, the 'partnership' had to be made to work.

CHAPTER X

The Brook era · *Boris Godunov* · Welitsch in *La Bohème* · mixed language performances · *Figaro* · Geraint Evans · Sylvia Fisher · *The Olympians* · Rankl and Brook in conflict · the Brook–Dali–Welitsch *Salome* · Boris Christoff · exit Brook

The very young Peter Brook was the first of a new generation in the theatre to make a mark, and Webster was thrilled to have him at Covent Garden. The boy might be outrageous, iconoclastic, but that was part of it – Webster was buying him for the excitement he'd bring to the house. He tactfully assured the Board that Brook had a 'first-class musical mind' and 'a first-class musical approach', though, if he did in fact prove a good musician and a good linguist, the work he'd done so far hadn't allowed him to demonstrate either talent.

Webster, from preliminary conversations, already suspected that Brook regarded opera as 'the Deadly Theatre carried to absurdity' (Brook's own description, twenty years later, in his book *The Empty Space*). 'All Change!' was quite obviously his motto. He was a risk, but one worth taking, and having acquired him Webster was of course prepared to back him fully. But, tactful as ever, Webster went out of his way to make it clear, at least to Rankl (the point didn't need emphasizing to Brook) that the Musical Director's was the senior post, and that Brook was going to be directly responsible to himself.

Actually, Webster was not unsympathetic to Brook's attitude, for to him too it sometimes seemed that opera house custom was still the same as in the days of Patti, when a maid was sent ahead to inform the stage manager where the diva stood and delivered and when and where she deigned to move. Flagstad actually sent her manager. 'At this point,' the gentleman once explained, when she was expected for a revival of *Valkyrie*, 'Madame Flagstad comes to the front of the stage and *turns left*. Except,' he reminisced, 'for one time in Gothenburg, when for some reason she turned *right*.' He shook his head wonderingly. 'I see,' Brook murmured ironically. 'The Gothenburg Variation!'

Brook might have been a risk, but then, where is the producer who is both talented enough and humble enough for opera? Webster knew Brook wasn't ideal, especially when it became apparent that he seemed almost to regard opera as something you have to improve. He did most certainly, at the very least, feel it necessary to assert himself, he wanted his hand to show in any production he took charge of.

And yet he seemed to promise a new look to an art form which gave every appearance of fading. Opera in the past had submitted either to the dictatorship of singers or of conductors. Patti, and Melba in direct succession to her, had together held sway at Covent Garden for a total of half a century. The present century had seen several ensembles of great singers held together by conductors of huge prestige – by Mahler in Vienna, for example. Webster was under no illusions, and knew that what he had was something entirely different – a company of more or less raw recruits stiffened by a few visiting stars – plus Karl Rankl. He knew that something different was needed, therefore, and he saw that the producer, with the designer as his right arm, had to be the vital element. The idea of the producer's dominance came much later to opera than to the theatre, but Webster anticipated it. Brook was an exactly calculated risk.

And there certainly was excitement in the Opera House. People sensed that they were participating in something new, and company spirit, for all the many moments of strain, was excellent. Watching rehearsals for *Boris Godunov*, the first of Brook's productions and the last of the second season, Webster was worried that he might be asking too much of his singers, for he wouldn't allow them to mark instructions into their scores as he made frequent alterations. 'Things unfold,' he told them. This was certainly a change for singers used to Schramm. He asked for a lot of movement during the singing, and there were swirling movements in *Boris* which would have taxed far more experienced choristers. But it was immediately clear too that Brook could be brilliantly imaginative.

There was nothing routine about preparation. The opera was best known in Rimsky-Korsakov's rescoring, but Peter Gellhorn persuaded Rankl to look at the Mussorgsky original, and it was decided to go back to the Mussorgsky version, which would be heard in London for the first time. This made the production already something of an event. And besides, Brook had asked Christian Bérard to do the designs, but Bérard himself had said that only a Russian could do the opera justice, and himself suggested Georges Wakhevitch, whose work was to be seen everywhere in Paris, and who had been responsible for the famous Cocteau ballet *Le Jeune Homme et la Mort*, which had been brought to London by the Ballets de Champs-Elysées.

The production was built to amaze and astound – Brook's first opera had to serve also as his huge and elaborate visiting card – and was clearly the most ambitious the company had so far mounted, its thirteenth not counting *The Fairy Queen*. Some of the detail he brought to opera was lost in a huge theatre. In this respect Guthrie would have known better, but the brilliant young Brook was comparatively inexperienced still. Wanting to enlarge the characters in *Boris*, Brook had them on platform shoes with large headdresses, but against the larger sets they were reduced to no more than normal size again. Some of the detail was more suitable to film.

As Webster had anticipated, the production, which opened in June 1948, did indeed prove a major event, focusing attention on the Opera House, and for once it was the opera, not the ballet, causing a stir. It was highly controversial, and the criticism it attracted was no longer merely contemptuous or dismissive, but downright furious. The staging was forever animated, and with the scenery tended to dominate the singers, including Silveri who made a very decent Boris. What was particularly singled out for comment was the long corridor of sliding doors which closed one by one behind Boris during the death scene. Brook's intention was to express terror, to create a visual counterpart to the claustrophobia which is in the music. The effect was certainly exciting, but it did make Boris a dying dwarf. Ernest Newman, who was to become Brook's main adversary, struck out for the opposition in the *Sunday Times*, against a production which he thought also dwarfed the work and 'touched for the most part the lowest depths to which Covent Garden has yet fallen'.

Webster persisted in being delighted, and put this production alongside Benthall's *Turandot* and Guthrie's *Peter Grimes* and *Traviata*: he was singling out the work of his Shaftesbury Avenue directors, and maintained that these productions represented a standard as high as anywhere in the world. He had nothing but praise for Brook's efforts to be extravagant and striking and, in the case of *Boris*, to create a grandeur in the production to match the grandeur of the opera.

He eagerly awaited Brook's next, which was *Bohème*, not an opera which lends itself to spectacular effects. This time Brook was going to have to make do with the original Covent Garden sets, copies of the Hohenstein sets designed for the Turin première in 1896, and against which Melba herself had first displayed her Mimi in 1899. So the excitement here was going to be provided, not so much by Brook, but by the participation of the glorious Ljuba Welitsch. She, you could say, was not merely Webster's but anyone's idea of a star. She had brought the curtain up on the third season with her Aïda, and Webster was somewhat taken aback when she asked to be allowed to infiltrate the cast as Musetta. Why did she want to do it? The second-act Waltz Song can stop the show, but it's a secondary role none the less. Elisabeth Schwarzkopf was cast as Mimi, and Webster had not been able to close his ears altogether to tales of prima donna rivalries: did Welitsch want to do a secondary role when Schwarzkopf was singing the lead? 'But I want to be reunited with my old friend from the Vienna Opera,' she insinuated maliciously.

Webster had no extra money to spare for a star Musetta. This didn't matter either. Welitsch would do it for very little money, for no money at all. She'd do it almost literally for a song!

Welitsch was a Webster darling. He was a man for favourites and she was one of them. There were few singers, indeed few *people*, to whom he so responded. She had a wonderful generosity of personality, a gargantuan flamboyance. She was a woman quite unlike, say, his own mother, from whom it was not easy to win a response. This was another brand of woman altogether – a fire-brand! She was also in an important respect so unlike himself too. He was so guarded that it was impossible to imagine him yielding to a generous impulse incautiously, while she was all impulse. Which meant that she needed protection: in one aspect of herself she was defenceless, for all her force, where he himself was carefully defended. And this was so large a part of herself as artist. She was not only big and bold, but she was also, Webster saw, one of those rare artists with the courage to create a stage persona which really encapsulates their essential nature, a persona resting on a firm base in the depths of their own psychology. Most artists don't reach these depths – they either fail to reveal themselves or actually, if unconsciously, protect themselves by concealment. A Welitsch is bravely, magnificently exposed on her every stage appearance, she lays her heart before her audience.

The core of the Welitsch persona was 'baby-doll' – instinctual, impulsive, greedy and generous, with no defences against corruption. It was as though she were forever licking from her fingers sugar from the marshmallows she'd just that minute been gobbling. It was round this core that she built her characterizations, which for all their careful differentiations had an identity her audiences, even if unconsciously, were quick to recognize. Her audiences felt themselves involved in what seemed to be a personal, unique relationship with the artist. This is also true of Maria Callas, with whom, too, Webster was to establish a warm and almost tender relationship – they were both his dear, vibrant, generous and defenceless children. He was thus, with regard to them, stable and protective. But they also returned him in memory to an earlier day, and other devouring ladies – they were almost a reminder of an umbilical cord, not really severed, and joined at its other end to Mrs Patrick Campbell herself. On a deep level of psychological conflict, these ladies represented to him the devouring female to whom he was happy also to be submissive.

And this was to be his Musetta. There was going to be excitement of another kind than *Boris* had provided. Schwarzkopf promised an affecting Mimi, but her voice then was not large, it had still to develop, and Welitsch was announcing here and there that *ziss time* Musetta was going to sing Mimi 'off ze stage'! At rehearsals Musetta indulged in outrageous and eye-catching horseplay – and who was Peter Brook to complain if anyone else managed to be outrageous? The meticulous Mimi, on the other hand, would turn aside her head and not see it. Conflict between artists on this level must come across to the audience, not as conflict necessarily – but a tension would be generated, and they would respond to *this* performance. In *Aïda* once darling Ljuba had gone so far as to put a lock on the arm of an eighteen-stone Amonasro. But her father in *Aïda* was one thing, her lover in *Bohème* quite another when the lover was the stalwart Silveri. He was not to be so easily managed, and it was within his capacity to put the bombshell across his knee and test whether it would explode or not when spanked. As anticipated, the audience had a treat. The Welitsch on-stage antics didn't please some of the critics any more than the Welitsch antics, on and off stage, had taken Schwarzkopf's fancy. To audiences she was irresistible. Schwarzkopf's Mimi was also admirable, but she was outsung: and she didn't take her curtain-call on the first night, though she too would have earned cheers.

The *Boris*, and now the Welitsch-*Bohème*; Welitsch rather than Brook, but surely Webster could feel he was having a success with his Director of Productions. So far all was well between Brook and Rankl. The real tension had been between the prima donnas. The everyday standard of the new opera company, which had been on show now for almost two years, wasn't high, so the Flagstad, the *Boris*, the Welitsch evenings were in their different ways all the more important.

Day to day it was still a story of inadequate rehearsal conditions and singers miscast. Webster had wanted Berg's *Wozzeck* done, and Rankl, quite rightly, had begged for postponement. 'It would be irresponsible for me,' he wrote,

> to promise a 'Wozzeck' performance next year, if I could not start with the singers right in October 1949. [Hans] Braun has definitely refused to sing Wozzeck, so we have to look for somebody else.

Wozzeck was postponed, but singers were often necessarily miscast. Webster one day met Geraint Evans walking in the street with his wife and he told him he'd be doing the Toreador in *Carmen* once more. 'But he's terrible in the part,' Geraint's wife felt bound to point out. 'Yes,' Webster casually drawled. 'I suppose he is. But he's the best we've got.' Singers were also overworked. Edgar Evans, who in the first season had taken over the role of Des Grieux from Heddle Nash, before very long was finding himself called on to undertake sometimes as many as four exacting roles in a single week, ranging perhaps from the heroic tenor of Calaf in *Turandot* to a Britten role. There was nothing Webster could do about it. In the company's first few years if not Walter Midgley or James Johnston for the tenor roles, then it was most likely to be Edgar Evans. It told. In 1955 he was away from the company for twenty weeks, suffering from nervous exhaustion. But this meant that 'events' were doubly important. When a new production was being prepared, it had the main share of rehearsal time and routine work suffered all the more – but at the same time the whole house shared in any excitement there was, and Webster was adept at making everyone, from the cleaners up, feel involved in the operation.

Language too was already a problem. And was increasingly to become one. The German Wagner performances could of course accommodate their guests easily enough, not only Flagstad and Hotter, but such other wonders as the bass Ludwig Weber. Otherwise it was officially English all the way, and accents might fall uneasily on the ear even when no foreign language obtruded. This was especially to be remarked when an English-singing cast was led entirely by foreigners. Brook's *Bohème* was a beauty of an example. Only the admirable Schwarzkopf could command English easily. The others, and especially Welitsch, couldn't really be said to *command* English at all. But by now mixed language performances were beginning – no new thing, by the by, in the history of opera. As far back as 1709 Italians and English had sung side by side, and W. R. Chetwood reported the occasion in 1749 in his *General History of the Stage*:

> Mrs Tofts, a mere Englishwoman in the part of Camilla, courted by Nicolini in Italian, without understanding one single syllable each other said or sung, and on the other hand Valentini courting amorously in the same language a Dutchwoman who committed murder on our good old English with as little understanding as a parrot.

Against *Camilla* can be set the *Aïda* which had opened the third season in the autumn of 1948. Webster had watched his already beloved Welitsch struggling with English for the first time in her career. An Italian, Franco Beval, was to have sung Radames in English, but he was ill, and Torsten Ralf, summoned in his place at short notice, treated the audience to a Nordic-like Italian. Webster was relieved to have the curtain go up at all. Elsewhere, besides the Bulgarian English of Welitsch, there were the varied accents of the Italian baritone Silveri and the Polish bass Nowakowski, with Edith Coates, the Amneris, providing the only authentic English of the entire cast. And when Beval did finally appear he too, with Ralf providing the precedent, sang in Italian. At some other later performances Marko Rothmüller was the Amonasro, a Yugoslav who sang in Italian but here and there threw in a word of English to help the story along.

This *Aïda* was the prototype. The same season also saw an English

Rigoletto, Tom Williams, replying to his Italian-singing daughter, the French soprano Solange Delmas, in Italian, but declaiming English to the other characters; while the season's *Trovatore* had as tenor the ecstatically lyrical and stylish Libero de Luca singing in Italian, with everyone else singing in English. The following season he returned to sing the same role, again in Italian, and this time his Leonora, Margherita Grandi, sang to *him* in Italian but to the baritone in English, while Coates's Azucena was in English throughout.

This casting, with its resulting language confusion, was more or less forced on the house. Where did you then find a heroic tenor for *Aïda*? And no one in the first two seasons, and only Eugene Conley in the third, in some *Bohème* and *Rigoletto* performances, had offered the house anything like stylish singing in the Italian tenor roles – and de Luca was also, which in that day was rare and exciting, authentically Italian. These first mixed language performances were to be explained to some extent by the exigencies of the situation, and sometimes as panic measures.

On the other hand, Brook's third production, *The Marriage of Figaro*, showed at its very best the policy of foreign guests and local artists singing together in English. His designer for this was Rolf Gérard, who had done the sets for his famous 'youth' *Romeo and Juliet* at Stratford. There were no visual distractions this time and, with expertly managed intrigues and carefully defined but unexaggerated class-distinctions, the complicated action was made beautifully clear. It was a thought-through production which did not lose its shape through many revivals. *Boris*, and the *Salome* to come, brought glamour to the house and focused attention on it, and also provided a frame from time to time for star performances. This *Figaro* in another way was as important, for the everyday of an opera house is repetition of the repertory works, and *Figaro* is a real repertory work that season after season can bring forward new and developing singers. Comparatively, it brought Brook himself, as well as Covent Garden, much less attention, and it is difficult to continue as an *enfant terrible* and to maintain a position as a 'star' director without constantly drawing attention. There was, for him, a sad lesson to be learnt – that good behaviour only wins modest pats on the back, but that a director's visiting card is more effectively dropped when the stage fizzes with business however distracting. The critics were virtually inviting him to indulge in future extravagances.

In the Salzburg Festival's *Figaro* that year Irmgard Seefried had sung Susanna with Schwarzkopf as the Countess, and this was the cast Webster wanted. Seefried was *the* Susanna, with her gaiety, youth, charm, daring, and she had already been Susanna at Covent Garden with the Vienna State, with Erich Kunz as Figaro. Webster wanted him too, all the more as he knew that Pomeroy was going after some of the Vienna artists, and these two in particular, for his opera company at the Cambridge theatre. Webster regarded Vienna as his, and with the agency run there by Diez and Joan Ingpen providing a pipeline, he was kept well supplied with the splendid Vienna State singers: and Joan Ingpen was helpful at the Vienna end in the still tricky business of securing passports for them. All the major opera houses were now in competition for the few outstanding singers who could do justice to the major roles, and Webster was fortunate in this contact.

But although Seefried sang Susanna at some later performances, it was Schwarzkopf who was the first Susanna in the new production: Kunz never appeared with the company, but two of Webster's own artists took the roles of Figaro and the Countess. And these were artists who were to be of great importance to the company in the future.

There was constant criticism of casting at Covent Garden, and complaints about the neglect of good English singers – in March 1949 Beecham was threatening to make out a list of the best English singers overlooked by Covent Garden, but in the end he didn't. Webster decided that it was best to have someone from outside attending auditions, which were held at the Opera House every Thursday and Friday morning, with Rankl present whenever possible. He himself had responded instantly when he heard young Geraint Evans audition in November 1947. Evans was about to sign with Pomeroy, but Webster persuaded him to change his mind. 'Don't you think you'll be better off here to start, than going there among the lions?' In spite of those Escamillos, Evans *was* better off. His first role was a tiny one, the Nightwatchman in *The Mastersingers* – but here he was, a year later, Figaro next to Schwarzkopf.

And the Countess? This was the Australian soprano Sylvia Fisher, recommended to Webster, like Joan Sutherland in the future, by Goossens. She had been auditioned four times and then sent on as Leonora in *Fidelio*. With this second great lady, the Countess in *Figaro*, she became at once the company's prima donna, its first. She had a gloriously warm and generous voice, a beauty of its age. Brook soon realized that he had a most willing and sensitive artist in this role, with not the voice only but also the spirit to imbue the music with the right dignity. On the other hand, her real dramatic instinct could be somewhat obscured by a self-destructive nervousness. Brook treated her most sympathetically: he positioned her carefully, moved her cautiously. He built the production round her. She 'went out' to the audience and they 'received' her gratefully. Webster was overjoyed. It was a joy for him too to see Geraint Evans making his first claim on the buffo baritone repertory in which, over the next many years, he was to have few equals.

This was exactly what Webster had wanted from the start. Here he had inexperienced singers working beside an established foreign star – Schwarzkopf was both a model of style and also an ideally helpful colleague who allowed herself to be perfectly integrated into the production. What could be more gratifying? Hans Braun, the Count, was replaced at some later performances by Jess Walters, an American member of the company. And Webster also noted the success on the first night of the newest-comer to the company, Adèle Leigh, in the tiny role of Barbarina. Next season she moved up to the larger role of Cherubino, and was eventually the Susanna, clearly benefiting from the example of Schwarzkopf. This was how it ought to be.

Webster could have hugged Peter Brook. On the one hand *Boris*, on the other *Figaro*. He didn't have the same hopes for *The Olympians*, the new Bliss opera which was to open the company's fourth season in September 1949. He didn't think that the time to launch English opera at Covent Garden had really arrived yet. The company wasn't ready, and in fact the English libretto had to be entrusted to a cast sprinkled with foreigners. And this was hardly the right way of expanding the still small repertory. But he was committed to putting on English operas, so, after *Peter Grimes*, which he so loved, came *The Olympians*, in which he grudgingly invested £10,000. He didn't expect the public to greet the new work very warmly, and he hoped that Brook was once again going to provide some theatrical excitement. But he wasn't able to screw the singers up to a notable pitch, the work didn't establish itself during the ten performances, and it wasn't given a chance in later seasons. This in spite of Ernest Newman's praise of it:

> Altogether it left me with no doubts that here is a composer with real talent for opera, and that in Mr Priestley he has been fortunate enough to find an English Boito.

If Webster was sometimes cautious about new music, it must be remembered how important the box office was, for it was a question of no audiences, no grant – as simple as that. And hence so many *Carmens* and *Aïdas*, which *could* be relied on.

After *The Olympians*, which absorbed the energies of the house, the repertory productions, inevitably that much more under-rehearsed, followed each other in somewhat dreary succession. All the more, then, depended on the forthcoming *Salome*, which was to sport not only Ljuba Welitsch (who had been the second-cast Salome with the Vienna State) but also designs by Salvador Dali.

Rankl had made his stand against guest conductors. No Serafin, then, and no Karajan – but names continued to come up. De Sabata for one, and in connection with *Salome* in particular, Fritz Reiner, the great Straussian who had conducted the first performance of *Woman Without a Shadow* in Dresden soon after its Vienna première in October 1919, and who was familiarly known to an admiring Stravinsky as 'L'Amico Fritz'. In the autumn of 1948 Ralph Hawkes had written from New York, 'It would of course be stunning to have him do *Salome* with Welitsch in October 1949' – and he'd in fact been willing to do both *Salome* and *Twilight of the Gods*. Without naming names, Webster had once more sounded out Rankl. But no. The Musical Director must conduct all productions by the Director of Productions. Came February 1949, and Reiner's success at the Metropolitan – and with *Salome* of all operas – made him instantly that much more difficult to secure.

Webster saw this as a wonderful chance lost. He regretted it the more bitterly as he saw relations between Rankl and Brook deteriorate – there had been times during *The Olympians* when the two were barely on speaking terms. A Reiner *Salome* was a certain triumph, if anything was certain. Now he stood to have a disaster with it. And he might in any case lose either Brook or Rankl or both. Not only was it painful for them to work together, but Brook was still not making headway with many of the critics, and was not short of offers in the straight theatre if he wanted to abandon opera: while the time was coming, and soon, when guest conductors would have to come, which Rankl, though now taking up the baton for *Salome*, might simply refuse to stomach. It was not a happy time for Webster either.

Salome rehearsals began, and the atmosphere was as unhappy as Webster had feared. And to add to his troubles, there was also trouble with the revival of *Boris*. A new bass, none other than Boris Christoff, had been engaged, a youngster with an implacable talent and unshakeable will before whom the capitals of the world were just about to capitulate. If about nothing else, Webster was anxious about the decision to allow Christoff to sing in Russian with the rest of the company in English. So far mixed language performances had not been given as a matter of policy, but through accident or *force majeure*. But Webster, while wanting to persevere with the present policy of opera in English, wanted also a greater degree of flexibility. Svanholm, for example, was allowed to sing in *The Mastersingers* in German with the rest of the cast in English, because a Walther was hard to come by and Svanholm was a catch. Early the following year Victoria de los Angeles, having just set the world by the ears with her broadcast of Falla's *La Vida Breve*, was engaged to sing an Italian Mimi in one performance, otherwise in English, of *Bohème*. This seemed reasonable. But Margherita Carosio, heroine of the San Carlo's visit in 1946, was asked to learn *Traviata* and *Bohème* in English; when she refused, insisting on singing in Italian, negotiations broke down. She wasn't engaged. Disappointment all round. Christoff's Russian Boris at the end of 1948 was therefore something of a departure.

Not that that was the main trouble: *The Times* thought his Russian 'an unfortunate but not a great price to pay for so fine an interpretation'. The trouble was that Brook was instantly in unresolvable conflict with Christoff too, and this Boris might easily not have been heard at all on this occasion. If the young lion Brook saw mange in the hair of his older adversary, Rankl, he snarled with relish at the opposition of a Christoff who, likewise new to his celebrity, was quite as determined as Brook to roar unforgettably at his audiences.

Brook was already wound up by the tensions of the *Salome* rehearsals, and he responded as like to like to the highly strung Christoff. He was further alienated because Christoff arrived knowing the Rimsky-Korsakov version of the opera, patches of which began to appear on the original Mussorgsky. Boris's death-scene, and not the scene of the Russian people before the Cathedral, brought down the final curtain now – since when Christoff sang it was the Emperor, and not the Russian people, who was the protagonist. Christoff particularly objected to the immense clock which ticked away the minutes on the stage, dominating his by no means puny efforts in front of it. He demanded, instead, the usual small ornamental clock. Webster, in the middle of it all, typically made no effort to play a heroic role. This he left to be divided among others. He instead played Queen Elizabeth I, amenable to all. He certainly couldn't be accused of being partisan, because he patently didn't commit himself to either side. He was asked whether it should be a large clock or a small clock. 'Why not, er, have both?' was his apparently reasonable and certainly mild suggestion.

Which hardly prevented a row. But he had ensured that it didn't break over *his* head. Brook slyly brought along to rehearsal not merely a small clock but the very smallest he could find, a miniature travelling clock, and hung it unmenacingly on the stage – but beside it was still the offending large clock, which he had made no undertaking to remove. Christoff stormed off. And Webster saw doom before him. The Brook–Dali–Welitsch *Salome* might never reach the stage, and now this *Boris* with Boris Christoff was threatened too – and these held all the promise of excitement the house, for the moment, was likely to know.

Happily, on stage was another bass, Nowakowski, who had already sung the role of Boris, in succession to Silveri, when the opera was first mounted. Webster saw a way. He had Nowakowski come forward, and rehearsals continued – and meanwhile he turned on the Tannoy so that the rehearsal was relayed to every dressing-room in the theatre. The voice of the Polish bass in *his* role of Boris assailed the ears of the Bulgarian bass as he paced back and forther behind his locked door. It was too hurtfully much a question of The Emperor is dead, long live the Emperor! and within minutes Christoff was back again on stage, rehearsing before the *two* clocks. Though the audience saw only the huge dominating one, in spite of which Christoff went on to have his first triumph in the house. He was to become one of the important singers of Webster's reign, as well as a particular Webster singer; so it was as well that Webster had hung back during the row between singer and director and made neither of them an enemy!

The Christoff row rocked the house only briefly. But during the *Salome* rehearsals a huge row developed and brought with it the first major crisis of the regime, which only Webster's famous tact managed to avert.

Brook hadn't been a star in the house for a while, not in *Bohème*, not in *Figaro*, not in *The Olympians*. But *Salome* was another opera in which he could display himself. Brook had decided that only Dali's natural style had the erotic degeneracy of Strauss and could also match the imagery of Wilde. Dali's first idea, the very revelation of which in the press once more focused attention on Covent Garden, was to turn the stage into a huge bed. Dali pretended to be serious, and Webster merely delighted in the attention, though he discouraged Brook from encouraging this other, perpetual *enfant terrible* to translate his fancies *too* nakedly to the stage. There had been a prophetically swashbuckling episode in which Brook, driving back along the Spanish coast from Dali's house in Cadaques, was ambushed by bandits, who happily did not see the value of Dali's designs painted on stiff boards three feet square.

But Rankl was soon to endorse the bandits' evaluation. He thought them excellent critics, and was soon himself, in great distress, cabling Webster, who was unfortunately in New York looking into the arrangements for the ballet company's first American tour:

> Saw Salome sets first time today – absolutely impossible for requirements of music and singers – even no room to put Jews in proper place stop no sound would be heard as singers placed too far back stage stop please authorize me by return stop work not yet started on sets until your return.

Webster, again, didn't take sides. And work did go ahead on the sets and work went ahead on the production. Rankl and Brook weren't speaking, and Rankl was right in considering so much waste paper the Royal Opera House's recent statement confirming that

Mr Rankl is the Senior Director under the General Administrator, and that in all matters regarding opera and the production of opera his decisions are final. This statement is agreed in this form by Mr Rankl, Mr Brook and the General Administrator.

What Webster had wanted was an equal partnership of Musical Director and Director of Productions, and this vitally important production he seemed, if anything, to regard as primarily the creation and responsibility of the Director of Productions. It was relevant that Webster had already reason to be uncertain about Rankl's future position in the house: and, hard to believe now, Strauss in those days, and for years to come, was, apart from *Rosenkavalier*, a doubtful quantity. Even in 1954, when it was arranged that the widow of Hofmannsthal, Strauss's librettist, should get £65 a performance, and she was shocked at what she took to be a breach of the contract which gave her not less than 7 per cent of the gross takings, Webster had to explain: 'Mrs Hofmannsthal would have been more shocked if she had been paid 7 per cent of the takings. She would have had a royalty of under £45 on that basis. Strauss is not popular in England.'

Webster, as always, had to consider more than simply the personalities immediately involved in any situation. Forfeiting Reiner, Webster had continued with *Salome* on the basis of Brook-Dali rather than of Rankl, and it was their contribution, as Rankl soon realized, that most concerned him.

But he was concerned about the placing of one of the Jews – namely Welitsch herself. Dali provided a central rostrum, with cliffs on either side, and a narrow road that went curling steeply up the side of the rostrum to the back of the stage. The basic idea was for the singers to spend their time on the rostrum singing while the production, so to speak, took to the road. But, dangerously, the sections of road didn't join up, and at moments judged suitable by the director steam rose from the gaps. (This was certainly not to be one of those productions which Dare Not Speak Its Name.) Webster, regaled with details, didn't actually commit himself to enthusiasm, which he tended to leave to others. He knew (he wasn't Scots for nothing!) how to lavish affection once success was assured.

But when he first saw the Dali set on the stage he had to control almost a sense of wonderment. The sheer cheek of it! 'But you can't expect Welitsch to stay on the rostrum for the Dance of the Seven Veils,' Michael Wood pointed out to him. 'What if she falls through?' For an instant Webster weighed up the value in terms of publicity of the prima donna's disappearance in these circumstances. But he was fond of Ljuba and he arranged for slats to be put over the gaps. Which

Margot Fonteyn as Ondine

Left: Michael Benthall and Erich Kleiber
Below: Rafael Kubelik
Right: David Webster and Otto Klemperer
Below: Giulini and Visconti discussing *Don Carlos,* 1958

Above: Sir David Webster and Sir Frederick Ashton
Below: after Klemperer's *Fidelio*, 1961. H.M. the Queen Mother talking to Jon Vickers and Forbes Robinson

didn't prevent the Welitsch foot going through occasionally to general consternation.

One production effect abhorred by critics was a stationary moon, which didn't move across the sky as the composer required and didn't turn red when the libretto indicated that it should. Another major effect was the descent from the flies of John the Baptist's head on a salver. 'I wish,' snarled Brook playfully, 'that that was Rankl's head.' Webster on the whole liked these varied excitements, and felt Lewis's and Metal Box all the better lost as his own pulse-beat speeded up to match them. But if he couldn't help being delighted by the pranks of his young protégé, he was very far from being delighted when Rankl, before the first night, stormed out of the Opera House never to return. His famous tact did persuade Rankl back, but the Musical Director expressed his disapproval eloquently enough on the first night by refusing to take a curtain-call.

Webster hadn't supported him. But then, this was a General Administrator who was ruthlessly expert at sifting priorities. The next day the box office was lively, though even then, Welitsch and Dali notwithstanding, full houses weren't guaranteed, and Webster was actually pleased to be able to report to the Board at least *one* sold out. Rankl's contribution alone certainly wouldn't have ensured even that.

The production was a *cause célèbre*, and Webster rejoiced that everyone once more knew that something was happening at Covent Garden. Welitsch herself produced wonderful sound in abundance, was thrilling in declamation, and quite overwhelming in her impersonation of an indulged child resentful of the corruption into which she found she had been betrayed. *She* certainly wasn't dominated by the production. It might have been argued that Welitsch alone would have provided enough excitement. But Webster loved the production, and he'd never accuse it of worse than being ahead of its time. The senior critics, though, reacted furiously against it, Ernest Newman's *Sunday Times* notice putting the case most succinctly:

> This young man seems to have persuaded himself that the issue is one between arthritic upholders of a hoary tradition and forward-reaching, height-straining young geniuses like himself. There is no such simple antithesis . . . progress is not synonymous with irresponsible larking about with a masterpiece.

Brook himself was not slow to give an answer to Newman's question:

> How much longer will the London opera public tolerate performances and productions which are for the most part an affront to their intelligence? How long, O Lord, how long?

Brook had had enough, and by mutual consent his contract was not renewed after its second year. Webster was in one way relieved, he was allowed to drop a Hot Potato. And he'd had the contribution from Brook that he'd needed and had engaged him for. Brook's engagement had, he considered, justified itself; though he regretted his passing, and within five years was inviting him back for *Otello*. The invitation wasn't accepted.

Webster also, deeply, regretted the *Salome*, Dali and all. There was henceforth no Director of Productions at the house (not until 1971 when the title was briefly restored for Peter Hall), and Christopher West, whom Brook had brought in from Stratford as his assistant, stayed on as Resident Producer. At least *his* status relative to the Musical Director's was clear. But *Salome* wasn't given the following season, and when it was revived it was in a new production by Christopher West and *sans* the also-offending Dali decor.

Such a production justifies itself, even if it can be put to only very limited use, simply by being a *cause célèbre*. But there are other productions, of quite another kind, less striking maybe, and having less obvious appeal for David Webster, which more gradually prove their usefulness over the years. There was for example Robert Helpmann's unobtrusively excellent *Madame Butterfly*, which was soon to provide a lovely frame for Victoria de los Angeles, and later on for others as fine: and it is still in use today. The same singer's charming Manon gave meaning to Ashton's production, while the *Rosenkavalier*, also from the first season, was now beginning to be one of the company's most important.

Meanwhile, with Brook gone, Rankl was the survivor. But, wondered Webster unhappily, for how long? It was coming up to 1950, time to make changes. Guest conductors, for all that Reiner had been lost, would have to be introduced into the house. Webster realized that he was going to have to square up to Rankl very soon. Was he going to prove adaptable?

CHAPTER XI

Webster's contract renewed · government takes over Covent Garden lease · guest conductors · Rankl's continued opposition · Kleiber's *Rosenkavalier* · *The Queen of Spades* · *Wozzeck* · Beecham's *Mastersingers* · Flagstad's farewell · exit Rankl

Through the eighteen months of Brook, Webster's own position had been shaky. While trying to keep the peace between Brook and Rankl, he had to think of his own contract, due for renewal in the summer of 1949, and of the new lease on the Opera House itself. Pomeroy had made his offer. Then in January 1949 Christie of Glyndebourne made his. (In Brook terms this was post *Boris* and *Bohème* and coincided with *Figaro.*) Christie's memorandum, 'The Operatic Problem', talked in somewhat muddled fashion of Covent Garden's 'failing' towards the past, and criticized, as was now commonplace, the inexperienced administration and the second-rate musical direction. 'Why should everything be held up by these Covent Garden failures?' Glyndebourne, it is true, had not had such failures even in its earliest days – but then, Glyndebourne had always been *festival* opera, and productions, and revivals too, might be given as many as twenty-four stage rehearsals. It was not a comparable operation. Webster ran into Christie once in a London club. 'I don't feel anything against you personally, Webster,' Christie told him. 'And what will you feel when my head rolls in the gutter?' was Webster's dry response.

Beecham meanwhile wasn't missing the fun. 1948 had been a sounding-off year for him, and 1949 began with the Incorporated Society of Musicians' annual conference at Brighton. He had included Boosey and Hawkes in his attack on Covent Garden, complaining that they were making money from the performing rights of scores held in copyright. It was true that they had indeed made some £1576 out of performing rights. But they had also, as Sir Steuart Wilson pointed out in his reply, 'rescued the Opera House from where Sir Thomas Beecham had left it – from becoming a dance-hall forever', and that operation had cost them the not inconsiderable sum of £35,000. And even though they'd arranged that from the beginning of the 1948 financial year their loss was to be limited to a maximum of £6000 per year, their six months' accounts to 26 June 1948 already showed a loss of £7385, and their losses had risen from there. After due consideration the Board decided *not* to sue Beecham. In March 1949 the word was that Beecham was collecting his list of British artists wrongfully not employed by Covent Garden.

And in March 1949 too the question of Webster's contract came up. It was decided that he should be transferred from the Boosey and Hawkes payroll and in future be paid by the Covent Garden Trust, and his new contract was to run for a further six years rather than for the five he had asked, which he considered a reassuring gesture. His salary was fixed at £4000, no huge sum considering the responsibilities involved, though there were of course 'perks', and not only in Dom Perignan. He was building up contacts in the social and business worlds which were likely to prove useful: and there were also, later, contacts in the expanding world of television.

Still, £4000 as salary could hardly be counted a very impressive sum. But Jimmy was now doing well in business, and money was not so much the problem. Webster's main concern was to keep the house open and to stay with it. In any case, his contract wasn't going to mean much if the Covent Garden lease couldn't be extended satisfactorily.

Covent Garden Properties Ltd came back to the Trust with new and unacceptable terms: so, waiving the Pomeroy and Christie offers, an important decision was made: namely, to approach the government and persuade them to buy the lease and sublet to the Arts Council. Waverley, in the subsequent negotiations, was once again a hero, and his good relations with Sir Stafford Cripps were fundamental to his success. It was happily concluded, before Boosey and Hawkes's tenancy ended, that the Ministry of Works should take the lease but sublet not to the Arts Council but to the Covent Garden Trust directly. The new lease was to begin on 1 April 1950, and to cover the interim, from 26 December 1949, Douglas Lund was named as proprietor of the house.

These were not unimportant matters. If the future still wasn't secure at least Webster had been given time, and Philip Hill of Covent Garden Properties Ltd, and Boosey and Hawkes, had at least the satisfaction of knowing that the scheme they had so generously implemented could still prove more than merely foolhardy. A little more acknowledgement might also, from time to time, have been accorded them – when Webster talked to the press, for example, or gave interviews on radio or television. But he wasn't one to give such acknowledgement if it seemed to serve no practical purpose. It was of a piece with his involuntary rejection of his own past. He wanted the Opera House beginnings, as much as his own beginnings as haberdasher, concealed, forgotten.

The Ministry of Works, taking on the lease, had virtually no commercial assets apart from the scenery and costumes, and certainly nothing they could sell easily. The Trust therefore thought it prudent to take a long lease from Covent Garden Properties Ltd – it was to run for forty-two years, until 1992 – and have the Ministry of Works step between. The Royal Opera House, merely using the Ministry of Works as post office, was to pay £13,500 a year, and to be responsible for the rates as well as maintenance and repairs: the Ministry didn't gain from the arrangement, but Covent Garden Properties Ltd were reassured by having the Ministry as their tenant to apply to in case of the Opera House failing.

This meant exit Pomeroy and exit Christie from the arena, with Webster comparatively more secure in the middle of it. Only comparatively. He still had to defend his own authority. A Treasury Report on the organization of Covent Garden drawn up at the end of 1948 was happy to announce that the Stage Director now had a staff of one hundred and twenty-four people working under him, which was near pre-war strength, and commented also on certain problems of the repertory system (lack of space for sets and props was one of them, and too many people too often idle and then having to go into overtime).

A Sub-Committee, which included David Webster and some Board members, now drew up a Memorandum, and among other things it was decided – certainly not by Webster himself – that an Artistic Director must be found for the house. Webster considered himself well able to absorb the duties of Artistic Director into those of General Administrator and he expertly delayed, suggesting that Ian Hunter, who was to follow Rudolph Bing as Director of the Edinburgh Festival, should come in as his assistant. To suggest an assistant to himself on this level implied that his own job was now beginning to be a considerable one. The appointment was intended to be an alternative to having an Artistic Director – but this particular threat was averted finally when not Ian Hunter but Sir Steuart Wilson was appointed Deputy General Administrator. It did at least prove a weapon when Webster had finally to broach again with Rankl the delicate matter of guest conductors, which the Sub-Committee grasped firmly like the proverbial nettle.

It happens, and is indeed a recurring theme in the history of the arts as well as of business and industry, that the very success of a young and developing organization displaces its founders. The Opera House grew and Webster grew with it. But Karl Rankl didn't. He wasn't able to adapt to the changing conditions which he himself had done so magnificently much to create.

For with the orchestra improving, the chorus improving, with singers getting to know their roles and improving in them, it was becoming happily, and sadly, inevitable that aspirations had to go higher. It was in one way a sad moment when the Opéra Comique, with whom negotiations had broken down in 1946, came to the house in June 1949 to give three performances of *Pelléas and Mélisande*. The Covent Garden orchestra played far better for Roger Désormière, the French conductor, than it ever had for Rankl. He showed that the instrument was there. But it was as though Rankl had created an orchestra which was too good, at least under the conditions in which he was forced to work, for him to conduct himself. In December 1950 Lord Harewood wrote in the *Daily Mail* that the Covent Garden Orchestra was providing the best string playing by any British orchestra since the war. And unfortunately the conductor, once again, was not Rankl himself, but this time the company's first guest conductor, Erich Kleiber.

Webster had used delaying tactics when it came to guest conductors just as he had on the question of an Artistic Director. The Sub-Committee recommended that Vittorio Gui, who had been in charge of some Italian performances at Covent Garden in 1938 and 1939, be invited on to the staff – but Gui was prepared to come only if he were allotted not the Italian but the Wagner and Mozart repertory, clearly an impossibility while Rankl was Musical Director. Capuana, who had been at Covent Garden with the San Carlo in 1946, was mentioned as a possibility for the Italian repertory, and Webster himself also suggested Cantelli, Toscanini's protégé, who did not surprise anyone, and certainly not Webster, when he declined because of the demands of his concert work. Finally, Webster went off unbeknownst to the Board, as was his wont, to have quiet talks in Switzerland with the conductor of his choice, Erich Kleiber; and he had already established a sympathetic rapport before he presented his case to them.

After *Salome* it was Peter Brook who had left the house for good, but it was Rankl, though surviving, who had been the more painfully mauled. He did not have youth, ebullience, even confidence in his own talents to help him recover. The rest of his time, given his nervous jealousies and his inflexibility, could only be spent trying against odds to block sorties against his authority – and by enemies who were striking at him through the very gates he'd forced open himself. It was, thanks to him, that the house was now worth the attention of distinguished foreign guests. He'd already protested against bringing them in, and he'd gained time. But how much time? How long could he expect Webster and the Board to be content with merely supplying him with assistants?

The attack was renewed early in 1950. Brook was clear of the house, so if not a Director of Productions then guest conductors were going to have to provide excitement. They couldn't be denied any longer. It wasn't a pleasant task for Webster, launching the attack on Rankl, but there was no one else to do it tactfully. Webster had timed it perfectly: his own contract and the lease of the house were both signed, and Rankl's contract ran only till the following summer.

He deliberated for some weeks, then dictated a letter to Muriel Kerr. 'It is remarkable,' he wrote to Rankl,

> that Cripps has been prepared to back Covent Garden so strongly in the teeth of considerable critical opposition. Deserved or undeserved, generous or ungenerous, knowledgeable or unknowledgeable, the criticism itself is a fact.

He developed his argument cleverly, this might-have-been-diplomat. Small wonder that it was so well known that you had to be very sure of your facts if you wanted to go against him. He explained to Rankl that there had been changes of personnel in the Treasury, that general economies were possibly about to be made, and that the Opera House grant wasn't safe. Waverley and the Arts Council were apprehensive. He continued with a pretence of flexibility:

> No one knows better than you how far our performances have come since 1947. Part of the improvement is of course due to the passage of time spent in actually performing. The bulk of the improvement is undoubtedly due, however, to your work. The only people who can be expected to realize this fully are those concerned with the actual day to day work of the theatre, but I know of no one connected with the Trust or the theatre who is not prepared to give you the fullest credit for this work: all of them are grateful to you. The best evidence is our desire that you go on working with us.

Webster then made a largely false analogy between the bringing in of a guest conductor and the appointment of an assistant for himself. No one could suppose that Kleiber in relation to Rankl was going to be the same as an assistant, whoever he might be, to David Webster:

> His name [Sir Steuart Wilson's] again from the public relations angle, is extremely useful to us, and his direct standing in the musical world is considerably greater than mine.

Not that Webster had been anything but reluctant to accept an assistant – but he was prepared to see Wilson's being seconded from the Board to the role of Deputy General Administrator as contributing to the good of the house. Here was the nub of the argument. *Couldn't Rankl regard Kleiber in the same way?* Webster was only asking Rankl to swallow the same pill he'd swallowed himself with a good grace!

> I was surprised at your view of Kleiber. He seems to be one of the few people who shares our views – he is all for encouraging local singers and

> he has done a great deal of this kind of work in South America. Then he believes in opera in English with the kind of exceptions we have already made . . . I think he may be a difficult man to work with but we have to stomach that for his usefulness. He speaks well of you.

Rankl fully appreciated the implications of the letter. He was being faced unmistakably with the proposition, exit Brook, enter Kleiber. Perhaps, it was suggested at this stage, as a guest for three months in the autumn. For the following season it might be desirable to have, at the head of the musical staff, Rankl and one other first-class conductor sharing equal status.

Rankl wrote back the same day:

> I have read your letter very carefully . . . The only question I should like to ask you is: are you presenting me with a *fait accompli* or are your proposals still open to a discussion between ourselves?

Webster of course was prepared to discuss – but this didn't mean that discussions were in any way going to affect the outcome. He was instantly dictating another letter to Rankl. Next season, Rankl's last under his extended contract – in other words, after Rankl's current contract had expired – the title Musical Director was going to be dropped.

In spite of discussions, Kleiber was coming. He was to make his first appearance in the house early in December, and he was to stay for three months. The fact of his being booked was to Rankl a defeat, and the still-Musical Director didn't expect to be any more comfortable with this guest conductor about the house than he had with a Director of Productions. Kleiber was already about the house in November, and it wasn't comfortable for either of them. They were very soon passing each other in the corridors without speaking. Webster made it his business to avoid being seen to take sides. But he wanted it to be as comfortable in the house as possible for Kleiber. This too was an appointment that had to be justified.

November was a bad month for Rankl, though for Webster, if not an easy one, it was at least full of exciting promise. For in this same month he had also to notify Rankl, again tactfully but resolutely, that another guest conductor would be coming the following summer. None other than Sir Thomas Beecham. *Beecham* of all people!

Webster had to use his accustomed tact in full measure, and Rankl first learned through the post of Beecham's engagement. Webster wrote to him to explain that Beecham himself had made the approach to Covent Garden – and, for all his tact, Webster didn't make any bones about the fact that he *was* going to be engaged. If it was over anybody's bones it would have to be Rankl's. 'Slanging,' he explained,

> is and always has been part of Beecham, I almost said part of Beecham's fun, and has little or no actual meaning. At the same time it is frequently impossible to regard him as anything but unpleasant. But whatever his character or his behaviour one thing is undoubted and that is his musical ability . . . Whatever he may think about us or whatever he says in the future, to have him do something in 1951 would be good for us as an institution. It is something of a triumph that the approach should have been made by him.

To Rankl, Kleiber and Beecham together represented a twin-pronged attack. Kleiber's first appearance with the company, on 6 December, was for Webster more significant than the day when Flagstad first appeared, or when the curtain rose on Peter Brook's first production, though those dates too had signalled changes and development. December 6, 1950 was an important day in the history of the house, and an important day in Webster's own life. He saw Kleiber hoisting the company to a new level – or, rather, he saw just what level his company was now capable of achieving. Flagstad and Brook in their very different ways had supported a tottering edifice, but Kleiber showed the future. A future of which Rankl was now a doubtful component.

Kleiber's first opera was *Rosenkavalier*, which was to become *the* house opera. Sylvia Fisher was the Marschallin, Shacklock the Octavian: Fisher had taken on her famous role only the season before, and under Kleiber instantly began to improve enormously, to become not only undisputed prima donna but one of the finest singers of her day. Had she only been invited to record, which in those days English singers weren't, her records would be treasured and her name celebrated worldwide. The Fisher/Shacklock *Rosenkavalier* performances over the next few years were at the very heart of the repertory, and more than any other showed the *company*. It was the happiest beginning, and the audience was duly grateful. On that evening of 6 December 1950 there was a particular atmosphere in the house, which it was sensed would not ever again be quite the same. The audience's welcome for Kleiber, their rapture when the curtain fell many hours later, was for more than the one man and the single performance.

The success of *Rosenkavalier*, and the promise of Tchaikowsky's *The Queen of Spades*, Kleiber's first new production due to open a fortnight later, prompted Kenneth Clark to write to Webster:

> We must do everything in our power to keep him [Kleiber]. He has made an immeasurable difference. But when all has been said, he couldn't have used the instrument unless *Rankl* had created it.

Yes, Rankl had created the instrument; and already, in his first weeks in the house, Kleiber was using it with an altogether more exalted poetic sense, a far deeper psychological awareness. He brought artistry, he revealed to the young company that there was more to operatic theatre than notes and music. He drew the singers, in the words of one of them, into a shared 'spiritual experience'. The audience too. There was a *Fidelio*, with Rankl in the pit, when the gallery heaped reproaches on his ageing head in the form of cries for 'Kleiber! Kleiber! Where's Kleiber?' The stalls rose in Rankl's defence, trying to drown the cries with their applause.

The Queen of Spades brought forward more house singers. Raoul Jobin had been asked to sing Herman, but suddenly Edgar Evans received an invitation to lunch with Webster, and arrived to find Kleiber there too, as well as Steuart Wilson and Constance Shacklock. There was a possibility that he might do Herman instead. He shook pepper nervously into his soup, the pepper-top and a deal of pepper fell in, but he made no comment and drank it just the same, and with burning mouth agreed to take on the part. The read-through was next morning at ten o'clock, and that evening at five o'clock he was asked to sing. The first bars were wrong. After five or six bars he wanted to give up. 'How can I do it?' 'Ah,' said Kleiber warningly, 'you have to be a superman.'

Kleiber was a tyrant if he didn't get what he wanted. There were only three weeks of rehearsal before going on stage, and the first night was four weeks away. Evans was given till next morning to decide. He rang Peter Gellhorn who agreed to teach him the role, and also advised him to tell Kleiber he'd need a few days alone. In fact Gellhorn taught him the role in a single day, going over it from ten in the morning until ten at night. The following day at eleven Edgar Evans went to Kleiber and they began on the second act. 'Mein Gott!' Kleiber exclaimed. 'He knows it.' A benevolent expression usurped his mask of amazement. 'Now you can be easy. I shall not worry you.'

Michael Benthall was the director, sustaining the melodramatic atmosphere of the work with fine but not irrelevant flourish, and Oliver Messel's ingenious decor progressed through the opera so cunningly from the realistic to the exaggerated that the audience seemed to be looking through Herman's eyes as he descended further and further into madness. And for Edith Coates, the Countess, there was a special triumph. 'Since the days of Chaliapine,' wrote Desmond Shawe-Taylor, 'I cannot recall a more sinister death scene on the operatic stage.' Edith Coates was also Kleiber's choice for the Witch in the production of Humperdinck's *Hansel and Gretel* he was hoping to do, but Webster was against the opera. Besides *Rosenkavalier* and

The Queen of Spades, Kleiber in his first season also conducted *Rigoletto*, *Carmen* and *The Magic Flute*, representing an extraordinarily complete range. If a superlative Straussian, he was no narrow specialist.

Now Rankl was furious to learn that Berg's *Wozzeck* was being held in reserve for Kleiber – the opera he'd refused himself because conditions weren't right for him to do it justice. He went to see Webster, who remained behind his desk, gracious but remote. It was, the General Administrator pointed out to him, a special Kleiber opera. Kleiber had worked with Berg himself on the opera, and had conducted its première in Berlin in 1925. Rankl knew all this perfectly well – better than Webster. He'd been in Germany at the time and had actually heard the opera under Kleiber. His period as Klemperer's assistant at the Kroll Opera in Berlin had coincided with Kleiber's as Musical Director of the Berlin State. He didn't need Webster to tell him about Kleiber and Berlin and *Wozzeck*.

When he'd first brought up the matter, Webster explained, he hadn't known that Kleiber might be coming to Covent Garden. It had been a possibility, true, that Rankl might have charge of the work. But surely, with Kleiber coming back to the house, it would be wasteful not to use his experience of Berg and *Wozzeck*? Surely Rankl could see that? Only think of the criticism that would be levelled against them both – General Administrator and Musical Director alike – if Kleiber were in the house and *not* used for *Wozzeck*. (By next year, of course, the title Musical Director was not going to be current any longer.)

Rankl saw his rival given preferential treatment. For *Kleiber* it was going to be possible to create the right conditions. There was the time when Kleiber was frankly – which meant vociferously – dissatisfied, and his displeasure was going to be visited. The Opera House might have had walls of glass, so clearly could storm-clouds be seen from a distance to be gathering. Miss Kerr, as usual, had first intimations, and relayed her fears to the Little Man in his Office. Kleiber was a veritable Fricka in his wrath, mounted on a ram-drawn chariot and driving recklessly up to the heights where this Brunnhilde, Muriel Kerr, was even then warning Webster-Wotan – who would have relished the analogy were he not fully occupied 'putting on a face'. Kleiber flung open the door, to find behind it a bland David Webster who welcomed him with apparent pleasure. Yes, he could certainly have those extra hours' rehearsal with the orchestra. Of course he needed them. Opera was to be presented to the English public in a manner appropriate both to the Opera House and to Kleiber himself. Rankl brooded. He wasn't given this kind of treatment. What would his own work at the house have been if he hadn't had to devote himself to teaching, and had been given way to in his demands as Kleiber was given way to?

There was also the awkward case of two trumpeters, which set the two conductors directly at odds with each other. On 9 February 1951, at 10.30 a.m., Steuart Wilson, in Webster's unfortunate absence, wrote to Kleiber, who was not to be gainsaid, that the two trumpeters he required would be at his disposal that same day at 12.40 p.m., 'and they can stay as long as you like'. That pleased Kleiber: but in order to please him Wilson had had to ride somewhat roughshod over poor Rankl, to whom, at 10.15 a.m., he had written to say that *his* rehearsal was to end at 12.30 p.m. He *had* to let the orchestra go. And if he wouldn't? 'If not I am afraid that I must exercise David's authority . . . and say that the two trumpeters must be here at 12.40.'

That's perhaps what Webster would have said in effect. But this would not have been his tone. It wasn't a tone he liked to take with anyone who continued in Opera House employment.

Beecham, that season, was as it were Third Trumpeter, bruiting abroad various ideas. For *Mastersingers* he suggested Los Angeles as Eva, but settled happily enough for Elisabeth Grümmer, and for Sachs he put forward the name of a promising young baritone, Dietrich Fischer-Dieskau (whose actual house debut was to be deferred for some fifteen years). Beecham's suggestions were not those of the tone-deaf. But much discussion was simply for the pleasure of discussion and the putting forward of self. He contemplated Gluck's *Iphigenia in Tauris* as well as a lighter opera, Lecocq's *La Fille de Madame Angot*, but the Gluck dropped out of sight while *Mamselle Angot* was replaced by *The Bohemian Girl*, the Victorian opera which, along with *Maritana* and *Lily of Killarney* made up the so-called 'English Ring', staple of the touring companies until the 1930s (an English Ring, as it happens of which two operas were composed by Irishmen, Balfe and Wallace, while the third, by Benedict, a German, has an Irish subject). Balfe's *The Bohemian Girl* was hardly what Webster had in mind for *his* English opera, but Beecham had persuaded the Liverpool Festival Authorities, the Arts Council and Covent Garden to produce it in the first place, before bringing it to London, as part of Liverpool's contribution to the Festival of Britain.

Michael Benthall was Webster's first choice for director, and he also recommended James Bailey, arranging for him to show his designs one evening. Beecham arrived in his car, couldn't find his way into Bailey's house, and drove round for three-quarters of an hour trying: Webster, needless to say, was soon having to look about for another designer. Furthermore Beecham, on whose sole insistence the work was being mounted, very soon grew dissatisfied with the score and decided to do an entirely new version which everybody had to copy out at night after rehearsals and somehow get finished before the first performance.

And there were casting problems too. 'I think the most practical way of going about this whole tiresome business,' Beecham wrote to Webster,

> is for you on your side to make a list of all those singers, etc., etc. who in your estimation are eligible: and I on my side will do the same. We will then exchange lists, perceive if there is any similitude or correspondence between them and after that meet in solemn and depressing conclave.

Lists were indeed made, and from them Elsie Morison, Richard Lewis, Howell Glynne and Graham Clifford were approved, though this didn't mean necessarily that they were actually included in the final casting.

The Bohemian Girl, with a revival of *The Fairy Queen*, made up a short season of native opera to follow on after the close of the opera season proper, in which Beecham's *Mastersingers* was a highlight. It was the orchestra – Rankl's orchestra – which drew highest praise from Ernest Newman:

> It is a long time since we heard a *Meistersinger* so pressed down and running over with all that makes orchestral listening a delight – ardour, passion, beauty, tenderness, thoughtfulness.

Beecham was as rapturously welcomed as Kleiber had been. There were four performances, and after the last of them Webster came out on stage with him to make a speech. Webster revered, and had never ceased to revere, Beecham the conductor. To have had him in his house, whatever their differences in the past, had been a great joy for him. In his speech he expressed both joy and reverence, and Tommy listened to it not unappreciatively. But all the while he was obviously screwing himself up for a jocularly abrasive speech to cap it; though the opera was over, he didn't feel his performance was yet at an end. He didn't, either, altogether like the stage usurped even for so good a purpose as praise of himself. But Webster, having rolled out his last words, folded his hands demurely and rolled up his eyes. Beecham raised his own eyes – to see the great curtain above them descend slowly. There was, of course, huge applause, but now it was partly Webster's too. Beecham's own speech, to his frustration, remained frozen on his lips.

The Festival of Britain summer was also memorable for Flagstad's series of farewell performances. She sang five Isoldes, but it was another guest conductor, Clemens Krauss, who was in the pit for the first four, not Rankl. Once again Rankl's orchestra responded superbly.

Krauss was yet another who had been at the house already with the Vienna State in 1947, in charge of their *Fidelio* and *Salome*. Krauss had not hesitated to go to the Berlin State Opera as Musical Director in 1935, at a time when the producer Wallerstein had proved himself no longer acceptable to the Nazi authorities: Krauss had subsequently proved himself perfectly acceptable, too much so certainly for Rudolph Bing who now, post-war, refused even to consider engaging him for the Metropolitan. Such considerations didn't weigh with Webster. If in the future negotiations were to break down with Kleiber, then it was Krauss whom Webster intended to go after. Himself a refugee from the Nazis, Rankl hardly relished Krauss's presence in the house, and he certainly resented giving up the first four *Tristans* to him. At least Webster had insisted that the fifth, on 30 June, be given to Rankl. This was to be not only Flagstad's final Isolde but her last performance of all at Covent Garden. 'I want to take things easily,' Flagstad told her audience at the end of the evening, after twenty-one curtain-calls. 'Please forgive me.'

It was a great evening, and the interest centred entirely on Flagstad – and yet it was also Rankl's last appearance in the house. For by now he had broken. He had announced his resignation on 7 May 1951. He was to continue until thc end of the opera season and then go on tour with the company in July. And one of the saddest aspects of the whole sorry business was that, once he had made known his decision to resign, his performances in the pit had improved almost perversely. It was not merely that the relief of shedding that huge burden of responsibility at last allowed him to put all his energy and imagination at the service of the opera of the evening; it was as though in this single act, by this one gesture, which had in it elements of the egotism and aggression of the suicide, he had managed to unburden himself of stored bitterness. His resignation was a cry of resentment against the unceasing criticism to which he had been subjected and against the very injustice which had deprived him of the balm of appreciation and praise. He had begun the first of the season's two *Ring* cycles on 4 May, just three days before announcing his resignation, and *The Times* notice matched the orchestra in responding to him with unwonted generosity:

> Dr Rankl seems to have turned over a new leaf in the matter of fidgeting and so rattling his orchestra. The tone of the playing was consistently sweet and the detail beautifully fabricated in a translucent texture.

Praise from Ernest Newman followed for *Valkyrie*. 'The orchestra under Karl Rankl gave us some very sensitive playing,' he wrote: and Sylvia Fisher too responded to it, finding a new freedom and fervour for her Sieglinde, which, Newman thought, was 'excellently sung, with an admirable variety of psychological nuances'.

Praise indeed. And Rankl maintained this form for his *Salome*. But it can't be said that he was regretted. His passing from the house was only briefly mourned, and the manner of his going made his return unlikely. He was never, in fact, re-engaged. His last performance with the company was in the provinces on 31 July, which happened to be the very day when *The Fairy Queen* was revived at Covent Garden. As the curtain rose in London, Rankl occupied a very small space in the minds of most of those present. Webster was reminded that when it was first performed four and a half years earlier he had had to persuade Rankl that it was not the right opera with which to present the new Musical Director to his audience. In 1951 Constant Lambert, only a few weeks before his death, was again in the pit.

There was another unhappy postscript. In 1953 Rankl was understandably dismayed to find that there was no mention of him in the Coronation programme. He wrote angrily to Kenneth Clark:

> I suggest this amounts to almost a falsification of historical facts. Apparently Mr Webster has seen fit to omit any reference to the man who, unaided by anybody and hampered by antagonism from all sides, nevertheless succeeded in building up from scratch the opera company that still exists.

The omission was not surprising. Rankl's name would not lend any additional glamour to the occasion, and however sympathetic were his feelings towards him, Webster was a positive Sophie Fedorovich of an administrator when it came to eliminating what was not immediately relevant and practical.

But it was feared Rankl might be in a position to sue on the grounds of the damage done his professional reputation; Webster had Rankl's letter sent to the lawyers, and meantime composed one of his own clever letters and dispatched it to the north, where Rankl was now in charge of the Scottish National Orchestra. The brochure, he explained, was primarily a piece of publicity for the Coronation season, and his article in it was only a statement of his aims as Administrator and a factual account of what had been done. No one's work had been evaluated. He pointed to the fact that his attitude to Rankl, his approbation, was on record, it was on record in the Board minutes for 1951 that he had declared: 'The value of Dr Rankl's work in the formation of the company and the building of the repertoire could not be overestimated.' Rankl would have preferred to have it estimated in a more public manner! It was small consolation to him to be informed that Kleiber, currently in his third season as guest conductor, thought that Covent

Garden now had one of the best opera orchestras in the world, or that by this time Rankl's discoveries were capable of supporting the routine performances, which is to say, those revivals for which stars were not imported. That Sylvia Fisher, Constance Shacklock, Jess Walters, Edgar Evans, Adèle Leigh, Monica Sinclair and others could between them provide decent evenings in the house without the help of foreigners, this was just one of the points that Rankl wanted credited to him publicly.

Rankl was not regretted; his going, indeed, was a relief. He had come to represent a humble past which slipped away as he himself slipped out of the bright circle. He was in charge of the Scottish National Orchestra from 1952 until 1959, and Webster cabled him in October 1952: 'Am very sad cannot be with you tonight. I hear great things about beginning of season wish you tremendous success at this opening concert David.' Between 1958 and 1960 Rankl was also Musical Director of the Australian Elizabethan Opera Trust.

People who had worked well for Webster were not likely to be entirely forgotten by him, and discreet letters here, words in ears there, expressed his continued anxiety about Rankl's future. In 1962, for example:

> I am very concerned about the position of Rankl, and would willingly write to a few people to see if they could do anything about him, but can you think of any special channels? It seems to me and from my personal knowledge I think it to be true that he does a very good job indeed, especially if he is not in residence. Freelance conductors of a reasonable price are not as common as all that.

And that was just *one* letter. But Rankl didn't conduct at Covent Garden again, and indeed was not to set foot in the house until the first night of *Moses and Aaron*, by his old master Schoenberg, in 1965.

It was an additional grievance for Rankl that his opera *Deirdre of the Sorrows*, one of four works to win the Festival of Britain competition organized by the Arts Council, was never to reach the stage. In 1963 he wrote to Webster: 'Only to remind you that it is twelve years since the completion of my opera *Deirdre of the Sorrows*,' and it was no pleasure for Webster to have to write, shortly after his death, explaining to his widow that, whatever she might have heard to the contrary, 'I am afraid there is no prospect of us doing Karl's *Deirdre of the Sorrows*.'

Rankl died on 6 September 1968. On the 11th *Rhinegold* was given at Covent Garden, the first opera in the first of a pair of *Ring* cycles being given that autumn, and before the curtain rose Webster stepped out in front and addressed the house. He announced that the performance of *Rhinegold* was to be dedicated to Rankl, and he paid tribute to him.

The tribute, to some of those in the audience who had known the house in its early days – these included the biographer – seemed altogether apt. But the very heart of it seemed to be not so much a tribute to Rankl himself as to the four artists in particular who had supported the regime in the difficult years. 'Flagstad!' Webster pronounced the name and projected it impressively into the auditorium. 'Hotter. Schwarzkopf.' And 'Welitsch.' Names which it was a joy for Webster's lips to form. Well and good – these artists, besides giving pleasure with their performances, had been an inspiration to their English colleagues. But it was the achievements of these English artists which were Rankl's best testimonial. The names Fisher, Coates and co. did not, perhaps, come so resoundingly off the tongue, nor would it have given Webster himself the same joy to recall the humble beginnings with a scratch orchestra and an unstageworthy chorus. Possibly Rankl borrowed glamour on this evening from the names put beside his own, and perhaps Webster unconsciously, in 1968, wanted to dissociate the house and himself from the very humbleness of those beginnings. But it was only by recalling them that justice could be done to the memory of the man to whom the evening was dedicated.

PART TWO

Building

CHAPTER XII

Webster's 'family' · his arrogance · personal life-style · gala performances · relations with the public · with artists · general benevolence · toughness · Webster and royalty · his understatements · meanness · bons mots

In the Festival of Britain summer Webster was forty-eight. He'd been still a young man when he received Gishford's letter and went along to that lunch at the Ritz, and now middle age was upon him. A group was growing within the house which was composed of men and women of different tempers, some of them difficult and quirky – but a bond between them was the feeling they shared for Webster, and if they became something of a surrogate 'family' for him, they in turn were rewarded by a comparable comfort of solidarity, and enjoyed a real gratification in being accepted by Webster himself.

Muriel Kerr, of course, was of it, and there was Joe at the stage-door and Gertie in wardrobe. Sergeant Martin, the commissionaire, became over the years a familiar figure, spreading inside his plum-coloured uniform and from time to time requiring a larger size. There was Bill Bundy, the Technical Director, and John Tooley who became Webster's assistant. The Orchestral Manager Morris Smith was a genuine confidant, and he and Webster frequently lunched together: Smith was one of the very few people to whom Webster could uninhibitedly, and safely, unburden himself. Smith's Welsh background, perhaps, as well as his very long operatic experience, led some people to think him as much manipulator as manager, but if he was, he manipulated to good purpose. Honor Thackrah, his assistant, who succeeded him when he was promoted to become Orchestral Director, was also of the 'family'. Lord Harewood, at the very heart of the organization through the exciting 'fifties, was of it, and there was too Edward Downes, a member of the musical staff who began to emerge as conductor around 1953. A fiery young man with a dangerous rumbling courtesy, he was supported through his difficult times by Webster and Harewood, and in his turn contributed to the family solidarity, which made for a good atmosphere in the house and was one of the attractions for guest artists who returned again and again.

The job of General Administrator to start with had been only as big as the man who agreed to do it, and it hadn't attracted men already distinguished. Now it was beginning to. There was never really any question of Webster's being replaced, but there were those who hoped.

Sir Steuart Wilson was not altogether pleased to see his name on the programme as Deputy General Administrator, and he didn't rule out the possibility that one day he might step up into the significantly higher position. Webster wasn't pleased either, having to see his Deputy named a knight in Covent Garden programmes. He'd have preferred to see himself Sir David. But he hadn't justified a knighthood yet.

Wilson, once a pupil of the singer Plunket Greene and himself a lieder singer of great refinement, had already held important posts in the Musical Establishment, Musical Director of the Arts Council and then, up to 1950, Head of Music at the BBC, and the little draper with Shaftesbury Avenue connotations was something of a foreign body to him. But it was the knight and not the draper who was to leave the house first.

Criticism of Webster continued for a while, much of it harsh and much of it personal. In spite of it he continued to impose himself, and gradually, as he ceased to be a doubtful quantity, more and more people ceased to be suspicious or condescending. Though as he grew to celebrity they were more sensitive in noting his reactions to them. His habit of guarding himself was – not for the first time – taking the form of superciliousness and snobbery, but now they appeared in sharper relief. A critic who had recently given an Opera House production a bad notice accosted Webster with the words: 'I suppose you're not on speaking terms with me?' Webster's cold eye registered him. 'If I knew who you were,' he said at last, 'I could answer that question.' The critic retired worsted, and for a while resentfully made Webster himself rather than one of his productions the target for his criticism.

Arrogance was one of Webster's weapons. Balanchine's *Ballet Imperial* was put on at the Opera House in March 1950, and Balanchine and Lincoln Kirstein came to London. A visit by their then fairly recently established New York City Ballet was a possibility, and by many it was eagerly awaited; but negotiations didn't go well. Webster found their conditions unacceptable, and soon he didn't seem to care whether they came or not. While Webster was out of London one weekend and not to be reached, Balanchine and Kirstein took tea sadly with the ballet critic Richard Buckle. 'Webster is always like that at first,' Buckle assured them.

And it was indeed a different story after the first night of *Ballet Imperial*, with seventeen curtain-calls and Balanchine handed a wreath on stage by the dancers. Balanchine gave a party in the Crush Bar afterwards and, assuming that there was to be no visit, he made his farewells. But the success of the evening had certainly done nothing to discourage Webster, who was *now* prepared to love the Americans to death. 'You can't leave London,' he told them, suddenly all smiles, 'not till you've put your signature to a contract!' And he allowed generous terms. 'Believe it or not,' he conceded graciously, 'I'm *happy* to have the New York City Ballet;' adding the rider, 'I assure you, however, *that London will make or break you.*' For Webster, London was the centre of the world, and the centre of London was already the Webster Opera House. He was blandly swollen, puffed up to the size of the house which was, after all, himself.

And he wouldn't sell it short. There was a possibility that in 1950 his company might provide the opera for the Edinburgh Festival. Rudolph Bing, then running it, suggested that Covent Garden bring *Otello* and *Wozzeck*, which would both have to be mounted specially, and *Bohème* in the existing production: but he also proposed that the orchestra be less than sixty, which automatically ruled out *Wozzeck*, and *Otello*, amazingly, was still considered something of a novelty.

There was subsequently the idea of doing the première of Stravinsky's *The Rake's Progress*, which the composer was still working on but which might be ready in time. Webster had already been out to see Stravinsky in California. Having been offered it by Stravinsky's publisher, Ralph Hawkes, Webster was somewhat dismayed when the composer, having poured him wine, at last reluctantly informed him that it had been promised to La Scala. Webster couldn't, therefore, be sure of it for Edinburgh, and in fact in the end it was Venice who had the opera first (and in England it went to Glyndebourne).

1951 came and went, and Covent Garden still didn't go to Edinburgh. If Webster was sorry he didn't show it. The opera company had so far still only been seen outside England in 1948, in Brussels and Paris with *Peter Grimes*. And in the end, Edinburgh now asking for an operetta which would also have to be mounted specially and wouldn't be of much use to the company afterwards, (and it certainly wasn't the way he wanted the company presented), Webster accepted an invitation to present the company in Rhodesia as part of the 1952 Rhodes Centenary celebrations. It wasn't a showcase in the class of the Edinburgh Festival, but the company could more happily flex its muscles there, with the artists appearing in roles with which they were familiar in a repertory selected by Webster and not dictated to him by anyone else. An Edinburgh visit was not subsequently arranged till many years later.

In 1954 Webster received outside confirmation of his own estimate of his house: one Ilgenfritz offered the Metropolitan 125,000 dollars on condition that an opera of his was performed, and when the Met refused his subsequent short list included the Vienna State Opera, the Paris Opera – and Covent Garden. Webster refused Ilgenfritz in good company.

Webster's personal life-style, within the limits ordered by his Opera House routine, was in the main commanded by Jimmy, and commanded to give him the greatest possible stability. In that 1951 summer of Beecham and Flagstad and Krauss, Jimmy bought the house in Weymouth Street, hitherto only rented: so they were settled. When Webster's father died his mother came south to live, for a while in a London hotel and then in Brighton, where Jimmy rented, and later bought, another house, and weekends in Brighton became a part of the routine. David continued to organize their holidays and travel – they'd rent somewhere abroad each summer – while Jimmy made the running of the house, indeed of both houses, and the household bills, his concern. Their social life too. He tried to bring to Weymouth Street a wider range of people than just musical people. He'd forecast accurately enough the inevitable changes in their life-style, and he wanted to prevent it narrowing too far. Lydia Lopokova once wrote to Webster:

> I want to give a treat to Maynard's old friends Duncan Grant, Vanessa Bell, Clive and Quentin Bell. What do you think it should be? *Cinderella* of course! I would like five grand tier seats, I am willing to pay, and afterwards will you please join us for supper in Gordon Square? I never had a 'yes' from you yet. Do forsake No in relation to me!

Never had a 'yes'? If Webster had had such an invitation in his Liverpool Busybody days a Yes would have been certain. Gallantry alone, it might have been supposed, would have ensured his acceptance of so charmingly composed an invitation. But it was No yet again.

Party-going was not the same thing as party-giving, and the Weymouth Street parties, unobtrusively organized by Jimmy and hosted expertly by Webster, turned their home frequently into an invaluable annexe of the Opera House. A yearly event of a somewhat different order was the Christmas morning party, to which there was no admittance unless accompanied by a child. The Christmas decorations were the wonder of the day, with presents for all round the tree. For the children it was like coming to visit Father Christmas himself.

Without this background of stability Webster could not so relentlessly have continued to grow, matching his house. His persona imposed itself gradually as he showed himself, as much as in its larger business, in the day-to-day minutiae of running the Opera House. It wasn't all going off for quiet talks with a Massine or a Kleiber, or being delivered of a Welitsch or a Callas. He impressed at Board meetings, where he tended to interfere little – he merely listened and gave conclusions. He proved himself, in business matters, the equal of the businessmen on the Board. The little man with lists showed his mettle in the undramatic, but absolutely vital, engagements with the Treasury, the issue being to persuade them that Covent Garden's needs were greater than they thought they were. Presenting the budget to them was therefore a campaign in itself. 'You know, John,' Webster said one day to John Denison, the Arts Council Assessor at the Board meetings, 'I'd like to go back to business – it's so much more honest.'

Not unimportant in this context are the Galas: organizing them upsets the routine of the house, but in so far as they are helpful to the government, in providing hospitality for diplomatic missions and so on, they to some extent help to justify subsidy and encourage purses to open. There are two kinds of Galas, the annual ones for the Royal Opera House Benevolent Fund and the Royal Ballet Benevolent Fund, and the great State Performances, of which there have been only seven or eight since the war, which are arranged as part of the entertainment for a visiting Head of State. The first of these, for the French President Auriol, was in 1950, and had been proposed by Lord Waverley to the Lord Chamberlain. For the occasion the Director of the Victoria and Albert lent some Louis XV tapestry chairs to furnish the Royal Box, warning that 'the chairs have not been sat on for 150 years and I cannot therefore guarantee that they are safe.' He forgot to mention that in that time they'd not apparently been cleaned, so that when the ladies of the royal party got up from them the backs of their white tulle dresses were grey with dirt.

This detail apart, it was an evening of great glamour; even Guthrie, though he thought the house 'an artistic graveyard', conceded that at least on such occasions it 'certainly pays a dividend'. And such glamour counted not only with the government. There were others who positively craved it. In 1952 the *Tatler* noted a visit to the Opera House by Somerset Maugham,

> who had lived to see the opera die in London, and now live again; and only a few weeks ago he could be observed leaning out of a box and drinking in the lovely scene, yes, still lovely as ever, if you carefully avert the eyes from the general sartorial level of the rows of stalls.

In the *Sunday Express* a couple of years later Beverley Baxter described a first-night audience as

> the best dressed that we have seen for some time. No tiaras, and the dinner-jackets outnumbering 'tails' by six to one, but at least the general

> effect was encouraging. The stalls (price £1.15s.) were also heavily sprinkled with grey suits, brown suits, and suits of no shade or character in particular . . . but there was one resplendent box where five men in evening dress were in attendance on two ladies in full regalia. Well done, my gallant seven!

The Gallant Seven were multiplied on these few gala occasions – and there were those who could then, and only then, feel the house at last opened to good purpose. Nostalgia for a past era, for the glamour of pre-war was, albeit briefly, satisfied. This could not unreasonably be claimed as at least a very minor function of the Opera House: and proving the house capable of rising to these occasions was another way of confirming its status. But meanwhile Webster was aware that the very fact of opera's being sung in English could, again in Guthrie's phrase, be dangerously 'snob-repellent', and he couldn't afford to repel anyone.

He was particularly delighted by one of the galas because it seemed, in addition, to confirm the growing status of the opera company within the house. 1953 was Coronation Year – the radiant young Queen Elizabeth II was being crowned, and for the first time since 1914 an opera, and not a ballet, was chosen for the Royal Gala. The year before Harewood – on the Board since 1950, but soon to join the Opera House staff – had been on a ski-ing holiday with Benjamin Britten, and they had discussed together the kind of opera that qualified as 'national'. *Billy Budd* had followed *Peter Grimes* at the house, and Harewood knew he could not carry back to Webster a better present than the promise of a third Britten opera, especially a Britten opera for this special occasion. The story of Elizabeth and Essex had appealed to Britten and, sure enough, he was soon asking the Queen's permission to compose it especially for the Coronation. Webster's fingers itched to be holding the finished score. But would it be ready in time? Britten cancelled all engagements between spring 1952 and June 1953, and he worked non-stop on *Gloriana*. It *was* ready in time. It wasn't, as it happened, well received. Harewood and Webster had been delighted to fall on to a subject that appealed to the composer, and the Queen had given her go-ahead – but it seemed to many that, dealing as it did with the sad declining years of the first Elizabeth, the opera was hardly a suitable choice for the occasion. But Webster liked it. If it didn't please in 1953 he was sure that one day it would be appreciated.

The efficiency of the administration, particularly in those early days, could be questioned even by those most sympathetic. Kenneth Clark, for example, always a strong support of Webster's, was once driven to writing to Waverley to complain that the administration was 'chaotic', and he associated Lord Harewood in the complaint and another member of the Board at this time, the autumn of 1951, Edward Sackville-West. Who felt obliged to write to Webster:

> As you are no doubt aware, I have grumbled frequently, to George [Harewood] and K [Kenneth Clark] and other members of the Board, about dilatoriness in signing up singers, leaving things to the last moment, and so on . . . I am well aware of the difficulties of running Covent Garden at the present time, although I do think that, by being slow off the mark, we sometimes have to make do with singers inferior to those we might secure . . .

Lord Harewood, in June 1970, in *Opera Magazine*, describes Webster as being practical, not a theorist:

> better at balancing next year's repertory, at devising a high-point on which to bring the company noticeably back from tour, at supervising the ratio of new to old, sweet to sour, imports to local products, than he was as a long-term planner.

His career as a whole is a nice exemplar of self-interest identifying itself with a practical idealism. Webster loved his public and they knew it. Having to cancel a performance was anathema, and he'd do anything to avoid it. This very reluctance appeared under the guise of love of his public. A cast change, of course, was sometimes unavoidable, but the public never felt that he was failing to keep faith with them, and whenever a difficult change had to be announced, he announced it himself. The audience invariably roared their approval. He handled them well, not simply with cleverness and calculation, though that too, but also lovingly, and whatever it was he was asking them to buy they thought he was doing them a great favour. In *Bohème* one evening the Rodolpho, Kenneth Neate, lost his voice in the first act – it simply 'cut out'. In the interval Webster came backstage with Rankl, and phone-calls were made. He found Parry Jones comfortably ensconced in a corner of the Savage Club and effortlessly winkled him out, and then went in front of the curtain to explain to the audience that in the second act Silveri, the baritone of the evening, would be singing not only his own role but also the tenor leads-in for Neate, who would just be walking through his part; this would give Parry Jones time to arrive and get into costume and make-up, and he would take over Rodolpho in the third and fourth acts. The audience didn't feel cheated. On the contrary, Webster gave them a feeling of being privileged, of participating in an exciting theatrical event.

This *Bohème* found Webster still a tyro, but able, when the situation required it of him, to act with a remarkably swift, as well as calm, decisiveness. The same swift decisiveness, the other face of his normal dilatoriness, was to be relied on throughout his career. It was in the 'sixties that, with an *Aïda* scheduled for that very night, the tenor let them know at the Opera House only at midday that he wouldn't be available. Webster summoned the Resident Producer and the Stage Director to his office, and Miss Kerr was there with her notebook. Within ten minutes all arrangements had been made. *Tosca* was going to be substituted for *Aïda*. It was already too late to get the *Aïda* scenery out of the theatre and get in the *Tosca* sets from wherever they were stored, so the opera was going to be done without scenery, against black velvet curtains and with only the *Tosca* furniture! The soprano Gabrielle Tucci, engaged for Aïda only, was going to be asked nicely to do Tosca instead. Off went the Stage Director to give orders regarding sets, curtains, furniture, and off went the Resident Producer to prepare a walk-through. As they left Miss Kerr was already dialling, and in moments Miss Tucci, asked very nicely indeed by Webster, was agreeing without hesitation to undertake the role under these difficult circumstances. Put to her by Webster, the prospect was exciting, a challenge. And that evening she, and the other artists, naturally somewhat nervous, sensed the atmosphere in the house as Webster went out front to explain imperturbably to the audience the nature of the crisis that had faced the management. Webster, as usual, gave them a feeling of being privileged, and disappointment was already turning to anticipation as, to grand applause, he withdrew, the lights dimmed, and the huge curtain rose.

Another time, a piece of the gallery roof fell in. It was five o'clock in the afternoon and the gallery had to be closed. There was an announcement on the six o'clock news, but the house was sold out and people were stomping about outside furious. They'd paid and they were entitled. Some of them had had long journeys, from Oxford, from Brighton. The boss was called for. He arrived, very polite, very courtly. He apologized. 'I'm very sorry,' he told them. And he was. 'I'm very sorry, but we're protecting you. We're thinking of what's best *for you.* After much soul-searching it was decided that we daren't risk endangering you.' The mood changed to one of calm tranquillity. People milled about David Webster gratefully, insisting on the privilege of shaking him by the hand.

He was known for his benevolence towards artists, but even this was against a background, where necessary, of ruthlessness. He could be dangerous, and this was known, and no bad thing that it should be – it restrained anyone's impulse to be over-familiar, and could only increase the growing respect in which he was held. People couldn't imagine that David Webster required, or was in any way dependent on, their good opinion of him – but equally no one could imagine that there was any pleasure for him in being brutal, except perhaps the pleasure of conquering himself, of forcing himself to act, against his deeper inclinations, for the good of the organization, for the family as a whole. He could be brutal in dismissing people. The buffo tenor, Hubert Norville, who sang in the early seasons, at the end of one of them simply found a letter at the stage-door informing him that his services wouldn't be required for the next. Norville wasn't the only one over the years suddenly to find he no longer had employment at the Opera House. But if they were hurt by their dismissal, they weren't allowed to remain to make their hurt felt – as in Liverpool, people dismissed went instantly. Though there was the case of the soprano given to nagging Webster for more and more parts who was finally given all she wanted. She was overtaxed, she oversang, and shortly afterwards she departed the Opera House to be heard there no more.

And Webster expected loyalty unstinted. Opera Manager Pat Terry applied to be considered for the job of Artistic Director of the Edinburgh Festival, and asked for a reference. Webster refused to give one. 'You wouldn't do the job well. You're not qualified.' Pat Terry resigned, but had second thoughts. He withdrew his resignation, and Webster said he could stay on – but with the resignation still pending. A year or two later Webster told him that the time had come, and he must go, and he claimed that he was not sacking him, but merely accepting at last the resignation he had already been offered.

Webster's brutality, though, was a minor aspect, if not an altogether insignificant one. In return for loyalty he gave loyalty and an extreme consideration. Men fired by him sometimes left his office feeling as though he'd given them a rise – and, the facts presented tactfully, there can be seen to be a benevolent aspect too in removing people from positions they're not equipped to fill. Sometimes people leaving – this had been as true at Bon Marché as it was at the Opera House – felt apologetic, as though they'd betrayed a trust. Webster was brutal in discouraging talentless people and, given that his estimation was correct, it needs no special powers of divination to understand that, in long term, he was bestowing a favour. If Webster saw his house grow in splendour, there had to be, for a number, frustration and rejection: the very growth of the house meant that many had to be outgrown by it. It was part of Webster's job to refuse opportunities to people who wanted them but whom he didn't think talented enough: he couldn't therefore always guarantee his own popularity, but it is no part of an impresario's brief to be popular, except in so far as it helps him be effective.

Most striking, however, was Webster's sympathetic understanding and his general benevolence. It gradually became known that there were singers who had given loyal service who stayed on the payroll for years after they had ceased to sing regularly – and conductors were often besought by Webster to use singers patently now past their best. His constant grief, throughout his time at the Opera House, was that he was not able to establish a pension scheme for his singers. In later years, when many of his singers were established internationally, he didn't resent their not being available for Covent Garden. 'No,' he said, 'I haven't got a pension scheme. I can't prevent singers going to earn money like that.' He knew that singers were at their maximum earning capacity only between the ages of thirty and forty-five, they had no security in the future, and even the tax-system didn't encourage them to work in England.

He worried too about the retirement of chorus members and the orchestra. There was an old chorister whose wife had died recently, and he was drinking. 'I'm not going to fire that man,' Webster said. 'What will happen to him? He'll drink himself to death or die having nothing to do. *I have an obligation to him.*' There was no pension either to cover the stage crew, and another time it came to Webster's notice, through a conversation overheard in a pub, that Ted Lilley senior was in bad straits. 'Who would know?' he asked. His son on the Opera House staff. 'Send him over.' There was at least a Royal Opera House Benevolent Fund, derived from the profits of the galas, to help members of the organization in need. When news came of the death of one of his company members, David Allen, in a car accident, Webster was seen to cry: and he arranged that David Allen's widow received £400 from the Benevolent Fund. He worried about the dancer Gerd Larsen when her husband, Harold Turner, died, and he arranged for Covent Garden to bear the funeral expenses. When the tenor Dermot Troy died, leaving a wife and three children, a fund was started by fellow-artists not only from Covent Garden but also from Munich, Hamburg and Glyndebourne, and, regretting once again that there was no pension scheme, Webster saw to it that £150 was put aside from the Benevolent Fund. And when it was suspected that Norman Feasey had TB, with the prospect of nine months in hospital, Webster visited him, and was soon assuring him, 'I'll pay your salary as long as I can' – he knew that worry about home and money must be foremost in Feasey's mind.

There was love. When in the autumn of 1958 Callas became embroiled in a famous 'row' with Bing at the Metropolitan, Webster said to Arnold Haskell:

> An artist like Callas has a perfect right to be temperamental but a temperamental manager is always wrong. Think of it, she can no longer make a reputation but she can lose one in a single performance.

His attitude to artists in general was far enough, not only from Bing's but also from that of Maplesson, the famous Victorian impresario, who wrote of one of his tenors, Giuglini, that he

> was in many things a child. So, indeed, are most members of the artistic tribe, and it is only by treating them and humouring them as children that one can get them to work at all.

Artists under stress can be childlike in their behaviour, but Webster recognized that an artist must on no account be dismissed as merely childish. When artists came to him he knew that any detail they wanted to discuss with him was of importance to *them*. He would not underestimate the importance of anything which was important to the artist, while at the same time he had to think of a total project and the organization as a whole.

There was, too, the public gesture. Beloved Welitsch, his favourite and the public's, was brought back to sing when she was past her best. She had put strains on herself, unable to believe that that wonderful instrument her voice would not last forever. It didn't – but she was back to do Tosca in 1951, singing in German with the home team in English, and an oddly unidiosyncratic performance it was. And she returned, even so, in 1953, when her Musetta worked only dramatically, while her Lisa in *The Queen of Spades* was almost embarrassingly pallid. This kind of loyalty can be criticized, but part of the atmosphere of the house was built on it. In 1956, on a first night – Muriel Smith was doing Carmen – Welitsch with her magnificently red hair brilliant against a jade green cloak, and with her dishy new policeman-husband at her side to show off proudly, made a superb entrance, not this time on to the stage but into the foyer, and the crowds parted for her, as they don't normally even for royalty. Webster greeted her royally. 'Come, my dear.' He half-turned and waved her to the grand staircase. 'Let us now take champagne.'

If artists trusted him he earned their trust. Kathleen Ferrier, most memorably, twice sang Gluck's *Orpheus* at the Opera House in 1953: twice only, alas. It was known that she was ill, already gravely ill, and she was therefore a risk, 'But if she is brave enough,' Webster said, 'surely we can be too.' She was in great pain when she gave the performances, and for the audiences, many of whom knew the circumstances, they were doubly moving. Shortly afterwards she died, and it seemed, unbelievably, that she had raised her own monument, her lament for Eurydice becoming a symbol for the loss her friends, and her audiences, had now to suffer.

Maria Callas too was a risk after the scandal of the Rome 'walk-out' – at the gala before President Gronchi on 2 January 1958 she wasn't able to continue after the first act of *Norma*, and the performance had to be abandoned – but Webster rejoiced, he *only* rejoiced, to have her at his house for *Traviata* that summer, even though he couldn't get insurance for her. Nor could he for her Medea the following year, owing to the 'impossibility of arriving at a satisfactory definition of ill-health'. And in 1964 she was virtually 'brought back' by him for her Tosca.

And Boris Christoff – when word got about that he had had a brain tumour and a slow recovery from it no opera house would risk engaging him. Except, that is, for Covent Garden, where the following year, 1965, Webster welcomed him back with accustomed warmth. In *Boris* he showed himself still, as he was to continue for many years more, an artist amazingly in his prime. Christoff's confidence in himself, and international confidence in him, was restored. He gave a party for Webster at the Savoy and invited the press. 'My whole career,' he announced to them (though his speech was not reported), 'is henceforth owed to this man.'

Artists could be confident of his support. Arthur Carron, who had been reluctant to commit himself at first, had been engaged finally for *Trovatore*. He could not manage the top note of the 'Miserere', so while Carron as Manrico stood at the small window of the tower in which he's imprisoned, Edgar Evans stood beside him, out of sight, to sing the note for him. But at the last performance in the series Webster urged Carron to risk failure and sing the note himself. 'I will,' Carron agreed, 'but only if Edgar is there next to me.' Edgar Evans clasped his hand firmly, and Carron managed the note.

Another reason that Webster made himself trusted was that he could be discreet about others as well as about himself. He enjoyed telling stories but he didn't gossip, and people were encouraged to confide in him. He was a repository for their secrets. His caring was the keynote, and this was not contradicted by an underplayed, throw-away flamboyance. Lord Drogheda, who was to succeed Lord Waverley as Chairman, in his *Financial Times* obituary notice of 10 May 1971 drew attention to 'the old-fashioned sociability which, never reaching the familiar and the free and easy, used to be called "clubbable".'

Webster had the style often to disguise his toughness. His mode of insinuating understatement allowed him to make his points often without menace. A young conductor came to him complaining of one of the singers in a performance he'd been given to conduct. 'If you don't like him you don't *have* to conduct,' Webster told him with a dry geniality. 'Of course,' he went on, 'it's easier to replace a conductor than a singer . . .' The conductor conducted.

People working in the house felt his presence. He might be sitting near the back of the stalls at a rehearsal, or they might happen at any time to pass him in one of the corridors. He knew what was going on, and if a singer behaved disruptively, there was a possibility that at the end of a rehearsal Webster might be there with his return air-ticket, and a substitute singer already on his way to the appropriate airport.

Toughness was needed to preserve friendships while keeping a balance, and he drove hard bargains but kept business and friendship separate: Helpmann, like Ashton, was one who remained a friend even though in Webster's office he was often confronted by the businessman.

For all the weight of his authority, he could be effete, with a kind of 'camp' which was almost over-deliberately not flamboyant. This was a basis of his mutually amused, cordial relations with, among royalty, the Queen Mother and Princess Margaret. An apocryphal story has Webster standing beside the Queen Mother at the party given on stage for the Bolshoi Ballet after their first night, and the Queen Mother whispers to him: 'Tell me, David, what do Russians think of Queens and people like us?' (In fact the dancers, most of them, were overwhelmed – they confided to the dancer Leslie Edwards, who speaks some Russian and was delegated to help them to food, that the splendour of the scene was too much for them, they'd never seen such people and they couldn't eat.)

Confirmed is another story, whereby Queen Fabiola wore a gold lamé coat with a train to one of the galas, and cast it off when she reached the Crush Bar, leaving it on a chair. Webster passed by with Princess Margaret. 'As soon as the national anthem's over,' he threatened, 'I'm coming back to try it on.' 'I don't believe you,' said Princess Margaret. 'I'll come back and watch you.' Webster, as always, was faithful to his word, and they did come back together at least to examine the coat.

Webster liked clothes and display, and in other circumstances it's conceivable that he might for the fun of it have slipped into the coat for a moment! One winter he was off to Canada and found that his old friend Sir Malcolm Sargent was to be on the same plane – and he instantly went into sartorial competition with that snappiest of dressers. 'I've got a lovely fur coat,' he boasted. 'So have I,' returned Sargent, looking down from his lean height. 'I've got a very nice fur cap to keep out the cold,' Webster continued. 'I'll be getting one too,' said the elegant Sargent. 'And may I ask,' Webster put it to him, man to man, 'what jewellery you'll be wearing?' For the trip Webster had actually borrowed a superb full-length Edwardian fur coat from a friend, and another had given him a mink lining for it – the best mink, unfortunately, and therefore too heavy. The result was that Webster put his shoulder out of joint, and he and Jimmy dolefully did sums and worked out how much that coat had cost them in osteopath's fees!

In lighter moments Webster remained apparently sagacious and still self-contained, his words as judiciously measured as when he conducted the most momentous negotiations. He was still the Administrator when, for example, someone looked along a line of girls in the corps de ballet and grimaced at their peg-top regularity and sexlessness, remarking, 'Those girls could do with having their bottoms pinched!' A momentarily loosened-up David Webster rather bravely responded with, 'And so could some of the boys!'

His drive towards concealment made understatement the readiest of his weapons. 'Why do you never say how good the orchestra is?' he was one day asked by his good friend Morris Smith. 'The day they aren't marvellous,' Webster unhesitatingly replied, 'I'll be the first to tell you.' And he had his mode of insinuating understatement which it was a pleasure to provoke him into exercising. Bill Bundy was sent to Munich with Leslie Hurry to see *The Ring* produced there by Hartmann, who was to do it at Covent Garden that summer, and Webster had recommended that they stay at the Four Seasons Hotel. 'The food in Europe's bad. The best, in my opinion, is at that hotel.' On his return Bundy went to Webster's office to have his expenses approved. Webster examined the accounts. 'Hm.' He looked up over the top of his glasses. 'I assume,' he said drily, 'that the *oysters* were very good.' The same year Harewood was sent to Hamburg to hear Maria von Ilosvay sing Fricka in *The Ring* there. Von Ilosvay was not only excellent, she was also the wife of Günther Rennert, at this time the Hamburg Intendant, and the day after she had sung the couple took Harewood and his wife to dinner. Next day Harewood sent Frau Rennert flowers, and put down the cost, all of £2, as expenses. This Webster, showing his still relatively provincial outlook, refused to allow, saying that he could not possibly get it past his auditors. It was in vain that Harewood explained that it was the invariable custom on the continent to send flowers when one had been entertained. Webster remained adamant, finally suggesting that Harewood put it down to drinks!

If he didn't gossip, he was certainly an anecdotist – had he lived on into old age he could only have declined into anecdotage. He knew Douglas Cooper, a noted art collector living in the South of France, and a sheep millionaire brother of Cooper's, over on a trip from Australia, rang to ask for two tickets. Webster refused him. He must queue at the box office like anyone else. 'I wouldn't dream,' he would afterwards explain, 'of asking him *for two free sheep!*' And he liked to create *mots* which others could repeat. He was at the Memorial Service for Norman Walker, the English bass who had performed nobly alongside distinguished visitors in the early Wagner performances. It was cold, and Webster was shivering. 'God,' he murmured to his neighbour, Geraint Evans, 'if it gets much colder we'll be at our own Memorial Service!'

Once his stories had found a form which satisfied him he didn't very much alter them. He enjoyed telling the one about Pavlova and Mrs Wishart, and there was another which was a particular favourite. He made a habit of dropping in to see the company on their provincial tours, and in 1956 once he caught a performance of *Valkyrie*, it might have been in Manchester and it might have been in Birmingham but that wasn't the point: it was somewhere in that provincial darkness out of which he had come himself. And the performance was a splendid one, conducted by Reginald Goodall and with the famous Hilde Konetzni as Sieglinde. He loved describing the moment of great ecstasy in the love duet when quite suddenly she performed a beautiful sweeping movement, one he'd not seen before, and ended kneeling at her lover's feet. He was deeply moved, and tears sprang to his eyes. He would go on to explain that what had actually happened was that the lady had *lost her tooth* and had seen it caught in the light – gleaming like Rhinegold! Her swooping joy was the joy of discovery, not the ecstasy of love. There was panic in the interval, with Konetzni not at all sure she could continue with a tooth missing. Stage Director Elizabeth Latham happily had an inspiration. Wouldn't chewing-gum keep it in? She sent out for some. It worked. It *just* kept the tooth steady for the rest of the performance.

If Webster had left the house at the same time as Rankl he'd have rated no more than a footnote in this century's theatre history, but by the end of the 'fifties he'd already made his main contribution and earned his place. For a long time he was still expected to justify himself. 'I've been asked yet again,' he once complained, 'what qualifications do I have to run this opera house. D'you know what I told them?' His answer was compounded of negatives. 'I don't want to conduct, I don't want to produce, and I don't have a mistress who wants to sing.' He knew that it was his achievements which would eventually have to speak for him, and it wasn't so very long before they were beginning to.

CHAPTER XIII

Foreign directors and designers · Kleiber again · *Rosenkavalier* · English singers abroad · *Wozzeck* and *Elektra* · Callas in *Norma* · her success and Webster's contributions · her importance to Covent Garden

Webster, without either a Musical Director or a Director of Productions, felt himself more than ever in charge. He'd justified the use of foreign artists, and now there were going to be more of them. Foreign directors and designers and conductors. He was a greedy provincial housewife let loose suddenly with a shopping-list in a top European store. Goods from everywhere sparkled in his eye.

So far there'd been only the two German directors, Schramm and Tietjens, in charge of the Wagner repertory and *Fidelio*. They'd been highly traditional in manner, and helpful to the younger singers in handing on to them something of a sense of the European tradition. Now in the early 'fifties the foreign entry included Rennert and Rudolph Hartmann, names respected in the major opera houses of the world. To Christopher West, staying on as Resident Producer, a subordinate position compared with Brook's, fell the extremely important but not always exciting task of rehearsing revivals and introducing new artists into them. He was highly regarded by Webster and Harewood, and both in revivals and in the new productions allotted him he was agreeably unwayward, something not always appreciated by the music critics. And so far, too, all the designers had been British, apart only from Dali and Wakhevitch brought in by Brook to make their spectacular contributions. Now foreign designers began to be brought in, and from 1953 new work from Wakhevitch was seen almost yearly.

But at first it was the contribution of guest conductors above all which marked this as a time of expansion. Beecham kept in touch, even sending in a list of works – he liked lists – from which he proposed that two new productions a year be mounted for himself. He was now in his seventies, and even though it was doubtful how serious he was about actually taking on performances, he liked to be embroiled in operatic affairs. But there were two further *Mastersingers* at the end of 1951, the first of them his two hundred and fiftieth performance at Covent Garden. Clemens Krauss returned for *Fidelio* in 1952 and in 1953 for *Mastersingers*, and Webster was discussing a further engagement for him at the time of his death in May 1954.

In the early 'fifties it was two artists in particular who imposed themselves. One a conductor and one a singer. The first of these was the first of the guest conductors – Erich Kleiber. He appeared during two more seasons only following his first, and then no more. Webster couldn't tie him down as Principal Conductor even, let alone as Musical Director, and Kleiber's association with the State Opera in East Berlin through the period when he was appearing at Covent Garden was one of Webster's greatest anxieties.

But Kleiber's importance to the house bears little relation to the time he was actually in it. His influence pervaded the house, and everybody, whether actually working under him or not, was affected. He was a keen psychologist; an opera conductor who was also a man of the theatre; a great conductor who was also a great teacher. He *communicated* with his artists (Rankl had been known to bark out during a stage rehearsal, 'Fisher, what do you think you are doing there?') Kleiber was a psychologist as much in his handling of people as in his understanding of the dramatic action of his operas. 'I have to know my singers,' he used to say. 'I must like them before we can make music together. The music is what we are working at – working *together*.' He was a superlative technician who could say to his orchestra, 'Gentlemen, if you can't hear the singer then you're playing too loud.'

He was loved even though he was always potentially frightening. Like Webster, he could allow moments of humour and even a kind of intimacy which didn't forfeit respect and which no one ever tried to take advantage of. He used humour as a tool, manipulatively, to create the atmosphere he required (though he could on occasion be misunderstood – when a replacement was needed for Wilma Lipp as the Queen of the Night in *The Magic Flute*, Kleiber asked Webster with insufficiently obvious irony if he had heard 'that *fantastic* Queen of the Night from Chile'? Unfortunately Webster hadn't, and, wrongly assuming Kleiber to have meant fantastically good, he went ahead with the otherwise inexplicable engagement of the said soprano for the role!)

But mostly Kleiber's humour worked effectively. Like Webster, too, he was scrupulously careful about not undermining an artist's precious and all-to-easily shattered confidence. He once asked Rhydderich Davies, playing the Attorney in *Rosenkavalier*, 'What are those rests for in your music?' Davies was none too sure. 'He's an asthmatic old darling, that's what they're there for,' Kleiber explained. Davies was soon almost choking himself trying to be asthmatic, and everyone laughed. 'I can't do it!' he protested. 'You *can* do it,' Kleiber insisted. 'You can do it because you're an *artist*.'

Webster had assured himself, when he first went to see him in Switzerland, that Kleiber was prepared to take an enormous interest in English singers; Webster knew that he had found a man who, like Rankl, shared his own faith in them. *Rosenkavalier* was the only opera

Kleiber conducted in each of his three seasons at the house, and its progress in Joan Cross's production almost of itself charts the company's progress. Not an 'event' in the same way as *Wozzeck*, but in its different way at least as important. Fisher and Shacklock continued in their roles, and in Kleiber's second season the Sophie was the Danish soprano Ruth Guldbaek; he considered the *blend* of these three voices to be the best in the world. That was a success for Webster to congratulate himself on. Next time, with Adèle Leigh and Howell Glynne, Webster could rejoice in an entirely home team. The praise earned by the production and the home team after Kleiber's departure continued to belong partly to Kleiber, whoever else might be conducting: and Webster could point to this *Rosenkavalier* as an exemplar of the success of his policy at the house.

Kleiber arranged for singers to study abroad and he promoted foreign appearances. Shacklock was the first. She sang in Amsterdam and The Hague during the Wagner Festival in November 1951, and in June 1952 she was singing Brangane under Kleiber at the State Opera, the first British opera star called in to fill a breach at the last moment, and the first English artist to enter Berlin after the war. Webster rejoiced in her success – it was also the company's, and his too. In Kleiber's 1952 Rome *Ring* Fisher was the Sieglinde and Otakar Kraus Alberich, with Edgar Evans and Frederick Dalberg also in the cast. Kleiber reported Fisher's success excitedly:

> She has been singing gloriously, and all the papers without any exception have singled her out as the best in the cast. This is true. It is her first experience on an enormously big stage, miles away from the conductor, and she has been reliable and splendid. Her voice has been praised for its limpid quality, its nobility, its passion and of course its perfect intonation and great beauty. We are terribly happy about her success and hope it means much to her and gives her more confidence and cheers her up for the future.

This was as important a letter as any Webster had so far received during his time at the Opera House. He had known there was ultimately no reason why English singers shouldn't be accepted as the equal of any. He had dreamed of the day when they would be in demand everywhere. But he would not have been able to forecast when that day, towards which he was working, would eventually arrive. He couldn't even be certain that it would be in his own time. Not until this letter, which Kleiber sent to him from Rome on 24 March 1952.

Fisher's success was a portent, but for many years to come the English singer had still his way to make. But *now* Webster was confident: even if for a decade at least every singer going abroad would still be an ambassador. Shacklock was booked to sing in South America under Kleiber in 1956, but his recent death meant that she worked under Leitner instead. 'Are there any more like you in England?' she was asked. 'Lots,' she confidently replied. And in 1962 Geraint Evans was engaged for the Salzburg Festival and Karajan, impressed by him, asked: 'Are there any young English singers you can recommend to me?' Needless to say, there were. And if each singer was an ambassador abroad during these years, he was also bringing back with him invaluable experience – wider horizons and a sense of opera as international, as well as the psychological 'uplift' of the approval of foreign audiences and glowing notices. English singers for a long time had to make their way without the help of recordings, for it was to be many years before record companies considered them marketable, and as distinguished conductors came and went in the house Webster was sometimes influenced in his choice by the hope that one or other might provide some of the company with the opportunity to record.

Another token of Kleiber's real involvement in the company's fortunes was the performance he gave in the summer of 1952 of Beethoven's Choral Symphony. This was intended to launch the welfare fund for the Opera House orchestra and chorus, who were used in the performance along with company soloists; unfortunately the idea behind the concert was not followed up.

The general development of the company was typified by the *Rosenkavalier* performances: but there were the 'events' too, which draw attention to the house and define its status internationally. If the history of the house asks to be written in terms of *Boris* and *Salome*, then the sequence has to be continued, through *The Queen of Spades*, to *Wozzeck* in January 1952. For its Berlin première in 1925 Kleiber had been permitted no less than thirty-four orchestral rehearsals for *Wozzeck* – nothing like this was possible at Covent Garden. (Though Kleiber was by no means undemanding. 'If there is no trouble in a house, then I *make* trouble,' was his boast. There was a tendency for arguments to be settled with the threat of 'Well then, I am going back to South America' – where, apparently, whatever Kleiber had wanted Kleiber got! Webster did his best, and a certain amount of rearrangement was often necessary.)

Designs were entrusted to Caspar Neher, who had been in Berlin at the time of the *Wozzeck* première, and, since Michael Benthall was not available to work with Kleiber again, Rudolph Hartmann was approached. In the end, setting his face against one of the 'clever young men', Kleiber accepted Sumner Austin, a baritone who had sung with Sadlers Wells before the war and directed several operas for them – though there was no detail which was not approved by the conductor, and not a few suggested by him. The overall conception was Kleiber's, and the presentation had a rare integration of its elements as well as musical sensitivity. (Directors known mainly at Sadlers Wells were rarely invited to Covent Garden, and then usually, as in Austin's case, when the pit contained such a maestro as Kleiber who would not tolerate self-proclaiming theatricalism to usurp the stage: it's no accident that Denis Arundell was invited only for the Beecham *Bohemian Girl*. Here was a weakness inherent in Webster's Shaftesbury Avenue orientation.)

Marko Rothmuller gave one of his most dynamic performances in the title role, but even more important from the company point of view was that Kleiber insisted on double-casting for all the roles, apart from that of Marie, played throughout by Christel Goltz. 'Here,' he told the company, 'we have no understudies.' The production was not the less important because it didn't do well at the box office, and even at times of financial crisis Webster was loath to cut back on new productions, pointing out that to shrink from these special efforts was itself too great a risk. But a *Wozzeck* had all the more to justify itself by its artistic success, and there couldn't be too many of them.

Kleiber's last new production was *Elektra*, in May 1953, (important besides as the first non-Wagner German opera to be given in the original language). This wasn't a box office success either, and Webster hadn't expected it to be; it had to justify itself in other ways. There were casting difficulties, and although Webster was used to negotiating with singers and making promises to conductors which he wasn't sure he could keep, casting for *Elektra* proved more difficult than usual, and it looked at one time as though Kleiber wasn't going to be amenable. Goltz was to have been Elektra, then Kleiber had wanted Astrid Varnay. Finally he'd been offered Erna Schluter. And that was only one of the roles – the same thing seemed to be happening right down the cast list. But all was well finally. On the night Schluter was a heroine using diminishing resources to great effect, acknowledged by Kleiber as well as by the none-too-large audience as one of the role's best interpreters in the opera's still short history. Webster was delighted, too, to note another success for Edith Coates. Later that summer Ruth Kleiber wrote to Muriel Kerr from Munich, where her husband was again conducting *Elektra*: 'I like Coates's Clytemnestra better the more I see of another in the part . . . And the Covent Garden orchestra *certainly* played better. There's no question about that.' This was the kind of letter Webster treasured. It gauged for him his company's progress, it gave him some idea of how his artists and his house were measuring up internationally.

But if the Kleibers were pleased with Erich's work at Covent Garden, he was not to be wooed back again after the summer of 1953. For Kleiber could find better conditions elsewhere and more money. Money of course *had* been a problem from the start. In his first season he'd settled for £120 per performance, rising to £150, but for his second he asked £200, and later increased his demands to £225. But by this time – these discussions were taking place in the summer of 1951 – Krauss and Beecham, and Knappertsbusch too if he came, were settling for between £100 and £150. (Like singers, conductors in the years to come were to up their fees dramatically, but in 1951 £150 was not a laughable figure.) Webster pointed out to the Board that Kleiber worked much harder than any other conductor, and it was agreed that he must be retained. It was agreed to pay him £250 per performance, and Webster prayed no one would get to hear about it. But Beecham did, and he too was soon asking for more.

By the summer of 1953 Kleiber was demanding double the rate paid to any other conductor whatsoever. And by this time some other large talents had been spending themselves in the house – Issay Dobrowen, Vittorio Gui and Barbirolli among them – and Webster now felt that no one was too big for him at least to approach. He was already well accustomed to paying his artists, in lieu of cash, with (genuine) love and admiration. From a possible point of view he was even the Unconscious Conman. Other professional men are not expected to reduce their fees – people don't ask solicitors to take less, or expect shop-keepers to ignore price-tags. Kleiber, regretfully, had to be let go. The Webster love and admiration had won wonderful service from Kleiber, and it is possible that, had Erich not had a devoted wife watchful of his interests, he might have won more. Not that Ruth wasn't appreciative too. In 1958, two years after Erich's death, she wrote to Webster:

> Nothing that happens at Covent Garden leaves me indifferent, and I want to be remembered to all who remember me. Papito loved the place, loved the orchestra – and I am sure that you are (and were) one of the few people in the world (in places of importance) who really, *truly*, knew what Erich Kleiber was!! And for that – as well as for the many times you were sweet and kind to us – I write today with special greeting and regards for Miss Kerr, too.

The fiftieth anniversary of Verdi's death, in January 1951, had come and gone without any celebration at Covent Garden. Webster felt guilty. *The Sicilian Vespers* had been discussed, possibly to be given in preference even to *Wozzeck* as Kleiber's second new production at the house. Webster would not have relished postponing *Wozzeck* again, but he liked the idea of a new Verdi opera, if only because it would help him strengthen the Italian repertory, which from the start had given far more trouble than the German. (Though *Sicilian Vespers* had actually been composed originally for the Paris Opéra, with a French text, it was essentially Italian opera and normally sung in Italian, not French.) Kleiber had conducted it when it was given in Florence as part of the Verdi celebrations at the Maggio Musicale. At Covent Garden the work was going to be sung in English, with Edgar Evans, probably, beside one or two outstanding artists from Kleiber's Florence production. Boris Christoff had been in it, he wanted to work with Kleiber again, and he spoke English. The soprano too spoke English, and although she was new it seemed that they couldn't do better: she'd caused quite a stir in this *Vespers* under Kleiber. She was Greek, and had subsequently made a successful La Scala debut. Like Christoff, she also was going to be asked to sing in English. Now, what was her name? Webster wasn't good on names. Oh yes. It was – a Miss Maria Callas.

These plans for a Covent Garden *Sicilian Vespers* came to nothing. But the young Callas wasn't forgotten. It is she, of course, who is the second artist of particular importance to Covent Garden in the early fifties (and after).

The agent Wilfred Van Wyck had written to Webster about her at the time of the Florence appearances:

> I know I'll never be able to persuade her to audition, as she is already the biggest attraction at the Opera Houses in Italy, and she has made her name in only two years . . . when she sang Traviata in Florence last winter, they had to call out the fire department and the police to control the mobs trying to get into the Communale.

But if she wasn't prepared to audition, she'd like to sing at Covent Garden, and would be available the following May and June if she were given enough notice.

Webster didn't delay. Callas in 1951 was established in Mexico and South America, but not outside Italy, in Europe. In Europe London was going to be her first non-Italian capital, and it was arranged that her debut role, though not under Kleiber, would be Norma, the Druid priestess in the Bellini opera, and the date was fixed as June 1952. But it had to be postponed.

Instead, *Trovatore* was given to welcome back a pre-war favourite, the mezzo Ebe Stignani. *She* didn't get a new production, but the opera was given in Italian for her, just as *Tristan* had been given in German in 1947 for Flagstad: it was Covent Garden's first post-war all-Italian performance. And indeed Stignani brought to Italian opera something of the might and majesty Flagstad brought to German. She was the kind of artist to elevate the status of the Italian repertory.

And meanwhile Webster had cabled to Callas at the Verona Arena:

> ALL GOOD WISHES FOR TONIGHT'S GIOCONDA STOP OWING TO YOUR MEXICAN COMMITMENT IN JUNE WE POSTPONED NORMA PRODUCTION UNTIL NOVEMBER AND WE ARE ABSOLUTELY COUNTING ON AND LOOK FORWARD TO YOUR PARTICIPATION.

Advance reports had whetted appetities, even if the new singer couldn't yet have the glamour of a Zinka Milanov, the Jugoslav singer from the Met who most nobly upheld the Italian grand opera tradition, or of Renata Tebaldi, whose tones had already been admired at Covent Garden when she sang Desdemona in La Scala's *Otello*. At first the demand for *Norma* tickets was not overwhelming. The opera had last been heard at the Opera House in 1930, when it had been primarily a vehicle for Rosa Ponselle – mustn't there be something wrong with a work unsung for so long? There must be good reason for its neglect, surely. Philip Hope-Wallace's *Guardian* piece expressed enthusiasm for the opera, but not aggressively, calling it a

> desuete masterpiece of the bel canto era which set the salons of the 1830s sighing and languishing with its innocent harmonies, its mild, suave accompaniments, and its marvellously extended, plangent melody.

The opera was only mounted, as a 'special', because it was part of the repertory rediscovered by Callas; she was the reason for its revival, but it was as well to have in the cast with her the proven Stignani, who would bring excitement and distinction to the evening even if the new singer were to disappoint.

Norma's first aria, her introduction into the opera, is *Casta Diva* – a prayer to the 'chaste goddess' whose shrine she guards. No more fitting introduction could have been devised for this artist who is a High Priestess of her art. There are those who look back on that first night (even if Ernest Newman found her 'slightly sub-Normal') as an event of supreme importance. Not merely in the fortunes of the Opera House but in their own lives too, for they found their imaginative lives extended, and their sensory and emotional capacity confirmed to them or revealed in a new intensity. It is given to few artists, only the greatest, so to impose themselves. Her audience could register imperfections here and there, but capitulate, many of them, to the noble and heroic spirit of the artist imposing itself *above and beyond* specific virtues, and in spite of faults or limitations. Her reign at the Opera House can be said to have begun even before the first night, for at the first orchestral rehearsal she had sung 'Casta Diva' with full voice and the orchestra, rare event, had applauded her.

She reigned – no other word is possible – for only a dozen or so years, and gave in all thirty or so performances of half a dozen roles. Little enough compared with a Patti or a Melba, who appeared season after season and whose reigns are reckoned in terms of quarter of a century. But, like Kleiber's, Callas's importance bears little relation to the time she was actually at the house. Through her virtually self-sacrificing intensity she demonstrated what is meant by ambition and aspiration in the arts. For this Dionysiac artist, exaltation on the stage was the normal mode.

This young singer came to what was still a second-rate house. Her success at Covent Garden was not unimportant in her own career, but it had an enormous effect on the progress of the still comparatively new regime at Covent Garden. She brought a splendour to the house, and she transformed it. The press recognized in her an exciting artist if not a perfect one, but the audience responded in a different way. It wasn't a question of making balance sheets, here a virtue, there a fault. On the one side a vocal blemish or two, on the other, well, a considerable list of virtues. Here was a magnitude in presence, in vocal style, in ambition. Opera lives, proclaimed the young Maria Callas in her performance on that first night, it is not a fading form any longer, more vivid in memory than in its present form. There were no heights, she suggested in her own person, that opera cannot now, in this day, scale. Heights were being scaled, this very night, and at Covent Garden. Webster thrilled to the excitement she had stirred up in his house, which was not going to be the same again. The first-night *Norma* was sold out, but there had been seats for all other performances. But not, he guessed, for long. Next day the rush for tickets began. It was good to show the Arts Council full houses, but that was only a small part of it. His house was not going to be the same again after Callas had appeared in it.

He was audience for Callas. He had joined the applause the orchestra accorded her at rehearsal, he capitulated to this great artist once and for all time. She was his 'love-child', and his relationship with her was to amount almost to a surrogate love-affair, while *she* was never more at home, working at the top of her bent, fully and gloriously extended, than when she was at Covent Garden. For Webster had a gift to bestow on her too – Covent Garden as a surrogate home, and a share in the 'family' which was beginning to be built at its centre. If she warmed the house with her genius, she was herself given a warmth of family feeling to which she responded gratefully.

It was a great love, that of Covent Garden and David Webster for Maria Callas. Webster could hardly *not* have responded. Like Welitsch, Callas was an artist of courage, and he *had* to respond: she was an artist who 'exposed' herself. He responded with a rare sensitivity and understanding. Callas, too, had something in common with Webster. She too was not given to exculpating herself. She liked to appear in disguise, to sail under false colours, thus putting people to the test. Would they, would they not, see her through her disguise? She too had the reserve of an essential loneliness, a reserve shattered magnificently, and heriocally, in performance.

There was perversity here Webster could savour. He experienced this reserve in Callas as a protective instinct born of terror and excessive sensibility and of a kinaesthetic memory of pain – which made her not only permit but wilfully encourage the growth of that absurd and banal image of the tigress. She was finally locked into a false myth. It is, of course, easier to conceive of a prima donna fighting with a manic selfishness for her own glory than it is to believe in an essentially frail and vulnerable woman fighting to preserve and exercise her genius against odds. Vulnerability was her keynote. *Could* she fill out this phrase, execute that action? To a degree that cannot be claimed by many other artists she had lodged within her imaginative eye the platonic idea of perfection in phrase and action – but could she *do* it perfectly? And were the people with whom she had to collaborate going to help her?

She sometimes felt, too, that she was liable to attack by that unconscious antagonism to the artist which is common in many people. This antagonism is not unknown in the non-artists who abound in the world of artists, though David Webster, as Callas soon sensed, was entirely free of it. And if not by antagonism, Callas was certainly, throughout her career, menaced by other people's inadequacy and non-comprehension, a non-comprehension which, like the complex Webster himself, she sometimes seemed almost deliberately to provoke. But Webster instantly sensed the reality of the Callas persona that day he heard her at the orchestral rehearsal, and he prepared to promote himself her protector.

When she first appeared gallant Philip Hope-Wallace thought her 'tall and splendid, like one of Millais's pictures of mid-Victorian divas'. The truth of the matter was rather that, with her brawny arms and her deliberate swagger, she was more like Popeye than a Millais, a Popeye surmounted by the head of Hermione Gingold. Gingold, as it happened, was there in the Opera House one evening to inspect the new singer – having perhaps had a resemblance reported to her? Callas's Norma asserted itself swaggeringly. She brought a huge sense of danger on to the stage with her, partly by anticipating danger. The tension in her performances was incomparable: and it was a pleasure for the audience merely to anticipate the relief from tension that would follow the resolution of the dramatic situations and the removal of danger. The rebirth of the emotional spring in performance was so alarmingly true that, uncomfortably, the drama seemed to be unrolling there and then for the first time.

When she returned in 1957 after three or four years' absence, and after her notorious weight-loss, there was still an essential element of disguise in her very slimness and elegance. Callas had, within that large form, shrunk timorously. Now she had become beautiful. And yet not beautiful. She was imposing herself on the world's hostile eye as beautiful while still feeling herself misrepresented. She carried within herself a sense of her unworthiness, almost of ugliness – if she wore a new mask it was still a tragic one, and she was pleading, even though too proud to plead, to be accepted as beautiful. She was a figure at once tragic and pathetic.

And here is the basis of her characterizations, into which she instilled the psychological basis of her own character. She habitually presented a figure who believed herself unworthy of love, and was therefore a solitary – a kind of emotional suicide. In her roles, when she loved she loved totally, her whole life bound up in this one love for which there would not be any substitute in case of disappointment or betrayal. A line from Donizetti's *Lucia di Lammermoor* characterizes all her heroines: *La spème, la vita, riposi in un cor* ('My hopes, my life, I pledged to this one heart'.) The mystery of having inspired love brought wonder to her heroines – there was an extraordinary intensity in her being surprised into both experiencing love and into returning it. An intensity extraordinary because she believed herself not worthy. The Callas heroine loved *desperately*, and it was despair when love was threatened which found its outlet in jealousy, which in a Callas performance was most importantly only another face of love.

Callas slim was the more exposed, the more pitifully vulnerable. Vulnerable even in the matter of her vocal imperfections. There was even a kind of poignancy in her agonized uncertainty; would she reach and sustain this or that note, would she be able to trace to its end, and colour as she so magically could, the phrase which musically and dramatically she had furbished to perfection in her imagination? Even the question of would her strength support her through the performance – the very question of would she actually be well, would she be there at the theatre for the performance – heightened the sense of her vulnerability. Jon Vickers, who is in fact shorter than Callas, refers to her as 'the *little* Maria'. He sang Jason to her Medea in 1959, and was struck by 'the almost masochistic way she'll drive herself into her part. She won't let the little Maria show through.'

The Tigress was the preferred image of press and publicists, and of herself. She was much more nearly a puppy-dog with a crushed paw. Nowhere was she more sympathetically welcomed than at the Opera House, where Webster and the 'family', that extension of himself, were ever-ready to shelter her, and to accommodate themselves to her. Webster's first protective act was performed during those first *Normas*. Stignani, the Adalgisa in these performances, had sung the role in the opera many times before, and was accustomed to taking her curtain-call at the end of the second act as Adalgisa does not reappear in the third. On the opening night she took her call as usual and went home – and at the end of the evening, though Callas's own reception was not less than overwhelming, the house called for Stignani. This was disconcerting to Callas, and Webster asked Stignani, the senior singer, if she would for the remaining performances stay to take a curtain-call at the *end* of the opera. She agreed – 'because Mr Webster is asking me.'

Webster, with his deep empathy for Callas, was ready from the very beginning, to assume that she was not a 'difficult' artist, at the same time acknowledging that she had a right to be difficult; and he accommodated himself in a way both protective and self-abnegating. In the warmth of the house she was given the confidence to be adaptive, and she wasn't difficult, apart from one single episode in which she had right entirely on her side. Minotis, head of the Greek National Theatre, had been brought in to direct *Medea*, and some months before the première he said that he wanted the slow dance at the beginning of the opera performed by a dozen members of the chorus, not by dancers. Webster and Harewood were doubtful, but Minotis insisted that this was the Greek tradition, that the dancing had to be done by the singers. When Callas arrived, she saw the dance and thought it ridiculous. Minotis, to his great discredit, agreed – and said that he had been denied the possibility of dancers when he'd asked for them. Callas raged, and all the more because she felt she had been betrayed. Webster was the man she had been wooed into trusting, he had promised her that she would be presented in a suitable manner. Her instinct to mistrust everyone was confirmed. She had been *promised* dancers. It was not easy to persuade her that Webster had kept his promise, and that Minotis had insisted on going against him and then used him as his alibi. Webster considered Callas justified in being angry. And this was the single occasion.

Callas didn't sing often enough at the house, but she was constantly being thought of, considered for this or that part – and there was prestige, and comfort, to be drawn merely from the knowledge that any approach Webster made her would be sympathetically received and at least given thought. Though in one way she actually made Webster's life considerably more difficult. Leading singers' fees in Italy, which they used as a standard, rose sharply in 1953 and 1954, and for this Callas, her success at Covent Garden not an unimportant part of her total success, was largely responsible. Against Italy, Covent Garden made a poor showing, and this was one reason why the subsidy, though growing, became increasingly difficult to manage on – costs rose alarmingly, and in this respect most of all. Callas's fees at the Metropolitan also tell the story. In 1951, before her greatness was acknowledged, Bing offered her $400 a performance. When she finally appeared there, in the autumn of 1956, she was given $1000 a performance, then the top fee at the house, and an additional $2000 travelling expenses. Soon afterwards the maximum fee ruling was relaxed, and $3000 was added as expenses for twelve performances spread over nine weeks. In 1964 she was offered $6000 a performance for Tosca!

From Webster Callas came to expect understanding and protection, and on his side he had an absolutely certain instinct for the degree of flexibility he must employ. When asked why Renata Tebaldi wasn't invited more often, his reply, 'We don't really like her voice, dear,' was, possibly unconsciously, dictated at least in part by his protective feeling for Callas and his personal pride in her achievements. Tebaldi's was hardly a voice you *couldn't* like. After her appearances with the Scala company as Desdemona she did in fact come again to Covent Garden, to do Tosca one summer, and if she was not given a new production she was at least given Tagliavini and Tito Gobbi as her fellow-artists: but the performance didn't catch fire, and the standard nobility of her gestures did not make the part a 'natural' for her, though it was one she had sung often enough and a reasonable enough choice for her. This starry evening was not, on the whole, more than routine on the highest level. Zinka Milanov, Callas's other 'rival' in the specific firmament of Italian grand opera, was also presented in a revival of *Tosca*, again with Tagliavini, and she did have something of a triumph. But the following year, returning in the same role, she had to contend with Corelli in his first youth, hardly a suitable lover for her, and Guelfi, whose voice, like Corelli's, was huge, and she was understandably out of sorts: while a definitely makeshift *Trovatore*, with inferior colleagues, found her in poor voice, though even then she showed herself at least gracious and stylish.

Webster was good, none better, at expending admiration and affection. But with Callas there was something different. To understanding he added the joy of worship and love. She was a great joy of the house under his rule, and her every appearance in it had the nature of a benediction. It was even a joy that she came to the house before Kleiber was lost to it, a greatness to succeed greatness. She was the very symbol of the highest aspiration in art, and seemed by her presence alone to guarantee a future full of glories.

CHAPTER XIV

Renewed search for a musical director · Kempe's *Ring* and *Butterfly* · Kubelik appointed · Ramon Vinay and Tito Gobbi · Otakar Kraus · the non-Gobbi *Otello* · triumph at last

With Kleiber gone, appointing a Musical Director became all the more important. Other considerations apart, there was no Artistic Director and it could easily seem that the General Administrator was shouldering too much responsibility. If Webster liked power, he didn't want it to be too apparent: he wasn't eager to divide power, on the other hand, and he was determined not to have anyone imposed on him. It would have to be a man of his choice.

Barbirolli was an obvious one, and for a while, so long as he wasn't pushed, he was prepared to work more at Covent Garden and to come into closer association gradually. He was English, that was one good thing. And he conducted Italian opera well – part of Webster's job in the 'fifties was to raise the standard of the Italian performances. Barbirolli's *Turandot*, which opened the season in the autumn of 1951 and brought him back to the house after an absence of fourteen years, treated the audience to playing in Italian opera which compared well with that heard during the Scala season, and subsequently Barbirolli was reserved almost entirely for the Italian repertory – exceptions were the Ferrier *Orpheus* and a *Tristan* notable for introducing, in Sylvia Fisher, the first British Isolde since Eva Turner's in 1937. But finally Barbirolli wasn't responsive. He limited himself, like Kleiber, to only three seasons in all, and didn't return after 1954.

Josef Krips was another possibility. He'd conducted the Vienna State's Mozart operas during their 1947 visit, and he was to have been in charge of *Billy Budd* in 1951, Britten's first new work for the house, though originally commissioned by Sadlers Wells. He was the composer's own choice, but in the end he cried off, claiming that he found reading the photostat score too much of a strain for his eyes: and it was nearly ten years more before he was heard again at Covent Garden.

Britten's own name was one that Webster often craved to see printed near his own in the Covent Garden programme, but he couldn't convince himself entirely that Britten would be the right man for the job. The Board too were given to toying with the name. But Leslie Boosey, his publisher, thought he wouldn't be able to give sufficient time to the job. And anyway, wouldn't it be a misuse of his talents? Lord Harewood invited Webster and Britten together one weekend to

Harewood House, where in the gracious Yorkshire calm the matter could be leisurely discussed. The weekend passed with no word of the Musical Directorship being so much as whispered. Webster was due to leave at ten o'clock on Monday morning. Breakfast was over – it was a *quarter* to ten and still nothing had been said. When Webster did finally speak his luggage was on the doorstep and his foot already half out of the door. For he didn't like striking before the iron was hot – if a decision didn't seem inevitable then he had no confidence in its being the right one. 'You shouldn't have to make decisions, they make themselves.' This one hadn't. His hesitation, partly neurotic, also represented an acknowledgement that in this case the facts were at variance with his own confused inclinations. Gratifying as it might be to have Britten, he *knew* he wasn't the right man for the job. There was employment for Britten at the house, but it was as a composer.

Webster was by now beginning to use young John Pritchard, a protégé of Busch's at Glyndebourne, where so far he'd only conducted Mozart. Happily, at Covent Garden he was proving apt for the Italian repertory. He also conducted, among many other operas, the première of *Gloriana* – he in fact was given too many operas to conduct, often, and especially for the repertory operas, without enough rehearsal time. He too often had under him casts not good enough in productions that were running down, so he wasn't always shown off to best advantage. But through this difficult apprentice period he too was passing in and out of Webster's mind as a possible Musical Director. He was another *English* conductor, and if he wouldn't bring the same glamour and glory with him to the job, Webster would have the glory of promoting a new talent.

But then there was Rudolph Kempe. He came first with the Bavarian State Opera of Munich, in charge of two of the three Strauss operas they brought to Covent Garden for their visit in the autumn of 1953. (One happened to be *Die Liebe der Danae*, which Webster had been offered as a world première in 1946. The work was none too well received in 1953 and he knew that he'd been right to refuse it.) Kempe was soon back again, conducting *Salome* on 29 October, his first appearance with the Covent Garden company. From Munich, only a few days later, he was writing to Webster: 'I have to tell you how happy I am to conduct at Covent Garden and how much I like the orchestra. I am only sorry that my duties in Munich make it necessary for my visits to be so short'.

For he was Munich's Musical Director, though he'd only had the job a year and had decided to make this second year his last – he wanted to be free for Covent Garden and elsewhere. But he made two more short trips to London during the season, first for *Elektra* and, in the summer of 1954, for *Rosenkavalier*, his fifth Strauss opera at Covent Garden within a year.

Kempe had scarcely, as yet, shown his range. But Webster had no doubts that here was a possible Musical Director for him. The Kleiber *Rosenkavalier* was so recent at the house, and in Strauss, and in this opera in particular, Kempe was entering into direct competition with the master. Perhaps for a while he was in Kleiber's shadow, but already, when he returned in the autumn to take on *Rosenkavalier* again, he had all but emerged from it. In this second season too, with *Fidelio* and *Tristan*, he began to take on other composers, as yet still within the German repertory. Here was Kleiber's successor in the house, then, and the obvious man for Webster to go after.

And in the summer of 1955 Kempe conducted two cycles of *The Ring*, and after this he was most certainly in no one's shadow. He was only in his mid-forties; and Covent Garden was the main scene of his unfolding. This was pleasing enough for Webster, a confirmation that if he took from his artists, he and his house had the knack of giving back too.

The Ring was, and always had been, from the beginning, important to Webster. If *Rosenkavalier* had become the heart of the repertory, Kempe's *Ring*, heard several times more through the 'fifties, can perhaps be called its backbone. The problem had been, how to do it? Bayreuth had opened its doors again after the war in 1951, and Wieland Wagner had taken a swipe at what by now had become a crude, old-fashioned realism. In a stroke he'd done away with scenery. The idea wasn't new in itself: Appia and Gordon Craig in their time, a half century and more ago, had advocated a theatre in which everything that stood between the work and the audience had to go. Wieland Wagner used gauzes and lighting effects, and gesture was more meaningfully visible in the emptiness. There was no 'method' here to be followed – Wieland Wagner's success was all in how he did it. What he did had to do with lighting and concentration on the psychological, essential action: what could be imitated was merely the negative, the doing-away with scenery.

Webster didn't find any of this appealing. It was too far from Shaftesbury Avenue, and Oliver Messel was thrown out with the bathwater. He wanted excuses for not doing it à la Wieland. He didn't go himself to the Bayreuth opening, but sent instead Reginald Goodall, whose conducting career at the house had disappointed him, but who was well-known by everyone there as the man with the deepest knowledge of Wagner. Elizabeth Latham and John Sullivan, Covent Garden's lighting man, went along with him. 'Reggie is in his element here,' John Sullivan remarked of this Wagnerian who was one day to reveal himself as Knappertsbusch's successor. 'But he really wants to go up the hill on all fours!' Reggie returned to London enraptured. This, he was certain, was the way for Covent Garden. When a new production of *The Ring* was mounted it couldn't, according to him, be done any other way.

Webster was reluctant, however. 'My audiences aren't ready yet,' he gave out cautiously as his own opinion – which was to attribute his own uncertainty to them. And it wasn't just that he was a Shaftesbury Avenue man, with a taste for Messel and Leslie Hurry – who cleaved to the theatre of, say, Gielgud and Ashton. He understood too that if the sparseness Reggie so enthusiastically described could work when applied by a Wieland Wagner, with someone less committed to non-realism, and working moreover in normal opera house conditions, the results might be *merely* sparse. He dreaded an empty stage.

Wieland Wagner himself offered to come to Covent Garden in 1953 to mount a production of *Tristan*. Here was the opportunity to judge the real Bayreuth at Covent Garden. But Webster didn't pursue negotiations with much enthusiasm; of course it wasn't in him to turn down such a celebrity, but he was never *sure*, and he preferred to continue negotiations and hope that their failure could be considered as the justification of no Bayreuth at Covent Garden.

Webster's first choice for the designer of his 1954 *Ring*, certainly not a foolish compromise, was no less than Henry Moore. If in his mind he'd rejected a celebrity whose association would lend lustre to himself and the house, in Moore he would be replacing him with another at least as prominent. Moore might excite even greater wonder than Wieland Wagner. Besides, Webster had seen one stupendous sculptor produce ravishing stage-designs – Isamu Noguchi, who had done *Orpheus* for Balanchine, and was besides celebrated as Martha Graham's frequent collaborator. The sculptor Moore could be counted on to come up with something massive and solid and not too representational either. Moore's style would be familiar enough and at the same time give a 'new look' to an opera stage, where it would appear daring. 'Safe daring.' Moore's 'modern' look for Wagner would actually relate to Bayreuth only in not being strictly representational, but people would be less likely to call Covent Garden old-fashioned. Webster would seem to be nodding at least in the direction of Bayreuth.

It didn't occur to him to wonder whether Moore might or might not be in sympathy with the composer. Kenneth Clark had sadly to inform Webster that 'He has never heard a note of *The Ring*, and is not particularly in sympathy with Wagner,' which pre-empted his refusal. Webster was not to give up sculptors so easily. Next season he brought in Barbara Hepworth to design Tippett's first opera, *A Midsummer*

Marriage, and the architect Hugh Casson was given *Troilus and Cressida* – works in which there was no tradition to be flouted.

In the end *The Ring* went to a Webster favourite, Leslie Hurry, who was neither the first nor the last to compromise between realism and non-realism. He was at once Bayreuth influenced and old-fashioned, which wasn't satisfactory, even to Webster, who hadn't wanted either to reject the old or embrace the new: in which he again showed, in slightly different guise, his indecisiveness. The look of the production never pleased entirely, and in many quarters was roundly abused.

However, in its second season Kempe was in the pit, and he made all the difference. He had only twice before conducted *The Ring* complete, but he transformed failure into success. The characteristics of his reading were lyricism, delicacy, beauty of texture, as those many who had so admired his Strauss by now expected. He combined the utmost refinement of balance and nuance with power and thrust, and in any one conductor's interpretation one cannot reasonably ask more. His reading had rapture and control, there was a solid architecture and, within it, variation and flexibility.

The Ring in a way also provides a measure of the company's advance, not only as regards orchestra and chorus, but in the excellence of the minor parts such as the Rhinemaidens and the Norns, all of them provided by local singers. In the early days, in 1948, Ernest Newman had been scathing about the Valkyries ('no one who loves a bit of good clean fun should miss the Swedish-drill turn of the eight Valkyrie girls'); but in 1956, on the contrary, he wrote of the 'magnificent turn by Wotan's eight Valkyrie girls – the most exciting performance of the full-blooded music I have ever heard'. This in its way was as welcome to Webster as the praise for Kempe himself or for the new 1956 Siegfried, Wolfgang Windgassen in his prime.

Kempe was the man for Musical Director, certainly the obvious man if an English conductor couldn't be had. He was not only a superlative technician, along with Kleiber the best controller of stage and orchestra the house was to know under Webster, but he was also a very complete conductor. In the autumn of 1955, following his first *Ring* cycles, he took on his first Italian opera at the house, *Madame Butterfly*, and Andrew Porter wrote in the *Financial Times* that 'by creating his interpretation anew and eschewing mere continuance of the "Puccini" tradition, Kempe did what Toscanini had done for *Bohème* and de Sabata for *Tosca*: made us listen with fresh ears.' But these are Italian conductors, and this praise is the more amazing in that it is given to a German, Kempe being one of the very few German conductors whose Italian opera thoroughly commands respect, and more.

And, like Kleiber, Kempe helped bring on the singers. This particular *Butterfly* presented Amy Shuard in her first appearance in the opera at Covent Garden, and she sang with a new grace and delicacy. When Liu in *Turandot* was proposed for her, Harewood wrote to Kempe that 'she would be overjoyed working with you again, not least because the experience of *Butterfly* was extremely valuable to her.'

From every point of view, Kempe was the man. But Webster couldn't cajole him into committing himself. He resisted all persuasion and Webster knew better than to risk losing him altogether by pressing too hard. Kempe contributed nobly, and continued to contribute, right through to the beginning of the 'sixties, so that Kleiber and he can be said, together, to have spanned Webster's great decade at the house. Kempe remained in close association even though he was given only three new productions, and none of them, whatever his contribution as conductor, a success. Kempe might, reasonably, have considered these failures in part a failure of the management to promote him, but he would then have had to acknowledge that his own reluctance to commit himself might also have had a bearing.

A Musical Director had none the less to be found, and at last *had* been found, even before the new *Ring* went on. He was to start in the autumn of 1955, ending the four-year interim during which Kleiber and Kempe more than anyone else had maintained musical continuity.

It was a surprise appointment, a man whose name had not hitherto been heard in discussions. 'I've been to Sadlers Wells,' Webster murmured to Lord Harewood one spring day in 1954. 'There was a conductor there: one of those conductors whose name begins with a K.' After Kleiber, and after Kempe, it was the Czech conductor, Rafael Kubelik, who had been conducting a revival of an opera by his compatriot Janaček. Not that this was Webster's only chance to assess the 'new' man, since he was often away in Paris or Vienna or New York, and his first meeting with Kubelik took place, just as it had with Kleiber, 'somewhere abroad'.

The Board, of course, was worried that Kempe might be lost to them, but Webster persuaded them that Kempe was readily available for Covent Garden, and that to try for a long-term agreement with him wouldn't show the right attitude towards the new Musical Director. The Board was by now used to trusting Webster in such matters – and indeed, Kempe not only continued coming to the house but Kubelik was delighted that he should. ('That Kempe is doing *Butterfly* was a great joy for me to hear', he wrote that summer from Elba.)

Webster had soon discovered that Kubelik's experience of opera was limited – he'd been in charge of the Brno Opera from 1939 to 1941 but had left to become director of the Czech Philharmonic, while in

England he'd done a broadcast or two and conducted the Glyndebourne *Don Giovanni* at the Edinburgh Festival in 1948. But Webster was convinced that opera was none the less his passion, that he had the most generous enthusiasm for the English singer and English opera. Webster was certain that in Kubelik he'd found a man who endorsed his own ideas for the development of the company; and soon after taking up his appointment Kubelik was declaring publicly that he liked his opera 'home-fed, home-cooked'. He was a foreigner, and that made him a risk – but a risk worth taking. Webster couldn't wait any longer for an Englishman both able and willing. To have waited longer would have been another kind of risk.

Kubelik was of course invited back to Sadlers Wells, to do another Janaček, and Webster knew he had to move fast or not at all. The Board had the name Kubelik put into their heads in June 1954, and on 7 October the appointment was announced. The following summer Kubelik made preliminary appearances at the house in charge of a new production of another Czech opera, Smetana's *The Bartered Bride*, which opened, only a few days before Kempe was due to begin his first Covent Garden *Ring*, on 4 May. The decor was by the Czech Jan Brazda, but the director was Christopher West and none of your 'clever young men', and the opera was sung in English and by an English cast.

In his letter from Elba that summer Kubelik also wrote about the projected *Otello*; 'I think I shall shout like an Indian on the arrival of good news.' His first season as Musical Director was to open with *Otello*, the greatest of all Shakespearian operas and the greatest opera based on an English play – its only rival in both aspects is that other late Verdi opera, *Falstaff*. Once again, after the Scala visit and after the Callas *Norma*, Italian opera was to be given in its full glory, performed on a level to compare with the best of Webster's German operas.

Otello also had a particular significance for Webster himself, and he was always about during rehearsals. In the 'twenties, a very young man, Webster had responded to those Bruno Walter *Rosenkavaliers* – and his house had now had its *Rosenkavaliers* under Kleiber and Kempe. When it came to Wagner, there'd been that succession of great Wagnerians at Covent Garden who still trod solemnly through his imagination – but Webster had given Flagstad back to the house, and now there was the Kempe *Ring* as well. There remained, then, *Otello*, which had been revealed to him in the Toscanini performances at Salzburg in the 'thirties. *Otello* in 1955 was also his own past recreated in the present, and perpetuated.

A decade earlier, Ralph Hawkes had reported back to Webster

from New York about a *Carmen* he'd seen at the City Centre: 'Don Jose was played by Ramon Vinai [*sic*], and I felt that it was a great pity he is not coming to Covent Garden, for he had a fine voice and is a good actor.' Had he been engaged for Covent Garden's *Carmen* no doubt the new company's way would have been smoother back in 1947. But perhaps it was good fortune for Webster that he hadn't been. Ramon Vinay (the spelling with which he became famous) had gone instead to study with Toscanini at La Scala, and there he had developed into a *great* actor. He could now be even more useful. Webster had dreamed of a Toscanini *Otello* as his own fiftieth birthday present, and in the person of Vinay he at least had Toscanini by proxy – for it was Ramon Vinay who was to be Othello.

Desdemona was to be the Dutch soprano Gré Brouwenstijn. She was a particular joy of the house in the 'fifties, becoming virtually a house singer. She was not an ambitious artist, and indeed tended sometimes to be lazy, having to be stirred to effort by a combination of circumstances. If conditions were such that the meaning of music and drama was obscured, then she was liable to fall below her own best. Outside her native Holland she was a star, a real star, only at Covent Garden. And even here she didn't begin well. But then, how could she have done? She first appeared at the house in 1951, an Aïda singing in English to a German Radames, then the *Trovatore* Leonora singing in Italian while everyone else sang English. She wasn't eager to return again, but Lord Harewood had enormous faith in her, having first heard her in Holland, and Webster too warmed to her. She returned assured of a welcome, and in *A Masked Ball* showed rather more of her potential. She'd already sung under Kubelik in one of his early broadcasts; and in *Otello* she was at last to be presented at Covent Garden in a carefully prepared production.

But the biggest star of all in this package was the Iago. Tito Gobbi. Incredible now, in the 'seventies, to think that with Vinay announced for Othello there could be another singer more eagerly awaited. But so it was. The name that sold the tickets, and had audiences glowing in anticipation, was Gobbi's. True, there were few singers *then*, or at any time, on a level with Gobbi – that rarity, an heroic lyric baritone, an Italian who not only brought to the stage what can be regarded as a typically Italian pleasure in the physical process of singing, of projecting tone lovingly out beyond the proscenium arch, but who had also, unlike so many Italians, a most subtle sense of character. He was an actor of subtlety who was not shy of the larger effect too. And he was one of the few singers celebrated outside opera, for he was also a film-star, made world-famous by *The Magic Mountain*.

Gobbi was eagerly awaited. He'd sung here before, first with La

Scala in 1950; but his few appearances with the Covent Garden company had been always in existing productions or, as in *A Masked Ball*, a last-minute replacement, when he'd not only sung in Italian with the others in English, but a different text too, the one setting the opera in New England (Covent Garden using the original 'Swedish' version). But at last this choice singer was to give one of his most famous roles in a carefully prepared major new production.

Kubelik was not enthusiastic about international 'stars'. As he explained, 'they come and go; they have no idea at all of real co-operation' (and hence his preference for opera 'home-fed, home-cooked'). He was fanatical about ensemble, he liked to cast from the resident company, and he didn't like to make changes even if replacements too came from the company. But Vinay was not that kind of 'star'. By 1956 he'd performed the role of Othello no less than two hundred and thirty times, and he was none the less ready, eager, to study it again with Kubelik and with Peter Potter, Christopher West's assistant, to whom had been entrusted the direction – decors were by Wakhevitch – and when Edward Downes took over in the pit the following season, Vinay was eager to hear what young Downes had to say too. Kubelik's enthusiasm, and the warmth he met with from Webster and the 'family', made the great Vinay a company member while he was singing at the house.

Vinay and Brouwenstijn had been in London since 3 October, but, so rumour had it, Gobbi was still in Rome recording. For whatever reason, rehearsals began and there was still no Gobbi. Webster ordered that Otakar Kraus, who was due to succeed Gobbi and sing Iago for the last four of the seven scheduled performances, should rehearse in his place. And cables were sent. At first there was no answer. Rehearsals continued without him. At the very first rehearsal Kraus had promised to create an immensely powerful Iago, one who would convince an audience that Othello, even in the mighty form of Vinay, could be carried along by him. Vinay at once appreciated a well-matched opponent, and at one crucial moment gripped Iago's chest-hair, painfully. Vinay happened to be a wild enthusiast for photographic equipment, and his wife, a Red Indian princess, was often in the wings filming him: she was present at this rehearsal, and afterwards assured Kraus, 'You're going to be all right together.'

Still Gobbi didn't arrive. But he did at least answer – and to the effect that he knew the work, he'd sung it countless times before. More, actually, than a hundred times. He didn't need so much rehearsal. 'He knows it,' said Kubelik. 'But we don't.'

Not for nothing has emphasis been laid on Kubelik's feeling for ensemble. If Vinay was the kind of star he could accept, Gobbi, a

Gobbi persisting in not coming to rehearse, seemed to be showing himself just the kind he couldn't. Kubelik asked for an ultimatum to be delivered. There must be a deadline. By a certain time Gobbi must be here – otherwise don't bother to come at all. It would fall to Webster himself, on behalf of the house, to do the delivering.

To challenge Gobbi was itself a challenge. Did he dare? To dictate terms to a singer of this stature meant that Covent Garden, suddenly, was virtually purporting to be another Vienna, another La Scala. It was surely merely laughable for a second-grade house to be giving itself such airs. Wasn't that how it would appear to everyone? Covent Garden was doing well for a beginner. It had its 'events' to boast of, and some company evenings which were a matter of local pride and held promise for the future. But it was a second-grade house still. And this was Gobbi! His was the voice they wanted to hear. He was the main attraction. When *Otello* was revived the following season, with Vinay and Brouwenstijn returning after enormous acclaim to their roles, but once again without Gobbi, even on the first night there were empty seats.

Webster paced, and he agonized. There was no one to consult. There was no peace to be made between warring elements because there wasn't even contact. Kubelik and Potter were working together – by challenging Gobbi Webster would be supporting the regime which he had himself so lovingly fostered. He didn't want to make excessive claims for his house – if by challenging Gobbi he *was* making excessive claims, then they were only incidental. But the principles by which he stood, in collaboration first with Rankl and now with Kubelik, were at stake. He seemed to have no alternative. Yet the voice of reason said, 'Don't fight him, Gobbi is bigger than all of us!' How the audience would react to the sacking of Gobbi was more than Webster dared envisage. Kubelik could surely be made to see that the most major *force majeure* was operating in the case of Gobbi.

None the less Webster did have the effrontery to cable Gobbi fixing a deadline. He hoped desperately that Gobbi would meet it. But he didn't. Came 5.30 on the evening of 11 October. Gobbi wasn't at London Airport, the new production would go on without him. It was the turning point in the history of Covent Garden post-war. The gauntlet was cast, and not merely at Gobbi's feet.

Otakar Kraus was a sensitive artist possessed of a supple intelligence and humour, and in his most memorable roles, of which his Iago most happily proved to be one, he used geniality to underpin the sinister. He was excellent casting. It would have to be Kraus for all performances, whether Gobbi arrived now or not. But Kraus was appalled at the idea of replacing Gobbi on the first night, of facing an audience who had paid to hear Gobbi, and who had for weeks been anticipating the treat. Summoned to Webster's office, he protested that he couldn't do it. He'd have to take the blame for Gobbi's being sacked – which is what the substitution amounted to – he wouldn't be allowed to finish the performance, he'd have the audience baying for his blood as soon as the curtain went up. And if they did let him finish there'd be nothing but boos for him at the end. 'But you're good. You've done good work,' Kubelik reasoned. Maybe. 'But they'll say we're two Czechs in cahoots.' Webster took thought. 'I never knew,' he said at last, 'that you were Czech. I thought you were some kind of Austrian.' He persisted, and brought the curtain down on the argument. Gobbi was out, and Kraus it was going to be.

The 'sacking' of Gobbi was self-evidently headline material, so Webster decided that no one must be told in advance. If the press got hold of the story and it was made public, pressure was bound to be put on Webster and his Musical Director. Even wardrobe mustn't be told, so Kraus's costumes couldn't be made until the last minute and he had to do the dress rehearsal in makeshift costumes.

And meantime Gobbi *did* arrive at last. The news which greeted him he found utterly unbelieveable. This is Tito Gobbi, and this Covent Garden! When at last he had to believe it, he invoked lawyers. There was an anxious meeting, anxious for Webster, who found himself, backed by his lawyer, ranged against Gobbi backed by his agent Sandor Gorlinsky and by *his* lawyer. Webster's tact, of course, was as important as the niceties of law, and the matter happily didn't go beyond the office.

But there was a dangerous rumbling in the house on the first night. 'If this doesn't work,' breathed Peter Potter, 'they'll tear the place down.' And Otakar Kraus was having to face not only the audience but also Gobbi himself – though fortunately he didn't know until after the performance, when apprised by a gentleman of the press, that Gobbi had been there in the stalls. By then it didn't matter. Webster hadn't had to use up much shoe-leather pacing anxiously behind the grand tier, because triumph had been signalled early in the evening.

Vinay brought to his role the splendour of a Titian portrait. He seemed naturally to assume poses of awesome weight, and his performance moment by moment had such a concentration of meaning that he imposed a continuous sense of the drama as a whole. His energy, like Callas's, was self-consuming – both great artists *had* to burn themselves out in comparatively short careers. Like Callas, too, at every performance Vinay found the emotional spring of the action, and even at rehearsals Webster had the sensation that, thrillingly, the drama was being made up for him as the performance unrolled. When Vinay was Othello, his commitment to Desdemona in the love duet at the end of the first act was total – the words 'If it were now to die, 'Twere now to be most happy,' were offered, as the dramatist intended, as a challenge to fate. Vinay also brought to his Othello a kind of braggadocio – he was immensely and outrageously noble, but, as though uncertain, he almost protested it too much, thus revealing the character as also vulnerable, a kind of Monarch of the Glen with a soft underbelly. His nobility was all but incomparable – his emotional responsiveness made him, as well as heart-rendingly vulnerable, deeply poetic as well. The spirit of Tamagno, the original Othello, had imposed itself on the role, and there were at the time a few who were not penetrated by the poetry of the performance, who felt that it was not a complete Othello who didn't also provide loud trumpet-tones (a frequent Desdemona of Tamagno's had commented particularly on 'the golden trumpet in his throat'). But Bernard Shaw hadn't been impressed by Tamagno, and Verdi himself had asked exasperatedly, 'Why doesn't he sing a *piano* note?' Vinay's was a performance that Shaw and Verdi must both have acclaimed, for it laid bare a masterpiece.

Brouwenstijn, with her nagging sense of the whole in any production, was released to perform as, at her best, only she could. Her Desdemona combined tenderness with sensuality; she asserted a kind of heroic womanliness while remaining comfortably within the limits of the character in the drama; and she projected an altogether unsentimental goodness without resorting to a single moment of merely generalized acting. Memory can scarcely recreate her Desdemona apart from *this* Othello in *this* particular setting, and imagination cannot improve it.

Verdi and Vinay made history together, it was a fulfilment of Brouwenstijn's talent, and it was beside these artists that Webster saw a member of his company, at the end, step out in front of the curtain. Upstart Kraus, enjoying the success of his life, shared the huge applause with his wonderful colleagues. Webster's decision was vindicated, his house was vindicated. This triumph justified the gesture of defiance from the second-grade house to which great Gobbi, however graciously, had condescended. After *Otello*, it couldn't ever again be safely assumed that Covent Garden *was* a second-grade house. Support for a Czech singer in an opera conducted by a Czech – in an Italian opera in which the leads were sung, in Italian, by a Chilean tenor and a Dutch soprano – had engineered a turning-point in the history of English opera. The single action, with success and not failure following it, brought the house worldwide attention, and gave singers worldwide a new respect for it. For them, La Scala had been a house to be won. But they expected

Covent Garden to woo *them*. But from this day forth Covent Garden was a house to be reckoned with.

It's also amazing that, after the first eruptions, Webster contrived to re-establish, and maintain, excellent relations with the rejected baritone. Gobbi returned often to sing at his house – the very next summer he was Rigoletto there. But he didn't appear as Iago until the 'sixties, by which time Vinay had renounced the role of Othello. The combination of Vinay and Gobbi in the opera was one Covent Garden was denied; but the combination of Vinay and Kraus was also superb. And it was Gobbi who was instrumental in securing Webster one of his many honours – thanks to him Webster, in 1965, became a Commendatore of the Order 'Al Merito della Repubblica Italiana'. Webster accepted honours with a serene pleasure, but this was a particular pleasure for him, the happiest footnote, years later, to this remarkable affair.

CHAPTER XV

Running an opera house · mounting criticism · financial crisis · a Beecham blast · Kubelik threatens to resign · increased subsidy · the ballet to the rescue · Ashton and Fonteyn · visit of the Bolshoi

Covent Garden was *always*, as regards money, in crisis. There was soon to erupt a particularly nasty row, provoked by an imperative need to go after more money, but for all its drama it was no more than one part of the continuous story of money troubles.

Day to day business at the Opera House could not be interrupted merely for a row. Webster continued through it, as at every other period, to be beset by a multiplicity of small problems, which could be solved only to be instantly replaced, Hydra-like, by others. He didn't expect respite, he only asked that, day after day, the curtain continue to rise.

The problem of storage, for example, became more acute as the repertory expanded. Rehearsal space too, an urgent problem because having to accommodate both the opera and ballet companies on the one stage could lead to clashes. The real breakthrough here didn't come until 1963, when the Opera House took on the London Opera Centre, for here it was possible to make out a rehearsal area of exactly the right dimensions. Webster had been adamant about not starting an opera school attached to the house after the pattern of the ballet school because there were already four music schools in London, and he considered he was better to concentrate on providing opportunities for singers who had already been given their basic training: Joseph Hislop, a distinguished singer in his day and then a teacher at the Opera in Stockholm, had been engaged as coach, to help the singers use these opportunities.

Touring was another problem. In the early days of government subsidy Webster had had to make a showing outside the capital, but he soon saw that only a few of the largest centres had theatres which could present the company properly, and in 1957 he managed to persuade the Arts Council to agree that tours be limited to four-week periods, taking in Manchester and one other town (in the early 'sixties the company was in Manchester a whole month). In the 'sixties tours were gradually discontinued, since regional opera had been developing and taking over the responsibility, as had too the Sadlers Wells Opera (renamed in 1974 The English National Opera).

On the one hand Webster had to scrimp, and on the other he had to be prepared to answer criticism of extravagance, grand opera being necessarily an expensive operation. Lord Drogheda, after he had become Chairman, worried about the price of the costumes for a revival of Tippett's *King Priam*. Webster took time to look into the matter very thoroughly, explaining finally:

> Opera costumes as a whole tend to be very expensive. They are made to be far more endurable [*sic*] than ballet costumes; there is very frequently an element of tailoring in them and when they are ornamented as many of the Priam costumes were, that of course adds to the expense and any form of armour costs still more. With a limited wardrobe and ballet costumes needing a particular skill which most costumiers don't have, preference is always given in the house wardrobe to the demands of the ballet, with the result that more opera costumes are made outside. All the Priam costumes were made outside. The designs were also late because we had to turn down Mr Kenny's designs and find somebody else to help.
>
> Having said all that I have taken the average cost of 1761 opera costumes in 16 productions, and the average price per costume is £42 and in the case of Priam the average would appear to be £51.

A day to day matter of particular importance was dealing with unions, both Equity and the Incorporated Society of Musicians. Webster had been given a Deputy partly so that some of the burden of constant negotiation would be removed from him, and Steuart Wilson as a former BBC head was no stranger to dealings with them. And John Tooley, Webster's assistant after Wilson had left in 1955, very soon showed himself a first-rate negotiator.

Webster's early socialist leanings helped him here. He believed in unions, and didn't necessarily feel always that he was dealing with enemies. And yet essentially he *was*, since their demands went against his interests. In so far as they were enemies, then his sympathy helped to give him insights. But he believed in artists' rights, and a necessarily unsleeping diplomatic wariness didn't preclude elements of goodwill which were recognized by the people he was having to deal with, and this too helped smooth matters. From 1948 Webster was Chairman of the Orchestral Employers' Association, (though he had to resign in 1965 when he was appointed Chairman of the London Orchestral Board).

Problems to be sorted out with the unions arose almost daily. In May 1948 arrangements had been finalized to broadcast Flagstad's hundred and fiftieth Isolde from the Opera House. A Committee appointed by the Ministry of Labour had recommended a certain fee, but on account of the work's length the Musicians' Union demanded double, and as a result the broadcast was cancelled. In 1952 Equity proposed a £2 a week increase for the chorus, which Webster referred to Sadlers

Wells, and in the end he settled for 10*s* a week. Another time, early in 1956, the stage-hands at the Opera House went on a work to rule – a wage agreement had recently been reached for stage-hands in the West End, but the staff at Covent Garden were in a slightly different position, since the many stage sets had to be brought in from outside and unloaded. They weren't going to take in any more. *That* problem was settled amicably.

But Equity was becoming increasingly tough through the 'fifties. In 1954 they gave the Ministry of Labour a list on which the names of foreign singers engaged by the Opera House were put against the names of English singers available, and the Ministry came back to the Opera House seeking to impose limitations. Both Mattiwilda Dobbs and Marko Rothmüller they considered 'over-engaged'. And a couple of years later an Italian singer of note, Melchiorre Luise, was cast in the small part of the Sacristan in *Tosca*, to bolster the production when Zinka Milanov appeared in it. Equity opposed the grant of a permit, pointing out that there were four British basses who could sing the role. The Ministry of Labour overruled their objection. Equity Council then called a meeting of members at Covent Garden. They refused to grant an Equity card to Melchiorre Luise, so that if he went on stage all Equity members were bound to walk off it. A resolution was passed endorsing the policy. The management resisted for two days, Webster arguing that three out of the four possible English basses, two from the resident company and one from outside, were none of them available. He eventually persuaded Equity to allow the foreigner to appear on the opening night, while the fourth bass, Howell Glynne, rehearsing *Martha* with the Sadlers Wells Opera in Bournemouth, was brought in at twenty-four hours' notice to do the remaining performances. Webster felt that he had a powerful case to present in the increasing number of English singers going abroad, and he hoped to persuade Equity to alter the arrangement by which they scrutinized each engagement of a foreign artist individually. But here he hoped in vain. That arrangement still stands.

Such problems, large and small, were likely to meet Webster as he entered his office any day of the week, and they can't be said often to have interrupted the smooth running of the house; but the smoothness was always the result of such problems being coped with. Webster sometimes had to achieve small miracles to provide a calm atmosphere for his artists to work in – but overall it was an atmosphere which, by comparison with that in most other houses, foreign guests could all the more appreciate. In August 1957 the chorus actually did go on strike, and not only at Covent Garden but at Sadlers Wells too. The rates had been £11.10s. per week at Covent Garden and a pound less at Sadlers Wells. A four guinea rise was demanded and Webster offered 30s. Equity came down to £2. But while Sadlers Wells planned a month of operas without chorus, Webster coolly went ahead with his plans unchanged, confident that he could bring the dispute to an end in time. The Sadlers Wells season opened – late – with single chorus-less acts of *Così Fan Tutte*, *Samson and Delilah* and *Bohème*. But Covent Garden went back to work. And this is the significant point: it was because of an overwhelming vote by the chorus in favour of return to work. 'We're going back because of Mr Webster,' they said. Webster and Equity together had talks with the Ministry of Labour, and the 30s. increase was made *immediate*. It was to be decided later whether a further rise should be allowed, Webster having already offered either 30s. or arbitration, but not, as Equity had demanded, both at once. What was patent was that it was love of David Webster that had determined the ladies and gentlemen of the chorus to forgo their advantage and remove the pistol from his head. They were persuaded to launch the season, as announced, and as Webster had been confident it would be launched.

Webster imposed a sense of his two-way loyalty, and at the same time his admiration and affection for his artists were not only genuine but were seen to be genuine, and these were Webster's most powerful weapons in his daily battles. If in the mid-'fifties he had such large concerns to occupy him as a gala to be arranged to honour a visit by Kruschev and Bulganin, or a proposed visit by the entire Bayreuth company (which didn't in the end happen), these wouldn't on any particular day necessarily clear the deck of other small concerns, and the harassments continued – there were wage-claims and go-slows and strikes which it was equally an achievement to resolve, and rehearsal problems and storage problems exercised him as much as planning the repertory and casting the operas.

A small event of November 1955 was prelude to a big money crisis. Vienna's new Opera House was opened that month, and Kubelik, by prearrangement, was to conduct one of the first new productions. But in order to be in Vienna for a rehearsal he had to be released from one of his *Bartered Bride* performances at Covent Garden, which was therefore taken over by the young John Matheson.

Webster had a pair of tickets for the opening, and when he and Jimmy boarded the plane, Vienna-bound, they found that they knew most of the people on board. They made a jolly party, soon the jollier for champagne. During the flight Webster was handed a newspaper and in it he read a criticism – was it right for the Administration to release the new Musical Director from his Covent Garden duties and pass the baton to a deputy? There was a stop-over in Zurich, and in the transit lounge the party continued. Jimmy kept the glasses filled, but Webster took his with him to a telephone-kiosk and spoke a letter directly to *The Times* in London. He had been known to give speeches of an hour and a half, without notes and without repeating himself, and he was equal to this occasion. 'Covent Garden,' he *said*,

> makes fewer changes of advertised programmes and cast than any other similar kind of opera house in the world. The changes for reasons other than illness are infinitesimal. It is reasonable to claim that this suggests good planning as well as a strong desire to keep faith with the public, especially as Covent Garden announces programme details much farther in advance than any other similar opera house. Programme details up to December 24th have been in the hands of the public for some weeks. Opera houses abroad usually announce details only ten days to a fortnight in advance. The decision that Mr Kubelik should remain in Vienna and not conduct here on Thursday night was not his, but mine. Fifteen months ago, when we invited Mr Kubelik to become our Musical Director, Vienna approached him to conduct one of the first new productions in the State Opera which opens this weekend. We agreed that he should accept the invitation which did honour to him and to us.
>
> Vienna at its opening festival is staging four or five new productions in almost as many nights, an enterprise which staggers any operatic management. I was asked a week ago by the authorities in Vienna if we would release Mr Kubelik for his engagement with us to undertake an important rehearsal which they were being forced to hold on Thursday. Vienna, to which the world owes so much, does not rebuild its opera house every day. Under ordinary circumstances it would not have been possible for us to agree but in these very special circumstances it seemed and still seems not unreasonable to make a gesture of good will and release Mr Kubelik. I cannot help feeling that the course we have taken has the generous approval of our public. *The Bartered Bride* on Thursday was in the capable hands of a young conductor who had studied the work with Mr Kubelik, and had in fact helped to rehearse it.

And back to the party went David Webster, to have Jimmy recharge his glass. End, so far as he concerned himself with it, of the affair.

He had of course to keep on good terms with Vienna. Negotiations were from time to time renewed for a return visit by the company, though they were never clinched, largely on account of expense. More than that was the matter of guest singers – singers he approached sometimes had to get leave from the Vienna Opera, and he was looking forward to the time when his own singers would be in demand in Vienna.

The real row broke out in the summer of 1956, when Covent Garden's booklet, *A Review of 1946–56*, was published. The booklet cost one shilling and was intended to back Waverley's demands for more money. A Draft Report had been in preparation since 1954, and it had been decided to give it to a practical outsider to write, with an eye on the Treasury rather than on the general public. W. E. Williams had been asked to do it; and it was finally entrusted to Wyn Griffiths, Vice-Chairman of the Arts Council. But the Report was never presented, as it was felt that it didn't finally give a strong enough sense of money well-spent, and the *Review* was published instead to put the case to the general public.

The background of the crisis was partly the crisis of the pound generally through the early 'fifties – the pound went on and on being worth less, and costs rose accordingly, as well as wage demands. Higher aspirations too meant higher spending, and every advance artistically implied an obligation to maintain the new standard. It was not altogether accidental that the 1956 crisis coincided with a period of artistic success – best represented by Kempe's second pair of *Ring* cycles, overall the high-point of the company's achievement so far – and of increasingly enthusiastic audiences.

The grant rose steadily, and with it standards. It was almost as though the very increase itself provoked a need for still more money. In May 1952 Kenneth Clark resigned from the Board to take up his appointment as Chairman of the Arts Council, so that the dialogue continued with someone who thoroughly understood Covent Garden's problems. In 1954 Webster had to insist on a minimum budget of £60,000 for new productions, feeling that any cutback here would be dangerous, and he had to resist the possibility of cutting down on orchestral strength, now up to eighty-seven: but none the less Kubelik, when he arrived, found among other inadequacies that the orchestra was still too small. He suggested at least ten relief players for the orchestra as well as twenty more singers for the chorus. And seat prices were still related closely to West End theatre prices, although they were raised gradually. But it was only for such events as Callas or *Ring* evenings that prices could go up significantly.

The *Review* of 1956 made the current situation clear, and it was not a happy one. It itemized expenditure, pointing out that 70% of the money spent on staff was controlled directly or indirectly by trades union agreement. The significant figures were those for total expenditure (1955–6), which was £730,000. Against this figure put income – £382,000. The grant of only £250,000, helped by ballet receipts in the United States and by increased ticket prices, didn't cover the difference.

It was emphasized that the Administration hadn't been idle or unimaginative. They had explored various methods for raising money, like trying to persuade the London County Council, on the European pattern of subsidy from the municipality as well as the state, to Cough Up. They hadn't.

A huge row followed. But, be it emphasized, day to day business, and the small harassments, continued at the Opera House. One large harassment didn't cancel them. And however distressing this row, the main anxiety for Webster was still, would the *outcome* be successful? The Opera House simply must have more money. If they got it, then it was worth the strain.

The *Review* was published on 5 June 1956, and Lord Waverley called a press conference. Waverley had finally to evoke the promise of Dalton's letter, with its guarantee of not letting Covent Garden down. He stated plainly, 'If the public wants what we provide, they must be prepared to pay for it.' If not – closure. He was almost deliberately challenging, for he and Webster both knew that the overdraft had by now become so large – it was not far off £150,000 – that to close Covent Garden, which would mean having to clear the overdraft, would put too heavy a strain on the Arts Council's funds. The following day there were leaders in the *Evening Standard* and the *Daily Telegraph*, the noise of Waverley's gauntlet hitting the floor reverberating in both of them.

There is a peculiar note sounding through criticisms of Covent Garden at this time. 1956 was the year of Suez and national humiliation, and this must partly explain what can almost be defined as a suppressed hysteria. Suppressed and probably almost unconscious. At such a time the very principle of arts subsidy – something still very new in England and certainly not yet thoroughly established – more than ever, to some, seemed to speak of decadence. To more than a few it must have seemed that the arts were being irrigated by the sweat falling from the brow of a humbled Mother Country. Many might have protested, the British Lion's teeth are being pulled! – and the instruments are being applied by these effete purveyors of *art*!! No one actually was brazen enough to suggest, Starve the arts and restore Britain's manhood, but this was a slogan which might have had its appeal. It was certainly one of the impulses behind the attacks at this time.

The *Evening Standard*, having worked out that everyone going to Covent Garden was receiving a personal Treasury grant of nine shillings, instanced 'notable examples of doubtful administration', among them both the Dali-Brook *Salome* and *Gloriana*. To avoid such mistakes in the future they thought that what was needed was 'a more aggressive, more vigorous management that instead of leaning automatically on the charity of the government will run Covent Garden with the aim of turning loss into profits!' There was, however, no formula given for achieving such results, though such a formula would have been gratefully seized on by opera houses throughout the world, *every one of which*, either from the state or from private monies, relies on subsidy.

The *Telegraph* objected to Waverley's hectoring tones, and thought he sounded too much like 'any chairman of a nationalized industry'. Sympathy might have been gained, they suggested, by pointing out that Covent Garden prices were lower than those of any major opera house in the world, and that no comparable opera house subsisted on so low a subsidy. (Webster could at least enjoy the implication that his was now a major opera house.) Incontrovertibly, the *Telegraph*, though regretting a possible closure, suggested that 'not everybody is prepared to avert it by paying a little towards something a large proportion of British people will never be able to enjoy.'

Controversy was shortly raging. Martin Cooper followed the leader in the *Daily Telegraph* with an article reviving the argument of the English singer's small voice and the suitability of a smaller theatre than Covent Garden for it: Covent Garden should be reserved for international seasons. No one had thought to mention, when this argument had been raised in the 'forties, that it wasn't so much the size of a singer's voice as its focus and projection that counted, but in the current row Harold Rosenthal, editor of *Opera*, wrote to the *Telegraph* pointing out that Patti and de Luca and Martinelli hadn't had large voices, and that latterly in Vienna Lisa della Casa, Seefried, Jurinac and Erich Kunz didn't have larger voices than English singers.

The arena was soon enlarged to take in the House of Commons. On 12 June Beverley Baxter, Tory MP, proposed, like Beecham seven years earlier, an enquiry into the running of Covent Garden. The Chancellor of the Exchequer, Harold Macmillan, refused, on the grounds that the Treasury wasn't the right body to conduct it. Webster, naturally a focus for criticism, when asked for a reaction merely murmured, 'I was appointed by the Board. If they were not satisfied, I can only presume [*sic*] that they would be the people to do something about it.'

The row was beginning to be widely reported, and Martin Cooper wrote in the *Telegraph* on the 16th that his article had brought him in a large correspondence from which he had learnt 'that there is widespread, deep and long-standing dissatisfaction not with the amount of money spent by the Covent Garden administration but with the way in which it is spent.'

This was the very day that Beecham, as though resentful that others were now usurping *his* pulpit, himself entered the lists, rhetorically unburdening himself in an article printed alongside Cooper's letter. He quoted the section from his 1944 autobiography, *A Mingled Chime*, about English voices being 'unlike those of other nations . . . the best among them are of comparatively moderate volume', and continued:

> The truth is, that the attempt to make Covent Garden a home for national opera has been a ghastly failure . . . the set-up there is botched by persons without experience of any kind, was founded in error and has been nourished in ignorance.

He wanted a company operating in a smaller London theatre and also in half-a-dozen larger provincial centres, thus satisfying 'the complaints of those who consider the capital to be unduly favoured by the public subsidy' (that the neglect of the provinces had by now become a common complaint suggests that Covent Garden was becoming more difficult to attack on other grounds: and the fact that it is not the principle of state subsidy for the arts but its *use* which was attacked suggests that the principle itself was beginning, however reluctantly by some, to be widely accepted). Beecham added meaningfully that 'the best brains available will be required for the task, and there should be no place in it for the dilettante and the amateur.'

Three days later the main stage was once again the House of Commons, where more questions were asked, this time by Dame Irene Ward, another Tory MP and also a member of the Board of the Carl Rosa Opera Company (which was being inadequately supported, and was finally, in fact, to be allowed, however reluctantly, to starve in favour of other beneficiaries, Covent Garden chief among them). She suggested that the Opera House be put under a new Board independent of the Arts Council, but the Chancellor this time replied that he found 'the interposition of the Arts Council quite a convenient instrument', as from letters and approaches made to him he had learnt that there were some people 'who want more money spent on Covent Garden and about an equal number who wish less to be spent'. More important was that MP Robert Boothby was one of the (apparently) few Tories who supported the Covent Garden regime, and he tabled a question in the House – would the Chancellor up the grant? Would he improve on the £250,000 the Arts Council was offering?

And this, in all the commotion, was what was going to matter. But now the range of the attack was extended, and Beecham, who had inveighed against Rankl's appointment, now turned on Kubelik in much the same way. On 23 June Kubelik published a letter in *The Times* which, with its passionate defence of English singers, was virtually a manifesto. He said that they had no inherent weakness either of quality or temperament, and needed only to be helped overcome their inhibitions and encouraged to project their voices. But Beecham in his *Times* letter four days later, stated that

> In my humble experience, I have always found that these two disabilities can be largely overcome by a due appreciation of the strong as well as the weak parts of our language . . . But how did the management of our national institution set about the task? In defiance of all common sense they engaged as Musical Director a foreigner, and let him loose upon the unhappy creatures who had been led to expect beneficial results from this monumental piece of stupidity.

It was again Harold Rosenthal who wrote the reply, quoting from the pamphlet Beecham had issued when his Covent Garden enterprise of 1920 had collapsed. 'For half a century,' it ran, 'we have talked English opera, we have dreamt English opera, we have wrangled about English opera, but we have done nothing.' Rosenthal recalled Beecham's earlier efforts in this field, which he had finally abandoned altogether, and ended with a rhetoric which seemed to take its tone from Beecham himself: 'Post-war Covent Garden has neither talked, dreamt nor wrangled. It has acted; and taken more than a first step to ensure the permanence of a British national opera.'

But Webster now was worried. This attack on his Musical Director was a serious matter. It might be a game for Beecham, but for Kubelik it was bound to be hurtful. Had real damage been done this time, Webster wondered. He was far more upset than he had been by any of the criticism aimed at himself.

And his fears were not groundless. Kubelik wrote to him offering his resignation.

> I can assure you that it is my love for the work I have started at Covent Garden which brought me to this decision. I admire British musicians and their friends in administration who are striving for a better future in the opera field in Great Britain. I hope that sooner or later they will unanimously find a way to work together with good-will towards new operatic horizons which some other nations have already attained.

The Board gave Kubelik its instant vote of confidence, and it was decided that Waverley should write to *The Times* to confirm their attitude in the crisis. Waverley wrote:

> The Board have informed Mr Kubelik that they are unwilling to accept his resignation. They have assured him that he has their entire confidence and that he can rely on their unstinted support in pursuit of the policy he has outlined during his tenure of his present office.

The Times was prepared to carry an article on their leader page, but only under Waverley's name, and eventually they decided that a piece on the financial structure of the Opera House would be more appropriate. And it was of course left to Webster to soothe Kubelik, and to persuade him to withdraw his resignation.

This was not an easy matter, for with Kubelik the hurt had gone deep. He had written to *The Times* as well as to Webster:

> In his letter of the 25th June Sir Thomas Beecham doubts whether I as a foreigner 'possess any of the qualifications essential for the creation of a truly national organization'. Having great respect for his 54 years' association with the lyric theatre and 46 of them as impresario, manager and musical director, I can assure him that I came to his country for the sole purpose of helping him with the development of something which I thought the majority of the British opera-loving public longed to possess: a British national opera. Since I see now that the British have not settled among themselves the problems of whether or not they want to have such a noble vista, and since I do not want to be in the way as a foreigner, I can set Sir Thomas Beecham's mind at rest: I have submitted to the Chairman of the Board of Directors my resignation as Musical Director of Covent Garden.

As soon as he learned about this letter, Webster phoned *The Times* and pointed out to them that this letter would sit very oddly beside Waverley's, it was already out of date and would they kindly suppress it. Happily, they did. Kubelik was persuaded to remain. The row was suddenly no longer of interest to the press or public, and died.

Though on 5 July, a month exactly after the *Review* was published, Beecham was interviewed by Charles Reid in the *News Chronicle*, a short interview containing little that had not been heard before apart for the statement: 'In 1951 I did a month at Covent Garden with *The Bohemian Girl* and also directed an inferior performance of *Die Meistersinger* with poor singers and an indifferent orchestra.' The 'poor singers' had included in their number no less than Elisabeth Grümmer, Ludwig Weber and Benno Kusche, and if the Covent Garden orchestra had indeed been 'indifferent', then it is all the more to be congratulated on somehow managing to draw such eloquent praise from Ernest Newman.

The crisis had also inspired champions of the Covent Garden regime. Colin Mason's long article in the *Spectator*, which appeared a week after the Beecham interview, took Kubelik to task only for his sensitivity.

> If he can maintain the astonishing rate of progress made by Mr Webster at Covent Garden during the last years in the building up of a really strong national opera company, he will do much more to overcome English resistance to English singing than by wasting his time on letters to the press.

And he summed up the present achievement in a crucial paragraph:

> If necessary, almost any standard opera could now be cast from the resident

Above: Callas and Sir David Webster after *La Traviata*, 1958
Below: Callas and Gobbi in *Tosca*, Act II, 1964

Above: Sir David Webster speaking at the luncheon given to mark his retirement in 1970. On his right, Dame Ninette de Valois
Below: Joan Sutherland and Sir David Webster

> company, with the exception of Wagner's and some of Strauss's, the vocal demands of which cannot be fully met by any opera company in the world from its own resources . . . to make our present lack of singers for Wagner and Strauss the basis of a general attack on the vocal capacity of English is an absurdity possible only to fatuous deaf xenophiles and Sir Thomas Beecham.

A joy for Webster to read! His Impossible Dream of ten or a dozen years ago was now reality. The case for the defence rested there, and Webster himself could not have improved it. His ambitions, in fact, did include an English *Ring*, and the idea of an English *Ring* at Covent Garden, never realized in his time, was one that haunted him. But he could, in 1956, rest satisfied with Mason's interim report.

Of course it was money – so long as the Musical Director wasn't lost in the commotion – which really mattered. Edward Lockspeiser had written in the *Tribune* on 15 June, before the row had blown up to the unfortunate Beecham proportions,

> The Treasury will no doubt be forced, reluctantly, to face the issue at stake – which is simply that Covent Garden has built itself up into a cultural institution comparable in importance to the British Museum or the National Gallery. Another £20,000 is not enough!

And the grant did go up. The Arts Council recommended a total grant of £300,000. The Treasury accepted the figure and threatened to peg the subsidy to this figure for three years – but Boothby's question in the Commons was answered by Macmillan with a Yes, and the grant, almost too much to hope for, was upped to £350,000.

The crisis was resolved. But this couldn't be counted as victory, simply because in this context victory *is not possible*. To be still *there* to continue the fight is the nearest approach. £350,000 ensured at least that the fight was going to continue.

And Webster knew how to turn this crisis past to good effect. When shortly afterwards he was making his end of the season speech, he said, 'We are going to open again,' and then, smiling broadly out into the house, he went on, 'As usual the opera will be relying on such *small Covent Garden voices* as Miss Amy Shuard's' (she had just sung Lisa in *The Queen of Spades*). The audience roared their approval. And he proudly announced plans for the following season, adding that he'd like to be able to offer more new productions. 'But' – and he pulled out the lining of his empty pockets – 'you know the answer as well as I do!'

One dependable source of money, which he'd come to count on, was the ballet with its full houses and its foreign tours, though the tours didn't bring in quite as much money as people thought, and less as costs rose in the 'fifties. Webster had a mixed attitude. He had been jealous of the ballet as a going concern, jealous of it as inevitably, and particularly at first, overshadowing his new opera company – grateful to it for the money it brought in, and for the renown it brought to his house. Jealous of that renown, and yet he would not happily have tolerated anything lesser for *his* house. He felt guilty about the use he had made of the ballet, and yet he refused even to countenance the idea that he had anything to feel guilty about. On the contrary, he considered that the Opera House setting he'd provided had been a vital factor in the ballet's development, and that much more acknowledgement was due to him for what *he'd* done for the ballet. He persisted in not publishing separate accounts for the two companies, money given to him by the government being intended for the benefit of the house, not for this or that company playing there; and he was conscious that however much or little of that money went to the support of the ballet company, and whatever use he made of the revenue that came to the house from the ballet, the ballet was still doing better financially than it would have done if it had set itself up, say, at Her Majesty's.

He continued to be proud of the ballet, though irked on occasion when reminded that it was never quite *his*. He had no great part in its running day by day. For the most part it was Dame Ninette working in another part of the house from himself, and for a long time Michael Wood acted virtually as liaison officer between these two busy people. And yet he was constantly involved – as in the mounting of *The Sleeping Beauty* and in negotiating the American tours with Hurok. Artists would come to him with their problems, and it was for him to soothe the artist who had not been given the promotion she thought her due. If an artist offered her resignation because she had not been Fonteyn's immediate successor in one of the great Ashton roles created for the ballerina, then it was Webster who was appointed to do the sweet-talking. The development of the ballet through these years has to be neglected in a history of David Webster – but none the less he was always *there*, holding himself in readiness to discuss seat prices and costings for a new ballet, to finalize arrangements for shipping scenery for a foreign tour, and to help determine repertory which would bring the company back effectively afterwards.

In particular, he was aware that the glory of the house was the Fonteyn-Ashton partnership. In 1956 Covent Garden to the world still meant ballet, and ballet at Covent Garden meant Fonteyn. It was impossible for him to resent Fonteyn and her supremacy. He responded to stars – he thought them wonderful people, and Fonteyn was a star of stars. The applause that greeted her on her every appearance was of the same kind as that which expressed the audience's gratitude for one of Callas's rare visits, or the return to the pit of a Kleiber or a Beecham. Fonteyn, appearing regularly, achieved the miracle of being greeted each time as though she were granting a rare privilege, like the most highly-valued guest. If Webster could persuade himself that Callas was not a 'difficult' artist, he could equally almost persuade himself that Fonteyn, too, was one of 'his' artists.

There was, and he couldn't blind himself to the fact, a danger that the ballet might come to rely too much on one artist, and that the company without Fonteyn might suddenly be revealed as a jewel-case without a jewel. The wonder-girl had married in 1954, and at that time expectations were only that she might continue dancing for perhaps another five years. Ashton created his ballets for Margot, a set of pearls to make a necklace for the star, and it was all the more important to encourage John Cranko, who had come to notice for his work with the Sadlers Wells Theatre Ballet, and Kenneth MacMillan, who had also been developed as choreographer by the smaller company.

In June 1956, month of crisis, Ashton created *Birthday Offering* for the gala, which in its way was a statement about the company's development up to that point. The work had its climax in the pas-de-deux for Margot and her partner Michael Somes, but it also served to present the company's other leading dancers, Beryl Grey and Violetta Elvin, the only ones who remained, with Margot, from the first generation of ballerinas. The second generation was represented by Nadia Nerina (who in that opening *Sleeping Beauty* had been one of the Maids of Honour standing beside the infant princess's cot) and by Svetlana Beriosova. Nerina and Beriosova had both to be given their own full-length works, and Beriosova's was in 1957, Webster having persuaded no less than Benjamin Britten to compose the score. This was *The Prince of the Pagodas*, choreographed by John Cranko, but unfortunately to his own silly and unworkable scenario. It didn't do what it ought to mark the new ballerina's status. Nerina had to wait till 1960 for *her* ballet, but this was worth waiting for. It was none other than Ashton's zestful *Fille Mal Gardée*, the length of whose two acts did not exceed invention by one second, and in which Nerina and her partner David Blair enjoyed, and gave, pleasure unlimited. Between the two, in 1958, Fonteyn herself had been given her apotheosis in *Ondine*, a full-length Ashton work beautiful in detail but entirely perfect only in its decor by Lila di Nobili, who combined fantasy on the level of Oliver Messel with taste and refinement to satisfy the most discriminating. If Webster wasn't exactly *that*, he was overjoyed to have this great designer working at her best in his house, and longed to appropriate her for his opera. Meanwhile the ballet worked beautifully in its presentation of the ballerina so long as that ballerina was Fonteyn, its inspiration. *Ondine* too was mounted on a commissioned score by which Webster set much store. One summer he'd taken a house on Capri, and he'd informed Jimmy that 'there's a *most* interesting young man coming over to have breakfast with us' – this was the then unknown Hans Werner Henze, who happened to live in Naples. Fonteyn was already flitting about in his mind while he talked to young Henze on Capri.

For all this Fonteyn-glory, there was no disguising the fact that boom-time, as de Valois had foreseen, wasn't going to last forever. The repertory, even taking into account the Ashton-Fonteyn creations, wasn't developing as excitingly and as interestingly as might have been hoped. If the company's fame and fortune had been based on presentation of the full-length classical works for which the Royal Opera House had provided a frame, in a sense it was almost trapped by its own success. Certainly a dancer's development in the company depended too much on her prowess in these classics, and how to enlarge this tiny repertory of full-length works was a question which absorbed too much thinking and effort. In fact, by the mid-'fifties it could be said that, for all its continuing success, ballet rather than opera was now the art form which seemed in danger of fading. It was ballet which needed a new look.

Hence the importance of the visit by the Bolshoi Ballet. In spite of the crisis, in the summer of 1956 Webster found the energy and the determination to conclude negotiations with the Russians – he had been over to Moscow the previous winter (to find Hurok there too hoping for pickings), and he had been firm in stipulating that Galina Ulanova must appear at least twice a week during the seven weeks' season, far more often than she did normally in Russia.

To add to Webster's harassment, through that long summer of 1956 this long-awaited event was on-off, on-off. The Russians did come at last, but, again delayed, they had to cancel their first night; and then the technicians had to work through an entire night setting up their *Romeo and Juliet*, the company rehearsing the whole of the following day before performing in the evening. Stamina they didn't lack, and nor did they disappoint, though a somewhat carping press hardly represented the public's enthusiasm.

A good part of the audience on the first night was an invited audience, and after the final curtain word went about that they should linger in the auditorium. The curtain rose again to show the stage now prepared for the party, and three gangways were put over the orchestra pit for the guests to cross. David Webster made a welcoming speech. Partisan he might be, but he did not respond to Ulanova less than wholeheartedly, and in the presence of his own stars he referred to her, awestruck, as 'the miracle that is Ulanova'. He *had* to delight in her art, and he could even, albeit briefly, envisage her as one of the 'family'. As he moved among the Russians, unable to communicate except by nods and smiles, he delighted in their reactions. They evidently shared his taste for glamour. Indeed, were clearly overwhelmed – the elegance and Royalty, people and clothes, the food and drink. This was wonderland to them.

Excitement didn't flag after the first night. It mounted steadily to near-hysteria. Ticket touts waxed fat. Seven weeks of Callas couldn't have served them better. For the audience, madly applauding, it was seven weeks of callouses. The critics too capitulated to Ulanova and *Giselle*. Hysteria could no longer be kept at bay when it was announced that the company would give three extra evenings of *divertissements* at the huge Davis Theatre, Croydon. Housewives queued through what might have become an unlikely Night of the Long Knives, for came the dawn they surged forward furiously, threatening the ticket touts, the roughish gentlemen, over-familiar throughout the season, who had encamped themselves prominently at the front.

All this attention was good for the Opera House at a difficult time. It helped Webster and Waverley who were turning themselves into unlikely Peter Pans exhorting their audiences, 'Don't let Tinkerbell-Covent Garden die!' And there was off-stage excitement too during the visit. The company was booked into the Shaftesbury Hotel, and had brought their own secret police with them for protection. One Saturday, lunching there, they were served with ice-cream, of which they were very fond. A dancer found a piece of glass in his. Then, so did another. And another. It *must* be a plot. Out they all marched. Webster, the instant he was informed, decided that Scotland Yard should be brought in to investigate. At once. The Russians protested – they wanted people from their own embassy. Here was a prospect before him of the season abandoned – an international crisis. But Webster didn't flinch. 'No!' he insisted. 'You're here in our country and *our* people must investigate.'

The English police arrived, and they went down with Webster to the hotel kitchens. The explanation was simple. The glass dishes for ice-cream were arranged on shelves, and one of the dishes on an upper shelf had fallen and smashed. The splinters had scattered, and the staff had carelessly put out the ice-cream without examining the dishes. End of this particular crisis. Trivial as it sounds, it might easily have had an altogether different resolution.

After the last appearance at the Davis Theatre there was another flurry, a more truly sinister one. The company were rushed to their waiting planes with almost indecent haste. Barely was the last plane in the air when news came that the Russians had invaded Hungary. And there was a doleful postscript. The Royal Ballet – as the Sadlers Wells Company had come to be known after 1955 – had been booked to give a reciprocal season in Russia, and the scenery had already been shipped to Leningrad. The season, of course, was cancelled, and sending the scenery and costumes and then getting them back cost the Opera House no less than £18,000, which had to be deducted from the £40,000 profit made out of the Bolshoi's London season.

What the Bolshoi had done, though, was worth more even than money. They had brought a new wave of excitement and enthusiasm to the art of ballet in England. Their repertory had been made up entirely of full-length ballets, if anything encouraging the Royal Ballet to persist in creating more of their own, which in the main was a pity. The Russians' modern chroeography didn't impress, and their designs, and particularly their costumes, were clumsily old-fashioned. Webster could support comparisons here with a certain smugness. But the dancing! The fervent *corps de ballet* in *Swan Lake*, not perhaps disciplined like our own, but a wonderful troupe of artists finding each her own way towards the same ideal! Unforgettable! Arabesques limitlessly extended, limitless like the Steppes which were the dancers' mental horizons. This was dancing clearly tempered by a landscape and a climate utterly different from our own. The home company was aflame with the wonder of it. The revelation of the male dancers' athleticism – the jumps and turns might not always have been quite precise, with toes not perfectly pointed, but the Khan's followers in the final scene of *The Fountains of Bakhchisarai* – the ballet admired by Keynes in Moscow many years before – transformed the Covent Garden stage, huge as it had once seemed, into a barely adequate pocket-handkerchief. Our own dancers could hardly wait till the end of the season to get back on to their stage and *try again*. Given this inspiration, this pacing, male dancing within the house improved by leaps and bounds – especially by leaps and bounds – almost out of recognition over the next few years.

And the Bolshoi didn't only inspire the ballet – it brought a new excitement to the whole house. Moving about in it, Webster happily smelt a more charged atmosphere. The opera company too shared it, and benefited by it. Webster was keyed up for the start of the new season, alert for the challenges which, as usual, he knew it must bring.

CHAPTER XVI

The Kubelik period · original language performances vs. opera in English · return of Callas · proposed merger with Sadlers Wells Opera · Jon Vickers · *The Trojans*

Kubelik, limited though his operatic experience had so far been, was from many points of view to prove himself a fine choice for Musical Director. He was no absentee director, he gave of his time generously. As he had shown from the beginning, with *Otello*, he was a courageous and fully committed company man, and he made good his expressed intentions by concentrating on company productions and not on those with guests coming and going. His three seasons show Covent Garden, advancing into its second decade under Webster, acquiring unmistakably the 'gait' of a first-rank house. It was a time by no means free of trouble, with crisis and confusions, and it was not the best organized period. Much of the energy and resources and available rehearsal time were given to the productions of which he took charge, or else to the new ones, and day to day repertory productions were sometimes makeshift affairs. But Kubelik's time will be remembered finally as a thrilling one, it will be remembered for its great achievements rather than for its occasional doldrums, and Kubelik himself, warm and generous man, is most lovingly remembered.

When Kubelik arrived the English singer was already 'on his way', as he readily appreciated. Glyndebourne's *Don Giovanni* that year had presented, next to the Donna Anna of Sena Jurinac, no less than five English singers, and three of them, Geraint Evans, Elsie Morison and Richard Lewis, were from Covent Garden: and Sylvia Fisher had been booked to appear in December 1955 with the Bayreuth Festival Company, their first Covent Garden artist. These were portents. Kubelik's refusal to take a solo curtain-call on the stage after performances except twice in a season, on the first night and the last, was a further gauge of his intentions – he wanted attention focused on the company, and to emphasize that any achievement was a company achievement. The opera he wanted more than any other to bring into the repertory eventually was the supreme ensemble opera, *Falstaff*. That could be the touchstone of the company's achievement, and he would be happy to have his work with the company judged eventually on the basis of an English *Falstaff*.

The *policy* was still, definitely, opera in English, with original language performances to be noted as deviations. Webster was already thinking of doing *The Ring* in English. The 1954 cycles had had Otakar Kraus and Frederick Dalberg in important roles, and during the 1956 tours the provinces were offered Sylvia Fisher's Brunnhilde and Kraus's Wotan, the one perhaps too sweet and lyrical and the other not ideally weighty enough, but it was early days for them in the great roles. The following year two extra performances of *The Twilight of the Gods* and one of *Valkyrie* were given outside the usual *Ring* cycles, (the three together were known familiarly as the *Ringlet*), and in *Valkyrie* Fisher's Brunnhilde was matched against the Wotan of Hans Hotter himself. Within a few years there was actually to be a group of singers at the house, led by Shuard, David Ward and Jon Vickers, who between them *could* have supported an entire English *Ring*. If it didn't happen, its very possibility is hugely significant.

In the Kubelik period the company was making huge strides towards Webster's goal, when they would be able to cope with virtually the whole repertory from their own resources, and Kubelik too was working to this end only. And greater flexibility in language matters only helped. Back in 1951 Hjördis Schymberg had been brought over in an emergency to do *Traviata*, which she knew only in Italian, and Kleiber had wanted Walter Midgley and Jess Walters to learn their roles in Italian to match her. Webster had refused to allow it. There had been special dispensations up to this time, but they were granted only in order to accommodate outstanding exponents of big roles – Boris Christoff had sung Boris in Russian, and Ludwig Weber been allowed to do it in *German*. Company members weren't allowed to sing in any other language than English. But on 20 April 1957 Los Angeles sang Butterfly at the house, in Italian, and the rest of the cast, all English, learned their roles in Italian to make a homogeneous performance – the first time a repertory opera had been given in the original language to accommodate a guest.

It was in any case becoming impossible – even were it desirable – to insist on opera in English. Everything worked against it. It was gradually becoming more and more common for all the great opera houses to give performances in the original. The Vienna State had brought their Mozart operas to Covent Garden in 1947 in German translations, but at home they had already begun to give one or two Verdi operas in Italian. It had still been possible, even in 1951, to consider inviting Maria Callas to sing in English in *The Sicilian Vespers*, but shortly afterwards no longer. She was prepared to learn roles only in the original language, and have them ready to perform anywhere in the world. In 1953 Webster was already finding that several singers offered their services for the Coronation summer season on the sole condition that they were allowed to sing in the original – it had been necessary, even then, for him to make the point with special emphasis that the basic policy of opera in English 'must clearly be continued'.

It was going to be more and more difficult to maintain an *exclusive* policy. Webster didn't at any time work out for himself just what degree of flexibility he wanted. It would depend on how things were at any particular time. There was no long-term plan. But at least some performances in English, if only to strengthen the identity of the firmly based company he *did* hope to hold together, were part of his plans for the future. He didn't always help the policy to work. He got good singers to learn roles in English, but then didn't always give them due acknowledgement. Hermann Uhde, invaluable singer, one of the best coming to Covent Garden in the 'fifties, learned the villain in *Lohengrin* in English but then was not asked back to do the role again after a single series of performances (and in English it was usable at Covent Garden and nowhere else). Uhde learned the four villains' roles in *The Tales of Hoffman* in English for a new production in 1954, and was replaced even before the first series was completed. Webster couldn't expect foreign singers to learn roles in English if it was going to be for a few performances only.

And for foreigners miscasting was all the more serious if they had to go to the trouble of the learning of the role in English. It was bad enough when Geraint Evans had to do Escamillo or Edith Coates Carmen, but home singers could reasonably be expected, as need arose, to step outside their normal limits. On the spot, they could more easily have it made up to them by a grateful Administrator.

The Italian repertory put most strain on the policy of opera in English. Webster was disturbed by the public response to the Italian seasons got up at the Stoll Theatre in 1952 and 1953. Not a jot did the audiences seem to care about 'scratch' productions and poor orchestral playing, there was some good singing and that was all that seemed to matter. Here were signs that no impresario could afford to ignore. Webster remembered too the grateful response in his own house. It was in answer to an evident need that, for this audience starved of real Italian opera, he started his own form of 'summer season' at the Opera House. But he didn't consider this a return to the pattern of the pre-war international season – his was rather a 'festival season' in miniature to be absorbed into the current, uninterrupted season of opera. The Stignani *Trovatores* in the summer of 1952 were the beginning, and there were 'festival seasons' of Italian opera every summer for the next five years, apart from 1954 when the new *Ring* was mounted. Performances on the whole were robust rather than sensitive or subtle, and if superlative singers were on offer there was certainly also a measure of poor casting (in the Stignani *Trovatores* both the tenor and soprano were roundly booed by an audience resenting the 'festival' prices exacted from them), and some of it was due to Webster's reluctance to commit himself too far in advance, at a time when, increasingly, opera houses in competition with each other booked singers farther and farther ahead and there was a queue for the services of the outstanding ones. Singers didn't always appear to best advantage in these 'get-togethers', not even Callas when, in Coronation summer, she appeared, this time with Giulietta Simionato, not only in *Norma* again but also as the *Trovatore* Leonora and as Aïda. Ernest Newman reported:

> I could never persuade myself that this was the Ethiopian slave Aïda. Had I been present at Pharaoh's court I would have assumed her to be the contemporary Duchess of Memphis, whose travels had taken her as far as the contemporary Hollywood.

Which hurt Webster at least as much as it did the diva!

The first time members of the Board scouted the possibility of a deliberate and avowed change of language policy came in April 1956, as a possible economy measure, and it came from Lord Moore (later Lord Drogheda) and Lord Robbins. The suggestion, similar to Pomeroy's when he made his bid for the lease in 1948, was for a return to two-month seasons of international opera with the house given to ballet for the rest of the year. Webster came back firmly with the answer that the Opera House's financial difficulties sprang mainly from inflation, which was general. He pointed out that in opera, though not in ballet, it was possible, if absolutely necessary, to economize by having less new productions, because guest artists in old productions could fill the house more cheaply.

The house was never reorganized in this way, but the situation alone is important as being the first positive expression of a significant bias towards a reversal of the language policy. And it came as early as 1956.

It seems relevant, even in this context, to recall once more that 1956 was the year of Suez and national humiliation. In the spoken theatre 'kitchen-sink' drama was in one way answering the needs of the time. It was a drama of drabness and disillusion, a drama of protest and scorn. But opera could, from one point of view, be seen as providing an escape from unwelcome realities – full-throated, plangent, gloriously technicolour as it could on occasion be, it answered other needs. For some people it could be almost a symbol of the glory that once had been.

The Opera House does itself afford a 'velvet and plush' East of Suez sensation. It has – any traditional opera house has – a feeling of 'exclusivity' and class-privilege about it, as from the first David Webster had been uneasily aware. He'd wanted *his* house, without sacrificing elegance, also to be 'popular'. He wanted *opera* to be 'popular'. He knew that some of those who were pushing for opera in the original were in fact aiming at keeping opera 'exclusive'. In his own early days at Covent Garden, when attracting audiences had been so urgent a problem, he had been painfully conscious that opera in English lacked 'snob-appeal'. He also knew that there was more to original language opera than merely its snob-appeal; but it worried him, in 1956, that perhaps its main appeal for some pushing for it was *precisely* this snob-appeal and the feeling of exclusivity it would bring to the house.

Even if it seemed, increasingly, to be going against the signs and portents, Webster persisted in opera in English, again persuading the Board in 1956 that it must still be the *rule*, whatever the exceptions allowed. *Jenufa*, the Janaček opera Kubelik had been asked to do at Sadlers Wells, was produced for him in English at Covent Garden, in December, with the same director-designer team as *The Bartered Bride*, Christopher West and Jan Brazda. Their work was modest and serviceable – here words of praise, for the stature of the opera was revealed, which isn't always the case with more glamorous but over-powering productions. Kubelik has an exact feeling for the rhythms of this wonderful music, and it was a success for a home team of singers. Shuard was Jenufa, the brothers were Edgar Evans and, after his success with Cassio in *Otello*, John Lanigan; while Sylvia Fisher, the Kostelnicka, stunned the audience, such as it was, into a deeply emotional response, earned only by artists 'opened' to a particular role. Had she been a guest, not a long-familiar local artist, she must surely have packed the house even in an unfamiliar opera. But houses were poor.

In January Kubelik was in charge of a new *Mastersingers*, and promoting this work in English had been a small campaign in itself for the General Administrator. Arthur Bliss, on the Board, had wanted it done in German. The Wagner Society had sent out a questionnaire to its members, who unequivocally preferred star casts singing in the original language and were perfectly prepared to pay vastly increased prices for them. Webster, sent the results of the poll, replied cautiously that 'he very much doubted if the cast that we shall put up for *Mastersingers* will be in any way inferior to a cast that would consist of a certain number of well-known names.' He now had the confidence to suggest that stars so-called were sometimes no more than 'singers who had the luck to be born in Germany'. He argued that *Mastersingers* is 'not a star opera, but an ensemble work which needs the kind of rehearsal that can in fact only come from the conditions that surround resident artists.'

The production was therefore important in making good Webster's claims for his company. But it wasn't a success. There were casting troubles, with Peter Pears a not very volatile David and James Pease no heavy-weight as Sachs. Webster had wanted his new tenor, Jon Vickers, to sing Walther, but he was already more than adequately employed, so Richard Lewis was cast. Then *he* couldn't. To save the show the producer Eric Witte, a well-known tenor but at this stage more satisfactory in character roles, had to do it. Only Geraint Evans came near ideal casting. Worse still, Kubelik's conducting didn't produce the steady flow and serene blossoming that this supremely lyrical score ideally requires (though things went better when Goodall, with his broader phrasing, took over the last two performances). Webster might go for solace to Ernest Newman's notice, who divined the spirit of the production when he noted that 'its outstanding feature was the organic union of all the features, musical, dramatic and scenic' – wasn't this *precisely* what they had gone after? – and Newman went so far as to praise Kubelik's conducting for its 'fine mixture of energy and sensitivity'. None the less, not the production that either the Wagner Society or the public at large wanted. It was a central failure of Kubelik's directorship.

But all was joy and success when, five days after the *Mastersingers*, opening, back to the house came Webster's beloved Maria Callas. Here was joy to compensate a dozen such disappointments. Callas, absent almost four years, returned no longer the Popeye-debutante. The Callas of 1957 was Callas svelte, and with the extra gloss and glamour of acclaim worldwide. She returned for two performances of *Norma*, once more with Ebe Stignani. Callas large had been a superb actress, but some of her acting had been lost within her frame. It had always been eloquent and beautiful, but now she presented images with linear perfection, and her audiences were deceived into imagining that she was now, actually, a *better* actress. But no, merely one more visible. The second *Norma* was on 6 February, and this time the last verse of the duet *Mira! O Norma* was encored; it had to be. The conductor, John Pritchard, couldn't get the performance going again. It was Covent Garden's first encore since the war, the first Callas had ever given, the first given by the veteran Stignani in *Norma*. Trinity of wonders! The only worries had been about getting Callas's dogs into the country, quarantine regulations, as Walter Legge had reported to Webster, being somewhat tricky to circumvent. Webster had written to him in reply: 'Mrs Patrick Campbell once told me that she got her dog into the country – once as her left breast and once as a diseased hip. After that she was baffled!'

It was a comfort and support for Webster to recall Callas and *Norma* when he found himself confronted by a second major crisis within a year. The cry was now, as Webster had feared it might be, for a merger of the two London companies, Covent Garden and Sadlers Wells. Right, said the Covent Garden Board, but only if this was the *only way* to preserve the lyric arts in London. And if it happened, then the Treasury would be responsible for destroying the identity of each house.

Webster was to make an estimate of what savings would be possible. He didn't see how it could be more than £40,000 per year. Meanwhile Norman Tucker, Sadlers Wells Administrator since 1947, resigned. An alternative plan was for a merger between Sadlers Wells and the Carl Rosa, which by this time had been off the road for three months. Sadlers Wells wasn't keen on *this*, which would entail thirty weeks a year touring outside London (in other words, Carl Rosa, augmented, would continue as before, while the conditions in which the Wells worked were to be sacrificed). It was a piece of luck for Webster, something for him to boast of, that, though Covent Garden's provincial tours were already by now curtailed, in 1957 Vinay himself was appearing as Othello in Manchester, the biggest operatic occasion outside London since 1951, when Flagstad had given her last Isolde of all in Liverpool.

There was no amalgamation. What happened in the end was that, sadly, the Carl Rosa, after its long history, was sacrificed entirely. By the end of 1957 the company was defunct, and the two larger houses, which together had made the Carl Rosa's function less important, continued their bumpy ways independently. A pity. But as V. N. Lucas had commented in 1946 in the *New English Weekly:*

> As a record of brave endeavour it is unique; as an example of a sustained fight for survival it is epic; but it is doubtful if at the end of the Carl Rosa's eighty years the public is any more opera conscious than it was at the beginning.

Ten years on and the public *was* more opera conscious – but thanks to Webster.

One result of this particular crisis was that the Governors of Sadlers Wells now decided that they wanted to shed responsibility for the Sadlers Wells Theatre Ballet, the smaller company founded at Sadlers Wells Theatre after de Valois took her company to Covent Garden. It was she who suggested that it be taken over by Covent Garden, and Webster concurred, notwithstanding that there was no chance of a compensating increase in the grant and the company had been costing Sadlers Wells £6000 a year to run.

But Webster saw a chance to use it advantageously. The ballet company at Covent Garden, while right for America, was too large for most European and British provincial theatres, but it had the big names to attract audiences. The company from Sadlers Wells Theatre was often too small, and it didn't have the drawing-power. The plan was a gradual amalgamation of the two ballet companies, to yield a touring group of some forty to sixty dancers, including big names, still leaving enough dancers for the main company at Covent Garden, where the touring group could also from time to time appear.

And now came *The Trojans*, the climax of Kubelik's second season. Never before had The Company been put so grandly on show. If *The Mastersingers* hadn't worked, and there was still no English *Falstaff*, then *The Trojans* was all the more important. The work had been composed mainly between 1856 and 1858, so that the Covent Garden performances marked its hundredth anniversary: they were also the first-ever stage performance complete! It had been a long-time ambition of Webster's to mount the work, which was, too, one of Harewood's great enthusiasms. After hearing Sir Thomas Beecham conduct them in radio performances in 1947, Ernest Newman had written in the *Sunday Times*, 'It is a pity we cannot hear works like *Elektra* and *Les Troyens* in their proper place, which is Covent Garden; but wireless performances are better than none at all.' He didn't have to wait long. *Elektra* in 1953, and with the same heroine, Erna Schluter, as in the broadcast; *The Trojans* in 1957. The company in hardly more than a decade was rising to the challenge of the gigantic enterprise, giving the opera in English as a company effort, with only the Dido, Blanche Thebom, brought in from outside. Cassandra, the heroic lady of the first part of the opera, was Amy Shuard, and it was a piece of almost unlooked for good fortune that Aeneas too could be cast from within the company – Webster having just acquired a promising new tenor.

Jon Vickers, in his own word, is 'a tenor discovered by David Webster one rainy Sunday afternoon in Toronto' – and how he came to be discovered is indeed a story.

In the autumn of 1955 the ballet company had been in New York, and Webster with them. A Canadian tenor was recommended to him (by Irving Guttman, who'd produced him in some television shows in Vancouver). But singers were *always* being recommended, and Webster didn't usually spring to attention. It happened, though, that he felt some slight obligation to Canada. In 1950 the ballet company had been in America for its second tour, which concentrated more than ever on the United States, and the Secretary of State for the Commonwealth,

Patrick Gordon-Walker, wasn't pleased that Canada, helpful during the monetary crisis, was feeling neglected. Only a few days before this 1955 visit to America Webster had published an article in *Music and Musicians* in which he had congratulated himself on his success with Australians – Fisher led a contingent which was soon to be made up to no less than ten – but claimed that Canadians went more to America and Europe. In Toronto he'd explained that he'd like to bring his opera to Canada, but suspected that 'operatically speaking, Canada is still inclined to be a little old-fashioned.' Political pressure wasn't being brought to bear, but, since he relied on government subsidy, Webster knew that it would be at least tactful, in regard to Canada, to be prepared to acknowledge an obligation of a kind.

He wrote to Vickers. He was going to be in Toronto. 'Can we get together?' His commendable speed promised to be of no avail this time. 'I've decided to quit,' Vickers replied. He wasn't making headway, and he was only continuing till the following summer to honour commitments already made.

A few days later, on 17 November, Vickers's phone rang at eight o'clock in the morning. It was David Webster again, but now he was actually in Toronto. 'I'd like to hear you sing at ten o'clock.' But Vickers had done a broadcast the night before, and he wasn't going to sing that day for anyone. Webster put the phone down a mite shaken. Didn't the boy know that Webster represented Covent Garden? Didn't *that* mean something in the world of opera?

Webster rang back. 'What about four o'clock this afternoon?' Vickers, this time, agreed. Webster heard him that afternoon, marked in his programme, 'Quite something!' and exhorted the boy not to give up singing but to move to London instead. He'd certainly offer him a contract. 'Then it will have to be a good one,' was Vickers's response. 'And what do you mean by good?' Vickers wanted a guarantee that if after eighteen months in England he'd failed he could return to Canada no worse off.

Webster went on to tell him that a contract with Sadlers Wells would present no problem but he couldn't be absolutely sure about Covent Garden. This certainly wasn't good enough. Webster was either misjudging his man – a rare event – or else merely sounding him out, he didn't himself know which. 'Unless you think I'm too good for Sadlers Wells,' pronounced young Vickers with superb confidence, 'I wouldn't *dream* of coming.' Characteristically, Webster began to whistle. 'You strike me,' he returned at last, 'as a man who knows the value of a dollar.'

Rapport was established, and it was to last. Vickers came over to London the following summer, in June 1956, when Webster's head was full of the Resignation Crisis. He had an ear for Vickers's London audition none the less. He sat forward attentively while Vickers sang 'On with the Motley' and the Flower Song from *Carmen*, and then asked for the *Tosca* arias. But Vickers hadn't sung *Tosca* for over six months. 'I'm terribly sorry. But I feel I've made a fantastic impression and I don't want to spoil it.' Webster was all graciousness. 'That's all right, Mr Vickers. *We were only asking for our own pleasure*.'

He'd heard enough – a heroic tenor voice big enough for his house. He concealed his excitement as he went on to explain: 'We asked for these things today because we think we'd like you to sing' – he paused just long enough – 'the part of Aeneas in *The Trojans*.' And this before either he or Kubelik had seen the new boy actually performing an operatic role! Vickers was offered a three-year contract – at Covent Garden – and ended by settling for eighteen months. He still wasn't sure about singing as a career and didn't want to become a resident in England subject to UK tax. And he wasn't sure about *The Trojans*. He hadn't even *heard* of it; though he'd registered Webster's pause. It had to be *something*. Still – 'I'd have to see the score,' he stipulated firmly.

Vickers's debut opera was *A Masked Ball*, which hadn't been a success in the repertory, but was a brilliant success for Vickers. It was brilliant and not altogether obvious casting. As Webster had foreseen, the boy was a treasure – a tenor with a trumpet-ring in his voice for heroic phrases who could also sing softly and expressively. But he hadn't been misled into assuming that the boy was by temperament exclusively, or even essentially, heroic: Vickers has in fact an uncanny instinct for hitting off neurotic heroes with a propensity for being dominated by women with a strongly maternal aspect, and if the point is not to be overstressed, his stage personality does gain an additional fascination because of it. In his interpretation, first seen on the company's tour in Cardiff in March 1957, and for the first time in Covent Garden in April, the king in *A Masked Ball* was a somewhat masochistic character who brought poignant doomed yearning to the guilty ecstasy of his love scenes with Amelia.

Carmen followed, this second success confirming to Webster that he had found himself a star, the crest of the wave of second generation singers at Covent Garden. The star of the first generation, Sylvia Fisher, was enjoying a fine flowering at the same time, following her Kostelnicka with Turandot, her first Italian role at the house. At the meeting of the Critics Circle in March Webster had claimed proudly that she was now internationally recognized as a dramatic soprano in the royal line of Emmy Destinn and Lotte Lehmann. He was already wondering how long it would be before he could make equal claims for his new singer in relation to Martinelli!

Above: Sir Frederick Ashton, Dame Margot Fonteyn, Cecil Beaton and Rudolf Nureyev looking at a first model of the set for *Marguerite and Armand*
Below: Fonteyn and Nureyev dancing in *Marguerite and Armand*

Above: Sir David Webster and Sir Geraint Evans at the vernissage of David Hockney's portrait of Webster
Below: Sir David Webster and John Tooley

And so to *The Trojans*, Kubelik's outstanding success at the house and one of Covent Garden's outstanding achievements, the most powerful case ever made for grand opera in English. Wakhevitch and John Piper were both approached for designs, and Picasso himself was considered but thought unsuitable. Eventually the director, John Gielgud, brought in Mariano Andreu, who had delightfully designed his celebrated *Much Ado About Nothing*. There were, to be sure, awkward moments. During rehearsals Vickers one day went to Webster complaining that the opera was being directed as though it wasn't centred on the hero, who was being used merely as a prop for the two heroic ladies! He wasn't going to settle for being a little-man prop. Webster came down with him, and he let Vickers see him in quiet confabulation with Gielgud – after which rehearsals progressed satisfactorily.

This was the scale of opera Webster had had in mind when he first opened the house after the war, and it was with this ideal that he had felt obliged to reject the Sadlers Wells Opera as the basis for his new company. After the first night Sir Eugene Goossens wrote to congratulate him. He had been 'moved and overwhelmed . . . Give us more opera in the "grand manner" like this!' he exhorted. Just the terms of praise to please Webster. *The Trojans* aroused interest worldwide. Webster's own trial period was surely over now, and surely too the testing time for English opera?

Lord Harewood, writing in *Covent Garden, 25 Years of Opera and Ballet*, the catalogue accompanying the 1971 Victoria and Albert Museum exhibition, summed it up:

> If one had to mention one production to epitomize Kubelik's regime it would be *The Trojans* in summer 1957 . . . it was enterprising in the sense that the work was one we all believed in strongly but which had in effect never even been given before in anything like so complete a form; and it relied on no gimmicks . . . In its way, *The Trojans* was an astonishing achievement precisely because the work's problems of length, complications, cost, lack of previous box-office attraction, were overcome entirely without recourse to over-dramatic expedients – a star-loaded cast, a 'trouvaille' of staging, publicity gimmickry. The achievement lay not only in the musical performance, which was considerable, but in proving honestly and convincingly that the work was viable for a big company in a big house and could not only be staged complete with relative economy . . . but without seeming unreasonably long to the audience – a danger in an epic of this kind as opposed to a Wagnerian music drama where motifs and their development make for a closer-knit whole.

The same article concludes with a testimonial to Kubelik, and speaks for the house at this time:

> Kubelik made a great contribution to music in London. With his ability to give unstintingly to colleagues, company, audience and above all to music, he was a pleasure to work for and with. In thinking of his own career, he might easily not agree with me, but I know that, if I were asked, I should find it hard not to nominate his three years at Covent Garden as the best of my life.

They could easily, in spite of crises, be nominated as the best in Webster's life too.

CHAPTER XVII

Centenary celebrations · exit Kubelik · Regina Resnik · Gerda Lammers in *Elektra* · Callas's *Traviata* · Leontyne Price · *Don Carlos* · Visconti and Giulini · an international triumph

The present Opera House is the third on its site, the second having been burnt down on 5 March 1856, at five in the morning. ('It is some time since we burnt down one of our national theatres,' *The Times* remarked: 'but this oversight has been amply repaired this morning.') The foundation stone of the present building was laid in 1857, and the house reopened in May 1858. It was a centenary to celebrate, and Webster looked forward to celebrating it. The present stature of his house required that he should celebrate in some style. He intended to.

In the autumn after *The Trojans* there was Kempe's *Ring* again, postponed from the summer because the Berlioz opera had taken up all rehearsal time. An extra attraction was the world's new Brunnhilde, Birgit Nilsson, and because of anticipated interest both at home and abroad Webster had decided to open booking no less than five months ahead. *The Ring* started the season magnificently, and began the build-up to the centenary celebrations the following summer.

Even now there were distresses. Lord Waverley died on 5 January 1958, a sad loss to the Opera House and a personal loss to David Webster. Like Lord Keynes, who had at least lived to savour the success of *The Sleeping Beauty*, Waverley too had known that the effort he'd made for the house had not been fruitless. He'd seen *The Trojans*, and he had known that plans were well forward to consolidate Covent Garden's position. And there was to be a loss of another kind, for by this time it was known that Kubelik would probably not be renewing his contract, which had only till the summer to run. The failure of *The Mastersingers* had particularly unsettled him: Webster could not but regret that Kubelik seemed perhaps, among his many virtues, not to include great stamina, or even a driving ambition. But he acknowledged that the burden of such a responsibility as that of Musical Director for an organization such as his was one that many, after a while, would want to lay down. Webster of course didn't try too hard to persuade a man not really willing, but he certainly bore no grudge. In later years Kubelik was to be deeply hurt that Webster never came to hear one of his concerts in London, but there was no significance to be drawn there – it was simply that, as Jimmy had foreseen, David had

had enough. He was over his ears in music already, and *could not* respond to more.

For all the excitement of the summer to come, this was an unsettling period, a period of change. Webster sometimes felt that the household about him was being pulled apart – though at the centre of it his 'family' remained strong. Waverley was replaced by Lord Drogheda (still Lord Moore) and he and members of the Board were now pressing harder to go over to original language performances. And the company was changing. They were like children growing up. Webster had *wanted* them to grow up, and it was with pleasure that he was more and more often now asking them to take over when a star guest had to be replaced. (Miss Kerr didn't any longer automatically reach for the phone to contact the agents of famous foreign singers.) He kept telling himself that it was natural for his own singers to want their chance of international careers – only natural that they should want to be free to work more abroad. Webster tried hard not to be resentful, and he worked at making himself graciously accommodating. He *did* understand – when, for example, Geraint Evans showed signs of restlessness. He'd been singing at Glyndebourne since 1949, and in 1957 he'd done Falstaff there under Vittorio Gui. His new Covent Garden contract was ready, but Webster saw that he was reluctant to sign, and quickly adapted to the situation. 'If you feel happier,' he said, 'I won't try to argue with you. Give it a try. But remember,' he added, '*if we want you, we have first choice.*' And Geraint didn't really leave. As he said at the party given in 1973 to celebrate his twenty-fifth anniversary at the house, he was always 'Sir David's boy' – when he went abroad he was always going *from* Covent Garden, and when he returned it was always a homecoming. Webster knew that there were good new singers coming on, and he let the established singers go, confident that he'd have them back as guests.

Naturally enough, too, English singers wanting their chance internationally needed to know their roles in the original language, and as much as foreign guests they too wanted at least some opera in the original. (The chorus felt very differently – for them it was more work and no extra rewards!) Gradually performance in the original language at Covent Garden came to be regarded as the gateway to abroad.

This was the point of the new production of *Aïda* which followed *The Ring* in the autumn of 1957 to open the season proper. It was in Italian but it wasn't a 'special'. It was something quite new in that Webster was mounting it to accommodate English singers as well as foreign guests, and was really a follow-up to the Italian *Butterfly* with Los Angeles the previous April. The new *Aïda* was not merely useful to the English singers but also flattering to them, since it implied a much greater equality between local and guest singers. *Aïda*, with many different casts, was a success. But Webster was at pains to emphasize that this greater flexibility did not mean radical change in language policy. *The Trojans* had shown that opera in English could be mounted on the highest level, and its revival was going to be an important item of the centenary celebrations. Webster was also contemplating other outstanding English events – Offenbach's *La Belle Hélène* with no less than Sitwell for translator, and Jean-Louis Barrault's name as director as further guarantee that this was aiming high. Unfortunately this project had to be abandoned because of a clash with the Sadlers Wells production, and the English *Falstaff* too had to be postponed (because of performances by an Italian company at the Stoll as well as those at Glyndebourne). That *Falstaff* would have helped knit the company together more strongly, and it was all the more to be regretted because, with Kubelik leaving, it was needed to round off his term of office.

The loss of these two operas in English somewhat upset the balance, and it was only balance that was in question. Poulenc's *The Carmelites*, with its graceful and restrained music, didn't make any great impression, but it was done in English and company members had their accustomed successes in it, and Poulenc himself thought it better than La Scala's. 'Why did no one tell me what opera here was like?'

Webster enjoyed reckoning up the pleasures to be found in the everyday repertory (at least when there were particular singers to lift a performance above routine). Jon Vickers, though in demand worldwide, was being thoroughly absorbed into the company – his presence helped cement it. When he and Shuard sang together in *A Masked Ball* their duet had a gorgeous, absolutely authentic vocal glamour, and young Joan Carlyle in the same opera made a page-boy with a delicious vocal glitter. For the first time they were showing how well Italian opera *could* go in English. And Vickers was also singing in *Carmen* opposite a newcomer, the American Regina Resnik. When she had sung in Britten's *The Rape of Lucretia* at the Canadian Stratford she recommended Vickers to them, and he now returned the compliment by recommending *her* to Webster. She arrived magnificently – an uninhibitedly sultry Carmen who put groin back in the opera. She became an instant Webster favourite. Her success meant all the more to her because she had only three years before moved down from soprano to mezzo, and with this Carmen began her real conquest of a new repertory. As she explained many years later in a *Guardian* interview, 'Carmen is my calling card all over Europe now, and I have David Webster to thank for that.' Pointing up Webster's achievement, all too easy to take for granted, she added, 'He got such an unusual cast together, all unknowns in those particular roles' – in 1958 the casting of Vickers and Joan Sutherland alongside Resnik counted as 'unusual'! – 'it was the beginning of my international career'.

A lead-in to the summer celebrations was given by a 'star-overnight' sensation that winter. Christel Goltz had been engaged for Elektra, but she fell ill a couple of weeks before rehearsals were due to begin. This still 'problem' opera relied above all on the glamour and histrionic ability of its leading lady to attract audiences, and Webster was doubtful about finding a satisfactory substitute. There were so few singers who could even get through it. But he hated cancelling performances. Lord Harewood had recently heard of an unknown singer who'd had success with the role in Germany. He recalled the name. It was a new one to Webster. But it happened, by an amazing coincidence, that this singer was in London at this very moment, about to give a recital – not a highly publicized one, and not in very grand circumstances, but still, she was here. The recital was to be given at the Mahatma Gandhi Hall, and thither Harewood repaired with agent Freddy Diez. He found her rehearsing, and he didn't interrupt her. Such a wonderful voice filled the hall as he could hardly believe. Surely there weren't unknowns with voices like *this!* He approached her. Yes, she said, she was available. It seemed a double miracle, that the singer could, if required, fit in all rehearsals and performances. Harewood couldn't book her on the spot, but he was certain it was only necessary for her to be heard. Next day she was at Covent Garden to sing for Kempe. Harewood introduced her – Miss Gerda Lammers. Was she going to be overawed by these grander surroundings? Kempe and Webster might have been smilingly tolerant of Harewood's youthful enthusiasm, but as Lammers began to sing Harewood knew at once that yesterday had been no fluke, and he watched delightedly as Webster sat forward, jaw sagging slightly. Webster 'flipped', Kempe 'flipped'. Lammers was engaged, and she began to rehearse. Now it was only a question, would she hit form on the night? The night arrived. And next morning, those who had sold their tickets, refusing to accept an unknown substitute when they had paid their money for Goltz, knew that they had missed a rare occasion. Lammers's Elektra, with its aspect of thwarted maternity and its suppressed and at moments gloriously outpouring lyricism, was a performance on an exalted level, the level even of Vinay's Othello and of Maria Callas herself in her great roles. She was ideally matched by her conductor, and for the first time the opera drew full houses.

Webster didn't have much money to spend on the celebrations. Lord Drogheda was scarcely in office before he was being called upon to show his financial mettle, in his very first month being obliged to relay to

Kenneth Clark at the Arts Council the sorry story of the shifts Covent Garden was put to. Provincial tours were being curtailed so that a film could be made instead, and maintenance had had to be postponed. The cyclorama was having to wait for necessary repairs and the orchestra for their pay-rise. If more money wasn't found, the theatre might have to close. It was Waverley's heir echoing Waverley. And to good effect. More money was eventually found, and once again disaster was averted.

Plans for the summer, though, had already been drawn up, and it was a question of making a splash with not too much money. There couldn't be any celebrations worthy the name without a contribution from Maria, and she *had* to be included, somehow, in the programme. Webster couldn't offer her a new production, so he was immensely grateful when she consented to appear in an old one. Guthrie's *Traviata* was by now run-down, and in its revival it did *not* come up good as new. Webster, however, involved in her work as always, was more than ever involved with her in this role, for the Callas-Violetta emphasized the daughter aspect, and very clearly made her motive for renouncing her lover, and with him all prospect of future happiness, the overpowering urge to be, albeit by proxy, dutiful daughter to her lover's father. Without any difficulty Webster could identify himself with the father-figure, and after the performance he greeted Maria, if anything, even more warmly than usual. It was altogether a deeply felt, a very special occasion, for them both. His adored Maria, who with the Mad Scene from Bellini's *I Puritani* also provided the centrepiece for the Centenary Gala in June, did, without rancour, suggest that in the future she would look more kindly on the idea of returning to Covent Garden if a new production were provided for her.

Leontyne Price, a very recent star, was another Webster was determined to present, another jewel to display to his audiences. No new production for her either – but her presence alone would ensure that the still-new *Aïda* would provide a gala evening. She was an extraordinarily vibrant and voluptuous Aïda at this stage of her career, and the Nile on these steamy Price evenings threatened to evaporate. Amneris was Resnik, who brought to her role that hint of corruption fermenting under a hot sun which was already virtually an artistic trademark. And Vickers, their man, was once again, as in *The Trojans*, happily heroic between his two heroic ladies.

Callas and Price, following Lammers, were certain wonders, a celebration equally of the house centenary and of the art of opera itself. But where the money went was on a single 'slap-up' new production. Just *one*. And this was to be *Don Carlos*, in many ways a most unlikely choice. Webster wasn't prepared to regard any season a failure which had a Callas *Traviata* in it, but if the new production failed then the celebrations would have a hole in the middle, and through it would be poured most of his money. Before embarking on the opera, Webster had weighed up the various considerations, and he'd justified the choice in his own mind at any rate.

This wasn't, like *Otello*, a work everyone already knew to be great. It hadn't made much of a showing in the 1951 Sadlers Wells production, and no one – Lord Harewood apart – seemed sure about it. Smetana's *Dalibor*, also an enthusiasm of Harewood's, was the other main contender for top spot in the centenary celebrations; it had already been proposed for Richard Lewis in 1954 and now was a possibility for Vickers. But Webster felt that the occasion demanded a production with a more gala feel about it, in the original language if that would help accommodate glamorous guest artists, and *Dalibor* could always be useful later as a house production. He also wanted to use the occasion to give the Italian repertory a lift. (Although Verdi had composed *Don Carlos*, like *The Sicilian Vespers*, for Paris, and set a French text, it too was essentially an Italian opera and it was decided to sing it in an Italian translation.)

This very opera, as it happens, had been the one chosen by Rudolph Bing to inaugurate his regime at the Metropolitan in 1950; but he had treated it as a 'singers' opera' and there too the work's stature had not been revealed. For if, like *Trovatore*, it does need superb singers (and was therefore a good opera for Bing, whose house laid the emphasis on the singer rather than ensemble and presentation), *Don Carlos* is also, in its way, ensemble opera as well as grand opera, and ensemble is of the essence if the work's dramatic structure and its true greatness are to be revealed. Before Bing it had not been heard at the Met for almost thirty years – and even a cast including Chaliapin, Martinelli and Ponselle hadn't won for it more than eleven performances over three years!

In fact the opera had *never* been a success. After its first performance in 1867 the *Illustrated London News* had remarked: 'We are not sure that the learned music of the opera will prove as grateful to the popular ear as the familiar melodies of his early days,' and its ninety years' history to date hadn't proved the writer wrong.

Don Carlos, then, was a risk. There were mutterings. People about the house were asking him, 'Are you sure?' 'Have you thought it over carefully?' He *wasn't* sure. He knew as well as anyone that it was a risk. But he'd taken risks in the past, and in every major decision he'd been right. So now he decided in favour of the work, and willed himself into certainty. There was Harewood's enthusiasm, that ought to justify a measure of certainty. Altogether, he was buoyant with a sense of adventure.

And moreover, canny as ever, he knew that it was now or never. All the more because the work was a risk, if it was to be put on at all it must be presented on the highest level, given all the help it could get; which meant at an expense which only this occasion could justify. It was a case of *Don Carlos* now, on the right level, or not at all, ever. He didn't, finally, feel he had any choice. He didn't feel he was making a decision, he felt that the decision had made itself. *That* meant it was the right one.

It was of course going to have the most glamorous cast, but also the best in the way of director and designer and conductor. And so – enter two more 'greats'. Visconti and Giulini. Luchino Visconti was from film and theatre and he'd turned to opera only four years earlier, inspired by Callas in *Norma*. Since then he'd collaborated with the conductor Carlo Maria Giulini in presenting her in several operas at La Scala. This connection with Maria was their best possible recommendation to Covent Garden. Webster, the two men already enhaloed by the love he bore Callas, was thrilled to have them continue their collaboration in his house.

Leslie Hurry's name came up for designer, but Webster also offered Lila di Nobili. Visconti refused her, not because he didn't appreciate that he was being offered the world's best; it was simply that he wanted to do his own. He was a director who shared Webster's own taste for a theatre of luxury and gorgeous display – but it was a theatre in which every fine detail worked to the one end, enhancing and illuminating the dramatic action, *not* distracting from it. At least it was so in *Don Carlos*. This was what Webster had dreamed of for his house in the early days of 'fidgit' productions, when the choice had seemed too often to lie between the nondescript and the irrelevantly showy. But Visconti loved the grandeur of grand opera. He accepted grand opera's conventions and he gloried in them, and he also had a fine sense of period style. His *Don Carlos* was the quintessence of David Webster theatre, and it was the most celebrated production of the Webster regime. As designer-director Visconti created a wonderful unity in his stage pictures, with a most imaginative and creative use of colour and lighting and groupings. While neglecting no detail he didn't at any time lose a sense of the whole.

Webster involved himself in the hour by hour excitement of the preparations. Early in 1958, with four months still to go, Visconti was writing to him:

> And finally, I need five baskets and some fake oranges and lemons for

> the Sito Ridente. I have dropped in at Scotts, in Tower Street, who has arranged to do the ones I want in five days for about five pounds, when he'll receive your OK to go ahead with them. Also, Balfour's and Co at Pollen Street have fifty 'oranges' in stock which they'll sell for the same amount . . . everything else is so satisfactory that it would really be a pity if these last details were not taken care of.

Visconti had a small obsession about ladies' gloves. Ladies weren't fully dressed without them, and the entire chorus wore gloves most of the time on stage; he held back the start of the dress rehearsal because the prima donna's had been lost.

In Giulini, quite simply, Webster thought he had found Toscanini again. He'd wanted Cantelli years before because Cantelli had been a protégé of Toscanini, and it was of Toscanini he thought when he first heard Giulini. The new Italian, in Verdi, combined refinement of textures with surging rhythms, with pulse and passion and power. And he shared with Kubelik that generosity of spirit which inspired and elevated those that worked with him. The stars assembled for the occasion became a team. Most of the singers were not new to their roles, and when Giulini arrived he was ready to start a stage rehearsal right away. But he found himself spending the whole day with Visconti and the singers just discussing the production.

Some of the singers were obvious choices in their roles, and the cleverness wasn't so much in choosing them as in getting them. And in getting them to work, at their best, within the production. First, there were the brothers-in-law, Gobbi and Christoff. Gobbi, surely the *only* Italian lyric baritone in the world, was obvious casting, though in fact Ettore Bastianini and Fisher-Dieskau were both brought into the reckoning. Webster at last had the pleasure of presenting him integrated into a good production and in meaningful relationships with the other characters on stage with him, and the pointedness and detail of his acting could now be fully appreciated. He projected the long, mournful melodies of his death scene lovingly, reaching right out to the back of the auditorium; with an equal technical and also imaginative grasp of the scene, he enveloped stage and audience in a positively ecstatic leave-taking. And this time he arrived early for rehearsals!

Christoff had been Bing's first choice for King Philip at the Met, but because of visa problems in the end it was Cesare Siepi. Webster was luckier, and this time Christoff it was. And once again, as in *Boris*, a lonely monarch provided Christoff with a triumph. He projected, with ruthless ferocity, a portrait of the *man*, not the king – a man powerful because of the loneliness which was a cancer in his very being, not a king who is lonely willy-nilly because of the isolation which inevitably goes with power. It was a portrait of pride corrupted, of mute egotism most eloquent; smudged only for the brief moment when, standing to receive his ovation after the study-scene aria, he allowed a huge smile to cut his face into two.

The lovers in the opera were not such obvious casting. Webster had considered Vickers and Amy Shuard, who had gone so well together in *A Masked Ball*. But he finally decided in favour of Vickers with Gré Brouwenstijn. Her musical intelligence and the richness and depth of her temperament, he knew, were best displayed when she was able to involve herself slowly in a production created to mean something moment by moment: and so it was with her in *Don Carlos*, when she sang and acted on a level with Christoff. She had at all times a sense of the whole unfolding drama of which her character was one element, and in the auto-da-fe scene, when Visconti had her posed on the Cathedral steps in a dazzling, oppressively stiff gold dress, she projected an overwhelming sense of a desolate spirit imprisoned. This was operatic acting and production on the highest level.

It was given, then, to Vickers to represent the company in the production. The company was well-enough represented elsewhere (Shuard was appearing again in *The Trojans*; and *Otello* in its second revival now had Edward Downes in sole charge in the pit, while Joan Sutherland replaced Brouwenstijn as Desdemona in the last three performances): in *Don Carlos* the company was sufficiently 'on trial' in the sole person of Vickers. Or was it really, in another way, the internationals who were on trial? Would they admit a local singer to their ranks?

Vickers had been carefully nurtured by Webster and Kubelik, and they weren't alone in thinking him ready to be launched on the international scene. He'd already been contracted to go to Bayreuth later that summer, to become their first-ever English Siegmund and Parsifal. *Don Carlos*, though, was his first blooding, and Webster was taking a further risk, infiltrating his new boy into this special among all 'special' productions. But he was more than ever aware that Vickers's obviously heroic aspect was leavened by the 'little-boy' element in it. This deeply interesting personality had worked so well in *A Masked Ball*. Was it going to work too in *Don Carlos?* It worked *superbly*. Vickers made a most fascinating neurotic of a Carlos. As sung by Vickers and Brouwenstijn, the second-act duet had an extraordinary melancholy compulsion; the ambiguous lover-mistress, mother-son, queen-subject relationship implicit in it was agonizedly projected. They have never been surpassed in their interpretations, nor anywhere near equalled, in all the many subsequent performances of the opera at Covent Garden, and nor will they be until a pair of equal magnitude, as well-matched and as sympathetically directed, is brought in for the roles.

It was not, finally, Vickers over whom hung the question mark. It was the Eboli. The casting of the role had presented problems, and in June 1957 Harewood had written to Giulini:

> It is very sad that Simionato cannot do this. I heard Cossotto rehearse for a moment at the Piccolo Scala, and everyone says she is very good indeed. The only snag from our point of view is that she is not yet at all well known. If she is a really splendid singer then this will not matter, but if she is only a very promising one we should probably do better with Barbieri from the point of view of the public.

Oralia Dominguez and Christa Ludwig were others thought of for the role, but in the end it did go to Barbieri. Webster was fond of her, she was popular with audiences and only the summer before she'd belted out a tremendous Azucena in *Trovatore*. It was naturally hoped that the enormous enthusiasm she'd aroused then would be carried over into *Don Carlos*. But a gipsy is one thing, a princess quite another. Her Covent Garden Amneris hadn't been quite right, and nor was her Eboli. It wasn't a question simply of stage deportment, but more of temperament and 'vocal deportment'. Good and exciting artist though she could be, she couldn't make Eboli aristocratic – she was essentially miscast, and this mattered more than the unfortunate last note of her final aria. Up to this last note she'd been going great guns, but she and Giulini had had a friendly argument about possible endings, and on the first night she got confused and went decidedly off whichever one she was half-aiming at. She was deeply upset, and didn't take her solo curtain-call. She even wanted to leave London forthwith and return home, but needless to say Webster provided her with the necessary reassurance, and she stayed on.

Don Carlos had been generally considered a flawed work impossible to stage effectively. Covent Garden, in answer to received opinion, had given the world a new masterpiece. The first-night audience was not slow to respond, and after the second interval, with the opera really rising to the heights in the study-scene, they too 'took off'. The none-too-happy history of Verdi and the Italian repertory at the house was now, finally, cancelled.

The effects of this inordinate success were far-reaching. It weighted that celebration summer heavily in favour of foreign-language opera, and gave the house a mighty heave along the path of opera in the original as policy. Webster was not too giddy with it all to register regret too for the plans for English opera which hadn't matured, and even to wonder how it might have been if they'd done an English *Dalibor* instead.

How *would* it have been, had Kubelik, besides *The Trojans*, also had

Dalibor or *Falstaff* as his new production, instead of *Tristan*, another 'compromise' Wagner production? Kubelik, for all the glories of the summer, wasn't really ending his term with a bang. Yet the successes of others must also, in any reckoning, be counted as *his*, his generosity in allowing the talents of others too to flourish being a measure of his success as Musical Director. *Dalibor* and the English *Falstaff* are all the more to be regretted on his account as the 'missing' operas of his time at Covent Garden.

The effects of *Don Carlos* can hardly be overestimated. Foreign conductors had already been coming thick and fast, even though John Pritchard was being well-used, and Edward Downes was by now taking more responsibility. But when it came to directors Webster had kept a balance, with Helpmann following that excellent *Butterfly* with *Coq d'Or*, and George Devine coming in for *Troilus*. But once Visconti had so emphatically arrived at the house this too changed, and doors were now flung open wider to foreign directors as well.

The entire opera world was dazzled by *Don Carlos*, which, in its international ratings, rivalled even the success of the Visconti-Callas collaborations at La Scala. It showed the world that a machine had now been created at Covent Garden. The production represented progress for the company as a whole and for the house, and from now on increasingly singers and conductors and directors were going to want to work at Covent Garden. Success at Covent Garden was henceforth to be significant in the progress of a new artist.

And, famously, a calm atmosphere was known to reign there. Leading artists in the world of opera were beginning to speak the name David Webster with increasing respect. In Vienna and Milan, in New York and San Fransisco, in Munich and Hamburg and Berlin, it was the same everywhere. Just such successes as *Don Carlos* make a house acceptable, and from *Don Carlos* onwards Covent Garden's was a steady progress towards higher and higher ratings. Towards being acknowledged as among the best, at the very least, of the world's international houses.

CHAPTER XVIII

Vickers spreads his wings · Joan Sutherland · *Lucia di Lammermoor* · Serafin and Zeffirelli · another triumph · Zeffirelli's productions · original language productions now policy · Klemperer's *Fidelio* · last skirmish with Beecham

The boundaries of administrative and artistic prerogative at Covent Garden were not clearly defined, and David Webster wanted a successor to Kubelik who wouldn't be too nice about having them defined. His Deputy Sir Steuart Wilson had left shortly before Kubelik's arrival, bringing to an end a relationship that had not been a happy one. Wilson had staunchly defended the house against Beecham, but once outside it he had threatened to launch an attack of his own. Webster was nervous at the prospect of yet more criticism, and all the more nervous because it was going to come from someone who had been on the inside and really knew some of the flaws in the organization. Happily, Wilson was persuaded not to make public his criticisms – and, furthermore, a new Deputy hadn't been appointed to replace him. Webster was well-pleased that it had been decided instead to provide him with an assistant, and he interviewed candidates himself. John Tooley was an excellent choice for this important position, invaluable in negotiations with the unions, and also, just as important, a loyal supporter of Webster's authority, not a threat to it. It continued to gratify Webster, too, that there was still no Artistic Director.

In his mid-fifties Webster was a man of tried and accustomed courtliness. How delightful it was for him, in situations which justified perturbation and provoked it in others, to continue imperturbable! Sometimes he would allow himself a telling contrast, and he could be positively foul-mouthed. But not often. His entertaining at Weymouth Street was courtly, and formal; and if there was something regal in the manner of his entertaining, it most certainly pleased him to be, as far as possible, absolute monarch at the Opera House. Rankl, and Kleiber and all the other Ks, hadn't weakened his authority, and he considered it vital that the new Musical Director too should be *his man*. Until such a man was found he was confident that Kempe, while refusing to be persuaded into the job, would continue to be once more both buttress and arch of the Webster regime.

The emergence of Jon Vickers at the head of the 'second generation' of Covent Garden singers had been vastly important to the regime because in him Webster now had his own English-language singer who *could* cope, in any house in the world, with the big roles. If Callas was his very own international star, Webster had brought on this house star in a sense to complement her – and he felt confident of Vickers for the decade to come. He had, surely, every reason to be confident that Jon Vickers would be leading his company for him through the 'sixties. But Vickers had his own plans. It had been an exciting summer for him too, and it wasn't altogether surprising, with his eighteen-months' contract coming to an end, that he should choose this time to 'square off' with Webster. He told his manager not to discuss a new contract till after his Bayreuth appearances, and himself wrote to Webster:

> It is my sincere hope that, whatever business differences we may encounter in these next few days, with their ultimate outcome, you will appreciate that I am attempting to fulfil a duty to myself, just as certainly as you are to your opera house.

Vickers's success at Bayreuth was immense, and he decided that henceforth he didn't want to be tied down. Not a weekly contract any more, but on a performance basis – and he wanted his salary brought up to match the offers he was receiving. This meant something like three times his current fee.

He put his demands in a letter which his manager delivered by hand. 'This is the first time,' the manager reported back, 'that I've *heard Mr Webster speechless!*' A long-held silence, from this man of few words, was eloquent. Webster was in danger of allowing personal feelings to overwhelm him in business affairs. But he mastered himself and at last broke silence. 'You know as well as I do I have to give in to his demands.' Vickers then decided to make partial amends by offering to sing the dress rehearsal and all four performances of Handel's *Samson* at the Leeds Festival for the price of only two.

The gesture wasn't badly received. Vickers called on Webster, who was standing at the window with his back turned, his favourite, and characteristic, position for negotiating. What inspiration, people were given to wondering, did its undistinguished vista afford him? As so often, Webster was whistling tunelessly. 'I'm very sorry that I felt I had to have a showdown,' Vickers said to him. Webster turned slowly – and his personality was now expanding into smiles unlimited. 'If you'll fight with me,' he said, apparently approving, 'then you'll fight with anyone.'

No one could accept defeat with better grace than Webster, nor bring it nearer victory. This was virtual victory, for Vickers now felt he had to accept any fee Webster chose to offer. At this stage, then, Webster could once more be certain of his star. He continued Vickers's mentor, strengthening the bond. Vickers's debut was arranged in Vienna, and on the eve he wrote to Webster:

> You have done far more for me than can really be appreciated – you have given me opportunities, experience, guidance, moral support, artistic and business advice, to such an extent that you have, so to speak, taught me the profession. And yet!! with all this, you have always treated me and my opinions with the utmost respect. You have forewarned me and calmed me, and yes! even fought with me a little, and this, so to speak, made me grow up. So! before growing up too much; in all my youthful enthusiasm, I want to say, Thank you.

And there was his Met debut, a complicated affair to arrange. Vickers had auditioned at the Met in 1953, as winner of a competition organized by Montreal Radio, but Bing had thought him a lyric, not a heroic, tenor, and had suggested he return to Canada and try Rodolpho in *Bohème*. Webster would no doubt have been delighted to be able to pour scorn on the head and faulty ears of the Austrian Rodolpho, Bing, towards whom he maintained feelings of unwavering hostility. But he'd forfeited the right. In 1957 the Met singer, James McCracken, a future Othello but still early in his career, as yet singing only small parts, had auditioned at Covent Garden. Webster and Harewood *had* thought him remarkable, though with little nuance – but the music staff to a man had insisted that he'd never get through the opera (*The Mastersingers*) as he hadn't the ability to pace the performance. Webster listened to his staff, turned down McCracken, and put himself, so to speak, in the proverbial glasshouse!

In 1958 negotiations between Vickers and Bing were becoming somewhat protracted, Vickers sensing that Bing was liable to despise people if he could get his way with them by flattery or subterfuge. At one point in the negotiations, in which Webster participated happily in an advisory capacity, Vickers remarked, 'I smell a rat.' 'Indeed, Jon,' Webster answered, 'you smell a very *large* rat.' Negotiations were eventually terminated satisfactorily, and Vickers, thanks to his careful and confident Webster-abetted handling of them, eventually established an excellent professional relationship with Bing. Webster didn't lose by his helpfulness, which was both personal pleasure and good business. Vickers was Bayreuth-approved, Vienna-approved, and soon the Met was to add its seal of approval – and he was still safe for Covent Garden, one problem the less for the approaching 'sixties.

Webster's promotion at this time of another singer gave him a second star for the 'sixties. But the rise to fame of Joan Sutherland was of a very different kind.

She had arrived from Australia in the autumn of 1951 with a letter of recommendation from Sir Eugene Goossens ('magnificent dramatic soprano voice . . . a grand natural voice'), which, if only taking into account the success of his earlier recommendation, Sylvia Fisher, ought to have guaranteed her an immediate audition. She sent Goossens's letter to Webster and had to wait seven months for a reply! And she made her quite unheralded debut in a small part in a repertory revival, as the First Lady in *The Magic Flute* on 28 October 1952. Her second appearance was at least on an evening with a more 'gala' feel to it – nothing less than the first Callas *Norma*, but she was not prominent in the proceedings, being only Clotilda, Norma's confidante.

She did soon move up to more important roles, but not, to begin with, of the trilling variety. *The Tales of Hoffman*, mounted in 1954, contains the most hysterically trilling role of all, that of the doll Olympia, but when Sutherland went into the opera, replacing members of the original cast, it was first in the other women's roles. She did finally sing Olympia (and even all three ladies in one evening): but she didn't so impress that she was asked to do it again in later seasons. There was no great shortage of coloratura sopranos at this time, and there were others to cope with the trills. One of the arias Sutherland had chosen for her audition had been '*Dich Teure Halle*' from *Tannhäuser* – and it had given promise of a big dramatic soprano, something the house needed more than a coloratura. And this was how Covent Garden, though not warming to her rapidly, chose to see her future development. She was at first groomed in the same stable as Amy Shuard; she was cast as Aïda, and certainly did well as Agathe in Weber's *Der Freischütz*.

But Webster remembered that she had also sung a Donizetti number at her audition, which had pointed to another possible way for her. And he was impressed by the way she found her way through the difficult florid music of *A Midsummer Marriage* at the beginning of 1955. True, she might be more useful to them as a dramatic soprano, but he saw a possible way to fame for her through trills. And if she thrilled with trills, it didn't have to mean she automatically renounced other kinds of roles altogether.

In February 1956 Donizetti's *Lucia di Lammermoor* was mentioned as an opera for Maria Callas. It was one of Maria's famous roles. Without Maria it would be hard to justify the opera at all. For where, in the 'fifties, in England at any rate, was Donizetti? In the *Guardian* in February 1973 Philip Hope-Wallace was to write of

> the contempt in which Donizetti as a composer was held in the late 'twenties and early 'thirties: grudging exceptions were made for *L'Elisir d'Amore* and for *Don Pasquale* where it was allowed that Donizetti's 'weak, sentimental and conventional' formulas were not inappropriate to the light-hearted intrigues; whereas, it was implied, these methods were totally inadequate to express such dramatic situations as those brought forward by *Lucia di Lammermoor* or *La Favorita*.

Callas had revealed Lucia as a figure awesome and exalted as a heroine of Greek classical tragedy. But that was Callas. It took both imagination, at this stage, and generosity too, to envisage promoting Sutherland outside the dramatic soprano repertory – and it took imagination indeed to promote her as the heroine of *this* opera, a risk without Callas, and surely a huge risk with a mere Miss Sutherland. But in June 1956 Webster was already putting her case to the Opera Sub-Committee. When it was put before the Board, though Kubelik supported the nomination they were every one of them totally opposed to the idea. The opera hadn't been produced at Covent Garden since 1925, when the heroine, as played by Toti dal Monti, had conducted the Mad Scene over the footlights with her fan! It hadn't been a success *then*, and had earned itself only a single performance. The second had had to be cancelled, the language of the fan, evidently, not having spoken eloquently enough. To trundle out the piece thirty years later, as a vehicle for mere Miss Sutherland, this surely was a piece of absurdity of truly operatic fancifulness!

Webster of course saw that it was a risk. But some of his very best successes had been eased gingerly from between the jaws of chance. Webster had faith in the opera, in spite of its sorry history here, because, alongside her other great *bel canto* roles, he'd seen Maria in it at La Scala. These operas, with Callas, directed by Visconti, conducted by Giulini or the veteran Tullio Serafin, *could* go splendidly. Done, at any rate on this level, they had an enormous glamour and theatrical excitement, and this was the level he was aiming at. Covent Garden had no more than nibbled at the *bel canto* repertory so far – it was represented only by its *Norma*, and that was always a 'Callas Night'. Webster acknowledged it a risk, but as early as 1956 he was sure that, in a properly prepared production, he had a very fair chance of making a 'Sutherland Night' out of *Lucia*.

He was determined that Lucia was to be the role in which, finally, Sutherland should be sprung on the world as a star. To this end, and over years, he mounted a relentless campaign. Three years were to pass, years of alarums and excursions, of expectations roused and hopes deferred, before at last, on 17 December 1959, she was revealed in the role, and as positively launched on an international career as Vickers himself. In May 1957 she sang Gilda in *Rigoletto*, and, more power to her trills, strengthened the case he was beginning to make out for her. And in that same month too the Italian opera season at the Stoll Theatre presented *Lucia* with Virginia Zeani: this meant postponing the opera at Covent Garden, and discussions didn't begin again until April 1958 – and by this time the Board was somewhat more amenable, both because the opera had done well at the Stoll even without Callas, and because Sutherland, having added Eva in *The Mastersingers*, Desdemona, and Madame Lidoine in *The Carmelites* to her repertory, was gaining ground. They stipulated that *if* she could be *assured* support from good Italian singers in the male roles, and *if* she had a first-rate Italian conductor, then *perhaps* she might seriously be considered for Lucia. More than that they wouldn't commit themselves to.

Giulini was in the house rehearsing *Don Carlos*. They asked him, would *he* do it? He refused. No progress was made for a while. Then it was decided that it would be done only if Serafin could be engaged. These were the two experts in this field, Giulini and Serafin. Serafin had conducted at Covent Garden as far back as 1908, and another debut that season had been Tetrazzini's, one of whose roles, though not under Serafin himself, had been Lucia. Better was the fact that Serafin had Callas-associations, and not only at La Scala – he had conducted for her when she made her Italian debut in the Verona Arena, and many times she'd recorded under him. He was her 'musical father' and it was he who had first introduced her to the *bel canto* repertory, thus beginning for her a 'second career', and with it the *bel canto* revival. Would he be a 'father' to Sutherland too? He was certainly, along with Giulini, something like the ideal choice. But it was hard that the Board should be making him the *only* possibility.

Sutherland was now taking on another coloratura role, the Israelite Woman in *Samson*. Webster emphasized to the Board both that her new 'profile' was beginning to assert itself, and that *Lucia* for her was surely coming to be a less outlandish suggestion. And also that if she wasn't given star treatment soon she'd probably be lost to them. So they agreed at least to the principle of a new production for her: if Serafin said no to *Lucia*, then it would be Charpentier's *Louise*, last thought of for Schwarzkopf. And if it was *Lucia* then it must be in English. It was a way of justifying the opera without Callas. A translation was commissioned from Christopher Hassall.

There was still the matter of getting Serafin. He didn't take long making up his mind. He accepted.

So – the go-ahead at last. Hassall's translation was completed, and Webster could count it a personal success simply to have got the project under way. But then Serafin protested, he'd only do the opera if it were done in Italian. The Board had insisted on English. Deadlock. The whole project could even now have been abandoned. Mercifully, the Board, though not without demur at first, gave way. The translation was 'ditched', and it was to be *Lucia* in Italian. The Board still needed reassuring, and to reassure them a defiantly confident Webster arranged for his future star to go to Venice to study with Serafin. It happened that her husband, the conductor Richard Bonynge, had already done a lot to encourage her to 'go coloratura', and he had also worked on the role with her. She had, indeed, studied it so thoroughly that Serafin found she only needed a couple of mornings' further study with him and the rest of her time in Venice was holiday!

The opera, with Miss Sutherland, was a risk. But every precaution was being taken. It would have been ideal to have, together with a Scala conductor, *the* Scala director, Visconti. That wasn't possible. But a Visconti pupil, Franco Zeffirelli, was engaged instead, definitely the next best thing. After the *Don Carlos* team of Visconti-Giulini, Webster couldn't envisage better than what he was offering Sutherland, this Zeffirelli-Serafin collaboration. But for *Don Carlos* there had been a cast of world-beaters, while *Lucia* is a prima-donna opera, and it was going to have to rely above all on one comparatively untried singer promoted for the first time to full prima donna status. A repetition of that earlier success seemed almost too much to hope for, yet nothing very much less would really count as success. Having got what he wanted, Webster realized that he was actually committed to a still bigger risk than before.

He assessed the situation as calmly, as reasonably, as possible. Crisis itself tended to make him calm. There *were* assets. High among them, he kept repeating to himself, were Serafin and Zeffirelli. Zeffirelli had directed Donizetti before, at La Scala, and to acclaim – though, true, it was so far only for *comic* opera that he was known. Webster also reminded himself frequently that this repertory *did* make stars. At the 1957 Edinburgh Festival Renata Scotto had taken over Callas's role in Bellini's *Sonnambula* for a single performance and was by next morning no longer an unknown. Not so much by words as by means of a deliberately projected aura, Webster conveyed his certainty of success to the many of little faith by whom he was surrounded at the Opera House.

La Scala was approached, would they lend Covent Garden their *Lucia* sets? Back in November came the answer, no, they wouldn't. Webster suggested James Bailey for designer. But Zeffirelli wanted to do his own. Was this a further risk? No. Visconti had also done his own, so it was, Webster decided, a good omen. He told Zeffirelli to to ahead. And had every reason to be happy that he did.

For the production turned out to be opulently romantic, wonderfully atmospheric, but also clean, economical even, in its detail. Zeffirelli built his production round Sutherland, treating her like the star she was soon to become. He gave her every help, paring movement down to the significant, and Joan had never done better and was never to do better again – partly because she was encouraged, decisively, to do as little as possible. The decisiveness of the production gave her an unwonted certainty on stage.

She was, besides, admirably cast. As admirably cast, it was very soon apparent, as Vickers had been in *A Masked Ball* and *Don Carlos*. The role, and not only because of the opportunities it affords for trilling, had a very particular appeal to her. Sutherland is not slight or fragile, and it is the greater pleasure, if it can be done at all, for one neither slight nor fragile to fine herself down for the impersonation of a heroine who can legitimately be exaggeratedly both. Such a fining down is hardly possible in naturalistic drama, but grand opera is another matter, and the Zeffirelli production was of the grandest. The sets were huge, but they didn't overpower the action and certainly didn't dominate the singer. Against them she looked all the slighter. And there is more than this. There is something in Joan's own personality to which the role of victim appeals, and this again is the more marked because nature has not seemed to create her to be a victim. It was as though she projected the victim all the more strongly – as Vickers did the neurotic – because it was the reverse side of her *manifest* nature. Webster knew when he chose the role for her that it suited her admirably and not merely because she could cope with the florid passages in the score.

Even before the first night Miss Sutherland had an ordeal to face. At the dress rehearsal, after the Mad Scene, she was informed that both Callas (Lucia herself!) and Schwarzkopf (a might-have-been Louise) were present in the theatre. They had heard that an event out of the ordinary was about to occur – and throughout her performance they had been sitting discreetly out of sight in one of the boxes. Sutherland, who after all was asking to share their top rung of the ladder, almost fainted. Suddenly it seemed to her that she had been pushed into too great a presumption. When the knock came on her door, and they were announced, it was surely her fiercest critics whom she was going to have to face! Schwarzkopf at least expended her talents in another repertory, but Callas certainly might be expected to be hypercritical of an aspirant to one of her own great roles. But these two high-aspiring artists could not but admire achievement of this order, and it was these two, Callas and Schwarzkopf, who were the first to confirm to Sutherland her success, and to welcome her to the heights. The first night audience, on 17 February 1959, had only to ratify their judgement.

They did. And it was a great night for Webster too. At the party afterwards Board members one by one approached him to offer congratulations. He had been right, they wrong. The success of the night was for him more than a personal success – whether his own or

Sutherland's. For where in *Don Carlos* the one house singer, Jon Vickers, had taken his place among world stars, in *Lucia* it was a house singer on her own creating a sensation in many ways comparable. It was an important date in the emergence of the English singer, and Sutherland enjoyed also the congratulations of her colleagues, who felt her success to be theirs too.

That success resounded in the world's press, and almost at once began the triumphant world tour which has continued uninterrupted ever since. Sutherland's travels the following season included a stop-over in Vienna for *Don Giovanni* and *Otello*, and in Italy she was created 'La Stupenda' in meaningless and involuntary opposition to Callas, 'La Divina', a singer she holds in awe and resembles not at all.

And nor were Webster's relations with Maria impaired. It was no tigress, but a dove, albeit a tall and smiling one, who walked through the streets of Milan one evening after a La Scala performance on George Harewood's arm; passers-by smiled and bowed, '*Buona sera, Signora Callas, buona sera, madama*,' and the while she was asking George why *she* hadn't been asked to do Lucia *first*. George explained that Webster and the house had responsibilities to Sutherland too. Relations continued harmonious, so harmonious that Webster could consider inviting her to do Lucia even after Sutherland, that summer when she came to Covent Garden for Medea. Maria suggested that another of her operas, *Sonnambula*, might be a good one for Sutherland, though hinting that perhaps she ought to do it at Covent Garden first and have Sutherland follow *her*.

Sutherland launched was, happily, a Sutherland secured. London was not left out next season when she was Lucia again, and also did *Traviata* for the first time. In December 1959 she wrote to Webster:

> I cannot think of anything before *Traviata*. This is a colossal role and my memory is *bad* – worse when I am pressed for time . . . You understand that since my very sudden 'rise to fame' things have become very complex for me – it will take a little time to adjust myself and to learn that I *cannot* sing too many new works at once.

Callas didn't sing *Sonnambula* at Covent Garden, but Sutherland did. It was the next new production for her at the house, and the first for her as undisputed prima donna. It was not a success on the level of *Lucia*: trills by the million but a somewhat anaemic impersonation, and the cause of Bellini in England none too well served. Serafin, once more her conductor, had suggested another kind of opera for her, Verdi's *Macbeth*. He had pioneered Callas's career, and before that Rosa Ponselle's, and if Sutherland and her husband Bonynge had not had such opposed views on how her career should go, her dramatic aspect might have been developed as well and an important corner of operatic history in our time been somewhat different.

Zeffirelli's success too was thrilling for Webster. He dominated production at the house for the next five years – and for the first time a kind of dramatic continuity was maintained. *Lucia* was notable not only for Sutherland, but also as the beginning of a virtual Webster-Zeffirelli entente, the Visconti pupil becoming the Webster protégé. Webster eagerly encouraged him to extend his range and expand his talents, and by the end of the five years Zeffirelli had no less than eight evenings' opera to his credit under Webster's roof – and Webster could almost persuade himself that he now had a house style of production. These successes certainly provided alternative excitements to Wieland Wagner and his gauzes, which he was all the more confident to eschew.

Webster could be guilty of *blind* confidence in his favourites, and it was, certainly, a mistake to entrust Mozart to Zeffirelli. *Don Giovanni* lacked purpose, and the sets were merely distractingly grandiose or totally irrelevant. Zeffirelli had already directed this opera at Dallas, but he didn't have an understanding of Mozart, and nor, to any marked degree, did Webster, who simply wasn't aware, when the production was first seen, that it wasn't working. This may have been partly because that first cast, headed by the unequivocally sensual '*beau garçon*' of Cesare Siepi, and with the superb Jurinac and a captivating Mirella Freni among his ladies, did *almost* make it seem to work; and it was certainly fair to credit his protégé with at least his usual skill in handling the singers.

But there was *Falstaff* at last. Not the English *Falstaff* that should have been Kubelik's – a very Italian one instead by Zeffirelli. Webster knew that it was just the sort of evening Kubelik wouldn't have approved: and indeed, as Webster was painfully aware, its very success virtually destroyed Kubelik's efforts. Following Zeffirelli's famous double-bill of *Cavalleria Rusticana* with its usual companion, *I Pagliacci*, the first opera mounted at the house in the original language for *all-English* casts, this Italian *Falstaff*, with several distinguished guests, finally confirmed opera in the original language as *policy*. No point now in pretending otherwise.

But Webster resolutely put Kubelik out of mind, and revelled in the evening. It was indeed an evening of revels, for the Zeffirelli Windsor was an Italian market-place of movement. The personages were up-graded socially, and it wasn't easy for Geraint Evans's ripe and riotous Falstaff to *condescend* to merchants' wives who were almost court ladies. But now at least Webster need have no doubts at all about presenting his own singers on equal terms with the most distinguished guests, his very own Geraint beside the seraphic lovers of Freni and Luigi Alva, to say nothing of mine hilarious hostess, Mistress Quickly, in the rubicund person of his almost-own Regina Resnik. This Falstaff, though *not* in the way Kubelik had intended, was none the less a progress report for the company as a whole.

And the sets had a timbery look; the basic set was a hollow U, so that the production could be regarded as a celebration of theatre, with Zeffirelli making his deep obeisance to the stage, a world unto itself, and to the Elizabethan stage in particular. Webster, relishing the suggestion, took it as a compliment to his own beautiful theatre. Giulini was in the pit, and it was he who brought elegance and style to leaven a production in some respects questionable. All in all, *Falstaff* delightfully 'came across', and Webster *was* delighted.

This was Webster's young entry. Vickers, Sutherland, Zeffirelli. They were young and to them Webster was a senior figure. Giulini was Toscanini all over again, but even he was only in his forties, and forty is nothing for a conductor. There was an older generation to whom Webster himself was young. He was also in contact with a great figure of the old generation, the one he, and Giulini and the other youngsters too, had grown up to revere. It set his blood racing, it made *him* young too, to be having dealings with no less than the great Otto Klemperer himself.

Webster had long had hopes of Klemperer. It would be the highest compliment to Webster and his house if, in his mid-seventies, Klemperer would consent to conduct opera again: for, apart from a short period with the Budapest State Opera, he had hardly set foot in an opera house since the war. He was now a broken Michelangelo figure, a veritable ruined Titan of a man. His face was a face which demanded to replace all those Presidents of America carved on Mount Rushmore. Negotiations had begun back in 1957, and one of the operas Klemperer had expressed an interest in was *Fidelio*. Though resident in Zurich, Klemperer was in charge of London's Philharmonia Orchestra and his cycles of Beethoven symphonies seemed at the time to be securing a tradition of Beethoven performance for another century to come. Webster would have been only too happy to settle for *Fidelio*. And then in 1959 Jurinac was showing herself ready to do her first Leonora anywhere at Covent Garden – though her terms were not easy. They included a new production and *either* Klemperer or Karajan as conductor. Almost unbelieving, Webster made the marriage. Contracts were actually signed. Klemperer was in charge of the production himself, jointly with Christopher West. Soon he was in the house rehearsing, and Webster held himself breathlessly at the ready to smooth problems as they arose. But there didn't seem to be any. Rehearsals continued. The first night approached.

Otto Klemperer was a figure wreathed in majesty, and even before the first night majesty was in the house. Everyone was inspired. In his single person Klemperer seemed to David Webster to stand in for Toscanini and Furtwängler, for Clemens Krauss and Knappertsbusch, for Kleiber and Bruno Walter. There were not many of them left. Mighty ghosts were stirring. Klemperer's entrance into the pit on the first night was a great moment both for the audience and for Webster, and he was stifled as much by memories as by expectations as the curtain rose. The production was spacious and unassertive, without any nods towards originality. In the pit Klemperer unfolded the score implacably, and Beethoven was given enormous weight. At the heart of the musical performance, to which Webster responded with tears, was a deep serenity, a confidence in the proceedings both musical and moral. The human and symbolic elements can never have been more thoroughly one and inseparable than in this performance, and a worthy centre was Jurinac's unabashedly feminine Leonora, a human not a heroic figure, driven desperately to deeds beyond normal strength, but driven by outrage and moral indignation as much as by love. That evening a tearful Webster had an inkling that the decade between the Kleiber *Rosenkavalier* and the Klemperer *Fidelio* contained his best years. He couldn't, he felt, have better. The best, by the end of this particular evening, must surely be in the past.

The love of this older generation made Webster more than ever determined to get Beecham back again. Exaltation, however, was not to be his reward this time. He'd been trying for so many years: both before and after the Resignation Crisis of 1956 proposals had been made, some by the Opera House and some implemented by Beecham himself. Nothing came of them. When Beecham neared eighty, and there was a possibility of performances to honour his birthday, he himself proposed *Bohème,* which he wanted done with his recent recording cast (but with the single exception of Victoria de los Angeles, his preferred Eva of 1951). Then his enthusiasm for *Bohème* waned, and it was *Tristan* instead. But he *insisted* on Ramon Vinay and Astrid Varnay while the Board stood out for Nilsson with Windgassen, for whom they'd anyway have to apply for permission to Vienna and La Scala. Webster kept telling himself, with Beecham it *couldn't* be easy. He settled back and tried to enjoy it. The Opera Sub-Committee would have given the go-ahead to *Faust* if he'd do it, and he riposted by bringing up another Gounod opera, *Romeo and Juliet*, and mentioning not altogether relevantly that Melba had sung it on her sixtieth birthday, and 'save for one note the voice was unimpaired.'

By this time it was hardly possible not to imagine that Beecham was deliberately making conditions he knew would be difficult to meet – and Webster still couldn't be entirely certain even when Beecham was actually engaged to conduct the second revival of *The Trojans*, in 1959, its first without Kubelik. He was actually announced for it, so now the public was alerted. Webster never ceased to have doubts. It would be wonderful *if* it happened. Beecham was hitting fine form in joyous interchanges inspired by the event, but the purpose of the long negotiations wasn't to stimulate correspondence. Webster recognized that the Beecham voice was unimpaired in *every* note as he raised it to wonder if it would be possible 'to get that wildcat Callas to sing Cassandra? It is just the crackpot sort of part for her, with any amount of screaming, cursing and somersaulting.'

Webster knew that there must be dangers. And sure enough, a call came through to him in Brighton from Walter Legge, at this time a Board member, and another with whom Webster could not always be said to maintain a very friendly relationship. Certainly not the best bringer of bad news as far as Webster was concerned – and it was bad news. The call somewhat violently threw a bombshell into the middle of his weekend. For Beecham had rung Legge from Canada, and was, it seemed, refusing to fulfil his engagement on the grounds that he'd arranged with Webster to do *The Trojans* in the original French, and had just seen in the Covent Garden programme that he'd been announced to do it in English.

Webster had made no such promise. He told Legge as much. He told Beecham too, whom he forthwith telephoned, to explain that putting an opera from one language to another was an enormous enterprise, which one didn't embark on lightly. Nor, he added meaningfully, did one abandon it lightly either. Suddenly Beecham changed course, and he was making another condition. He wanted to do the huge work in its two separate parts on successive evenings. This too, Webster told him, was not possible. Whereupon Beecham began shouting down the phone. Webster became cajoling. 'Don't let's carry on like this. I'll leave England tomorrow. I'll travel via New York to Toronto and I can be with you sometime Tuesday.' Beecham growled his goodbyes.

Webster arrived in Toronto to find Beecham ill in bed. They met for dinner, and out came the true story – Beecham had been told by his Canadian doctor that he was in no fit condition to rehearse and conduct the opera. So much for objections to doing it in English and for wanting it spread over two evenings! Webster insisted, before he left, on having a letter explaining Beecham's medical condition. He was going to need it. When Beecham's scheduled appearances were cancelled there was going to be uproar. It meant a storm of criticism once again for the General Administrator – who, if he hadn't made this trip to Canada, would have had to take the blame himself entirely. There would still be tedious scenes and patient explanations to endure.

So Beecham was to be no more than an off-stage voice. But if his eightieth birthday wasn't marked at the Opera House, it was none the less Webster who was called upon to propose his toast at the luncheon given for him at the Dorchester. 'A brilliant amateur, the papers called him,' Webster reminded the guests, giving it as his opinion that Tommy was rather 'the greatest old pro'. He read out the many telegrams, most of them from other artists, and the last of them from Sibelius. 'Nothing from Mozart'? Tommy gruffly enquired.

The Trojans illness was the beginning of the end for him, and he died early in 1961. But he didn't die without preparing a posthumous squib. Webster had visited him at the Connaught Hotel and tried to cheer him up by making plans for what he might do when he was better, though both of them knew that he wasn't going to get better. Towards the end of the visit Beecham turned the conversation to his income tax. It riled him that, though resident abroad, he still had to pay more tax than a foreign conductor working in England. Could Webster do anything about it? Webster was doubtful, but he promised to discuss the matter with someone who could put it directly to the Head of Inland Revenue. He'd at least get an authoritative answer. Beecham then claimed that he'd already tried this, and mentioned the name of a supposed intermediary. Webster ventured to give it as his opinion that there was no reason to assume that this particular intermediary would be effective. The discussion developed, with other names mentioned and other possibilities explored.

It was only after the old funster's demise that Webster learned, with some distress, that the conversation had been secretly tape-recorded. The tape had been sent to Beecham's manager, and this long and unguarded conversation discovered on it. Webster, a man who had spent his life being guarded, found himself exposed! Something rare in his experience and he didn't like it! But Beecham too was someone he had not ceased, even through their stormiest passages, to revere – and he still kept upstairs at Weymouth Street a stack of Beecham's old seventy-eights, the records with which he had first journeyed into music. And even now he could not but relish the idea of Tommy meanwhile laughing all the way to the Heavenly Gates!

Beecham died on 8 March 1961, while Klemperer was in the middle of his *Fidelio* performances. Bruno Walter was to die a year later, and Knappertsbusch in 1965. Klemperer was the last of the 'great' generation. He was heard several times more at Covent Garden, in a revival of *Fidelio* as well as in new productions of *The Magic Flute* and *Lohengrin* (which were not, unfortunately, on the same exalted level). Miraculously, it seemed, he was once again in the pit in March 1969, the opera once more *Fidelio*, and this time the life-enhancing Anja Silja, in glorious form, as his Leonora. It was fitting that *Fidelio*, one of the greatest achievements of his long career, should be his last opera. His death soon afterwards marked the extinction of the whole great school of conductors – and Webster himself, as it turned out, was not to survive them long.

PART THREE

The Last Years

CHAPTER XIX

Drogheda as chairman · growing accord · Solti · a bad start · Webster restless · knighthood · congratulations

Webster was nearing sixty, an age when a man might be expected to resist change. He could certainly be resentful, but at the same time he had not lost his life-long habit of adaptability. He could still be as adaptive as ever so long as he had made up his mind he had a worth-while object.

The new Chairman was posing him a problem. For Webster found, to his frequent irritation, that Lord Drogheda was not a man he could always have his way with. He certainly represented change, the nature of which Webster himself winkles out in the letter he was, much later, to write to him. Waverley had been content not to use the powers that went with position. He made finance his role. Not so Drogheda.

> You were a shock at first. Here was someone who wanted to know every detail and have a hand in everything. You revelled in detail and expected all the Board and your officers so to revel. You have a great love for Covent Garden. You have a tremendous flare [*sic*] for writing letters in which you make it clear to each of us exactly what you think. In time these letters have become known as Droghedagrams. Your enthusiasm has been a fund of strength. If you took up an idea in which there is something you should follow through with the authorities for Covent Garden then nothing will deflect you from your aim.

True enough. Lord Drogheda has a passion for the Opera House which matches Webster's own. The very fabric of the lovely building has become virtually an extension of his own drawing-room, and in his range of interest and active concern he was indeed a contrast to his predecessor. A Droghedagram might read:

> Just to remind you about painting the walls above the amphitheatre slips a light colour, preferably the shade of the dome, instead of that glossy chocolate,

and there was an interchange, on the subject of flowers being presented on stage wrapped in Cellophane, which spreads itself over several years. A Droghedagram on *this* subject reads:

> Everything is so very good about Covent Garden that these strike a most jarring note.

Webster could be most unaccommodating when he chose. He liked decisions in his own house to be his own. But there was a constant Drogheda watchfulness on every subject to do with the Opera House, large or small, be it financial or artistic. It was the financial support Webster was grateful for – but Drogheda was ready to be alerted too when it came to public relations and the creation and maintaining of the house's image, or when it came to building up and maintaining audiences, and there was a degree of anxiety, an almost depressive element of regret, if things had not turned out for the very best. The Drogheda energy and attack made Webster sometimes wonder himself, did people perhaps think, some of them, seeing the contrast between Drogheda and himself, that the house which he had built had finally outgrown him, as it had Rankl in the past. Were the times passing him by?

At the beginning, certainly, there were sharp differences between the two men, and there is in fact an element of comedy in the occasional collision of these two devoted gentlemen. In part it was simply that the extreme opposition of their two temperaments was bound to occasion collision: in the English capital, Irish charm was breaking itself impulsively on the granite of Dundee. The two men were even aware themselves, on occasion, as they enforced decorum and a dignity of utterance commensurate with their respective high offices, that within were screaming to get out a little Mime and a little Alberich, the Wagnerian goblin brothers who confront each other to such good purpose in *Rhinegold* and *Siegfried*. Difficult, though, to envisage the rangy Lord reduced to dwarf – easier here to personify the figure of Webster.

Webster's habit of ignoring problems and not answering letters was one that could not be more opposite to the life-means of the impulsive Irishman, who leapt to pen or telephone as naturally as he breathed. In the early days of his Chairmanship, and no doubt with perfect accuracy, he was writing to Webster:

> I find it most depressing that I have only to support an idea for you to oppose it – especially questions of rep and singers . . . If my suggestions were frivolous, it would be quite another matter. But they are not, and you invariably pay lip-service to them. That, however, is the limit of it, and I can assure you that it adds little to the joys of being chairman.

Many of the suggestions, no doubt, were not at all frivolous, though some of them might have seemed to Webster to be concerned with matters too small to be worth consultation together. On the other hand, he was not beyond persuading himself, feeling his authority in *his* house challenged, that they were frivolous, in order to justify ignoring them.

But if the two men grew into accord, which eventually they did, and without subverting their own essential styles, it was because they had sufficient motive in their mutual love of Covent Garden – which was the first redeeming feature they arrived at acknowledging in each other!

For a while, it wasn't certain that Covent Garden was ever going to get another Musical Director. As soon as it was known that Kubelik wasn't likely to renew there'd been meetings and discussions, ponderings and lists. Webster and Drogheda both wanted one. But no major talent was available, that seemed to be the inescapable conclusion. Webster worried too, how much more power would he have to give away? A man of the right stature, this was becoming clearer, wasn't likely to come at this time without something near complete control. Webster had wondered about a troika consisting of Kubelik in harness with Kempe and Giulini. He couldn't implement that pleasing idea. At the end of 1958 it was decided to ask Britten to act as 'musical consultant', and he agreed to make himself available for informal advice. That was something gained, but not enough.

Discussions became more intensive again in the summer of 1959, and they were concluded with a strong recommendation that the musical strength be augmented by additional guest conductors of the first rank. In fact three such conductors did make their Covent Garden debuts the following season. Georg Solti, whose name had first appeared on a list two years earlier, was one of them, and the other two were Krombholc and Santi, all three in charge of important revivals, and all successful.

Webster didn't see one debut as more important than another. But it was Solti – invited by Drogheda – who was to be their Musical Director. The two men were introduced by Solti's fellow-Hungarian, the pianist Ilona Kabos, in the Connaught Hotel – which, as the scene of the Beecham tape-recording session, promised to be an ill-luck venue for Webster! The Lord issued his invitation to the maestro almost at once. Part of the power of madly impulsive people is that the entire force of their will and of their charm is invested for the moment in any commitment they make. Solti, a handsome man with will and charm of his own, was not insensible. His head is set slightly low on his shoulders, with a forward inclination, and his demeanour suggests that he is ready to use this head, if necessary, as an instrument of battering.

He had already had many years of operatic experience, six years as head of the Munich opera and nine at Frankfurt. He wasn't sure that he hadn't had enough of opera. Nice of Drogheda to ask him. But he wasn't free to accept the offer anyway because he was already contracted – to the Los Angeles Orchestra.

Regrets on both sides, and the two men parted amicably, Solti to return to Los Angeles. Where events were conspiring. A small clause in his American contract stated that all final decisions had to be referred to the orchestra's principal conductor, but Solti returned to find that Mrs Chandler, President of the Trustees, had in his absence appointed an assistant conductor, Zubin Mehta, whom Solti had himself invited to appear with the orchestra *as guest*. Nice timing. Solti resigned after a row. So now he was available for Covent Garden.

What happened next had something in common with what had happened in the past, but was not entirely of a pattern with it. Webster, as usual, went off alone, quietly, to meet the new man. The meeting was in Luxembourg. But things otherwise weren't at all the same. He'd wanted Kleiber and he'd wanted Kubelik, and he'd worked hard to ensure that those negotiations had been successful. Here he wasn't meeting his own man. An experienced negotiator can always manipulate. Negotiations with Solti could easily have broken down.

But they didn't. For if still equivocal in his attitude, Webster did realize that Solti at the beginning of the 'sixties was something unique. He'd had enormous practical experience running an opera house, and he'd even worked with Toscanini at Salzburg in 1937 and 1938, no mean recommendation. His work at Frankfurt had amply demonstrated his musicianship, and he had brought up the ensemble there to a high pitch of excellence. But if he already had prestige, and a European reputation, he had still not grown his full lion's mane. A man less advanced in his career might not have quite the prestige for the job on offer, while any other man of like achievement was going to be too far advanced and not to be pinned down. He would certainly want control if he came to the house. Webster's authority was in danger of being hedged still further. Webster found himself with a diamond in his hand, but one with perhaps a cutting edge. 'I've never met anyone,' he was shortly to acknowledge, 'who works with such enthusiasm': but this didn't mean that Solti was transformed into a Webster man. It would be truer to say that it was *Webster who made himself into Solti's man*.

Solti still couldn't be sure. Webster suggested he think it over. 'How long can I think it over?' 'As long as you want. We haven't got anyone else.'

Drogheda, meanwhile, was almost inevitably having to write to Webster: 'Your unwillingness to consult or inform one is chronic. Beyond a certain point it can become insupportable.' It must certainly have been insupportable while these all-important negotiations were under way!

What Solti did next was to consult with Bruno Walter. When offered the job himself sixteen years before, Walter's position and circumstances had been much different from the younger man's, and Covent Garden hadn't been at all the same thing either. He advised Solti to accept.

Solti did accept. But to start with he committed himself to only three years. He regarded the house he was coming to as *Webster's* house – and if in later years Webster was not always in health to act forcefully, it never, for all that, was to seem to him anything else than the House that Webster Built. 'A painting by the School of Rembrandt is still a Rembrandt.'

In December 1959 Solti had come as guest for *Rosenkavalier*, with a magnificent international cast led by Schwarzkopf and Jurinac. When he returned early in 1961 it was to take charge of a somewhat contrasted evening – a new English opera, Britten's *A Midsummer Night's Dream*, with a fine cast of English singers. Webster was presenting him carefully, still nervous that there might be criticism of Solti as another foreigner. There was no such criticism.

They got off to a bad start together, Webster and Solti. One evening Webster invited him and his wife to see an act of *Rosenkavalier* in a subsequent revival of the opera. Solti had watched the performance with rapt attention, and as the curtain fell Webster asked him casually, already flushing with pleasure at the praise of his 'children' he was sure would follow, 'How d'you like it?' 'Terrible! Terrible!' the new Musical Director spluttered in return. Webster was deeply hurt. True, Régine Crespin had been in the earlier performances of the current series, and she had had to be replaced; perhaps the best of the several celebrated Marschallins who have graced *Rosenkavalier* since the war, she would no doubt have made a difference. But Webster couldn't admit objective judgement in something so close to him as the doings of his 'family'.

To Solti it was, simply, a terrible performance. And in the house soon to be his responsibility. He'd signed, it had been announced that he was coming. Webster was more than deeply hurt – he was insulted, and he would not take into account for one second Solti's natural apprehensiveness at this juncture. Solti was convinced he'd made the biggest mistake of his career so far.

Webster was insulted. But the Soltis were his guests, and a table was booked at a restaurant. Thither they repaired, silently. The silence was broken when the Soltis were invited to chose from the menu placed before them. Webster ordered. Then silence again. They ate. The meal finished, the bill paid, they parted.

This was hardly a good beginning – except in so far as it gave Solti a sense, when he looked back on the event, of the loyalty and unquestioning support he could expect when his own work was put before the public.

A depressed David Webster wondered whether he wanted to stay on at the house. There were moments when he thought he'd had enough – moments like this. It wasn't as if he was permanently fixed at the house, and a marvellous alternative offer had suddenly come out of the blue for him, comparable with the one he had turned down in 1944. Arnold, later Lord Goodman, was a long-time and trusted friend, and the two men would lunch together occasionally. Normally afraid to confide his doubts and depressions, Webster was grateful to have someone else besides Morris Smith he could trust. Goodman happened also to be a lawyer to Southern Television, and it was through his suggestion that Webster was invited to become the company's Managing Director (he had been a director since its beginnings in 1957). Sir John Davis, the Chairman, put the offer to him, and it was an attractive one. There would be power and prestige, and a sackful of money to bear home at the end of each month, more, certainly, than he had ever been given at the Opera House.

But terms were never finalized. In spite of David's unrest and the obvious attractions of the offer, Jimmy was loath to see him give up the Opera House. However heavy a burden it might sometimes be, it was his love and his life. Jimmy wondered, too, why this kind of offer should be made to a man David's age. 'We've been so busy chasing youth and new ideas,' Davis explained, 'that we find we're lightweight on wisdom.'

In spite of this assurance of a most canny appreciation of his worth, as well as of more money, Webster declined. As in 1944, he opted for opera and for less money – he stayed on, he was going to accommodate himself to what was almost a new regime. There were moments when he looked back. Had he made the right decision? Could it be reversed? Anyway, there were openings if he wanted them, that was proven.

He sometimes felt, at nearly sixty, that the burden of ceaseless work was beginning to weigh on him, that the criticism over so many years must also be at last taking its toll. Power seemed to be slipping away. He *could* adapt, but was it worth the effort?

If he'd left much earlier, at the beginning of the 'fifties, say, then he'd have earned himself no more than a footnote in theatre history. But now his place in it was sure. By the end of the 'fifties, it even seemed to him, his work, essentially, was done. The Opera House, continuing to flourish, under other leadership, would remain his testimonial. So would the improving status of the English singer. There were laurels to be worn, and, away from the Opera House, he could wear them in tranquillity. Indeed, for quite a while now, people had been wondering about a knighthood for him. He'd earned it, and surely couldn't be denied it much longer? About *Don Carlos* time Ruth Kleiber had written:

> I keep reading your name in newspapers and magazines and reading of the grandiose happenings at Covent Garden – nothing that happens there leaves me indifferent . . . I long to read your name in the Honours List – and I know that I shall soon be writing Sir David!! I know it! Although it will not change you or make any difference to your achievements, still it is a token of recognition which simply must come.

And come it soon did. The 1960 New Year's Honours List saw him at last Sir David (Hugh Dalton at the same time being made a life peer). David was well-honed in his last moments as plain David, on his way to the Palace accompanied by his mother, up from Brighton, and his aunt. Jimmy stood down for the occasion. A prince being shortly to be born, the Queen herself could not conduct the ceremony, and David was knighted by proxy – but before the little party launched itself from Weymouth Street, Ruth Lynam appeared with a toy cardboard sword to suggest a 'do-it-yourself' knighthood instead. Mrs Webster, not one to betray her feelings, was certainly not *visibly* moved by the ceremony.

But many people were, as the letters pouring in testified. There were letters from the great in the world of the arts, from theatrical knights and dames as well as from such musical figures as Otto Klemperer. From Benjamin Britten came

> Heartiest congratulations! I am very glad that at last there is this public 'thank you' for all your terrific work these last years. Let us hope it may strengthen your hand in all your troublesome battles of the future.

And Harewood cabled from Venice: ESULTATE CONGRATULATIONS SPLENDID NEWS, 'Esultate' being the first word uttered triumphantly by Othello in Verdi's opera. Like Othello, Webster had passed through storms, and as Britten had noted, they were not necessarily past. Another friend, Isador Caplan, wrote with a nice understanding of the achievement,

> Maybe you would have been happier at the announcement of greater financial encouragement from the Treasury, but your friends are delighted at this measure of personal recognition of the tremendons job you so unperturbably carry on without any sign of flagging under the strain.

And Desmond Shawe-Taylor summed up the sentiments of most when he expressed his delight that Webster's labours had 'now been crowned by so splendid a diadem'.

There were letters out of his past too. From Tyson-Smith, the sculptor who long ago had made the plaster cast of Epstein's 'Genesis' for the Sandon revue:

> In the Sandon there are not many of the old ones left who were there in your time. Maud Budden is as full of enterprise and life as ever . . . One of my recollections of you is flying you off the stage at the end of a sofa, and dropping you neatly in the wings attired in a few bits of leopardskin and safety-pins.

And Edith Rose of the Liverpool Repertory Opera Company wrote: 'Am regretting this late letter, but at 89 am not feeling well, and thankfully am not entirely bed-ridden.'

Lillian Byers's was another letter out of his Liverpool past:

> Congratulations on your knighthood, I note by your photograph in the Daily Paper you are still watching your weight. I still have a photograph of you and I taken together at the Bon Marché sports day outing at Aigburth when they were guessing our combined weight, that was a few years ago. I always knew you would be successful, as I once told Mr Harold Cohen you were the best manager I ever had, and I had a few as you know.

And there was a striking one from Dame Edith Sitwell, who when she first invited him to a party shortly after his arrival in London had assured him most forcefully that she was confident of his future success:

> You probably won't have time to think (considering the thousands you must have to answer). But if you *did* have a moment, you must have thought me out of my mind. And I myself take a pretty dim view.
>
> I shouldn't have written now, but for a dream I had late yesterday afternoon. (I have been laid up for six weeks after a very bad accident.) I dreamt that a woman I knew came into my club in London and said, 'Really, Edith, I *do* think you are extraordinary not to have written one word of congratulations to David Webster about his knighthood.'
>
> I said crossly, 'But nobody connected with the arts has got knighted or damed this time!'
>
> When Osbert came to say goodnight to me I told him this dream. He looked at me with absolute astonishment. 'But *of course* he was knighted. Haven't you written to him?' I said No. Because I had no idea of it till this dream.
>
> Well, dream or no dream, nothing could *possibly* give me greater pleasure than the reality – so *richly* deserved. When I think of the superb work you have done, I feel very proud that I knew you when you were 25, and had quelled the audiences of Liverpool and Manchester so that they did not so much as dare disturb a performance by breathing loudly.
>
> And so it has gone on, from triumph to triumph.

Karl Rankl too wrote offering congratulations, adding: 'I hope this has increased your magnanimity towards my *Deirdre* and that you will feel inclined to give it a performance in the near future.'

And what very particularly pleased Sir David was the appreciation of his audiences, from whom letters also arrived in large numbers. From Jan Lindsay Wellington, for example: 'May I tell you how delighted I was to see in this morning's Honours List that public recognition has been given of the magnificent work you do for us – the community.'

Or from Myles Proctor-Gregg: 'May I thank you for the many pleasant hours you have given me in the Opera House. But may I also ask that you will encourage and further more and better broadcasts of your operas; you are turning "the people" into a conscious lover of opera – at last!' Which was surely testimonial enough in itself.

CHAPTER XX

Solti at Covent Garden · difficult days · Solti and the press · *The Force of Destiny* · a chapter of accidents · disaster

Solti's first appearance with the company as Musical Director was in the 1961 Edinburgh Festival, in charge of the new production of Gluck's *Iphigenia in Tauris*. He had wanted to be known more grandly as Musical and Artistic Director; the Board, given that he was at first contracted only for three years, had hesitated, suggesting that perhaps Director of Opera would do instead. In the end he'd settled for plain Musical Director. These discussions about title did nothing to reassure Sir David.

Solti was demanding. He wanted enough rehearsal time, and especially for his own productions. He wanted a lion's share, being a lion, of the new productions, and he expected to be the main force in determining policy. Webster had anticipated nothing less. No one in 1960 asking less would have convinced that he was a big enough man for the job. Of course there were times when Webster felt that he'd given his empire away. But he could also appreciate how well they'd done to get Solti at all. Musical leadership was a problem everywhere, it wasn't peculiar to Covent Garden. In his memoirs Rudolph Bing writes:

> By the 1960s I had lost the war to secure the best conductors for long seasons, and finally I became more than willing to take even six weeks' commitments from conductors like Georg Solti, Leonard Bernstein, Herbert von Karajan and Colin Davis. The days when a Busch would commit himself for eight months at Dresden, or a Walter to six months in Vienna, or a Kleiber to seven months in Berlin, had vanished in the jet-stream of modern aircraft.

Yes, Webster told himself repeatedly, they were very lucky to have Georg Solti. And he was full of admiration when he saw the new man trying to improve discipline and organization. Solti also had definite ideas about how he wanted the repertory expanded. He thought it neither balanced nor complete, and it says much for his tenacity that of the long list he compiled only two operas, *Faust* and Berg's *Lulu*, had not been given by the end of his sojourn, which was to extend itself, finally, to a most generous full ten years.

Webster never had doubts about the talent; but he very soon divined that dynamic Solti, in 1961, was not the most relaxed or self-confident man. In his early Covent Garden days a tension was sometimes to be detected in his work which, while not diminishing its excitement, was none the less a sign of his lack of confidence. Webster could try to ease it. To give the new man more confidence.

For some time Solti was most certainly not at ease in the house. This was in large measure because he came from German opera houses and his way of working was very Prussian. His association with the Chicago Symphony Orchestra in the 'seventies is perhaps the most joyful and unrelievedly harmonious of his entire career, and it is relevant that the orchestra was founded by Theodor Thomas and was taken over by Stock, its Musical Director for forty years. It has an entirely German tradition. But in Covent Garden Solti found a house which seemed to him in many respects amateurish. One among the many reasons for his unease was, for all his insistence, inadequate rehearsal time. He'd heard the orchestra on ballet evenings, playing, as he thought, poor music poorly. How could they be expected to follow a ballet evening with *Valkyrie?* He wanted the orchestra reinforced, and, finances permitting, Webster would happily have obliged. Webster, had of course, been over this ground before.

And the chorus. Solti thought them the second-best raw material in the world, but he also thought that Chorus Master Douglas Robinson needed extra assistance. Webster again made conciliatory noises. By all means – if Pitz, creator of the Philharmonia Chorus, wouldn't accept a post at Covent Garden he *might* be induced to come in for special events. Solti wanted Rotter brought in from Vienna to advise on lighting, and Webster countered with the promise that the lighting system was going to be replaced in 1964. What had brought Solti to London, after all, was the opportunity to present opera on a higher level than he had been able to do in Frankfurt. Webster dismissed nothing lightly, including Solti's complaint that his own name was being played down in publicity material, his treatment quite shabby by comparison with the way Walter Legge had built up Klemperer and Giulini and William Glock had built up Dorati.

Webster was at pains to convey his full appreciation of Solti's passionate involvement in every aspect of opera presentation – without actually acknowledging faults in his house he even managed to convey that he almost *approved* these dissatisfactions, which after all, more than anything else, indicated a love of the house and a desire to do beautiful work in it.

But there was also a deeper unease of which all this was in part an unconscious expression. The very atmosphere at Covent Garden was totally different from what Solti had been used to. Here, though people knew their place in an organization, there was a kind of camaraderie that was to him entirely strange. Sir Frederick Ashton might be sitting in the canteen beside stage-hands calling him Fred . . . it was difficult for Solti to believe that under such circumstances a stage-hand could remain a stage-hand. Germany is full of titles. It is Herr Diplomatischer this, Herr Diplomatischer that, and titles are rigidly adhered to. In England it is nothing out of the ordinary for choristers and orchestral players to be called by their first names. And at Frankfurt boss Solti had only had to ask for something and it was done, while in London his ears were being reluctantly opened to the words, 'can't be done, guv'nor,' followed by hopeful attempts to make it possible. It was something Solti had to learn, that here you were not respected for your title but for your achievement. Germany rated you according to your title – hence Solti's initial concern over nomenclature – and title saved your face even if you were incompetent. In England respect wasn't automatic but it could be won. And it was none the less respect for being perhaps friendly and even casual. All this had to be learnt.

And more. Solti could not be really conscious of the newness of operatic tradition here. Before Webster, London had had an opera house with an exalted history, but it had been one without a tradition. Nor was he immediately aware just what it meant that London in any case is a general arts centre, not a musical and most certainly not a specifically *operatic* centre; the importance of a General Administrator as well as of a Musical Director is therefore relatively not the same at all as in Germany, where the opera house is the centre of the artistic life of the community, and where the Intendant and the *Generalmusikdirektor* bestride their city.

Those first years of Solti and Covent Garden were something of a trial marriage, with Webster the cautious broker. Even before Solti took up his appointment there had been difficulties. In Germany he had been used to rehearsing morning and evening, and between rehearsals he would go home to lunch and rest until five o'clock. This was how he had organized his schedule when he came over for the *Dream*, and people involved in his rehearsals hadn't known how to fill the time between sessions. Webster was anxiously aware of the unrest, but he hadn't wanted to ruffle the man shortly to become his Musical Director. He waited, two days, then three; then he spoke to Solti and schedules were changed.

There was one problem, perhaps the most irksome of all, which nobody saw fit to explain to the new Musical Director because, simply, it was beyond anyone's grasp that it represented a particular problem. And this was the press. The plain fact was that no one here knew what the press on the continent is like. On the continent, the press is *con-*

sistent – if you start there by getting bad notices you continue to get them. Solti didn't understand that the press here is open-minded, and that there is no question of first judgements being final. It's not even a question of the treatment of this or that Musical Director – in Germany the press wouldn't write about the President as here, daily, they write about the Prime Minister. In Germany a Musical Director, a town dignitary, tends as a matter of civic pride to get well reviewed. Unfortunately, there were events in Solti's first year or two which were not beyond criticism, but he thought the press over-eager to register criticism, he felt that their reaction was not only untoward but even personal. He'd come with good intentions, to elevate the status of the house, and what seemed to be happening? He found himself, a lion, transformed into a bear at a baiting.

Solti had made a good impression at Covent Garden while still a guest, but once in the job he seemed almost perversely unable to make good that promise. He was pained enough by deficiencies without the press attacking him for them. *Iphigenia* was not particularly successful, for if Rita Gorr's reverberant Amneris might have justified her casting, in the event the heroine's music lay rather high for her. *Don Giovanni* followed. Mozart was now the big problem of the repertory, and in 1959 Giulini had been all but contracted to take charge of a new Mozart cycle. But negotiations had been suspended while talks went ahead with Solti, and he had unhesitatingly yielded the opera (Solti reciprocating by letting *Falstaff* go to *him*). *Don Giovanni* didn't, unfortunately, bring in better days for Mozart, and it didn't show the Musical Director to be a natural Mozartian.

A further problem, which held Solti back, was that he didn't know English theatre, which the Opera House had been used to raiding for its directors. At first he often had to take what he was given on trust, which didn't mean exactly that he was given rubbish, only that he couldn't know in advance whether he was going to feel that director and opera had been matched. For the triple bill including Ravel's *L'Heure Espagnole* Webster suggested Peter Ustinov, who convinced Solti, when they met, that at least he had a musical mind. But the nature of their collaboration is rather suggested by that moment during rehearsal when Ustinov, having implemented a particularly intricate piece of staging, was asked by Solti if some time might now be found for the music!

So far Solti had not had a good press. The new *Ring* was the big chance. It was to be phased over successive seasons and not, as before, disgorged in one huge mouthful. Pains weren't going to be spared, and success in the huge undertaking could make good the failures. But the question still was, how to do it. Webster had turned his face away from Bayreuth and gauzes, and if he'd been in touch from time to time with Wieland Wagner he had pursued him at most half-heartedly, and had at times been insolently casual. But the only tradition for Wagner that the house had established through the 'fifties was a dismal one of 'compromise' production.

Solti felt that the time had come to move away from neo-Bayreuth and back to a greater naturalism. This suited Webster's taste well enough. Solti himself wanted Hans Hotter for director, and Webster once again approached Henry Moore for designs. And was again refused. In the end the job went to Herbert Kern, from Munich. Hotter's work was not much liked, and Kern's designs, alas, were so heartily disliked that even Leslie Hurry's for the 1954 production, also abused in their time, now came in for some praise. The Kern designs weren't allowed, like a malignant growth, to spread to the other operas. They were scrapped, and a new designer, Günther Schneider-Siemssen, took on the whole cycle, beginning with *Siegfried* the following season. His work wasn't admired either, but at least it didn't provoke a demand for the reinstatement of Herbert Kern.

So much for staging. The musical performance, happily, was something else. It was apparent at once, with the first instalment, that this *Ring* was going to be nothing like Kempe's, Solti's gift being essentially dramatic, not lyric. He can screw up a performance to a wondrous pitch of excitement, and he did, even if in these early performances his nervousness occasionally brought with it some over-emphasis and inflexibility. His *Siegfried* and *Twilight of the Gods* at Covent Garden were, surprisingly, his first-ever.

Webster hadn't been able to get Birgit Nilsson, whom the ambition of the enterprise demanded, because last time she'd sung *The Ring* the press hadn't given her her due. There was one notice which had enraged her. How well she could have sympathized with Solti's feelings about the press. In her fury she had vowed that she wasn't coming back. Anyway for *The Ring*. She had no need to. A star such as Nilsson could expect to be royally received: she didn't need to fight for money and acclaim, it was hers everywhere. She certainly was given more money elsewhere. If the press attacked her then there was simply no point in coming. Never again.

But, as all singers knew, Webster could be persuasive. The following year she came back for the new production of *Siegfried* only. Webster hoped, little by little . . . but alas, she was never again to appear in a complete *Ring* at Covent Garden. A year later Solti's first-ever *Twilight of the Gods* was given a wonderful boost by Nilsson's presence in it – but it was also the last Covent Garden was to hear of her Brunnhilde. This *Twilight* was thus also Twilight of a Goddess.

Siegfried was mounted in Solti's second season, and with a second *Ring* opera it was clear that once more a somewhat tarnished hoop of gold was being forged. But the musical level, over of a first-ever *Siegfried* for the conductor, gave virtual guarantee that *The Ring* was going to remain as important as ever in the repertory.

Shortly after *Siegfried*, in September 1962, came *Force of Destiny*, over the years frequently discussed, much looked-forward-to – and, in the event, Disaster! Sufficient of itself to break Solti at the Garden. Webster brought in Sam Wanamaker to direct, on the strength of his success with Tippett's *King Priam*. That production had been sparse, jagged, stark, and not at all to the taste of Webster, who had sympathized with those who during rehearsals had dubbed it *Priam Agonistes*. But the critics had liked it. It was wonderful that they had liked something in Solti's first season – it was the only unqualified production success. Not without doubts, Webster none the less 'sold' him to Solti. Sean Kenny had designed *Priam*, and his mastery of stage-machinery had impressed (particularly lovers of Meccano!) – but Webster was confident that he was doing better by Verdi in bringing in Guttoso to work with Wanamaker, for Guttoso was a very celebrated Italian designer and painter much more likely to be in sympthy with the ideal of nineteenth-century grand opera. It wasn't any fault of Webster's that Wanamaker and Guttoso quarrelled, for he followed his usual policy of not interfering with his people once he'd given them jobs to do. When he learned of the quarrel, it was too late to try and mend it. He found himself with an important new production pending and no designer. And, a bad time, a *Solti* production. 'Get someone else, then,' he told Wanamaker. This certainly wasn't mere casualness, and in fact he was desperately anxious. Hopes of keeping Solti after his initial term were fast receding, and a success was vital. But he adhered to his policy, letting his artists work as far as possible unimpeded. And he hated any project, once embarked on, to be abandoned. And this one had been planned, originally, on such a gratifying high level.

What happened was that Wanamaker, instead of casting about for a new designer, came up, like another Zeffirelli, with designs of his own. But not ones that impressed David Webster. They were, to him distastefully sparse, not at all the backing for grand opera, not at all the sort of thing Zeffirelli would have conjured up for him. Cleft stick for an impresario! If he didn't accept them he'd have to scrap everything. So he accepted the designs on his own authority.

It happened that since Drogheda's assumption of the role of Chairman, two new sub-committees had been formed, and one was a Design Sub-Committee under a Board member, Colin Anderson.

Webster made a point of being very careless indeed about letting them know what was happening, and they didn't even know that Wanamaker wasn't working with Guttoso any more. But he thought the Sub-Committee liable to interfere in the often sensitive relationship of director and designer. Most un-Websterish! He didn't want *his* relationship with them interfered with either. After *Force of Destiny* the point was strongly made, all designs for new productions *must* be shown to Colin Anderson and approved by the Sub-Committee. (In spite of which directive, it remained patently ineffective and Webster was not ill-pleased when it was disbanded. The other new Sub-Committee, for Finance, continued to work well, and with his full approval, under Lord Robbins.)

The trouble wasn't only the sparse designs. It was rather that the production seemed to suggest that Wanamaker, ripped from a theatre in which Berthold Brecht was currently an idol, was trying to give nineteenth-century grand opera a Brechtian gloss. Both Verdi's opera and Brecht's *Mother Courage* have the Thirty Years' War as background, and if Brecht had revised *Force of Destiny* he would no doubt have set the vivandière-as-Mother-Courage in opposition to the gentry, whom he'd have reinterpreted as selfish and ludicrously old-fashioned in their preoccupation with outmoded chivalresque codes. This might have been Brecht's way with a *written* text. But the Verdi score approves the gentry and exults in their high-romantic passions, and his opera provides material altogether intractable to Wanamaker's apparent purposes.

To make matters worse, Jon Vickers and Leontyne Price had been hoped for, and neither was finally in the cast. Carlo Bergonzi came in place of Vickers, which at least reassured Solti that the proper level was still being aimed at. No actor, Bergonzi – and now, alas, Wanamaker made a cardinal error in trying to make him act. On the first night the duel scene had elements rather of Chaplin than of Brecht, Bergonzi first losing his sword and then suffering further embarrassment when his visor dropped. Bergonzi, though, has a fine larynx, and it was Leontyne Price who was more sorely missed. Her replacement was Floriana Cavalli. On Giulini's recommendation Lord Harewood had engaged her to sing in the Verdi *Requiem* in the 1961 Leeds Festival (which he'd run from 1958): she'd sung beautifully, and Harewood recommended her to Webster. But when she appeared at Covent Garden, only a year later, she was in poor voice. 'Don't you think we ought to do something?' a disturbed Webster had murmured to Solti during rehearsals. At times now he was wondering simply, from which direction was disaster going to strike? But Solti wanted to persevere with a singer once cast. On the night she sang disastrously flat and more or less without voice. The huge aria of the final act was awaited with dread, and as the poor thread of a voice uncertainly emitted an approximation of the last notes, another voice, from the gallery, hissed out, charged with venom – 'This is *disgusting!* Where's Shuard?' The unfortunate Cavalli came before the curtain at the end of the evening, and as her body bent in a bow it seemed as though she was being broken by the weight of booing. John Shaw, in the baritone role, also had his share of boos, largely because a section of the audience had been incensed by the management's decision to terminate the contract of another Canadian, Louis Quilico, in favour of keeping Shaw at the house. Wanamaker, smartly erect, was totally unbowed by *his* boos, and returned the widest of smiles to this almost Roman audience. Easier, of course, for the director to smile. He doesn't have to come back another evening to do it all over again.

Webster did his best to remind Solti that, despite *Force of Destiny*, he was a proven Verdian. The revival of *Otello* he'd been in charge of, the one in which Gobbi at last gave Covent Garden his Iago, had been a real success. He was a proven Wagnerian too.

One more new production to go before this second Solti season ended. It ended none too happily with *Figaro*, carefully prepared, and with a distinguished cast. But next morning a very gloomy Webster was reading *The Times* headline – 'Mr Solti Skating over the Score'. He felt that he'd been pushed back over fifteen years, he remembered how he had dreaded newspapers when, in his first season, one production after another was condemned. He dreaded his Musical Director's reaction, and quickly induced the Board to give Solti a vote of confidence.

Webster was determined to keep Solti, and transform this dismal progress into triumph. He admired his stamina and will, and his staying on and ultimately succeeding had by now become almost a personal challenge. But Solti had been battered by the press. There was more too – he'd been booed from the gallery, and only later learnt that the booing had come from a very few people only. There was the time when he'd left his car, a very recognizable white Mercedes, registered GS, and with a left-hand drive to help identification, at the end of the paved alleyway opposite the Opera House, in Drury Lane, and he'd come back to it after the performance to find it daubed and the words 'Solti must go!' *scratched* on it.

But more than anything it was the press. 'I'm not coming back,' he said when asked to renew his contract. 'I can't take your music critics.' He'd had such ambitions and his problems had been so little understood! Webster knew the feeling too. But as Peter Hall later described in a radio interview, Solti had asked him to come to work at the Opera House in 1961. Peter Hall couldn't because he was at Stratford, and Solti had exploded:

> It's all very well, I come here to this house, and I'm going to try to help opera in England and all you producers are so busy with your bloody theatre you won't come and help me. How am I to do it?

Fair question! Peter Hall also comments:

> If Georg had managed to surround himself with a group of producers in 1961, he would have made not only a musical style but an operatic style during his musical directorship.

Webster, who at the beginning hadn't been sure he wanted Solti, in 1962 was giving up hope of being able to persuade him to stay. One more season and yet again it would be a house without a Musical Director.

And Solti was amazed to find that the press, when they discovered he wasn't renewing, wanted to give a party for him! A farewell gesture – a sign of their appreciation! They'd taken their time showing appreciation. But it was too late. If nothing else, this surely told Georg Solti that he would never understand the English, and never be able to settle down among them.

CHAPTER XXI

Nureyev defects · the Nureyev–Fonteyn partnership · four Juliets · pricing policy · Solti stays · Callas in *Tosca* · Webster vindicated · Peter Hall · *Moses and Aaron* · *Arabella*

In the summer of 1961 London was looking forward eagerly to the visit by a second Russian ballet company, the Kirov. When they arrived, however, one of the dancers announced to appear was no longer with them. He had defected in Paris at the end of the company's season there – had actually made his dramatic dash at Orly Airport as they were about to board planes for London.

Audiences here hadn't singled out young Rudolph Nureyev in advance as a dancer they particularly wanted to see. Most knew nothing about him, and he had not been expected to play an important part in the season. There were plenty of other dancers senior to him. But this was the first defection by a Russian dancer – England's own Russian dancer, Violetta Elvin, who had retired only a few years before, had been allowed to leave Russia when she married an Englishman. The drama at Orly was a headline affair throughout the world, and everyone was now suddenly eager to see Nureyev.

England had not long to wait. Nureyev was first seen here not at Covent Garden but at Drury Lane, where on 2 November 1961 Fonteyn organized a matinée in aid of the Royal Academy of Dancing. She invited the young Russian to participate, though not as her partner. He danced a solo specially created for him, to Scriabin music, by Frederick Ashton; and after this single appearance de Valois had no doubts, he must come to Covent Garden at least as a guest artist, not because of his freak value but because of his value as an artist. Webster shared her enthusiasm. But they were agreed, caution must be used in introducing him even as guest, for the feelings of the artists of the Royal Ballet were going to be easily ruffled.

Nureyev first partnered Fonteyn at Covent Garden on 21 February 1962, in *Giselle*. The two went well together, and Webster noted that Fonteyn was clearly 'charged' by this new conjunction. If a partnership could be established, and if it really worked, it might even mean a new phase in Fonteyn's career, though it was still not certain just how much longer she was going to go on dancing. In 1954, when she'd married, expectations had been fixed on perhaps another five years. Her partner of a decade, Michael Somes, had recently retired. These were factors. Another was that Nureyev was already being compared to the pantherine Jean Babilée, and even, by those with longer experience, with Nijinsky himself. 'The temperature rises when he's about,' Webster commented.

But caution – he was still far from proven. When he returned to Covent Garden in April Fonteyn was away in Australia, giving guest performances there. She had taken with her David Blair, normally Nadia Nerina's partner, and Nerina's first choice to fill the gap would have been the Bolshoi's Fadeyechev, who had been her partner when she herself had gone to Russia as guest. But she knew there was no guarantee of a Russian's actually arriving even if all arrangements had been made, so she suggested instead the Dane, Eric Bruhn – equivalent in dancing terms to a *bel canto* singer. He'd been seen at Covent Garden with the Royal Danish Ballet in 1953, and recently he'd been giving concert performances round the world in a quartet of which the other male dancer was none other than Nureyev. The two came together, and brought a huge excitement to ballet and to Covent Garden. Again the art form was given a 'lift'.

De Valois and Webster were now more definite about wanting Nureyev for the company. Definite but still cautious. There were going to be problems politically, not only international, but within the company, for company politics also generate passions. Webster, however, was determined. He knew wherein lay the best interests of the house. Imposing Nureyev on the company was going to need all his accustomed tact and the now huge weight of his authority.

If Webster saw Nureyev's value to the house, he was scrupulous about not rushing in. Lord Drogheda suggested higher prices be charged for the Bruhn and Nureyev appearances, and Webster's long reply shows just how tactful, just how circumspect, he felt the need to be.

> Nobody realizes more than I do that we need to pile up takings. But nobody has asked us to get all the money we can irrespective of all other considerations except money . . . Of course N is a draw, just how much of a draw is not yet known but he *is* a draw. But being a draw isn't the only consideration.
>
> I am absolutely certain that Bruhn is not at the moment a draw but he may become one. Some people think he is the finest male dancer in the world but he clearly does not mean that to the great British public. He is not booking badly but people are not rushing to see him. I hope he may become so but at this stage he is not well-known and to put up prices for him does not make sense and to run the very considerable risk of poor houses is to say the least of it a mistake. Give him a chance to get his public – then we can do what we like. This is surely sense. You must have a public to get the money and to put a barrier against a possible

asset is not a grave risk, it is a mistake. To charge extra for the unknown is not an asset for the unknown. N with Margot is an undoubted success. N in *Giselle* is an undoubted success. There is not proof that he will be such a success in other parts. I am doubtful. He is very young, incomplete ... In any case we did not ask him here to put up prices but to see if he was all right for the company. He is being given the same as Bruhn, in other words a reasonable guest fee. To transfer him to a salaried member of the company would not be difficult nor *in terms of money* have great repercussions. N is a very astute boy, make it clear to him he is a huge draw at special prices and you will probably not get him as a member of the company. If he is to be a valuable asset in the future he needs the company. We will make money out of him in the future, and to lose the extra on six performances now does not immediately matter.

While N could be an asset to the company he equally might start its dissolution, or at least the first big break away.

He comes to us at an odd time. We are facing a considerable period of adjustment in the ballet company. In ballet as it is not in a way in opera, THE COMPANY is the thing.

On Wednesday N asked a boy not to come on with him at a given moment, the boy like a fool did what he was asked. That is the sort of thing which if he gets away with it could cause havoc. Suppose we brought into the company a young ballerina of enormous potential and considerable immediate appeal but not fully developed, what do you suppose would be the effect on Nerina, Beriosova and cie? Supposing we immediately put the youngster with not very great support into the special price category which would give her great prestige within the company? Do you think this would make for good relationships? I am quite certain we would lose almost immediately certainly Nerina and Beriosova. We can do anything we like with Margot and she with us, because she is in a completely proven special category and jealousy if it is felt simply does not raise its head.

I am sure it is in the best interests of the company and our takings to play him slowly. I can hear you say well the company must get used to these things ... If we stir up jealousies in the company at this moment we are in for trouble.

Nureyev was back at Covent Garden in the autumn, and the partnership with Fonteyn began in earnest. There was *Swan Lake* and *Giselle* together, in November 1962; the pair coruscated in Petipa's *Corsaire* pas de deux, produced by Nureyev himself; and in March 1963 came the Ashton *Marguerite and Armand*, more or less an extended pas de deux for the pair based on the *Traviata* story, but with Michael Somes, Fonteyn's former partner, as her new partner's father. By this time the partnership was already indissoluble. That Nureyev was brought, and reasonably smoothly blended into the company, was a triumph of diplomacy. Even then, the proposal to bill Nureyev as the star of the company on its next American tour was a dangerous one, and there were protests, and threats of resignation – precisely what Webster had feared – unless the dancers were listed in alphabetical order. The dancers *were* so listed. The incident proved Webster right in being anxious.

After his first success at the Opera House, Nureyev, shy and nervous, didn't want to talk to the press. But when the company went to America with Nureyev, in the spring of 1963, press officer Bill Beresford managed none the less to get cover stories in both *Time* and *Newsweek* – and in the same week. Sidney Nolan executed the *Time* cover, and a Zoe Dominic photograph was the cover of *Newsweek*. It was a publicist's dream. Aglow with success Beresford came wordlessly to Webster's office and put advance copies on his desk. Webster looked from one to the other, 'Fancy . . . ' he was just heard to murmur. This man who was famously *not* easy to prod into compliments.

Webster had been right in judging that if Nureyev was to become a valuable asset he also needed the company. The company not only provided him with a framework, but also gave him, uprooted and still 'incomplete', a home and stability. And Webster was his godfather. Of this Nureyev was not insensible, and he was later to dispatch his agent, Gorlinsky, to Cartier's, to 'get anything' for Sir David. Gorlinsky bought suitably expensive and decorative cuff-links, which it gave Sir David a good deal of pleasure to show off.

The Fonteyn-Nureyev conjunction brought the Opera House more attention than any other item of the Webster quarter of a century, with the possible exception of Callas's appearances. Fonteyn was into a new and almost unlooked-for phase of her career. It had been expected that she would see out the 'fifties at the head of the company, but nothing more had been taken for granted. With Nureyev she was launched into the 'sixties. Even then, every extra year was a kind of bonus. Webster would not have cared to predict that she would still be with him ten years later . . .

There were dangers. Dame Ninette had realized that company policy must not be too much dictated by any one artist even if that artist was Fonteyn. It was wonderful to have her still – but the company as a whole must be developed. However far into the future this amazing career could be extended, it was important that the company should now be ready for the time – which must come – when they would have to continue without her to lead them. A second generation of dancers, led by Nerina and Beriosova, had already emerged, and yet another, a third, was now coming along. It was easier for Webster to register them while Fonteyn herself was away; and in fact, it was while she was in Australia that Eric Bruhn had produced some dances by the Danish choreographer Bournonville, the Napoli *divertissements*, and they had strikingly presented three young and contrasted dancers, Lynn Seymour, Antoinette Sibley and Merle Park, as well as an Anthony Dowell so young and undeveloped that he seemed almost an outline in the air waiting to be filled in. Webster knew then that there were responsibilities to these dancers too to be met, and that with them, perhaps, lay the future – possibly after he and Fonteyn both had shed their responsibilities. He didn't anticipate serious conflicts. Eighteen months later Nureyev himself produced an act of the Petipa ballet, *La Bayadère*, for the Royal Ballet, an imperial vehicle for himself and Fonteyn. It made an ideal double-bill with the two-act ballet, *The Two Pigeons*, which Ashton had created for Lynn Seymour and her partner Christopher Gable. One partnership didn't seem to Webster to fight the other, any more than Ashton fought with Petipa. It was richness to set beside richness, with gain for everyone.

Conflicts couldn't always be avoided, and sometimes it was matter of choosing the path of least risk. As when Kenneth MacMillan created his full-length ballet *Romeo and Juliet* in 1965. The history of modern full-evening ballets was a somewhat doubtful one at Covent Garden; and this one used the same Prokofiev music as the Bolshoi's, on which the choreographer Lavrovsky had worked in close collaboration with the composer, and would have to bear direct and dangerous comparison with it. Lavrovsky's Juliet, when the ballet was first seen at Covent Garden, had been Ulanova, succeeded by other fine dancers. Webster was determined that MacMillan must be given the support of the company's prima ballerina in her famous partnership. The other excellent young dancers could follow her.

But MacMillan had created the ballet for Lynn Seymour. No matter, she must follow. That was a Webster decree against which there was no appeal. Seymour's partner Christopher Gable had to teach his role of Romeo to Nureyev (whom MacMillan thought would make an ideal Mercutio). The curtain rose, and Fonteyn and Nureyev lent their glamour to a success – which was what most mattered. In due course, Seymour and Gable appeared in it, to acclaim. Sibley and Park also took turns as Juliet in the ballet's first season.

It was arranged that all four Juliets should be photographed together one morning. Three of them duly arrived. They were already in costume and full make-up before it was noted that one of their number hadn't arrived yet. Where was Lynn Seymour? Telephone calls had to be made. Had she overslept? And if she had, it might have been interpreted as an involuntary protest.

Webster recognized that there was a balance to be maintained. And he considered that he'd maintained it. Even when in the second half of the decade MacMillan left to direct the ballet in Berlin and Seymour went with him. It was a pity, but she was, after all, to MacMillan what Fonteyn had been to Ashton. He was sorry that Christopher Gable gave up dancing to be an actor. But none of this was because he hadn't maintained a balance. He considered that Fonteyn-Nureyev, and the youngsters coming along brilliantly too, were blessings of his last years.

It was nothing new to charge more for distinguished guest singers, but ballet audiences paid, not for this or that dancer, but for the privilege of seeing the company. While Fonteyn was a company member prices didn't vary even when she was dancing. But in the autumn of 1959 she'd gone on to a guest contract, which meant that she was paid per performance, instead of by the week for a stipulated number of appearances: and from 1959 onwards a 'Fonteyn Night' was priced higher. Nureyev, because he wasn't a British subject, couldn't join the company and he remained a guest, though when he returned in the autumn of 1962 it was to become virtually a company member. But Webster watched Nureyev, the audiences, the company too – and higher prices weren't charged for Nureyev alone, *sans* Fonteyn, until March 1965.

There was an anomaly in opera pricing. When a series of performances was 'kicked off' by a celebrated guest or two, their roles might be taken over before the end of the series by house singers. But the higher prices remained. Webster wouldn't lower the value of house singers, in their own eyes as much as in audiences', by, as he saw it, selling them short. But anyway costs were continuing to rise alarmingly, and prices generally were affected. They weren't any longer so closely related to straight theatre prices – they'd 'broken loose'. Higher prices generally, and higher still for special evenings, in turn affected the nature of audiences, which Webster saw with some dismay, in the lower parts of the house, becoming somewhat more 'social'. The boom in the tourist trade too, with the very often favourable exchange rates for visitors, also registered. The box-office needed them, but foreign languages were increasingly heard in the stalls as well as on the stage.

Nureyev's first appearances at the house occurred during Solti's first season. The *Corsaire* pas de deux exploded on a stage which barely a month before had heaved under the weight of that *Force of Destiny*, and *Marguerite and Armand* drew cheers during that anxious time when Solti's new contract was being discussed. It was too much like the old days, with Massine putting the house in credit after the opening *Carmen*.

But Solti *was* persuaded to extend his contract. There was time for recovery.

It was Webster, above all, who persuaded Solti – even though Solti was perfectly well aware that to start with Webster hadn't wanted him.

Only to start with. Afterwards there had been unstinted support. Without Webster's support it is quite certain that Solti would have been lost to the house. Webster knew it. It confirmed to him that he had been right, he could have achieved nothing comparable if he'd gone to Southern Television. This sixty-year-old still had a lot to give the Opera House!

The two men were one in their determination – to transform present failure into success. Webster could hardly conceive, now, of a time when he *hadn't* wanted Solti. He'd kept him partly, he knew, by small tactfulnesses, and by a graceful yielding to necessity, quite as much as by a large understanding and through imaginative sympathy. He knew how to make giving, even when he knew he *had* to give, a pleasure for himself as well as the recipient. (He'd had a good training with Erich Kleiber!)

Solti, thanks to David Webster, was saved for the house. He gained ground slowly. By 1964 things were better – but even now the major excitements were being provided by others. Webster managed to keep the house warm, giving his Musical Director *time*. There was the still-new excitement of Fonteyn-Nureyev. And, as though to help them in their troubles, Maria Callas herself agreed to return to Covent Garden.

This was a great surprise. Maria had last been in the house in 1959, for Medea. Shortly afterwards she'd gone into semi-retirement, and her appearances since had been few. A somewhat doubtful Medea at La Scala in 1962 had had the press all but writing obituary notices. Giulini was asked to consider her for the new Covent Garden *Trovatore*, proposed for the following year, but naturally everyone – everyone, that is, apart from David Webster – was anxious and uncertain.

Callas's agent, Gorlinsky, wrote to Webster on her behalf:

> Madame Callas has pointed out to me that until now her fee at Covent Garden has been very low, and considerably less than she receives in other opera houses, and this time she really wants a fee in accordance with her reputation and box-office draw.

This was not unreasonable, far from it: somewhat ill-timed perhaps. But Webster understood that it seemed rather than anything else to express an unacknowledged reluctance on the diva's part either to accept the offer or to reject it and thereby perhaps interrupt the dialogue between herself and Covent Garden. It certainly confirms that Webster had very often to pay his artists with love (his own) rather than with money (the Treasury's).

A Callas *Trovatore* was for a while a possibility. The production was in any case postponed until the end of 1964, but Webster, with his habitual, and be it said sometimes blind, loyalty, continued to be enthusiastic about having Callas sing for him, at a time when other opera houses were decidedly reluctant to commit themselves to her.

And then, late in 1963, Callas herself announced that she was prepared to undertake Tosca. Webster was overjoyed. He'd been so often in correspondence with her, and there had been so many ambitious plans. *Tosca* had been one of several loving prospects – back in the autumn of 1958, shortly after *Traviata*, he'd written to her:

> I was appalled last Friday morning to discover that you had left an hour or so before my call as this is the second time you have been in London and we have not met . . . Anyway I hope you enjoyed yourself in your recording and the television which I did see and enjoyed: you looked absolutely beautiful. I suppose in two or three weeks' time you are away in America where I hope you have a triumphant time.
>
> Are your plans for the 1959/60 season any more definite than they were when you were last here? At that time you were saying that you felt you would only appear in operas which had been specially produced and rehearsed for you. If you are still of that mind what would you like to do with us? Is *Anna Bolena* a possibility with you or have you any other special desire? There is of course still one part that we should absolutely love to see you in here which does not square with the special ideas that you have in mind, and that is Tosca. Is there any possibility of your doing that with us June/July 1959? If there is I will rush over to Italy and discuss it with you.

It had taken him five years, but now he was to have his Callas *Tosca* at last. Webster was overjoyed. He refused even to notice the lack of comparable enthusiasm about him. She was virtually in retirement? Then they must take it as the greater compliment that she chose Covent Garden for her return! She was a risk? Could there be a more worthwhile one? But he refused even to acknowledge that she *was* a risk.

She even agreed at the same time to do *Norma* again, in the following season. Better and better! But this Solti was against. He didn't feel that the opera was priority for a new production. Webster told him that a production could be borrowed from Paris against the exchange of the new *Tosca*. Solti countered that even then the repertory would be thrown out of balance. With a Callas performance on offer, Webster wasn't one to think of balancing the repertory. But Solti was very much against choice of repertory being determined by any particular singer – even if that singer was Callas. A new production for Joan Sutherland was being planned, which would mean another opera from the *bel canto* era. He stipulated that it had to be either *Norma* or the Sutherland opera but not both. Webster knew when to give way,

Scene in the Crush Bar following the Farewell Gala for Sir David Webster. In front, Tito Gobbi, Sir Georg Solti and his wife; looking on (right), Lord Drogheda and (left) John Tooley

The Royal Opera House cast and staff bid a backstage farewell to Sir David Webster after the Farewell Gala

Above: Jimmy Cleveland Belle and Sir David Webster on their way to a wedding
Below: Sir David Webster and Lord Drogheda

but this was a painful quandary for him – solved when the Callas *Norma* ceased to be a possibility any longer, and *I Puritani* for Sutherland became uncontested winner.

Nothing was going to get in the way of *Tosca*, though. Zeffirelli was at the house already, directing *Rigoletto*. Good. He was just the man for *Tosca*. Webster arrived excitedly at a production meeting with the letter from Callas in his hand. Yes, he announced, it was definite – she'd actually consented to do Tosca for them.

No one present seemed to greet the event as excitedly as he had. And he wasn't really surprised. He carefully gauged the reaction when he told them that she'd only do it if it was *now*. He sensed that there were one or two present who would have been happy if it was *never*. 'I know,' he told them, 'you're all going to say there's no rehearsal time.' He didn't give them time to say it. 'We'll find time!' he informed them. And everyone at once recognized that Webster was giving them a directive which could not be refused. It would be futile for any of them to argue with him. There was no gainsaying Webster when he was in this mood. *Tosca* had to be: and it had to be *now*.

They had six weeks in which to mount the opera. Designs and casting were done at the double. Normally three Sundays were put aside for set-up and lighting on the stage. *Rigoletto* rehearsals were going ahead at the same time, in a most elaborate production and with gorgeous settings and costumes by the unsurpassed Lila di Nobili. So for *Tosca* there could be only one Sunday.

But, for all the initial reserve, the house was committed to the enterprise, and Webster's enthusiasm fired everyone. It was an exciting time. Solti was in the pit for *Rigoletto* and Carlo Felice Cillario came in for *Tosca*. Zeffirelli was everywhere about, in several places at any one moment – emptying his mind of one sequence of fascinating problems to leave it free to cope with another! There was a unity, and friendly rivalry, as the two productions rehearsed under their two conductors and one director. One production paced the other.

Tosca was revealed for the first time on 21 January 1964 and it was, in spite of everything, a glory. Once again, a triumph was born of risk. Callas had returned with a vengeance. The decor was by Renzo Mongiardino, and rich stage pictures – with a fire blazing for picturesque effect in Scarpia's huge fireplace in midsummer Rome! – were maintained by Zeffirelli as a respectful frame for Callas, whose genius was displayed in many a fine stroke from which nothing was allowed to distract. Handsome was the word, for Callas herself, for everything in the evening. Handsome was the word for Scarpia in the person of Tito Gobbi. How often in her career had Callas had to *will* herself, an insistent small martyrdom, into belief of this one as lover, that one as father, that as villain. But in Tito Gobbi she had a villain she could *adore*. Callas, with Gobbi and Zeffirelli, confirmed that the art form was being maintained on its highest level. Their collaboration successfully challenged the preceding history of the art, whether lodged in memory, on record or in idea; they confirmed the possibility of a future in which tradition was perpetuated, not traduced. It was partly this sense of history encapsulated, of past combining with future on the one particular evening, to which the audience responded so gratefully and affectionately.

Next day came a telegram from Rudolph Bing, who wanted Callas to do Tosca at the Metropolitan. Callas exclaimed indignantly. 'What's the matter? Isn't it a good offer?' Webster asked her slyly. Her eyes flashed in good imitation of the prima donna style expected of her. Yes, it was a very good offer indeed – $6000 a performance, no less. But he'd only made the offer after he'd read her notices! It was Webster who'd given her the chance to *show* – Bing risked nothing. She appreciated Webster's faith and daring. So did many others, and not least others who had had experience of musical administration. Peter Diamond (later Harewood's successor at Edinburgh) wrote to him most appreciatively:

> I believe I can somehow realize the great risk you took when planning this performance: nobody could foretell, when you invited Maria, in what form she would be in – in fact, whether she would appear at all. Many, very many, of those who admire Maria had become careful, even doubtful. That you felt an artist such as Maria worth any risk – that to bring her back to the stage would not only provide her audience with a unique experience but will also undoubtedly help her to resume her task which she, temporarily, seemed to have neglected: this deserves the greatest admiration and sincere gratitude from all those who believe in opera and feel that there is no operatic artist comparable to Maria.
>
> In shouldering the great responsibility which this performance, in more than one way, entailed, you have set – certainly not for the first time! – an example to all those who prefer the line of least – or less – resistance!

Callas had as warm a reception from the press as from her public. Peter Diamond's letter, more privately, consistuted Webster's 'press'. But if more privately, the letter does speak for the particular kind of esteem in which Webster was held in his own world, among those whose own experience could tell them of the basis on which Covent Garden's successes were built.

As it happened, everything had gone right for that *Tosca*, while *Rigoletto* had been harried by misfortunes. No part of the blame was Solti's in the pit; and in revivals the virtues of the production could be seen more clearly. Rigoletto himself was Geraint Evans for the first time in his career. It is not a role for a buffo-baritone, but as a star of the house he was entitled to use it to test his limitations and extend his range. But he was, besides, in poor health when the first night arrived, and unable to do all his scheduled performances. Anna Moffo, the Gilda, was also in poor health, and actually fainted at one performance. The not-so-frequently uttered words 'Is there a doctor in the house?' were actually heard in the vast theatre. Five presented themselves at the stage door, one or two of them highly distinguished, and one stammering young man who declared, 'I'm a qualified doctor but I've never practised. But if I can help I will.' This was in fact Dr Jonathan Miller, who was one day to do productions of his own.

The first scene was particularly sumptuous, an authentic tableau teeming with life – almost, one could say, a life of its own. The production's very richness did not go uncriticized. Webster was making a speech at the Royal College of Music, once again demonstrating the excellence of his outstanding physical feature, his (speaking) voice. A student commented on the extravagance of Opera House productions. 'I haven't noticed any exceptional extravagance,' Webster replied with his effectively supercilious drawl. 'Of course we have a high standard. I'm careful not to let down that standard.' The young critic refused to be patronized. 'What about the Zeffirelli production of *Rigoletto*?', he insisted. 'With all those dwarfs in the palace scene.' Webster sighed with a slow impatience. 'I can assure you, sir,' he returned, 'that's it's very inexpensive to hire troupes of dwarfs.'

These first months of 1964 had seen a small Zeffirelli festival at the house. *Tosca* in January, *Rigoletto* in February, in March *Puritani* for Sutherland in his production borrowed from Palermo. It wasn't the Musical Director who was yet providing the major excitements – though he did bring *Billy Budd* triumphantly back into the repertory, fulfilling one part of the promise of his early appearances as a guest still, when he had had charge of *The Dream*, another Britten opera. But it was *The Ring* which proved to be Solti's first major achievement at Covent Garden. Its segments had already been seen separately, but it was given complete for the first time in 1964, in September: Solti had now completed his first three years and was beginning his extended term. Critics and public alike had become used to its staging and were ready to look past what they *had* to see to take in the musical performance. Solti's triumph can be considered the greater in that it was a triumph in spite of the visual aspect. Webster registered this success with enormous relief. How would he be feeling if Solti hadn't renewed? Who would have been in charge of this *Ring?* And what would the verdict have been on the late Musical Director after his brief term? Webster would no doubt have come in for a share of criticism himself. And there'd have been the weary business of looking about for a Musical Director all over again. 1964 was being kind to him.

The contract had been extended to evidently good purpose. The 'sixties were to be the decade when at last the day to day standard became notably more even. It was already beginning to be. In the 'fifties, the same orchestra that, with special rehearsal conditions, played superbly for Kleiber or Giulini might on another evening under someone else be mediocre. One of the features of the 'sixties was to be simply this, that orchestra tended to play well whether Solti was in command or not. For his own productions he would sometimes have Downes in the pit during rehearsals while he moved about the theatre checking balance. It was this kind of ambition which also raised the everyday level of orchestral performance.

1965 brought with it two outstanding productions which were both Solti's – and at last it was the Musical Director providing the main excitements. His fourth season, begun with *The Ring*, ended with an unlikely success.

When he arrived Solti had agreed to one new production each season of a foreign work in English, and it was a policy which continued after his first term. These productions included among them interesting extensions of the repertory, so far, most importantly, Shostakovich's *Katerina Ismailova* under Edward Downes. But Solti so far hadn't shown much interest in involving himself in them. Nor had he when *Moses and Aaron*, the Schoenberg opera, had been proposed. If it was to be English opera with local casts, then he preferred Britten, (which was, after all, still opera in the original). A long list of directors had been named for *Moses*, starting with Felsenstein, and it wasn't until after frequent postponements that it devolved on Peter Hall, whom Webster had approached before, as had Solti, but hitherto without results. Now Hall was free, and it was a work he was interested in doing. And he was chosing wisely for his Covent Garden first – not a classic with a long tradition of performance against which he would be judged! There was a large bonus in that the postponements had also found Solti free to conduct it.

This was a piece of luck for Webster. The collaboration promised to be an important one, and he did his considerable best to provide the right conditions. Peter Hall wouldn't commit himself to a gigantic project unless he was assured of them. He wanted his Stratford designer, John Bury. And seven weeks' rehearsal, no less. The routine of the house was dominated by the *Moses* effort, and was sometimes disrupted by it. Worth it. In more ways than one, at a stroke the activities of the house were being enlarged. The orgy scene aimed at getting beyond

Cecil B. de Mille into greater realism, at times almost too real for some of the young ladies involved – their frantic and not always successful attempt to escape their pursuers on stage did bring a degree of hoped-for realism, and several of the same young ladies, assembled later for a revival, were dismayed to hear Peter Hall asking them 'to remember what you did last time'.

This, on the whole, delighted a Webster who *could* be prim. But the theatre-man in him responded. Before, it had been Shaftesbury Avenue he'd brought to Covent Garden. Now it was a different kind of theatre, Royal Shakespeare theatre, which he recognized as the current advance away from the theatre he himself was most at ease with. He'd attended performances at Stratford and the company's London home, the Aldwych, and he registered the type of audience attracted and the kind of response elicited from them. His Opera House couldn't ignore such things.

And Hall in collaboration with his Musical Director – Solti who had worked for Toscanini. What was current in the 'sixties was being grafted on to a very safe trunk of tradition. This was the right way. A collaboration to nurture. What hadn't, in the old days, worked with Peter Brook and Karl Rankl – what he couldn't make work with Zeffirelli because he'd arrived at a time when there wasn't a Musical Director – perhaps *now?* If Webster's energies were flagging, he could concentrate them for an ambition like this one!

And there was, besides, *Arabella*. With this Strauss opera Solti at last fulfilled the promise of his other appearance as guest, with that early *Rosenkavalier*. *Arabella* was directed by Rudolph Hartmann, and had spacious and magisterially traditional sets by Peter Rice. Not the kind of production that could *ever* be old-fashioned. It was a rare and wonderful harmony of director/designer/conductor. Of course, with the overall standard already becoming higher, it would soon be more difficult to see the peaks. But *Arabella* must always be one. A great production in a house which had become accustomed to wonderful Strauss. A wonderful production which, like *Don Carlos* in the 'fifties, was among the best anywhere in its decade. Wonderful singers – Dietrich Fischer-Dieskau in his house debut, Lisa della Casa, one of the best of all Strauss sopranos – wreathed by Solti and Strauss in beautiful sound. *Arabella* will be recalled, Webster knew, whenever the name Solti is spoken. Arabella/Casa descending the staircase in the final moments . . . if the lights had had to go out then for David Webster, he would have gone happy into the dark. He could have asked for no more beautiful sounds in his ears before final silence. For the new regime, it was *Arabella* which was the culmination, and a fulfilment of his own service in this decade.

CHAPTER XXII

Failing health · English singers established · Callas's last appearance · the Solti–Vickers disagreement · productions of the last years · Webster and Goodall · a triumphant *Mastersingers* at Sadlers Wells · Colin Davis and Peter Hall

By 1965, Sir David Webster was already wearing the house with a difference. Not so jaunty now. In failing health, sometimes grasping at authority, frequently irascible and forgetful – often, these days, an unquiet showman. It was fortunate for him and the house that Solti was now secure. Supporting him through the awkward years was Sir David's last sustained effort. He couldn't have persevered for so very much longer, and it wasn't in him to make another. He was fortunate too in his 'family'. He could count on their tact and support. Enid Blech, Solti's secretary, was its latest addition: she had instantly 'fitted in'. And Solti had wanted his agent, Joan Ingpen, to come to Covent Garden with him as well. She was Controller of Opera Planning, a job which in the person of Lord Harewood, now running the Edinburgh Festival, had come to mean something.

How much longer was Sir David going to shoulder the burden – whose eventual laying down was a frightening prospect? Could his retirement be very far off? In 1963 he'd seen Dame Ninette retire and Sir Frederick Ashton take her place as Director of the ballet company...

Day by day Muriel Kerr saw to it that he was well-briefed for meetings. John Tooley, good negotiator (and his eventual successor), now showed himself an admirable prompter as well. Much of the business of the house was in his hands, and fortunately Lord Drogheda was able to continue the fight for money effectively. There were days, even weeks sometimes, when the important papers, the ones needing attention, were most of them on Tooley's desk. Not that Webster liked his desk to be empty. When he invited anyone to his office he liked to be discovered fiddling with papers, or perhaps signing cheques. After a busy moment or two he'd look up, over his glasses, and in the well-accustomed and expected manner ask, 'Oh yes, and what can I do for you?' If a visitor found him busily reading a letter – and from the other side of the desk it was patently clear that the letter was being held upside down! – no matter; he commanded automatic respect, and there wasn't a visitor who wasn't tactful.

His prestige was unassailable, and he had his good days too. Each year the heads of all the opera houses of the world would hold a meeting, and Webster, more and more deferred to, had gradually become something like a chairman. On one of several occasions when a projected return visit by the Vienna State had to be abandoned because it would have cost too much, Webster opened negotiations with the Hamburg Opera, whose Intendant then was Rolf Liebermann. Years later Liebermann was to ask someone who had worked with him, 'Tell me about Sir David. I've never understood why I took a piece of advice from him when I don't even know him very well.' Liebermann was adding to the legend, and the legend was armour for Sir David in his declining years.

He'd usually call in at the Salzburg Festival for a day or two; and there he'd sit, outside the Golden Ox. Intendants of this or that opera house would be about too, sitting with him or coming up to pay respects. And the word was, what have *you* got for *us?* The visit was more valuable for promoting his own artists than for finding new ones for Covent Garden.

The achievement of the English singer was known and acknowledged – acknowledged as above all Sir David's achievement. There were signs everywhere, large and small. Gwyneth Jones had become Vienna's favourite Verdi soprano, and she was a Covent Garden singer. In Berlin the visitor was liable to be asked, 'But do you know *Charles Craig's* Othello?' Covent Garden's new production of *The Trojans* had an English Dido – this time it was Josephine Veasey. Long ago a chorus member, she had left for a year or two and returned as a very junior soloist. She had been one of the artists who, as vivandière, had been cheered not booed at the end of that *Force of Destiny*. And she was now a star. Then there was the case of Michael Langdon, another of the very few singers to get out of the chorus. He'd been Ochs in the *Rosenkavalier* which had so offended Georg Solti. He might not have been very good then, but it was early days for him in the role, and he'd got better. It wasn't long before he was being invited to sing it in San Francisco. Geraint was often in San Francisco too – but then, Geraint was everywhere. There were English singers at Bayreuth and Salzburg and in Buenos Aires . . .

But there were regrets in the last years. Webster was perpetually irked by his failure to set up a pension scheme for his artists. It would have meant Covent Garden putting money down – and there wasn't any to spare. (It was finally established, but not till after Webster's departure.) And he'd very much wanted, too, a second, smaller house built, to take the smaller-scale works. Such a house might have at last solved the Mozart problem. It was needed too to make it possible for new works and experimental works to be mounted more cheaply and more often. The site he favoured was at the top of Portland Place, in the gardens set in the middle of the Nash Terraces of Regents Park

Crescent. Just five minutes walk away from Weymouth Street as it happens. But his powers of persuasion didn't work here.

He used his powers of persuasion on Maria Callas rather too effectively, so that her last appearance at the house was a sad occasion. In March 1965 she was in New York for the two $6000 Toscas she'd agreed to, and Webster cabled her in exuberantly breezy style:

> HOPE YOU KNOCK NEW YORK AND THE MET FOR SIX STOP BEST WISHES STOP LOOKING FORWARD TO SEEING YOU ON RETURN LOVE DAVID.

The $6000 compared most favourably with what she was accustomed to getting from Webster. But she was returning to London none the less that summer, once more for Tosca, and not for only two performances but for four.

She'd never had a contract with Webster and she'd never let the public down in England. Rarely, indeed, elsewhere, in spite of the impression the press was wont to give. This summer was the first time. Her voice had gone, she wasn't in a fit condition to sing, and she had to cancel all her London performances.

One of them had been planned as a gala in the presence of the Queen. Webster went to see Callas in Paris, where she was living: he begged her to appear at least on this one gala evening. For love of David Webster, no other reason, she did appear. And her performance did show clearly enough that she had been crying off for good reason. It's not on record that she ever needlessly disappointed her public, and the present occasion was not any different from any other on which she'd been reluctant to sing.

This Callas Tosca caused the only serious difference between Webster and Solti, who felt that the public who had queued for long hours for tickets had as much right as the Queen not to be disappointed, and that Callas ought either to sing for them too or not sing at all. Marie Collier sang the other three performances in Callas's place, and like that earlier Callas-substitute, Renata Scotto, she earned herself favourable attention in the press worldwide.

A cartoon duly appeared in the press, showing cows on their way to a dairy show. One of them remained behind, refusing to go. 'She only appears before royalty,' another cow was explaining. There is a 'rival' soprano who for a long time had this cartoon pinned to the wall of her dressing-room.

This last Tosca represents a somewhat bathetic coda to Callas's reign at Covent Garden. David Webster had for the benefit of his house persuaded an artist against her own best interests. Ironic that it should be the one among them he perhaps loved best of all. The occasion would have been all the sadder for him had he known that it was to be her last appearance at Covent Garden. He was ready at any time to bring her back again. And he never ceased to hope for her return.

If only he could have been as effective in persuading Jon Vickers and Solti to make up their quarrel. He'd had huge hopes of their collaboration – Vickers the hero of many a Wagner evening under Solti's galvanizing direction. And as Othello too. With Vinay no longer singing the role Vickers promised to be the world's best. Webster was determined that London would see it first, with Solti his ideal conductor.

So he invited Vickers to lunch one day, and, assuming that accustomed casualness that could not be expected to deceive anyone who knew him, he proceeded confidently to sound him out. Had there been no quarrel, or had Webster been able to resolve it, this might have been one of the most important interviews of his entire quarter of a century.

'When are you going to sing Othello for me?' was the first blow of the first round. 'When do you want me?' 'June 1962,' was the prompt answer. 'OK,' said Vickers. Pause. Webster waited: how was Jon going to parry. 'On condition, though' – Jon played the game with relish – 'that you mount a new *Force of Destiny* for me.' No problem. He was being asked for an opera they'd already decided to do anyway. He agreed without demur. Who better than Vickers for it? But now *he* had a condition. 'In return you must do *A Masked Ball* for me again.' Vickers too agreed without demur. *His* condition this time was that he be given Othello in the Shakespeare Centenary Year, which was 1964. He found Webster once more not unprepared. 'But of course, dear boy. That's *precisely* why I'm asking you to do a preliminary series of performances in 1962.' And as an afterthought – hardly more – he added that he'd deem it a favour, it would be most handsome, if Vickers could perhaps spare the time to throw in a few *Fidelios* for him. And possibly a *Valkyrie* or two?

Alas for well-laid plans. Vickers sang in *Valkyrie*, that unhappy first instalment of Covent Garden's new *Ring*. The Kern sets were scrapped: but far more serious was that this first collaboration between Vickers and Solti was also their last. Vickers wasn't galvanized – he felt he was being bullied. On his side Solti felt that Vickers was unco-operative and obstructive, and, after carefully drafting it and rejecting several versions, he wrote him a letter:

> I feel that I must say first of all that I am very disappointed with our collaboration in *Walküre* especially as I felt that your co-operation was

somewhat lacking. I regret this very much because I feel very strongly that each individual vocal part must fit in to the whole scheme in order to make a homogeneous performance. Don't misunderstand me – I don't want to enforce my own ideas, but to have the opportunity of exploring the singers' potentialities and to understand their conception, thereby achieving a happy compromise and enabling the singers to combine to make a fine performance grow from our collaboration.

For a wide variety of reasons we lacked time together but I must be perfectly honest and say that I felt that I met with a rejection of almost every suggestion. I am sure you realize that each conductor has a different interpretation and the interpretation may even differ with time. Mr Hotter, who has sung his part with me many times in Munich, found himself also presented with new ideas and we succeeded in making adjustments. I feel very strongly that we must have time together to work out Othello and that we approach the problem with the mutual desire to make a fine performance not only of the part but of the whole opera.

I would like to know from you that you accept this point of view and that the enclosed schedule is possible for you. As regards *Ballo in Maschera* I know that we cannot have enough time together and I will therefore ask another conductor to take it on.

Vickers sang in *A Masked Ball* under Edward Downes: and he was distressed to find that, for whatever reasons, with the change of conductor had come alterations in the schedules. Two weeks had originally been set aside for rehearsals and now they were reduced to less than one. Vickers's distress did not help to reduce the breach between tenor and Musical Director, and overall this *Masked Ball* was certainly not a soothing experience. Ande Anderson, Resident Producer in succession to Christopher West, was in charge of the revival, and there was no complaint here: but the very atmosphere in the house disturbed Vickers in his present unhappy frame of mind. Drogheda, going backstage after the first night, described to David Webster how he had

witnessed a strange scene. Vickers had retired to his dressing-room before the end of the applause, and was fished out by Anderson to take a final call. He came back, and then after the curtain had finally fallen, burst into tears in Shuard's arms. (It should have been the other way round for she had just lost her father.)

When Drogheda phoned him next day to congratulate him on his success he found Vickers past consoling. He told Drogheda

that he had made a decision regarding Covent Garden, that in future he would treat us as though we were any other house in the world. He would demand exact dates and details of performances, etc., etc. before he would sign any contract.

Webster was still more distressed than the tenor. He found for once that his famous tact wasn't equal to the situation. Replacements had to be found, and for *Force of Destiny* it was Bergonzi. The great moment arrived for the Vickers Othello with Gobbi as Iago, but Vickers was not to be persuaded. Covent Garden could have its *Otello* with either Vickers or Solti, but not with both. So – no Vickers. A great deprivation. (His replacement was Mario del Monaco, and Covent Garden's subsequent Othello for the 'sixties was James McCracken.) Vickers told Webster, 'Georg Solti has done me a great favour. He has shown me what is my value in this house. While he is here my fees will be Del Monaco, Carlo Bergonzi fees.'

Webster found it hard, at first, to believe that the breach was not healable, that that Siegmund in *Valkyrie* was to be Vickers's only role under Solti. He continued to work for a reconciliation, and he was delighted when, at the beginning of 1963, Solti wrote to Vickers:

> I was sorry that I did not know until afterwards that you had been in the house a few days ago, as I would have liked to talk to you.
>
> I am hoping very much that you will be able to sing Siegmund for us in the new production of *Walküre* which will form part of the complete *Ring* cycle newly staged by Schneider-Siemssen, with Hotter producing and myself conducting as before.

Webster too was still hoping. But it was not to be. Vickers did appear again at Covent Garden in the 'sixties – but not as often as he might have done, and never under Solti. He was in the new *Aïda* of 1968, and there was something of an uproar when he refused, because of the continuing quarrel, to appear in the television performance. Webster was already tearing at his remaining hairs because the designer, Nicholas Georgiadis, had *quadrupled* his initial budget of £20,000: and the uproar was an additional embarrassment, a public token of his failure to heal this vexatious breach. He could have done without it. (A consolation – the production had got back its expenses within only two years!).

Webster suffered disappointments with other friends too. After the little 'festival' early in 1964, Zeffirelli returned to the house no more. Not because he had fallen out with anyone. But opportunities, thanks in good measure to his Covent Garden successes, were becoming increasingly available to him, and outside opera, in theatre and films.

Giulini too was becoming restless, though he was not yet lost to Covent Garden. Drogeda, in Rome to see the Visconti/Giulini *Figaro*, wrote to Webster:

> Fortunately for us you have succeeded in making them both very happy to work at Covent Garden. Giulini prefers it to anywhere else – except

> that of course Rome is his home. He finds the *spirito de corpo* something unique, and this is a great tribute to yourself.

However, Giulini's interests were turning more and more towards his concert work. Nothing could be done about *that*. Webster had to remind himself, he mustn't become petulant, mustn't nag. Just hope.

It was natural, as he grew older, that Webster should cleave to familiar people; and, however receptive he might force himself to be of new ways and new ideas, to familiar ways. He couldn't revive former glories, though, when at last, after five years, he got Visconti back for the delayed *Trovatore*. Then followed an art-nouveau *Rosenkavalier*. Costume designs were so late coming that Webster was forced to wire pleadingly: 'We are becoming used to the idea that the cast will appear naked.' When the designs did arrive they proved not altogether worth the waiting. The production was questionable, and, once again, former glories weren't revived.

But Webster wanted more. He had hopes of the Visconti/Giulini *Traviata* planned for the beginning of 1967. This time designs weren't late – but they were in black and white, after Beardsley. Webster uttered to the effect, very nice, but what is the colour going to be? No colour, he was told. It was to be Beardsley all the way. Drogheda wrote anxiously to Webster:

> You have said that we may not get Visconti back if we do not accept the designs for this *Traviata*. One could, of course, argue that if he is going to use Covent Garden for whimsical experiment we really do not want him back.

Perfectly reasonable so to argue. Webster wrote to Visconti advising him somewhat gloomily that he considered Beardsley 'a doubtful fellow'. But he clung to the idea, surely this team, as in the past, must bring glamour and excitement to an opera by Verdi.

Up to a point he was right. The stage pictures were exquisite and the production had a certain distinction. Yet it was only on Giulini's contribution that no doubts could be cast. (What refinement, what sheen and suavity, and withal such a sweep and passion!) The production, again, was questionable.

On the first night Maria Callas, greatest of Traviatas, made an appearance, if not on stage, at least, and above all to Webster, most welcome as part of the audience. The crowd in the foyer parted for her, and Webster greeted her with his 'Shall we take champagne, my dear?' routine. He'd so wanted her to work in his theatre with the two friends creating this *Traviata* for him. Was there still a possibility?

No. And not because of Maria alone. This was the last of Visconti, and of Giulini too, at his house. Without them all, a whole special 'Webster wing' would have to be closed. And with this *Traviata*, closed it was.

Not long before Webster had been across to New York for the opening of the new Metropolitan. It was said to be stupendous. With actual Marc Chagall murals. The opening production – *Cleopatra*, a new opera by Samuel Barber – was being directed by Zeffirelli. Cleopatra was Leontyne Price, who was now too expensive for Covent Garden.

A music reporter, Raymond Ericson, spotted Webster among the celebrities who made up the first night audience. Knowing that Rudolph Bing was not exactly *persona grata* with David Webster, he asked the *New York Times* critic Clive Barnes if he'd approach the English administrator on his behalf. He wanted a quote. What did Webster think of it all? Sir David welcomed the opportunity. 'I think it's all unspeakably hideous!' He glowed warmly, full of goodwill. 'And it's one of the happiest nights of my life!' He beamed on Barnes, on everyone. And added regretfully, 'But of course, you can't *quote* me, dear boy!'

Back in London Webster was again asked for his impressions. He'd had time on the plane back to give them final form, and now described his sensation as 'rather like sitting between two giant pairs of golden dentures'.

On his return from New York, Webster, as always, was given a warm welcome. He was 'coming home', everyone made that clear to him. Yet by this time he knew that there was seldom any need for him to hurry. He could take his time, dawdle even. Everything was working without him. The house was now a machine which functioned, seemingly without assistance. Though he knew it was being helped along. By John Tooley. By Lord Drogheda. By Georg Solti, settling down now among the English, and well on his way to earning the eventual knighthood. They were a triumvirate he could happily leave in charge while he was away. The 'store' was being very well looked after.

What he was doing in his last five years, in terms usually applied to stage artists, was 'nursing his resources'. 'Coasting', even. Saving himself for those occasions when effort was unavoidable.

Covent Garden in the late 'sixties was – what? It was a picturesque and elaborately decorated wagon, streamers flying, which *seemed* to be going uphill without being either drawn or pushed. Sir David watched its progress, often, now, distantly. He didn't, as he'd used to, get tense when big events were in the offing. In the old days so much had seemed to depend on a single production, a *Salome*, or a *Trojans*. But not any more. Big events too had become routine.

Josef Svoboda, a Czech designer making impact in London's spoken theatre, was coming in for the next Strauss opera, *The Woman Without a Shadow*. Webster watched to see how it would turn out. Svoboda provided a great flight of steps and nothing much more. It was the kind of thing people admired nowadays, and *Woman Without a Shadow*, it was soon evident, was to be counted among the major productions of the decade. Fancy . . . Pierre Boulez came in to conduct *Pelléas*, and again the designer was Svoboda. *Pelléas*, with its magic swirls of colour, Webster rather liked. Another famous production.

He was careful to cosset Solti and Peter Hall when they got together again, after *Moses*, for *The Magic Flute*. They were allowed to hog the stage, and the ballet *Raymonda* had to go on without enough stage rehearsal. But it was a fair price to pay if they were kept happy. They would have been happier, of course, if the production had been more of a success; aiming at majestic gravity, it had seemed to Webster, as the evening unrolled, to be merely increasingly gloomy. (He'd been doubtful all along about John Bury for designer.) This was Webster's fourth production of the *Flute*, it seemed to be impregnable as far as he was concerned. But from Solti's point of view, at least, it was his best Mozart so far.

Something had to be done about Mozart. Webster tried to persuade Joan Sutherland to take on *Seraglio* – but no, neither she nor that young husband of hers, Bonynge, would agree to it. What they wanted was another Donizetti, *The Daughter of the Regiment*. There was no question, these days, of the repertory being determined by the availability or wishes of this or that singer. Solti was adamant on the point. Even Teresa Berganza, captivating Rosina in *The Barber of Seville*, an instant house darling, hadn't been allowed what she wanted (which was a second Rossini role, Cinderella). But Sutherland was an exception, the point was waived, and *Daughter of the Regiment* it was. Webster was getting used to the idea that her conductor was going to have to be Bonynge in future. It did seem sometimes that the young man was not ideal – but then, it was undeniable, his presence in the pit gave her confidence. Webster was soon persuaded that really, taking all considerations into account, it was a good thing to have him. The new opera gave her an opportunity to cavort rumbustiously instead of languishing, which was fun; besides, John Tooley was able to lend the production to Dallas, subsequent scene of triumphant cavorting for the diva, and then it was advantageously sold to the Met. Everyone was happy.

Webster was happiest, perhaps, on 'diva evenings'. Sutherland's, or Birgit Nilsson's, whom he'd got back for Turandot. She did Elektra too, under Solti, a thrilling performance, and quite a contrast to the ones he'd used to enjoy so much, the ones with Lammers under Kempe.

And, at last, a Mozart which really worked. The 1968 *Così Fan Tutte*, with elegant scenery by Henry Bardon and costumes by David Walker – theirs was work Webster *could* enjoy without reservation. The director was John Copley. He'd come in years ago as Christopher West's assistant and this was his first major assignment. The general effect was one of intimacy though the opera was projected tellingly enough into the large house. It showed it could be done. Many people thought Solti in the pit in sparkling form.

Webster was grateful that his Musical Director, after two or three years, had come more and more to interest himself in the possibilities of the English singer. He hadn't nagged him and finally there'd been no need to. Solti had been assiduous in providing them, where possible, with recording opportunities, and he didn't necessarily give preference to foreign guests in important productions.

The English singer had arrived, indeed, at being *dangerously* in demand, offers following success at Covent Garden too rapidly and in too great profusion. This could bring problems, and Walter Legge (who resigned from the Board partly because he felt Webster's attitude to him to be too obstructive) confided to Lord Drogheda his concern for Gwyneth Jones: 'A voice as good as hers needs the care usually lavished on orchids or Sèvres porcelain.' But Webster was confident that his house had a good record as regards nursing singers, with Norman Feasey, the Chief Repetiteur, and the music staff really fighting hard to prevent forcing.

And certainly Covent Garden continued famously free (comparatively) of intrigue. Artists seemed usually only too happy to return – so long as the press didn't misbehave. As they had once more when Fischer-Dieskau sang Falstaff. *He* wasn't coming back.

The wagon rolled on gaily and smoothly up the hill, and Webster watched it, sometimes cheerfully. If only he felt stronger . . .

He was still not at a loss for the courtly gesture. Another champagne occasion at the Opera House was the party given in celebration of Dame Eva Turner's 75th birthday (on 10 March 1967). In her own words:

> The guests (there were about twenty) were asked to assemble in the anteroom of the Royal Box where pre-lunch cocktails were served. In the house itself there was a dress-rehearsal of *Cavalleria Rusticana* in progress. Out of the blue Sir David said, 'Come with me, Eva,' and took me to the front of the Royal Box. At this point the rehearsal stopped, flood lights were

> switched on to the Royal Box and as a man the whole of the cast, principals and chorus, turned towards the box and Bryan Balkwill conducted the full orchestra in 'Happy Birthday to You'. The glorious sound of the orchestra, full cast and chorus was a most moving experience. When that ended Sir David addressed everyone and said, much to my amazement, 'How would you like to hear Eva Turner sing again in the Royal Opera House?' This suggestion was cheered to the echo and one of my recordings was played (I forget at this date which one). This was followed by *In Questa Reggia.* Sir David himself had gone into the house very early in the morning to supervise the wiring for this wonderful happening.

It *was* a wonderful happening. Twenty years before Dame Eva had sung Turandot on the stage of the Opera House, representing a level of achievement to which it had then seemed almost absurd for the young company even to aspire. In the meantime Sir David and Dame Eva had seen many changes. Dame Eva had herself coached Amy Shuard in her role of Turandot . . .

Retirement was not far off. It had been fixed for the summer of 1970.

One day during his last winter at the Opera House he was walking in the market. It was icy weather, and slippy underfoot. Suddenly he fell – heavily. No fuss was made and he was taken home, not to hospital.

Not many people knew about the accident. He had a few days in bed, well-attended. There was a certain amount of worry, had there been any brain damage? Careful examination said no, no cause for alarm, there hadn't been.

Shortly afterwards, talking about Webster on BBC television, Maria Callas was to observe: 'He has locked in a vault of his own, I'm sure, all the wonderful things we have had, which are intangibles and tangibles together.' He did indeed treasure his memories, and by now there were many. A reason more for going. He didn't need them added to.

As he lay in bed, memories crowded in on him. But they weren't only the lovely ones. He brooded too. There was the case of Reginald Goodall, who, after conducting the first performance of *Peter Grimes* at Sadlers Wells in 1946, had come on to the staff at Covent Garden, and had been on it ever since. He was one of Webster's failures . . .

'He came to us when we first opened,' Webster later wrote to Drogheda,

> with the shine of the first performance of Grimes about him. It is not without importance that shortly after that Britten lost his opinion of Goodall and has not used him for the English Opera Group in any way at all.

> We were faced here after a time with many protests from artists of his conducting in terms of time and accent and it was because of this that we tended to drop him. He was much praised for a performance of *Walküre* in Golders Green or on second thoughts Croydon and the praise came from Andrew Porter. On the other hand it cannot really be maintained that we have been short of Wagnerian conductors. For Wagner we have generally had pretty decent to excellent services from our resident conductors with the very occasional guest.

Goodall had been invaluable as a Wagnerian coach, and a whole generation of singers had passed through his hands. His achievement here was vastly appreciated, by the singers themselves as well as by the Opera House administration. He had a little room way up under the Covent Garden roof to rehearse in – the charladies' dressing-room, referred to on the call-sheet as the Upper-amphi. He'd had a little upright piano put in there because he couldn't bear people about him when he worked.

It was as a conductor that he'd been neglected. Thinking that he might do better elsewhere, Webster had even suggested to the Board that they drop him. Goodall stayed, but from the early 'fifties on, as guest conductors came to the house, he was used less and less as a conductor.

But there was, now and again, a *Valkyrie*, at Croydon and in the provinces too (with Hilde Konetzni the Sieglinde in some of them), and a *Mastersingers* or two at Covent Garden. They remained in the memory of four critics in particular – besides Andrew Porter, also Edmund Tracey, David Cairns and Peter Heyworth – who persisted in drawing attention to Goodall's neglect, which they felt to be both wasteful and wicked. Wasteful because it meant bringing in guest conductors unnecessarily, wicked because Goodall's confidence was being undermined. 'I still see cracks from time to time in the press,' Drogheda wrote to Webster in 1962, 'about our failure to use Goodall. Can you see a satisfactory solution to this problem?' No one at the house could.

It was true that Goodall was not suited to coping with the normal day to day working conditions that pertain in most theatres, and he was often, apart from the frustration of not being given operas to conduct, far from happy. He didn't always make things easy for himself. He stood in, during Solti's first season, for some rehearsals of the new *Valkyrie*, but his tempi were so different from Solti's that, at Hotter's request, he was replaced: and subsequently he was not to be persuaded that he had not provoked Solti's hostility. In Solti's second season Kempe was engaged for a series of *Mastersingers*, and as he was going to arrive late he asked that Goodall take charge of the first rehearsals.

The understanding was that Goodall would conduct the performances if Kempe should finally not be able to come. Kempe in fact did come – but by this time Goodall, having at first refused to take the rehearsals because he had convinced himself that Kempe too didn't like him, had announced that, if he did take rehearsals, he still wouldn't be prepared to conduct the opera, Kempe arriving or no. The 'sixties scarcely promised to be a happy decade for Goodall. Webster was not even certain that this apparently fragile little man had the stamina to get through an entire evening in the pit.

What actually happened is part of the larger musical history of our day. In 1956 Edmund Tracey went to work with the Sadlers Wells Opera as musical equivalent of Literary Manager, and he proposed that Goodall be brought in to take charge of their new *Mastersingers*. At Covent Garden Goodall had taken over existing Wagner productions, and they hadn't, any of them, been really *his* conceptions. It wasn't going to be so here. The project was to begin and end with Goodall. He was given the conditions he needed to function fully, and every adaptation was made to him – as though he had already become the acknowledged master-Wagnerian in the pit as well as in the classroom. Goodall wanted a year's preparation. He wanted to coach each singer, and to teach the orchestra in sections, so that when finally he assembled the various pieces he would know individually not only each singer but each orchestral player. Everything – *everything* – was under his personal direction. What ideally he would have liked was to have his singers, and even the orchestra, encapsulated under his command and taking no other work for the entire year. Their world would have been Wagner and nothing but Wagner.

At Covent Garden they wondered. Many were doubtful.

In 1968 the opera went on and its acclaim went round the world. It seemed to many that, unequivocally, here was the world's Wagner conductor. His was widely recognized, at the very least, as an interpretation to put beside any other of the day, or indeed any within memory, and he was talked of commonly as a Wagnerian in the great line of Knappertsbusch. The production continued to draw superlatives when in 1970 the Sadlers Wells Opera moved to the Coliseum, a much larger theatre, and in the West End. (In 1974, now under Lord Harewood, the company was to be renamed the English National Opera.)

Webster could not but recognize that the Goodall case was 'sad and difficult'. He wrote to Lord Drogheda:

> I am afraid that I am still dubious about Goodall for miscellaneous works in the repertory but maybe we should have paid greater attention to his Wagner. We are incidentally using him for *Parsifal* next season.

Webster considered it extremely bad luck that Goodall's altogether unlooked-for success – unlooked-for by him, at any rate – made his non-use at Covent Garden a central failure. It irked him that others had solved a problem he couldn't, and whatever had gone wrong through the years it was now too late to put right at Covent Garden. He'd been prompted belatedly to allot a *Parsifal*, scheduled for 1971, but that alone hardly made good the long neglect.

It irked him too to recall, lying in bed, the fortunes of his own new *Mastersingers*. It had gone on a year after Goodall's had first been heard at Sadlers Wells, and he couldn't bear to admit to himself that it had been, in comparison, almost a flop. Solti had wanted to do it. But if anything he had seemed slightly miscast. As conductor he had lacked, perhaps, the humour for this ideally most relaxed and warmly, richly humorous masterpiece. Webster preferred to blame rather the almost voiceless Sachs – that was why this *Mastersingers* hadn't worked. Norman Bailey, the Sachs acclaimed at Sadlers Wells and the Coliseum, had come in as substitute for one performance, and Webster, as he announced the cast-change to the audience, was fully aware of the irony of the situation. He explained that they'd asked all round Europe for a replacement before trying 'down the road'. Bailey had had a wonderful reception at Covent Garden too. But the Board had none the less hastily decreed that their *Mastersingers* was 'an outstanding success', and Webster had hastened to communicate the intelligence to his Musical Director.

To make matters worse, Sadlers Wells was no sooner installed in their new home than they were announcing plans for a complete *Ring* under Goodall (with a new translation commissioned from Andrew Porter). It was too late for Webster, on his way out, to prepare counter-measures. But he'd so long wanted to do an English *Ring* himself. He'd discussed it with Peter Hall four years earlier, and if it hadn't happened then he hadn't given up hope. Any *Ring*, English or German, ought to be at Covent Garden and nowhere else. Or so it seemed to him.

When he got back to the house, Webster seemed, somehow, a shrunken figure. His 'family' about him was cautious. Everyone was cautious and considerate. A girl working in an office passed him one day in the corridor. She had to put out a hand to him – support, in case it was needed. 'Oh, Sir David!' she exclaimed. She couldn't help it. He seemed so . . . well, reduced. Ill. Webster was often aware that voices were lowered when people spoke to him, as though he needed to be insulated against sudden noise, against shock of any kind.

Yes, it was time for him to go.

The Coliseum *Ring* began with *Valkyrie* – a success. The cycle wasn't completed until after Webster's death, and in some respects it represents the ideal towards which his efforts had been directed. It wasn't achieved under his roof, but it is there finally as further evidence of his own success. Brunnhilde, Rita Hunter, and the Siegfried, Alberto Remedios, are both from Liverpool, and one can say confidently that it was a good thing for them that Webster had got to London first. Had Webster not prepared the way, there might not have been a Coliseum *Ring* at all.

It had been a matter of pride to him when Janet Baker in 1969 had taken over as Dido from a sick Josephine Veasey. He was proud to be contributing to her career. Not that she wasn't already a complete singer, a very *English* singer established in the glorious line of Isobel Baillie and Kathleen Ferrier: Britannia in her most compelling form. Webster had a right, though, to feel a measure of pride, however little he and Covent Garden had contributed directly to her development. Without his work she might well not have found her opportunities in *opera*, and made her career mainly, like her predecessors, on the concert platform.

He'd once said to Anthony Gishford, 'I would like to know who is going to be the next Frederick Ashton, who the next Benjamin Britten.' And if possible before he retired, Kenneth MacMillan (who was going to succeed Sir Frederick as Director of the ballet company)? John Cranko? He wondered what John Cranko's career might have been had he stayed on at Covent Garden. Years ago, in 1958, the Ballet Sub-Committee had decided that he was inventive but lacked a strong enough sense of theatre. Webster had assured them that if it was true at the time Cranko was certain to mature with experience. In the mid-'sixties he'd left England, to go to Stuttgart to direct the ballet there. He'd been a loss – another failure of the administration?

In 1964 there'd been a possibility that Cranko might have composed his ballet version of *Eugene Onegin* at Covent Garden: the Board had said no. An insult to Tchaikowsky, even though he was going to the composer's other music and not touching the opera. So he'd finally done it for his Stuttgart company. And this was the ballet which opened the company's short Covent Garden season in 1974, their first. Had Webster been alive, he'd certainly have seen his confidence justified. A superbly musical and theatrical piece, and a superb piece of balletic story-telling. But by this time, alas, Cranko himself was also dead, and that first-night *Onegin* was given in his memory to an audience ready to mourn him anew.

Webster was confident that Britten's work now provided the basis of a new repertory of English operas – to which Michael Tippett's operas also contributed. He'd been grateful to Solti that, besides bringing *Billy Budd* back after its long period of neglect, he'd also kept *Grimes* and *The Dream* prominent season after season. (After *The Dream* Sidney Bernstein of Granada had considered commissioning a second Shakespeare opera from Britten, *The Tempest*, with Gielgud again directing. Another might-have-been!)

If Webster left Covent Garden seeing no certain successor to Ashton or Britten, he did try, a last campaign, to make a gift of another kind to Covent Garden's future.

This was a partnership between Colin Davis and Peter Hall, which his skills and remaining energies had been devoted to establishing. In the autumn of 1971 Davis was following Solti – an English Musical Director at last. For Hall Peter Brook's old title of Director of Productions was being revived, which was itself a statement of intentions. Was it going to work? A sharing of the empire – and, perhaps uniquely in the history of opera outside festivals, musical and dramatic standards on the same level.

Webster had sounded out Hall as carefully as, in the past, he'd sounded out potential Musical Directors. What Hall wanted, mainly, was adequate rehearsal time, not only for new productions but also for revivals. And he envisaged a somewhat different future for the Opera House, with more performances of less operas. An opera is now played for six, maybe eight performances, and then disappears till its next revival: Hall wanted each series of performances extended to perhaps sixteen, and singers induced to give their services for longer periods in return for the conditions offered them. Virtually festival conditions, in fact.

Webster knew that it would be difficult to meet Peter Hall's demands. But he was convinced that the best for the house in the future lay in an equal partnership of Musical Director and Director of Productions. His major decisions over a period of twenty-five years had been right ones, and this last scheme, if it had been followed through, might have worked well. He did his best to create a favourable atmosphere for what was a kind of revolution. For a while it promised to succeed, and the collaboration was well-begun with the new Tippett opera, *The Knot Garden*, which went on a few months after Webster himself had left the house. But soon, while Colin Davis remained at Covent Garden, Peter Hall decided to leave, and went instead to the National Theatre. Webster's final effort was not, after all, crowned with success.

EPILOGUE

Webster's Farewell Gala · retirement · KCVO · positively last appearance · death · memorial service

A Farewell Gala was mounted for Sir David Webster on 30 June 1970. Benjamin Britten composed a Fanfare, and his programme note explained that it had been

> based on a series of rising fifths which celebrate the Royal Opera House (C. . . . E. . . . G. . . . .) and its retiring General Administrator (DA. . . . . . . .EB. . . .E. .). Over these are scraps of nine of Sir David's favourite operatic tunes, with one thrown in for historical reasons. No prizes are offered for their identification.

Solti conducted the Fanfare. Edward Downes and John Pritchard, whose talents had developed through the years of the regime, both appeared in the pit. Colin Davis too; and young David Atherton, a Solti protégé at the house, was given charge of one item. Reginald Goodall conducted the Prelude to Act Three of *The Mastersingers*; Richard Bonynge conducted his wife Joan Sutherland in the *Lucia* Mad Scene, which the soprano herself had decided at the last moment to substitute for the previously announced *Casta Diva* from *Norma*. The gala was staged by Ande Anderson.

At the end Webster came on to the stage to acknowledge the applause, which he was accustomed to deflect to his artists. Habit dies hard. He made a speech, and concluded with thanks to the Queen Mother, who was beaming down at him from her box, for her continued support; and this time it was to her, rather than to his artists, that applause was deflected. She was given an ovation, after which the curtain descended slowly, cutting off Webster from view.

He had hoped until the last moment that Maria Callas would be able to be present. But a cable had to suffice:

> WITH ALL MY AFFECTION AM WITH YOU THIS EVENING MAY YOU ALWAYS REMEMBER ME AS YOURS DEVOTEDLY MARIA CALLAS.

While Peter Hall had written: 'Thank you for giving me an exciting future in the House . . . You have transformed Opera and Ballet in England.'

Ruth Lynam wrote most sympathetically, concerned about what such a break must mean to David, and about how he would adjust to it.

> What a fantastic night! We were (and still are) so very proud of you, and do hope your 'farewell' pleased you. But how wonderful that it is not farewell at all . . . we are so absolutely thrilled that you will be staying on as that very proud thing . . . CONSULTANT!
>
> . . . I feel just a tiny bit proud of having been a minute cog in the early workings and when I remember how few of us there were and when I think of what you have achieved . . . well, it is simply staggering.

The Friends gave a Luncheon for him on 15 July in the Ballroom Suite at the Dorchester, and he didn't manage to control emotions right through to the end of his speech. 'I blubbed, I have to admit,' he said afterwards. What had disturbed him was the prospect of leaving his 'family' – the ladies in wardrobe, the cleaners, all of them. He was going to miss them all.

On 24 July David was present at another Farewell Gala, this time as a member of the audience. He was there to pay tribute to Freddie Ashton. Another room was being sealed up . . .

The artists and staff at Covent Garden, and artists who had come as guests, made a special collection to buy a present for David. They inscribed their names in a handsome presentation album, and David put most of the money into the Hockney portrait, which was going to be hung in the Opera House, and there was enough left over to buy two fine claret decanters, which now stand on a sideboard in Weymouth Street.

David retired full of honours: and to mark his retirement the Queen made him Knight Commander of the Victorian Order. This is a second knighthood which it is the prerogative of the monarch alone to give, and the monarch was on hand herself this time to confer the honour. David's mother had been alive to take pleasure in his first knighthood, but she'd since died; and it was Jimmy who accompanied David to the Palace for the ceremony in 1970.

But there had been another honour conferred which was as much as any of his own a tribute to David Webster. When the Royal Italian Opera Covent Garden became the Royal Opera in 1892, reference was to the building alone. But in 1968, when the Home Secretary, James Callaghan, had translated the Covent Garden Opera into the Royal Opera, it was *the company* housed in the building which was named. This was, for Webster, to have his success ratified. The future of the company was surely now secured. It would have to be an unimaginable crisis which could transform the house once more into a furniture store or a dance-hall.

Jimmy also retired in 1970, at the same time as David. They wanted to enjoy their retirement together.

If leaving the Opera House was a wrench it was also going to be a relief from the constant tension. David needed to recuperate, not only from the fall, but from the strain of the long years. Slow promenades along the front at Brighton were part of the recuperation.

While the house was his Webster hadn't permitted himself to comment unfavourably on the artists working in it. But after his retirement he was watching a performance one evening with Jimmy beside him, and he at last felt less need to restrain himself. 'She's not very good, is she?' he whispered to Jimmy. The particular soprano wasn't, but that seemed no reason for Jimmy to be heaving with suppressed laughter. Jimmy managed to whisper back gratefully, 'I've been waiting *twenty-five years* to hear you say that!'

When David began at the Opera House Jimmy had wanted him to buy something, a set design or a costume design, from every production. He looked forward to the time when perhaps they might have a large enough house, maybe in the country, to be able to put aside one room for these mementoes. David had never followed through the idea. They had the original painting of one of James Bailey's *Manon* sets, and Wakhevitch had given Jimmy a drawing of one of his *Carmen* sets. Jimmy gave David a John Piper painting one year as a Christmas present. But that was all. It wasn't very much.

David persisted, when he retired, in worrying about money. Jimmy found it very difficult to persuade him that this at least was something that needn't worry him. Webster had money coming to him from four sources. There was his interest in Southern Television, he had a pension from Covent Garden, and he was to be Consultant until his seventieth birthday, in 1973. And in 1965, following a recommendation in the Goodman report, the London Orchestral Board had been formed, its purpose to divide the subsidy made available from the Greater London Council and the Arts Council, and to co-ordinate the activities of the London orchestras. Lord Goodman himself had promoted Webster's appointment as Chairman, and he was reappointed shortly before his death. The reappointment was a gesture, since he had asked for it. But it appeared by no means certain that he could cope.

Jimmy did his best to assure David that, even without this income, they would be all right for money. He would see to that.

When he retired, David was already in poor health. He was weary, glad not to be overstretched any longer. Though he missed the job none the less. It had been more than a job: he was giving up his life.

By the autumn of 1970, the first of his retirement, David was slowing down. This could be at least partly attributed to the difficulty he was bound to experience in adjusting to a different life. But was government, now that the market is being moved, is paying £6,000,000 for two sites beside the Opera House, to safeguard its future development. That development might provide a more public place.

It took time also to arrange for a plaque in St Paul's Church. When David Webster died, there were only one or two spaces left. Gladys Cooper had died about the same time, and her Memorial Service was held in the church: at one time it seemed that she too might be a candidate for the last plaque. Neither she nor David would have relished a posthumous battle, and David would most certainly, and most graciously, have wished to yield place had it been necessary. It wasn't. Gladys Cooper's family renewed a derelict sun-terrace in the public gardens at Henley-on-Thames, which overlooks her house further along the river, and her plaque is there. And another row of plaques was added in St Paul's Church. There was permission to be granted, though, and formalities. Jimmy fretted, while knowing that David would have laughed at the idea of so much trouble being taken. First the portrait, now a *plaque*. Muriel Kerr patiently wrote and answered letters. On 23 January 1974, after a service, the plaque was finally unveiled. It is at the end of the row, on the left as you go out, with Ivor Novello's above. And then there was no more to be done.

He is gone. The Opera House remains, with changes in it. It will cease to be Webster's: but he will be remembered, because the foundations, whatever the house becomes in the future, will always be his.

DAVID L. WEBSTER
KNIGHT

General Administrator of the
Royal Opera House
Covent Garden 1945–1970

BIBLIOGRAPHY

Harold Rosenthal: *Two Centuries of Opera at Covent Garden*, Putnam, 1958
Harold Rosenthal: *Opera at Covent Garden, A Short History*, Gollancz, 1967
Harold Rosenthal and John Warrack: *Concise Oxford Dictionary of Opera*, Oxford University Press, 1964
Edited Harold Rosenthal: *The Maplesson Memoirs*, Putnam, 1966
David Franklin: *Basso Cantante*, Duckworth, 1969
Rudolph Bing: *Five Thousand Nights at the Opera*, Hamish Hamilton, 1972
Herman Klein: *Golden Age of Opera*, Routledge, 1933
Dennis Arundell: *The Critic at the Opera*, Ernest Benn, 1957
Clive Barnes: *Ballet in Britain Since the War*, Thrift Books, 1953
Edward J. Dent: *Opera*, Pelican Books, 1940
Edited Anthony Gishford: *Grand Opera*, Weidenfeld and Nicolson, 1972
Arnold Haskell: *Balletomane at Large*, Heinemann, 1972
Stendhal: *Life of Rossini*, translated by Richard N. Coe, Calder and Boyars, 1956
Berlioz: *Memoirs*, translated by David Cairns, Gollancz, 1969
Ninette de Valois: *Invitation to the Ballet*, Bodley Head, 1937
Tyrone Guthrie: *A Life in the Theatre*, Hamish Hamilton, 1960
Thomas Beecham: *A Mingled Chime*, Hutchinson, 1944
Charles Reid: *Thomas Beecham*, Gollancz, 1961
Peter Brook: *The Empty Space*, MacGibbon and Kee, 1968
J. C. Trewin: *Peter Brook*, Macdonald, 1971
Stelios Galatopoulos: *Callas; La Divina*, Dent, 1966
Lincoln Kirstein: *The New York City Ballet*, Black, 1974
Joan Hammond: *A Voice, A Life*, Gollancz, 1970
Ivor Newton: *At the Piano*, Hamish Hamilton, 1966
R. F. Bisson: *The Sandon Studios Society and the Arts*, Parry Books Ltd, Liverpool

INDEX

INDEX

there something else? One or two people wondered about that fall.

The last sight some of his friends had of him was at a party in Weymouth Street in the spring of 1971. Ruth Lynam, whose comment on Webster has provided the title of his biography, was among them, and she recalls him, this last time, appropriately among friends, informally. He retired early that evening, walking up the stairs and into the small study which, like a balcony, overlooks the fine drawing-room. 'Goodnight everybody,' he said quietly. He moved away, then turned and added, 'I love you all.' A small gesture of the hand, an echo of the past restrained flamboyance, accompanied the words. And then he was gone.

That weekend he was in Brighton with Jimmy, as usual. And he was taken ill. He was brought home. Now there were strong doubts, as people thought back, about that fall in the market. Had it been a stroke?

He died within a few days, on 9 May 1971. When she received news of his death, Ruth Lynam recalled his goodbye to his friends at the party, and she couldn't help wondering – surely he must have known, that evening, that he wouldn't see any of them any more.

As he had wished, he was cremated.

John Pritchard was with Joan Sutherland in New York when they received the news. They sat together at a café table. John Pritchard had first appeared at Covent Garden on 23 October 1952, almost twenty years before. On 28 October he had conducted the performance of *The Magic Flute* in which Joan had made *her* debut. They talked together quietly in New York about the man who, they agreed, was responsible for their being there in New York, as stars. They couldn't have made their careers without him.

There were many, scattered throughout the world, who thought of him at this time in the same way.

Jimmy received many letters. Benjamin Britten wrote to him:

> He has been so much part of our lives for so many years (do you remember our evening together early in the war in Liverpool?) – we will miss him dreadfully. But how marvellous that he carried Covent Garden so triumphantly to the end of his time, left it in such a flourishing condition, and in such good hands. He must have felt very happy about it.

Peter Hall wrote: 'I was hoping that David would have many years of peace and pleasure. There is no justice.'

George Melly wrote:

> Marvellous to think what he achieved. All that bitching and sneering from the musical establishment and he, so determinedly pressing forward to unassailable triumph. He *did* die young but he *had* done so much.

Tippett had dedicated *The Knot Garden* to David Webster, and had given him an autographed score. When David died Jimmy gave it to David's godson, Lord Harewood's son Jeremy Lascelles.

A Thanksgiving Service for David Webster was given on 2 July 1971. St Paul's Church in Covent Garden would have been the obvious place for it, but there wasn't enough room there, so the Service was given in the Church of the Holy Sepulchre in High Holborn: a musicians' church, with a window in it dedicated to Melba (whose voice we invoked at David Webster's christening). The Reading was given by Dame Ninette de Valois, who chose some Yeats. Jon Vickers sang an aria from Handel's *Samson*, the opera of which he'd once given David Webster a dress-rehearsal and four performances for the price of two. Webster's successor, John Tooley, read the Lesson. Birgit Nilsson was in London for her two Isoldes in Solti's farewell production. The second of them was the following day so she didn't feel she ought to sing at the Thanksgiving Service – and Webster would have applauded her decision. His audience was owed a Nilsson in fresh voice. But she made her contribution, teaching Heather Harper, who had never sung it before, the *Tristan* Liebestod, with Solti conducting. Geraint Evans gave the Address. Solti also conducted the Awake Chorus and the final chorus from *The Mastersingers* (A Thanksgiving Service was later given for Lilian Baylis at Southwark Cathedral, on the centenary of her birth, and there too the Awake Chorus from *The Mastersingers* was heard.)

Joan Sutherland was in London recording. She was to have sung '*Libera Me*' from the Verdi *Requiem* at the Thanksgiving, but couldn't manage to arrange sufficient rehearsal time. She arrived, escorted by Hardy Amies. 'Never mind the "*Libera Me*",' she whispered, pointing to the choir. 'I ought to be up there with them.'

The choir was made up of some of the principals of the Royal Opera as well as some chorus members. And among them was a young Maori girl from the London Opera Centre, Kiri Te Kanawa. She was to be the company's next new star. The story was continuing.

It remained to find a place in the Opera House to hang the Hockney portrait. It's oblong, and no public place could be found for it. (Someone suggested that it be cut in half, and the Webster half only hung, but *that* suggestion was ignored.) It took time to settle on even a temporary place, but at the moment it hangs on the staircase leading up to the Royal Box. The walls are white, suitable for a modern painting, and there's enough room for it. But it can't be seen by most of those who contributed towards it, nor by the public.

If Webster had been able to get a second house built, perhaps at the top of Regent Street, there might have been somewhere for it. The